The American History Series

SERIES EDITORS

John Hope Franklin, *Duke University*

A. S. Eisenstadt, *Brooklyn College*

Regina Lee Blaszczyk
UNIVERSITY OF PENNSYLVANIA

American Consumer Society

1865–2005
From Hearth to HDTV

HARLAN DAVIDSON, INC.
WHEELING, ILLINOIS 60090-6000

Harlan Davidson, Inc., has made an effort to trace and contact the copyright owners of
all images used in this book. Copyright owners that have been found are fully credited.
If additional copyright owners make themselves known, the publisher will acknowledge
them in future printings.

Library of Congress Cataloging-in-Publication Data

Blaszczyk, Regina Lee.
   American consumer society, 1865–2005 : from hearth to HDTV /
Regina Lee Blaszczyk.
       p. cm. — (American history series)
Includes bibliographical references and index.
ISBN 978-0-88295-264-2 (alk. paper)
1. Consumption (Economics)—United States—History. 2.
Consumer—United States—History. I. Title.
HC110.C63B53 2009
303.60973—dc22
                                          2008019218

Cover photo: RadioShack catalog cover, 1963. Courtesy RadioShack
Corporation

Manufactured in the United States of America
11 10 09 1 2 3 4 5 VP

For Lee, who follows his own fashion

FOREWORD

Every generation writes its own history for the reason that it sees the past in the foreshortened perspective of its own experience. This has surely been true of the writing of American history. The practical aim of our historiography is to give us a more informed sense of where we are going by helping us understand the road we took in getting where we are. As the nature and dimensions of American life are changing, so too are the themes of our historical writing. Today's scholars are hard at work reconsidering every major aspect of the nation's past: its politics, diplomacy, economy, society, recreation, mores and values, as well as status, ethnic, race, sexual, and family relations. The list of series titles that appear on the inside covers of this book will show at once that our historians are ever broadening the range of their studies.

The aim of this series is to offer our readers a survey of what today's historians are saying about the central themes and aspects of the American past. To do this, we have invited to write for the series only scholars who have made notable contributions to the respective fields in which they are working. Drawing on primary and secondary materials, each volume presents a factual and narrative account of its particular subject, one that affords readers a basis for perceiving its larger dimensions and importance. Conscious that readers respond to the closeness and immediacy of a subject, each of our authors seeks to restore the past as an actual present, to revive it as a living reality. The individuals and groups who figure in the pages of our books appear as real people who once were looking for survival and fulfillment. Aware that historical subjects are often matters of controversy, our authors present their own findings and conclusions. Each volume closes with an extensive critical essay on the writings of the major authorities on its particular theme.

The books in this series are primarily designed for use in both basic and advanced courses in American history, on the undergraduate and graduate levels. Such a series has a particular value these days, when the format of American history courses is being altered to accommodate a greater diversity of reading materials. The series offers a number of distinct advantages. It extends the dimensions of regular course work. It makes clear that the study of our past is, more than the student might otherwise understand, at once complex, profound, and absorbing. It presents that past as a subject of continuing interest and fresh investigation.

For these reasons the series strongly invites an interest that far exceeds the walls of academe. The work of experts in their respective fields, it puts at the disposal of all readers the rich findings of historical inquiry, an invitation to join, in major fields of research, those who are pondering anew the central themes and aspects of our past.

And, going beyond the confines of the classroom, it reminds the general reader no less than the university student that in each successive generation of the ever-changing American adventure, from its very start until our own day, men and women and children were facing their daily problems and attempting, as we are now, to live their lives and to make their way.

John Hope Franklin
A. S. Eisenstadt

CONTENTS

I hate the bus.
I want my own car.
A car with a heater.
I want a big TV set and more.
A big old house. . . .
In every room a TV and my own telephone.

—Emmie Thibodeaux,
a maid's daughter in 1960s Louisiana,
from the Broadway musical *Carolyn,*
or Change

INTRODUCTION

Shopping for a Perfect Self

Everyday, tens of thousands of Americans shop at Target, one of America's largest retailers. In 2004, this general merchandiser had 1,300 stores across the United States. The store's brand tag line — "Expect More. Pay Less." — reflects its commitment to selling well-designed products at affordable prices.

Target exemplifies a big-box retailer geared to middle-class consumers looking for "something different." Some people love Target's clever products, like the novelties in the One Spot bins, while others appreciate the shopping environment, seeing it as a fancier, brighter, and tidier version of Wal★Mart. Still others think Target is ideal for one-stop shopping: why run all over town for flip-flops, dog food, and shampoo when one big store has everything? Indeed, Target *combines* quality, low price, and convenience, merchandising concepts introduced by mass retailers more than a century ago. Back then, department stores like Lord & Taylor sold expensive luxuries like fur coats to wealthy women, while five-and-ten cent stores like Woolworth's catered to indigent immigrants who needed cheap dishes, socks, and fabric. Target has mixed these strategies into a new model. It sells popular luxuries like Sony HDTVs and Simply Shabby Chic home décor as well as everyday basics like Dove deodorant and Scott paper towels.

Target's marketing speaks to something distinctive about twenty-first century American culture. Americans live in a "consumer society," buying Ford pickups, Prada shoes, Tommy Hilfiger jackets, and Nokia cell phones, defining themselves by their purchases. Possessions tell everybody who we are and how we wish to be treated. It's a world where Razrs, Hummers, Oprah, and Hello Kitty have personal and cultural meaning.

The Passion for Possessions

Americans developed a taste for possessions and the shopping experience over the last 150 years. This book examines how this consumer society emerged, evolved, and changed, and the implications for American culture. It focuses on people as consumers, advertising, and the houses, furnishings, fashions, magazines, cars, music, and electronics people bought and used.

Changes in social attitudes, values, products, and institutions help divide the past century and a half into three periods: the late Victorian era, 1865 to 1900; the Modern era, 1900 to World War II; and the Boomer era, 1945 to 2005. These periods aren't based on the political benchmarks of most U.S. history textbooks, but suggest a new way of looking at America through its consumption patterns. Each period has a unifying theme, summarized briefly here and explored in depth in the book's three sections and nine chapters.

In *Victorian America*, industry and commerce expanded, and new types of retailers appeared: department stores, mail-order houses, and five-and-tens (a precursor to the dollar store). Economic growth enabled *some* people to shop for a wider selection of factory-made goods. A standard "consumer identity kit" evolved to symbolize the "middle-class" lifestyle. A person's identity kit contained artifacts—the products of civilization—such as the single-family home, cozy furnishings, and fashionable clothes. Those who could afford to do so saved up to buy their own homes and put together fancy parlors filled with knickknacks, overstuffed furniture, and lace curtains. Americans loved fashion and splurged on the latest Paris and London styles. In this way, they defined themselves as part of a group, the middle class. In *Modern America*, more and more people were able to become part of consumer society. New cultural concepts, such as "personality" and the "self," eroded lingering resistance to the getting and spending of money. It was now more socially acceptable to envy and covet. Phrases like "keeping up with the Joneses," "the standard of living," "purchasing power," and the "American dream" entered the language, connecting material comfort to upward social mobility. Entrepreneurs brought to market products Americans never knew they needed or wanted. Illustrated magazines like the *Ladies' Home Journal* and the *Saturday Evening Post* introduced full-page color advertising. Products like Quaker Oats, Kodak, Ford, and Marlboro transformed the consumer experience by making people desire a brand rather than a commodity.

In *Boomer America*, mass consumption expanded its boundaries beyond "middle America" to a much broader swath of the population and began fragmenting it in the process. In the prosperity that followed World War II, typical middle- and working-class Americans had steady incomes and relatively high earnings, allowing them to enjoy the American dream. As factory workers entered the middle class, their taste for big Buicks and Cape Cod cottages had an impact on mainstream design. The development of synthetic fibers helped create a market for stylish casual clothing. An explosion in consumer electronics (televisions, hi-fis, and computers) led to an even bigger explosion in marketable content (records, cable TV, and software). Most important, niche marketing now directed at teens, yuppies, urban blacks, and others supplanted the very concept of the "mass market."

Dissonant Voices

As Americans earned more money and enjoyed more leisure time, anxious social observers worried about the impact of the trend. Thorstein Veblen's famous 1899 book, *The Theory of the Leisure Class*, was a stinging indictment of nouveau riche Americans who loved to flaunt their costly possessions: fancy clothes, carriages, and mansions. Veblen, an economist, considered these expenditures of energy and resources as wasteful, describing them as "conspicuous consumption."

Good ideas captured in snappy expressions often take on lives of their own, and "conspicuous consumption" was no exception. Countless social critics followed Veblen, their eyes fixed on society's flagrant displays of wealth, their sharp wits ready to condemn extravagance. Conspicuous consumption worked its way into the American lexicon as shorthand for reckless materialism, both up and down the social ladder.

Recent critics have turned their attention to consumerism's adverse impact on the environment, and to the maldistribution of wealth. There is worry about pollution, toxic waste, and the depletion of natural resources, and they question the sustainability of mass production and mass consumption in the context of global warming. Critics of companies such as Standard Oil, General Motors, and Wal★Mart rightfully decry the dangers of monopoly power and social injustices like price fixing and exploitative labor practices.

Other observers see consumption more benevolently, appreciating its potential for eradicating poverty, darkness, and discomfort. Journalist Virginia Postrel, who writes for the *Atlantic*, asks Americans to reflect on the advantages of a consumer culture, emphasizing the importance of style and glamour as cultural forces that give meaning to people's personal lives. Sociologist Sharon Zukin believes that consumption is a pleasurable experience that helps people understand themselves, their communities, and their nation. "We dream of shopping for beauty, truth and perfection," Zukin writes in *Point of Purchase*, "and if we do not shop for a perfect society, at least we shop for a perfect self."

Treasures and Throwaways

Consumer society, which rests on the accumulation of things, has never been static, but it has changed dramatically over the past 150 years. Most significantly, the Victorian idea of consumption as the purchase of a material thing has evolved today to include the purchase of evanescent experiences.

The Victorians lived in a culture that treasured things, while contemporary Americans throw things away and treasure experiences. Earlier generations of consumers spent a larger percentage of their incomes on necessities, and they took pride in those purchases. Students looking at Victorian interiors sometimes recoil at the clutter: the patterned carpets, needlepoint pictures, and china bric-a-brac. But what Generation Y may perceive as excess, the Victorians valued as badges of success. The treasure chest idea began to disappear in the late twentieth century with the birth of a throwaway culture. As retailers competed primarily on price, the new generation of consumers began to see their purchases as being temporary. A new family in 1870, 1925, and 1955 scrimped to furnish their home or apartment, investing in things they would keep for a lifetime. In contrast, the newlyweds in 2005 shopped at IKEA for starter furniture, expecting to upgrade again and again as they journeyed through life.

In addition, content is now as important a signifier of identity as material things. Cultural "software" has started to replace cultural "hardware" in the consumer identity kit. The generations of Americans who grew up on throwaway brands, global tourism, cable TV, and portable electronics began to redefine mass consumption around their experiences. Many preferred to download songs from iTunes, fly to Florida for spring break, tatoo or pierce their bodies, or ingest designer drugs rather than spend their money on prom gowns, record collections, or muscle cars. The traditional ways of getting and spending didn't disappear, but experiential consumption added a new dimension to consumerism. This content revolution is still underway, and the students reading this book will play a vital role in shaping it.

From Knickknacks to Kickin' Back

In consumer society, the great shift from knickknacks to kickin' back brings us full circle to Target and points to some of the most important themes in consumer history. When a customer buys a stuffed Valentine's Day teddy bear at Target, is she buying what she wants or what Target is telling her she needs? Is the relationship between the American people and producers like Target, Wal★Mart, Home Depot, and Macy's adversarial or complementary?

This history of consumer society shines a light on the joy earlier generations took from the things they owned. It then explores the evolution of the relationship between what Americans purchased and how they expressed their collective and individual identities. There is a great difference between the human desire for comfort, convenience, and beauty, and the yearning for instant gratification.

Although the story of American affluence is complicated, intriguing, and exciting, the stories of factories, advertisers, retailers, and brands are often left out of traditional U.S. history books. The factors that shaped our materialistic outlook—the American passion for comfort, convenience, and beauty—may seem slippery and hard to pin down. If we look in the right places, however, we can learn more about them—even about ourselves.

This book explores the changing conception of American affluence by watching Victorian women put on their corsets, farmers drive to town in their Model T's, and teens swoon over Beatniks and The Beatles. The chapters watch Martha Stewart create "good things" in the home, Frank Woolworth stock his dime store, Olivia Newton-John get physical, and Starbucks invent itself as a brand. They describe how men, women, and children used possessions in their private and public lives, how manufacturers and retailers determined what to make and sell, and how government stepped into the process as a referee and peacemaker.

Part One, Victorian America, begins this tale in the stores, factories, and streets of the 1870s.

PART ONE

Victorian America, 1865–1900

Between the Civil War and World War I, the United States became an industrial powerhouse *and* a giant among consumer societies. Mechanization, urbanization, immigration, and westward expansion transformed the American economy and recast social expectations. The gross national product (GNP) doubled, and much of the population migrated from the country to the city. Most important, more and more Americans identified themselves as *middle class*, using their possessions—clothing, furnishings, houses, musical instruments, pets, and sports equipment—to define their social status.

Victorians, Hierarchy, and Progress

Political historians often label the last thirty years of the nineteenth century the *Gilded Age*, the title of a book by Charles Dudley Warner and Samuel L. Clemens (Mark Twain). This 1873 novel satirizes business and politics of the time, and historians concerned with these subjects have adopted the memorable phrase as a synonym for the period. With its booming steel industry, towering skyscrapers, and technological wonders such as the telegraph, telephone, streetcars, and electricity, the era shimmered with a gilt veneer. The immense wealth of entrepreneurs like John D. Rockefeller, Andrew Carnegie, and J. P. Morgan captured public attention, as these giants ran corporations that dominated entire industries and lived in stupendous New York mansions. However, beneath the golden veneer of the Gilded Age lay a rotting interior: child labor, scandalous business practices, and racial, ethnic, and gender discrimination. One of the grimmest hallmarks of the period was political corruption throughout all levels of government.

Cultural historians use another term, *Victorian,* to discuss these decades. This word is borrowed from Great Britain, where it describes the times of Queen Victoria, the empire's ruler from 1837 to 1901. The phrase *Victorian* is relevant to this study because of the *transnational* character of European and American consumer culture and its shared preoccupation with respectability and domesticity. Queen Victoria's twenty-one-year marriage to Prince Albert provided a model of domestic harmony that had wide cultural influence on both sides of the Atlantic Ocean. For the first time in centuries, romantic love and familial accord were associated with the British monarchy, and an ideal of cozy Victorian domesticity became fashionable in both England and the United States.

Like the phrase *Gilded Age*, the term *Victorian* also is useful for describing other aspects of Anglo American culture of the late 1800s and early 1900s. Whether in England or the United States, Victorians believed in a predictable universe, an objective truth, and a stratified social order. These assumptions rested on the notion of *progress*, an idea that esteemed science and technology as the peak of human achievement. The related doctrine of Social Darwinism, popularized by the British philosopher Herbert Spencer, incorrectly modified the evolutionary theories of Charles Darwin to explain human civilizations. Spencer's writings and lecture tours popularized the concept of the "survival of the fittest" as applied to social order.

Victorians who subscribed to the ideas of progress and social evolution believed that everyone and everything fit into a hierarchy, with some people simply more qualified than others for leadership and success. In America, these beliefs limited upward mobility in the business world for those who didn't "fit in," traditionally women, immigrants, or people of color. At the same time, they asserted that *anyone*, principally white men, could yank themselves up by their bootstraps and succeed in America. The Victorian ideal supported the mainstream belief that the United States was the "promised land" of opportunity and plenty, a cornucopia overflowing with delicious fruits and profits. Victorian progress defined man-made goods as signs of human creativity and held that all civilized people had the right to enjoy these products. Victorians put Western cultures at the pinnacle of the social pyramid, identifying industrialized nations as "civilized" in part because their citizens enjoyed a high level of material comfort. Billowing smokestacks testified to economic productivity, while the ownership of factory-made goods showed that a person had "made it" in industrial America.

Early European Antecedents

Americans weren't the first people to relish their possessions, and they certainly won't be the last. Globally, earlier agricultural and industrial societies displayed a rudimentary consumerist mentality, going back several hundred years. There had always been a small minority at the top of society with consumerist tendencies, but these elites spent their money on goods that conveyed lasting prestige, rather than on fashions or fads. Indeed, the endless creation of novelties and the constant production and promotion of anything "new and different" are the marks of a full-blown consumer society.

Scholars debate the appearance of the first true consumer societies in the modern world, but the consensus focuses on mid-eighteenth-century Western Europe. Before then, only the *crème de la crème* of certain European societies showed consumerist behavior. In Renaissance Florence, wealthy banker-princes made their *palazzos* into showcases of luxury products, fine art, and cultivated pursuits. At Versailles in seventeenth-century France, King Louis XIV inaugurated state policies to encourage the luxury trades, creating jobs for skilled artisans and providing courtiers with a steady supply of exquisite wine, diamond jewelry, painted coaches, and fabulous shoes. The aristocracy and upper classes owned luxuries and were beginning to appreciate novelty, even as everyone else still suffered from a basic want.

In the seventeenth and eighteenth centuries, consumerist impulses emerged in regions with commercial economies and access to international trade, which introduced exotic products like sugar, coffee, tea, silk, and porcelain. During Holland's golden age from roughly 1580 to 1670, profits from the overseas trade established an urban middle class that could afford large townhouses, elegant furnishings, and exquisite paintings. The great symbol of seventeenth-century Dutch prosperity—the tulip—became the focus of a collecting craze in the 1630s and 1640s. Yet while tulip mania foreshadowed consumerism, the frenzy didn't reach ordinary people and didn't lead to another fad. Only during the next century in Georgian Britain did the world's first true consumer society appear. Born out of industrialism, colonialism, and world commerce, Britain's prosperous middle class had sufficient discretionary income to build fancy houses, buy Staffordshire china, and wear waistcoats made from embroidered French silk. For the first time in modern Europe, people other than those at the very top of society could indulge their fancies and follow cultural trends that were *in fashion*.

Most of Europe remained socially stratified, however, and people didn't expect to advance beyond their birthright or to own things that singled them out as individuals. Nearly everyone had a predetermined role from cradle to grave. Slivers of affluence—visible in the real-estate developments of the Royal Crescent and the King's Circus at Bath and the impressive country houses of the aristocracy—contrasted with widespread poverty in mining towns, farming communities, and port cities. Shop windows glistening with baubles suggested change and the promise of a better life. Still, most people simply got by, living from season to season and hand to mouth. Those who did have something extra channeled the surplus into land or community activities, such as improving the town hall or building a taller church steeple.

Opportunities for Display

American consumer society emerged in the late nineteenth century and broke away from these patterns in important ways. First and foremost, the range and intensity of events in the United States, particularly after the Civil War, made the antecedents pale in comparison. In Victorian America, not only did many more people *aspire* to enjoy a comfortable lifestyle, but many actually *achieved* this goal. For the first time, ordinary people had both the aspiration and the access to move up in society. Steady wages or farm income allowed them to buy the fruits of abundance, while the desire to improve one's lot in life led them to see material goods as badges of success. Whether in fields or factories, Victorian Americans developed an appreciation for the symbolic function of possessions, which they used to anchor themselves to their desired stratum of society: the middle class. With a love of material things, the Victorians associated middle-class status—or "respectability"—with accumulation and display and, in doing so, initiated the fundamental cultural practice that would be refined, politicized, and given new meanings in the Modern and Boomer eras.

The proliferation of goods wrought by industrialization and international trade offered a viable solution to the distinctive problem of American mobility. As a former British colony, the United States had been part of a stratified European society where tradition dictated personal success or failure. In the new nation, birth proved to be less important than luck, pluck, and networking skills, and most free white men used their wits and contacts to navigate American society. European visitors like the Frenchman Alexis de Tocqueville, author of *Democracy in America* (1835), commented on the fluidity of American life, which contrasted sharply with the immutability of European society, despite the stain of slavery. The Civil War and new immigration after 1880 further scattered Americans across the land: from North to South, East to West, from the country to the city, and from job to job. Under these conditions, Americans were always meeting new people, and they needed some means for evaluating the trustworthiness of strangers. Social contacts, reference letters, and printed calling cards provided some assurance, but the Victorians developed other ways of "reading" each other.

Living in a society of strangers on the move, Victorian Americans drew on their British legacy to establish a consumer-oriented republic that cherished respectability: domestic harmony and middle-class manners. The British traditions had shaped gentlemanly experience in the colonies and meshed with the tenets of republicanism to spread the behavior of the gentility among the lower classes. Yet during the Revolutionary era, some colonists had expressed ambivalence or outright hostility toward consumerism, associating the "baubles of

Britain" with moral corruption. Later Americans, seeking to shed their rough-and-tumble image, let go of their reluctance to spend their way into respectability. Even families of modest means learned to use houses, parlors, furniture, etiquette books, and sentimental novels as tools that demonstrated their mastery of polite behavior. Although it came from British conventions, the culture of refinement evolved into something distinctively American in the decades surrounding the Civil War. Rapid industrial and commercial growth reshaped gentility into "middle-class culture," which further advanced the idea of mobility while blurring and obscuring the boundaries of class. In this way, gentility begat refinement which begat a consumer culture that celebrated a claim to a social stratum based not on birthright but on the acquisition of the "right stuff."

The consumerist spirit of Victorian America rested on the twin pillars of emotion and economics. Although some may have longed for wealth, most people were happy with the promise of just being better off than their European ancestors, whose status was established at birth. The prospect of respectability energized consumers, who assembled their identity kits as their budgets permitted. Owning the accoutrements of the middle-class lifestyle and buying things from the new stores that began to dot the city streets soon seemed like second nature, an expected part of the American experience. A homesteading family in Nebraska who temporarily "made do" with a sod house filled it with valued possessions that would eventually go into more permanent quarters: an upright piano, matching dishes, and dainty lace doilies. Jewish immigrants in Brooklyn cherished their parlor set, even though it embodied the values of the Anglo-Saxon Protestant culture from which they remained outsiders. Through the pride of ownership, these consumers saw themselves as joining the mainstream, accommodating to it in some way, or bending it to suit their own needs and subcultures.

Victorian shoppers did not live in a throwaway world as do twenty-first-century consumers. They cherished their possessions. Yet the foundations of desiring seasonal colors, disposable plastics, and wave after wave of novelty were laid during this era. The cornerstone may be found in a celebration of progress and innovation—the 1876 Centennial Exposition.

1876 Centennial Exposition, the Industrial Cornucopia

In 1876, the United States celebrated its hundredth birthday with parades, fireworks, and extravaganzas. Among the most important tributes to independence was the great world's fair held in Philadelphia. Now relics of a bygone era, from the 1850s through the 1960s world's fairs were an exciting way of showcasing a nation's growth, accomplishments, and progress. The 1876 Exposition was one of the largest world's fairs ever held, and it highlights both the differences and similarities of Victorian and twentieth-century America.

The Centennial Exposition was equivalent to an Olympiad, with 30,000 exhibits attracting nearly 10 million tourists between May and November. Like circuses and carnivals, the fair featured music, games, and attractions from around the world. Many people first saw elephants, tigers, giraffes, bears, and lizards at the Exposition's zoo. The Japanese exhibits introduced visitors to Asian culture and a stupendous oriental garden.

Besides these exotic attractions, the fair had several noble missions: to commemorate 100 years of independence, unify North and South at the end of Reconstruction, promote American industry, and link technological progress and mass consumption in ways that stimulated and legitimated the Victorian desire for a better material life. In a tribute to progress, booths displayed new technologies that would become common: Alexander Graham Bell's telephone, Thomas A. Edison's electric light bulb, and Fleischmann's Yeast. The new commercially made yeast produced delicious fluffy breads that fairgoers could sample at the Fleischmann concession, The Vienna Bakery. The fair also introduced attendees to bananas, popcorn, root beer, and ice-cream sodas—all destined to become part of every American's diet. Most important, the 1876 fair showcased infinite varieties of consumer products pouring out of English, German, French, Japanese, and American factories.

The Exposition emphasized the links between industrial production and consumer society, displaying goods in enticing ways. Like earlier world's fairs in London, Paris, Vienna, and New York, the Philadelphia fair exhibited the newest furniture, porcelain, sewing machines, dress patterns, ready-made clothes, and clocks. The fairgrounds had five large structures and 250 smaller buildings. Some consumer goods were marketed in specially designated buildings, but people could buy soda, food, and souvenirs almost everywhere they wandered. The main building alone comprised twenty acres of space—larger than New York's contemporary Javits Center—dedicated entirely to consumer goods. Many exhibits showcased foreign cultures and built people's interest in exotic goods like Persian rugs and Japanese porcelain. In addition, the fair introduced the "model room," an innovative technique for showcasing interior furnishings as one might arrange them in the home or office. Mounted by furniture factories, model interiors awakened people's desires and exposed them to basic aesthetic principles, such as color coordination and the judicious use of space. They provided important object lessons, showing that the best household interiors had an overall harmonious effect. Exhibits by sewing-machine manufacturers and major patternmakers, such as Demorest and Butterick, reinforced the idea that personal style in dress could be accessible to all. Overall, the Centennial showed American visitors how to outfit their homes and themselves in proper fashion, drawing on goods from around the world.

The tourists who flocked to the Centennial lived in exciting times. Innovations in transportation, communications, commerce, and industry were driving the economy. The exhibits were a tribute to these changes. Everything about the fair—the meticulously landscaped grounds, the spatial arrangement of the buildings, and the choice of products shown—spoke to the Victorian faith in a precise social order, the great potential of industry, and the promise that material goods would help people improve themselves. One of the fair's foremost tourist attractions—the gargantuan Corliss steam engine that heated and powered the Main Building—was the embodiment of American engineering prowess and ingenuity. In short, the Centennial Exposition was a microcosm of Victorian America's hopes and ambitions that rested on material progress built on transnational connections and industrial growth.

The United States had started to industrialize in the early national era, but the Civil War sped up the process that produced the abundance and novelty of goods at the Centennial Exposition. War mobilization stepped up industrialization and stimulated a rapid increase in the production of capital and consumer goods. Capitalists pooled their resources to create joint-stock companies, or corporations, in publishing, railroads, shipping, insurance, and textiles. The government encouraged the formation of corporations by passing laws that gave them special status and limited the liability of investors. Magnates like Andrew Carnegie and Henry Clay Frick grew successful partnerships into gargantuan firms that often came to dominate their economic sectors. Big businesses never eliminated small businesses, but the managerial and technological innovations the former developed had a wide influence and established the standards for how many companies operated.

Industrialization and the rise of big business were separate, but related, phenomena. Both were new; together, they transformed Victorian American. They accelerated changes to the social order that had been developing since the colonial period, creating a large new middle class as well as new extremes of wealth and poverty. Yet the American economy and social structure retained many *old* characteristics. Small retail stores, craft workshops, farms, fisheries, and other family-run businesses persisted. Many people continued to live in rural areas and small towns. And it still remained difficult for outsiders—African Americans, women, and recent immigrants—to reap economic gain.

The Allure of Cities

In the Victorian era, most Americans lived in the industrial heartland, where thousands of factories, mills, and workshops in towns and cities churned out products for the national market. During the Civil War, all of the nation's major cities were on the eastern seaboard, but just forty years later, a great urban manufacturing district stretched from the Atlantic Ocean to the Mississippi River. Its northern border was the Great Lakes, its southern boundary, the Ohio River. Today, this region is unflatteringly called the "Rust Belt" because the dramatic decline of manufacturing in the late twentieth century destroyed its vitality. Between 1860 and 1900, however, approximately 65 percent of Americans lived and worked there, and the Smokestack region was America's economic hub and population center.

Industrialization created thousands of jobs in factories and offices, offering opportunities that galvanized all manner of people who wanted better lives. The nation's manufacturing cities became magnets for rural people, white and black, desperate to escape the backbreaking toil of farm life. Although agricultural productivity grew tremendously, American farmers barely earned a living. Declining prices for crops and repeated natural disasters—floods, insect invasions, and droughts—created a life of drudgery and isolation on the farm. As a result, many rural Americans turned toward the nation's cities. Peasants who arrived in America after 1880—Greeks, Hungarians, Italians, Mexicans, Poles, Russians, and Slovaks—left their homelands for different reasons. Some wanted to escape starvation, the devastation of war, or religious persecution, but all of them envisioned greater opportunities in America for themselves and their children.

" American Dream"

Regardless of motivation, migrants and immigrants alike flocked to industrial centers to look for work: the garment district of New York City, the slaughterhouses of Chicago, the steel mills in Gary, Indiana, and the coal mines of West Virginia. Many took the dirtiest jobs, which still provided a better paycheck than that they had earned back home. The experience of the Irish, who immigrated *en masse* in the nineteenth century, is a case in point. In New England, Irish immigrant families found jobs in Lowell's cotton textile mills, working long days for little pay and living in shantytowns on the edge of the city. In Boston, Irish boys worked as day laborers in construction, helping to build the luxury development known as Back Bay. As a lad in 1910–12, Frederick Thomas O'Neill, for example, carried buckets of beer from local taverns to fellow Irishmen building the elevated railway through Roxbury. Young Irish women who spoke proper English took jobs as household servants, living with American families who needed help with cleaning, washing, cooking, and child care. With a little capital, Irish entrepreneurs might establish small businesses, such as grocery stores, taverns, breweries, or boardinghouses. We will examine in Chapters One and Two how the most successful immigrants could decorate their homes with a few goods that pointed toward middle-class respectability or wear ready-made suits that showed how much they had risen since leaving the old country.

New arrivals were awed by urban life, with its fast pace and exciting public entertainments. The throngs on the streets of New York, Chicago, or Philadelphia were themselves a great attraction. People from all walks of life rubbed shoulders on a commercial thoroughfare like Broadway, where in 1857 a Russian visitor noted the "magnificently dressed women" and men "rushing about on business." By 1900, few intersections were as busy as that of Eighth and Market streets in Philadelphia, where three giant department stores attracted thousands of shoppers at rush hour. Amusements complemented the street life. By the turn of the century, a large American city had stores of every size and variety, penny museums, parks and zoos, vaudeville theaters and nickelodeons, restaurants, saloons, and dance halls. Before the arrival of zoning laws, printed and painted advertisements—handbills, posters, signs, and billboards—lined the sides of buildings and fences, creating lively and colorful streetscapes. Peddlers and pushcart operators hawked everything from newspapers to vegetables. Even smaller cities like Rochester or Buffalo had these attractions. Their streetlight-lined Main Streets, illuminated first with gas and later with electricity, were magical sights to people who had grown up in rural isolation and darkness.

The Rise of the New Middle Class

In 1858, the poet and journalist Walt Whitman noted, "The most valuable class in any community is the middle class." In antebellum America, the middle class had consisted of Protestant householders, mostly of English and German descent, who had a "passion for physical comforts." Male breadwinners worked as bankers, doctors, editors, farmers, lawyers, merchants, ministers, teachers, skilled artisans, and minor entrepreneurs. After the Civil War, economic growth enlarged this stratum, as white-collar workers employed in industry and commerce joined its ranks. These office workers redefined middle-class culture, becoming an influential cultural force that shaped the direction of consumer society.

The beginning of the twenty-first-century service economy starts with these Victorian office workers. Early government statistics describe the composition of the U.S. labor force and highlight the changing nature of work. During the 1870s, 52 percent of Americans worked in agriculture; 21 percent in manufacturing and mining; and 27 percent in other occupations. By the 1890s, the distribution had shifted: 41 percent in agriculture; 22 percent in production; and 37 percent in the service sector. Between 1919 and 1940, the most dramatic change occurred: farmers only accounted for 21 percent of workers; service occupations, a whopping 54 percent.

The growth sectors in Victorian America—manufacturing, transportation, publishing, finance, retailing, and wholesaling—created jobs in offices, factories, warehouses, and stores. Growing businesses needed thousands of employees to handle paperwork. The new office jobs provided men, who headed most households in the United States, with the means for upward social mobility. At a minimum, the jobs required sobriety and integrity. They also demanded an excellent command of the English language and skills in reading, grammar, penmanship, composition, and mathematics. Men educated by the expanding public school system—offspring of the old middle class, well-spoken country boys, and second-generation immigrants—found that the white-collar world provided them with decent salaries, clean places to work, and social respectability. While blast furnaces roared and textile looms thumped, the office buildings of Victorian America bustled, as layers of clerks and their bosses kept track of the nation's business.

By the 1880s, the American middle class had three sectors: professionals such as lawyers and doctors, business owners, and white-collar workers. Precisely where an individual stood in relation to others depended on a complex set of factors, but the breadwinner's occupation played a formative role in defining the social standing of most households.

Some examples from the 1880s and 1890s illuminate the variety of occupations found in the Victorian middle class. Men like Charles Yockel, a Philadelphia entrepreneur whose small foundry made molds for glass factories, belonged to the middle class, as did lawyer Henry James and office worker Walter Teller Post, both of St. Paul, Minnesota. James was an attorney, a member of an old and well-respected profession; the upstart Post worked for the Northern Pacific Railway as a junior clerk, a relatively new occupation roughly equivalent in duties and status to a customer-service specialist or data-entry clerk in the twenty-first century. Yockel and James owned their own homes. In contrast, Post held on to middle-class status by the skin of his teeth, his ambitions for home ownership circumscribed by his modest salary.

Among middle-class occupations, annual salaries and weekly wages varied widely and income often determined whether a household might realize its dreams of prosperity and progress. Several factors, including the deflationary economy, affected economic status. From 1865 to 1896, a long decline in prices created an environment friendly to capital investment and consumer spending. Capitalists got more for their dollars when they built factories, railroads, stores, telegraph lines, and warehouses. As the transportation infrastructure developed and productivity increased, urban prices fell relative to prices in rural districts. Deflation had a positive impact on purchasing power. For many people, annual earnings in real money increased by nearly 80 percent between 1865 and 1900. As a result, many middle-class households could keep up with their neighbors, buying pieces of the identity kit that marked the middle-class lifestyle. But some, Walter Post included, struggled to keep up appearances.

By the end of the century, white-collar workers had grown in number, visibility, and cultural influence, and they congregated in cities. In busy ports such as Boston, Milwaukee, Philadelphia, and San Francisco, white-collar workers headed between 25 and 40 percent of all households. Although the middle-class was not the majority in terms of numbers, it occupied a cultural center stage. In the classic scenario, the "breadwinner" should earn enough to provide his family a comfortable lifestyle, and his wife should not have to work to bring in extra money. Instead, she should keep house, care for the small children, perhaps with help from relatives or some hired servants for the heavy chores, and shop for and buy the household goods that established the family's status. Chapters One and Two will show how this model middle-class family could save enough to buy one of the new single-family homes fast becoming the ultimate status symbol, as well as proper dress for Victorian success.

Labor's Consumerist Turn

Opportunities aside, living in the consumer society of Victorian America wasn't easy for everyone. Recessions plagued the economy and thwarted many dreams of upward mobility. The boom-and-bust economic cycles were an integral byproduct of the nation's rush to industrialize. A spurt of economic expansion typically lasted four to five years, followed by a slump. Banking crises and financial panics in 1873, 1893, and 1907 caused severe and lengthy downturns, but there were smaller ones nearly every decade. As these downturns wreaked havoc among small businesses, new business methods threatened age-old practices and professions. For example, the rise of specialized companies that handled routine law work—title searches and debt collection—eroded the livelihoods of many small-town lawyers. Unemployment and medical insurance didn't exist, and many people never earned enough money to save for a rainy day.

Reacting to the deflationary economy, industrial workers pursued better living conditions by connecting to consumer culture. More than others, factory workers and artisans felt themselves slipping economically when employers cut costs to keep up with the competition. Previously, artisans had defined themselves as "producers," as a labor aristocracy entitled through skill and tradition to a privileged place in the social order. By the 1880s, the idea of a labor aristocracy faded. Factory production forced smaller workshops to close, and artisans who once sold their skill and expertise found themselves wage laborers selling their time. The new generation of industrial workers, organized into early unions such as the American Federation of Labor, formulated a platform of workers' rights that hinged on a stable family life, home ownership, and access to consumer goods. In negotiations and strikes, union leaders demanded that employers reduce the ten-hour workday to eight hours and pay sufficient wages to enable workingmen's families to enjoy some standard of comfort. Adopting the rhetoric and tone familiar to capitalists, living-wage advocates reoriented the labor movement around access to consumerism.

Through this "consumerist turn," to borrow the words of historian Lawrence B. Glickman, union workers battled for their right to stand on equal footing with white-collar employees and live better than had their parents. It would, however, be misleading to say that Victorian workers fully accepted the tenets of middle-class culture. Many didn't find these values appealing and were reluctant to exchange their independence for nicer surroundings. Nonetheless, the consumerist turn helped to eliminate lingering British conventions that preserved the social hierarchy and limited upward mobility, legitimating the idea that all people should have access to modern conveniences. Although gradual, the reorientation of the American worker would have a lasting impact on consumer society in the Modern and Boomer eras.

In this volatile economy, white-collar workers may have been less vocal than the blue-collar labor force because they suffered less—and often had more options. Even among the comfortable sorts, however, economic uncertainty bred insecurity. Bankruptcy constantly threatened small entrepreneurs, while cost-cutting measures in large corporations resulted in routine personnel cuts that forced clerks to move from job to job. Nothing guaranteed that those who had brought home the bacon in boom times would be able to sustain their incomes or to improve their future lifestyles.

Buying American or Pursuing Empire?

As the industrial juggernaut moved forward, many politicians, executives, and consumers rallied around postbellum America's single most important policy debate: the tariff. These fiery deliberations—about whether protectionism or free trade was best for the United States—are immensely important to the history of consumer society. The debates hinged on deeper concerns about the role of government in economic life and, consequently, in shaping American consumer society. Should Congress erect tariff barriers that protected the U.S. market from inexpensive imports, or should it permit the unrestricted flow of goods and capital across borders, allowing "the market" to dictate successes and failures among industries, firms, and worker-consumers?

The question of imports had preoccupied policymakers since the birth of the nation, but it became the subject of heated partisan debate in the late-nineteenth and early-twentieth centuries. Protectionist William McKinley, who as a U.S. Congressman was the Republican party's leading tariff expert, told fellow members of the House in the 1880s: "The farmer, the manufacturer, the laborer, the tradesman, and the producer and consumer all have a common interest in the maintenance of a protective tariff." In theory, the protective tariff, which levied taxes on imports based on a fee schedule set by law, was designed to discourage merchants from flooding the domestic market with foreign goods that could undercut prices for American materials and products. By upholding prices and limiting imports, protectionism could help American industries grow while encouraging factories to pay workers the living wage they needed to participate in consumer society.

In the other camp, free traders opposed protectionism for reasons that echoed Social Darwinists' mantra of survival of the fittest. They believed it was beneficial to open the U.S. borders to international trade, permitting the unrestricted flow of goods from around the world, the concomitant export of American commodities abroad, and effecting lower prices everywhere. As some American businesses expanded, they looked to Asia and Latin America, where raw materials and ready markets were ripe for the picking. American firms like United Fruit, McCormick Reaper, and Singer Sewing Machine became the nation's first prominent multinationals, investing in plantations, factories, and distributorships overseas. Drawing from Adam Smith's classic treatise *The Wealth of Nations* (1776), free-trade advocates believed that the global market would determine which competitors would survive.

From 1861 through 1913, protectionists prevailed and trade barriers remained in place. Yet foreign goods continued to enter the American market, despite the high duties on them. Some imports, including raw wool, were encouraged through low tariffs because American supplies were limited, and industry needed these materials. Luxury goods like Bohemian glassware and Paris fashions were of the finest quality and, regardless of duties, found ready buyers among upper-class customers who could afford to pay a premium. Culturally, the high retail price added to the perception that European goods, the products of old world traditions, were precious luxuries.

Advertising Abundance

Against the backdrop of the tariff wars, the question of what to buy played out culturally, as consumers pondered architectural styles, fashion choices, and interior decoration. In the face of the heated tariff debate, many well-to-do consumers filled their houses with foreign wares. Whether from China or France, imported luxuries helped wealthy Americans define themselves as cosmopolitan consumers who knew how to appreciate European craftsmanship and Oriental exoticism. For this group, imports served as symbols of distinction, a type of "cultural capital" that set them apart from the swelling ranks of the middle class.

Other American consumers didn't always make their purchases with this level of self-confidence. Newcomers to the middle class found it difficult to know what to wear, where to live, and how to decorate their homes to give the right impression. It would be a mistake for a young railroad clerk and his wife to invite co-workers home for dinner, only to learn later that the boss thought the table linens and china were garish and the menu was all wrong. Was it preferable to buy things made in America or imports from abroad? Should a family invest in miniature versions of the Japanese and English showpieces at the Centennial? What messages did different goods convey, and how might consumers know which things they should use in performing their new roles on the stage of middle-class life?

Of course many new arrivals to the middle class learned how to select and use products simply by looking: by studying those of higher status and emulating how they dressed and decorated their homes. In a small Midwestern city like Springfield, Illinois, the elites set the standards that everyone else watched from a distance. It was more difficult to learn by looking in a large eastern city like New York, where access to the upper crust was more limited. Imitation could be impossible if there was no direct contact with trend setters. More Americans had the resources to spend, but many remained perplexed about what to purchase.

This cultural puzzlement led to the development of commercial mechanisms that taught people what to buy. Chapters One to Three will focus on several of them: books that illustrated architecture, furniture, and interior design; fashion magazines with colored plates of Parisian styles; and new types of stores that tempted shoppers with a great variety of stock and stupendous show windows. However, many historians still agree with David M. Potter's classic argument, articulated in *People of Plenty*, that advertising has long been the quintessential "institution of abundance." This section will conclude by examining advertising at a moment when it turned to the use of persuasive imagery, and Chapter Four will develop a deeper analysis of it for the Modern era.

Victorian businesses used several types of advertisements to place their products within the context of middle-class respectability. Nineteenth-century advertising differed from later efforts, including national magazine and television campaigns, in important ways. Retail advertisements were generated locally, geared to the needs of consumers in a particular city or town. Local stores stressed themes and products with community appeal. Advertisements for brand-name goods, like Lydia Pinkham's patented medicine for "female complaints" and Sapolio soap, were created by the national manufacturers or distributors. Consumers saw colorful printed labels on wooden boxes, tin cans, and paper packages. Flyers, billboards, signs, and trolley placards punctuated the public landscape. Stores displayed manufacturers' posters on the sales floor or in show windows. Newspapers advertised the products of local businesses from breweries to gun shops. Main Street retailers gave away colorful trade cards as collectible ephemera, while distant mail-order houses landed catalogs with the newest styles into consumers' mailboxes.

The proliferation of advertising media brings us back to the quintessential Victorian value known as progress. Mainstream Victorians saw the products of industry as evidence of their cultural superiority, as a sign that human civilization was achieving perfection. Industrial nations were perceived as being better than less-developed countries, and the fruits of industry were proof of their ingenuity. Popular advertising images portrayed the factory as the ultimate symbol of human achievement, its billowing smokestacks as emblems of progress. Victorian iconography also depicted consumer products as symbols of fecundity, tangible proof that America was a fertile land of plenty.

While this iconography appeared on many types of advertisements, pictures of plenty most often entered the Victorian home on trade cards. Such advertising cards were small pieces of paper, typically 2" x 4" or 3" x 5", with colorful images on the front and plain black lettering on the back. Typically, trade cards were designed, manufactured, and distributed by chromolithographers in the large industrial states such as Illinois, Massachusetts, New York, Ohio, and Pennsylvania. These establishments hired artists to generate hundreds of stock images, which were reproduced by the hundreds of thousands and sold across the country through catalogs or commercial travelers. A printer in Des Moines would purchase a supply of trade cards, which he customized for local businesses by adding the retailer's name and address, often on the reverse. Shoppers, in turn, acquired advertising cards as premiums in packages of brand-name coffee, tea, or soap, or as over-the-counter novelties given away by retailers who wanted to build customer loyalty.

Between the 1870s and the 1910s, there was a craze for collecting such trade cards, and it taught consumers to read the visual iconography of abundance and hone their ability to make aesthetic judgments. The trade-card collecting hobby heightened consumers' powers of observation and taught them to critically assess what they were seeing.

Trade cards not only expanded consumers' awareness of color and design, but exposed them to the wondrous new world of goods. Advertising cards for durable items like sewing machines, parlor organs, and upright pianos suggested where consumers might place new dream items in the home. Soap cards pictured how these cleansers eased the burdens of domestic life, while showing the rooms of the house. Regardless of what they advertised, trade cards frequently included enough detail about interiors — the corner of a room, or simply a sketch of its draperies or carpeting — to alert readers of appropriate household arrangements. By picturing domesticity, trade cards showed how goods could reinforce the family values at the heart of Victorian consumerism. Consumers could now demonstrate their superior knowledge of middle-class culture by purchasing the right stuff, whether Singer sewing machines, Wedgwood china, New York fashions, or Caribbean sugar.

•••

In the Victorian era, several factors combined to lay the foundation for contemporary mass consumer society. Historians generally agree that the seeds of Western consumerism were sown in early modern Europe, but the growth of industry and a continental market gave the United States important advantages during the late 1800s, pushing American consumer culture to the fore. New cultural institutions — world's fairs, widespread advertising, mass-market retailing, and the democratization of fashion—combined with changing expectations for gender, home, and work to give birth to the world's first *mass* consumer society.

Certainly, these new institutions and forces were not unique to the United States, but the distinctiveness of American circumstances created opportunities not available in the same concentration elsewhere. As Europeans struggled to establish nation-states and a democratic order, Americans emerged from their own Civil War poised to take advantage of political stability, a large internal market, and economic progress. Certainly, the tradition of social stratification, racial prejudice, and gender stereotypes prevented some Americans from participating in consumption, but breakthrough concepts such as "the middle-class" and "the living wage" planted the idea that every citizen's birthright included access to goods. For the first time in modern Western history, ordinary men and women who dreamed about comfort might actually find it.

CHAPTER ONE

Home, Sweet Home

Martha Stewart was America's first billionaire businesswoman and its queen of the home. This former fashion model turned caterer ultimately established Martha Stewart Living Omnimedia in 1997. Fittingly, Stewart toasted her firm's initial public offering on the New York Stock Exchange with fresh-squeezed orange juice and homemade pastries. While the press chattered about the conflict between business and the home, Stewart continued to promote gracious living to American homemakers.

Martha Stewart Living Omnimedia has become America's leading corporate supplier of "Do-It-Yourself" information on decorating, entertaining, gardening, cooking, and child rearing. Its success spotlights the importance of the home in contemporary American life. *Martha Stewart Living*, the firm's flagship magazine, instructs readers on home beautification through cooking, handicrafts, antiques, and Martha products. It celebrates the "domestic arts as well as the homemaker," providing "inspirational ideas for anyone passionately invested in the subject of everyday living." And while Stewart's avid fans—college-educated, home-owning women aged twenty-five to fifty-four—know their houses will never rival the settings in *Martha*

Stewart Living, they squeeze what elements of domestic arts they can into tight budgets and schedules. They welcome Stewart's guidance, which empowers them to make their surroundings seem luxurious, inviting, and unique.

Stewart's fortune rests on the assumption that the home is a show-case for personal taste and a tool for solidifying one's middle-class identity. As an entrepreneur, she understands how consumers shape their living spaces into private palaces, acquiring objects in stores and arranging them in distinctive ways to reflect their self-image as individuals and as members of the middle class. America's domestic maven knows how consumer society works and where the business of domesticity fits in it.

The Martha Stewart look is distinctive—a signature "simple life" aesthetic. This brand identity has roots in Victorian times, when design was a tool for market segmentation. At the time, mainstream consumers began to surround themselves with things that were identified with the middle class. Sometimes, people's possessions reflected their place in society, but just as often con-sumers made purchases to indicate their aspirations. These same forces are at work today. Affordable products like Martha Stewart Everyday, a line of home goods sold by mega-discounter Kmart, make middle-class aesthetics available to almost everyone. Con-sumers study *Martha Stewart Living* and display the advertised goods at home to show their newly acquired good taste. In many respects, these contemporary working women are pretending to be Victorian housewives, whose middle-class status allowed them to stay at home, employ servants, and practice genteel domesticity.

Separate Spheres

After the Civil War, a heightened emphasis on domesticity began to transform a nation inclined toward materialism into a nation driven by consumerism, and the home became one of America's most impor-tant places. Many believed that nothing nurtured the mind, body, and soul better than the single-family dwelling, appropriately furnished with the right artifacts—acquisitions symbolic of class. Antebellum Americans embraced the idea of the private family home as a fortress, a retreat for a nation of people always on the move. Victorian Americans modified this notion, repositioning the home as a showplace for consumer taste.

This middle-class reverence for domestic life stemmed from a set of beliefs now widely known by historians as "separate spheres," referring to the division of the sexes by assigning specific gender traits to different spaces. Men dominated the "public sphere," which consisted of the marketplace and the political stage; they were in charge of earning the family's income by working in jobs outside the home. Middle- and upper-class women, by contrast, were confined to the "private sphere," or the hearth and home; they were not expected to earn money at all. Many household tasks, often shared by men, women, and children through the 1850s, became the woman's exclusive domain. Through this gendered division of labor, the home evolved into an environment that, if properly furnished and managed, would influence the family's well-being.

Early promoters of the gendered division of labor linked separate spheres to the Protestant values of health, economy, and morality. A good mother had to create a loving home that served as a bulwark against urban poverty, papist immigrants, and other perceived social evils. Domesticity's biggest advocate was Catherine E. Beecher, who together with her sister Harriet Beecher Stowe, of *Uncle Tom's Cabin* fame, wrote the 1869 best seller *American Woman's Home*. Beecher celebrated the hearth and home despite her career as a school principal, lecturer, and writer. She touted it as a place for teaching morality and cultivating good manners and was one of many advisors cautioning women against temptations like overshopping and following the trends of fashion. Nothing less than the future of the republic and national progress was at stake.

By the late 1800s, the notion of the home as a moral retreat receded and a secular alternative promoted greater consumerism. The new model still equated women with the domestic sphere and did little to advance their political and economic rights. Yet, the new way of doing things redefined women's household responsibilities to allow for greater personal creativity. The home became the linchpin of consumer society.

Victorian media experts—novelists, architects and builders, advice-book authors, and advertisers—guided women in their home-making role. As industrialization threw open the doors of consumer society, more people sought advice on how to act and outfit their homes. Cultural authorities used the media to promote the perfect home. They idealized it as a place for the rejuvenation of the spirit, the cultivation of manners, and the display of proper sensibilities. Martha Stewart is capitalizing on this legacy, which lay at the heart of Victorian consumer culture.

Dreams of Home Ownership

In Victorian America, the home provided shelter, fostered family solidarity, and signaled belonging to a social class or community. Many people evaluated each other through this prism, sizing up a residence to determine its occupants' place in society. They took cues from a home's location, size, style, condition, and interior decoration. In a boom-and-bust economy, purchasing a home required hard work, sobriety, thrift, and discipline. Home ownership was a mark of supreme accomplishment, denoting American values, community ties, and a steady income.

Scholars acknowledge that the Victorians valued home ownership, but they know far less about who bought their own residences, how they financed the purchases, and who failed in this endeavor. Property ownership had a precedent in Anglo American law, which valued real estate as a form of wealth; land was an investment, a fitting legacy from father to son. For those without capital, home ownership was possible only after years of financial sacrifice. People strapped for cash, excluded by law, or on the move—women, artisans, and immigrants—often had a tough time buying property. Because ownership was elusive, the home was lauded in popular culture as an emblem of success. Sentimental icons like John Howard Payne's 1823 song "Home, Sweet Home" may have inspired people to settle down. If not, they could at least decorate their rented apartments as reasonable facsimiles.

Victorian popular culture presented a remarkably consistent vision of the ideal family home. Books and magazines promoted the single-family dwelling, often a two-story structure in the center of a landscaped lot. The perfect house was a few feet back from the street and raised off the ground. It consisted of a warren of single-purpose rooms, each dedicated to a special activity. The first floor of a large house might have an entry hall, parlor, library, dining room, kitchen, and pantry. Upstairs were several bedrooms, a nursery, and a sewing room, while the attic held servants' quarters. A smaller house would have fewer rooms, but its floor plan was similarly compartmentalized. Stylistic elements of the houses stressed solidity, comfort, and tradition: mansard roofs, bay windows, and ivy-covered walls.

Idyllic depictions of such dwellings were popularized by Victorian magazines, how-to books, and architectural manuals. One volume that achieved wide circulation was Samuel B. Reed's *House-plans for Everybody* (1878), illustrated with architectural plans that were first published by a farmers' magazine, *American Agriculturalist*. This inexpensive plan book, sold by mail order, targeted rural people, encouraging them to build homes reflecting their aspirations. In Reed's view, a man's house was "an index of his character," an expression of "the owner's ability, taste, and purpose." The book showed forty houses that cost between $250 and $8,000 to build, from the humble cottage to the majestic mansion.

This vision of domestic bliss contrasted with the reality of Victorian America, where people lived in many different types of spaces, including rental units. In rural and small-town America, people resided in sprawling farmsteads built over multiple generations or temporary structures that indicated transitory status. As urban America grew, cities adapted to spatial pressures by expanding vertically and horizontally. Before zoning laws, commercial, industrial, and residential properties coexisted in the same neighborhoods. Housing stock was varied. People from different income groups, unmarried men and women, couples, and families lived in apartment buildings, boarding houses, cottages, duplexes, row houses, and tenements.

Between 1860 and 1900, 14 million immigrants and countless migrants from rural America caused the urban population to soar. In older port cities, congestion reached an all time high. In Boston, New York, and Philadelphia, gridlock was common, as pedestrians, horses, and vehicles vied for passage in the streets. The absence of zoning laws and environmental regulation meant that breweries, slaughterhouses, tanneries, and factories generating noise, smoke, and pollutants existed next to residential buildings. Chimneys belched smoke into the air, covering buildings with black coal residue. Horses and other urban animals produced foul, noxious waste. Overcrowded, unsanitary living conditions encouraged the spread of water- and airborne diseases like cholera, smallpox, tuberculosis, and typhoid fever. Still, many Americans had no choice but to seek their fortunes in crowded urban neighborhoods.

Transportation innovations relieved some, but not all, of the population pressure by helping to create low-density neighborhoods known as "streetcar suburbs." From Boston to Chicago, new transit systems—commuter railroads, horse cars, and later steam and electric trolleys—connected the city to surrounding land targeted for residential development. Nearby rural areas that once had farms mushroomed into America's first suburbs. Beginning in the 1870s, Boston expanded outward by two to twelve miles per decade, along the electric transit system. Smaller cities, like Cincinnati and Columbus, followed similar patterns. In each place, distinctive neighborhoods evolved, reflecting regional building styles and local consumers' pocketbooks.

Speculators saw the opportunity to amass real-estate fortunes by creating less-populated neighborhoods on the urban outskirts. In Chicago, real-estate investors pooled their resources, purchased large tracts of land, and laid out new subdivisions. Most of these syndicates were risky, short-term investments created to develop a single property within five years. After that, taxes eroded their profits and syndicates had to sell the lots quickly. Many targeted as buyers recent immigrants, who were strongly predisposed to home ownership, and were offered easy payment plans. Developers left the responsibility for installing streets, sidewalks, sewers, and utilities to the towns. If unable to pay the taxes for these services, families lost their property to the municipalities. Nonetheless, real-estate syndicates accounted for the successful, rapid development of the new, blue-collar districts in the Windy City.

Other aspects of Chicago's growth show the follies of making broad generalizations about nineteenth-century urban America. For example, new neighborhoods near factories, built with money from local industries, had sewer and water services before the upper-class suburbs, where residents didn't want to pay for these improvements.

Although people of different incomes, religions, and ethnic origins continued to live side-by-side, a new urban geography reflecting America's hierarchical social structure emerged in some sections of the country. For the first time in some locales, each economic group was relegated its own neighborhood in the streetcar suburbs. Wealthy people moved to spacious, tree-lined sections. Some white-collar employees who worked downtown continued to stay within walking distance of their jobs, while others commuted to them by streetcar. Blue-collar folks lived in factory districts on the urban periphery. By the 1880s, Milwaukee followed this course. The affluent lived north of the city along Lake Michigan; the lower middle-class Polish and German families lived in the southern and western districts.

Whether factory workers or physicians, Victorian property owners had to figure out how to pay for their homes. Today, a first-time home buyer with a good credit rating, a down payment, and a steady job can secure a mortgage from a bank. A century ago, thirty-year mortgages and first-time buyer incentives didn't exist. People were constrained by the limits of their personal financial circumstances, and they often had to rely on the combined resources of families, friends, and banks to buy a home. A new institution, the savings and loan, appeared in the Victorian era. Readers may recognize it from the 1946 Hollywood movie classic, *It's a Wonderful Life*. This Frank Capra film tells the story of George Bailey (James Stewart), who runs the Bailey Building and Loan in small-town America—Bedford Falls, New York—during the Great Depression and World War II.

By 1915, every state had these people's banks, serving more than 3 million members and having assets of more than $1.5 billion. Building-and-loan associations capitalized on deficiencies in the banking system. Most mortgages originated with an individual lender, such as the seller, and came due within three years. They covered half the purchasing price, and buyers had to scrape together the rest as a down payment. Most ordinary Americans couldn't meet these terms. In contrast, building-and-loan associations were membership organizations where depositors were shareholders. When someone put money into these associations, they purchased shares in a mortgage company that generated income by lending to borrowers. Savers earned competitive interest rates and received access to mortgages on favorable terms.

Whatever the difficulties of financing, many Americans clung to the idea of home ownership as a symbol of *success*. They continued to tighten their belts to buy homes. Two examples illustrate how working men managed to buy their dream houses. In 1879, a Roxbury, Massachusetts, coachman began saving part of his $35 monthly earnings with the goal of purchasing a home. In 1885, he put $200 down on an eleven-room dwelling that cost $1,900. His monthly payments accounted for more than half of his pay. A St. Paul, Minnesota, tailor joined a savings-and-loan association in 1876. He saved $10 per month until 1883, when he purchased two lots on the city's outskirts for $700. Two years later, he hired carpenters to build a two-story house for $1,860. His mortgage payment was $26 per month for eight years. Pleased as punch, the tailor compared his house to the posh mansions of the elite, who lived closer to St. Paul. "I have as fine a view as any of the nabobs of Summit Avenue," he boasted, "and can see up the river half-way to Minneapolis."

By embracing the home as an *idea*, Americans came to unify and differentiate themselves not only through the traditional means of religion, politics, and ethnicity, but also through the newer mechanism of consumption. The dream of home ownership promised everyone access to an American lifestyle based on the accumulation of worldly goods.

Womanly Creativity and the Art Craze

The rise of the single-family home influenced family behavior, gender roles, and consumption habits. In urban areas, commuting became part of the daily experience for men. During rush hour, the trains, streetcars, and sidewalks were crowded with clerks, lawyers, artisans, and teachers. Many wives stayed behind, their routines revolving around the management and care of the home.

By the 1870s, Charles Darwin's evolutionary theories, which addressed notions of hierarchy and difference in the natural world, were misused to continue justification for separate spheres. A man's rational inclination and aggressive disposition, it was believed, suited him for the bustling business world. For Victorians, a woman, seen as emotional, sentimental, and nurturing, had characteristics best suited to child rearing and housekeeping. In *A Plea for American Decorative Art* (1895), Cincinnati art teacher Benn Pitman summarized popular wisdom: "Let men construct and women decorate."

In this equation, the "fairer sex" held responsibility for beauty and aesthetics in the home. However, separate spheres generally denied women the chance to apply their artistic abilities to public projects such as architecture, sculpture, landscaping, or engineering. Those professions were reserved for men. In 1890, only one in forty women worked in factories, stores, or other people's homes for wages. The vast majority of them were homemakers, who managed a domestic system of ritual and symbolism that was increasingly associated with style and taste.

The emergence of the creative homemaker owed much to two demographic shifts that reduced the burdens of motherhood and housekeeping. For centuries, women had spent most of their adult lives bearing, feeding, and nurturing children. Between 1800 and 1900, the average number of children borne by white women who lived to menopause dropped from 7.0 to 3.7. The declining birth rate, ushered by a gradual decrease in childhood mortality and the spread of birth control, began to free women from the burden of continual childbearing. Another change reshaping the population began in the 1870s, when immigrants and migrants swelled the labor pool in the Northeast and the Midwest. Many of these female newcomers took low-paying jobs as household servants. Soon, nearly every middle-class household employed at least one servant who did the washing, cleaning, ironing, cooking, and baking. Now with domestic help, the mistress of the home had time to pursue aesthetic homemaking.

The focus on household taste developed from an "art craze" that swept across America as the economy rebounded from the Panic of 1873. Collecting was no longer the exclusive purview of elite men such as the oil baron John D. Rockefeller. Ordinary families could take pleasure from buying stylish products in the stores or collecting trade cards and pasting them into scrapbooks. The deflationary economy kept prices low and fed this fascination for beautiful things.

Women took part in the art craze in several ways. They could register for courses in engraving, drawing, painting, and wood carving at local art schools. They saw advertisements for new styles in newspapers, magazines, and billboards. They read books that linked aesthetics, femininity, and domesticity. Best sellers such as Clarence Cook's *The House Beautiful* (1878), Charles Locke Eastlake's *Hints on Household Taste* (1883), and Candace Wheeler's *Household Art* (1893) told homemakers how to create beautiful rooms. The craze extended to all social classes. The publisher's preface to George A. Martin's 1888 book, *Our Homes: How to Beautify Them,* noted: "It is not alone the mansions of wealth and luxury which have experienced the results of this decorative advancement, but the humble homes everywhere through the land reveal the beautifying touch of taste and skill."

Where Catherine Beecher had linked domesticity and morality, the art craze encouraged women to indulge in material goods for the sake of pleasure. For the first time in American history, mainstream culture—the education system, the media, and the retailing network—linked aesthetic experience to consumerism.

The artistic home became an important tool for displaying the family's wealth, dignity, and social position. Victorians understood that interior decoration—the furnishings, textiles, and bric-a-brac—represented a household's achievements. The astute observer, versed in the symbolism of the period, sized up an ensemble of objects to formulate an impression of the occupants. Through associative thinking, the visitor linked the objects in the home to larger cultural beliefs, ideas, and values. In *The Lady's Guide to Perfect Gentility* (1856), Emily Thornwell argued that taste proceeded "from the power which objects have to recall other ideas to the mind." The intuitive person knew how to follow the subtle links from object to idea. Victorians literally took their "object lessons" to heart.

Victorian women were responsible for choosing and managing the goods that furnished this symbolic world. As they transformed the public rooms of their homes into miniature museums, they faced considerable challenges, needing to combine store purchase, natural history specimens, and homemade crafts into unique, tasteful statements. The resulting aesthetic interior reflected the family's economic success while providing a retreat from the harsh outside world. A properly decorated interior not only applauded progress by spotlighting consumer goods made in distant factories, it also honored womanly creativity by displaying feminine handicrafts and a woman's ability to construct an aesthetic home.

The artistic homemaker, less burdened by tiring chores than earlier generations, was expected to develop an individual taste. Her servants could wash the laundry; the homemaker had to create and maintain a stylish interior that reflected her family's affinity with mainstream values. Wifely duty had been redefined around a new set of skills. As the arbiter of taste, the woman became less a housewife and more a shopper, fashion expert, and interior decorator. In short, she became a consumer.

The Victorian Parlor

Several rooms in the home held particular meaning for Victorian consumers: the hallway, the parlor, and the dining room. Here, homemakers displayed their prized possessions, showcasing their husbands' purchasing power and their own skills as interior decorators. These rooms became the essence of Victorian consumer culture.

Consumers used the public spaces of the ground floor to impress visitors—whether acquaintances, friends, relatives, or strangers. Many new Victorian homes had a hall, a substantial entryway that measured six to eight feet wide by twelve or more feet long. The hall functioned as a transitional space connecting the public and private spheres, meshing the masculine world of business and commerce with the feminine domain. Most halls had an elaborate front door with stained or frosted glass, a grand stairway, fancy lighting fixtures, and specialized furnishings designed to make an impression.

Two now-obsolete items found in the hall—the hallstand and the card receiver—suggest how this transitional space was used. A large piece of case furniture, the hallstand featured a plate-glass mirror, a seat, hooks, and an umbrella stand. Family members used the mirror to check their appearance before leaving and to store their hats, overcoats, and raingear after coming home. The card receiver—often a metal dish with a pedestal foot—held the cards of female visitors, who by convention filled up their afternoons by calling on each other.

Adjacent to the hall, the parlor was the home's aesthetic showcase and what Katherine C. Grier, author of *Culture and Comfort*, terms the "memory palace." To Victorians, the parlor represented the pinnacle of the family's achievement and taste. Families used this room for entertaining visitors and marking rites of passage, such as birthdays, weddings, and funerals. The parlor presented the family's best face to the world through the careful display of prized possessions. The precious atmosphere was *intentional*. This was a ritualistic, aesthetic space that made a house into a home and a statement.

Interior decoration gave the parlor its distinctive look and conveyed information to visitors. It was a mix of textures, colors, and materials: velvets, fringes, ribbons, florid wallpapers, portrait photographs, and every knickknack imaginable. To Victorians, this busyness conveyed urbane sophistication, a worldly familiarity with the latest styles. The overstuffed sofas and chairs, copies of French rococo furniture, suggested that the family understood European elegance. Imported Belgian carpets or American imitations of them added to the room's color and warmth.

The bric-a-brac, or "what-not," shelf embodied the parlor's role as a repository for the family's trophies, memories, and relics. In *Life on the Mississippi* (1883), Mark Twain wrote about riverside homes in which every parlor had a "pyramidal what-not in the corner, the shelves occupied chiefly with bric-a-brac of the period, disposed with an eye to best effect." Twain noted the family's precious treasures: seashells carved with prayers; an unusual piece of quartz; a locket containing an ancestor's hair; and young ladies' artwork. In poorer homes, consumers displayed their relics on a mantel or a small wall shelf, which served as a makeshift what-not cabinet. This unique piece of furniture was used to fulfill the artistic goals set by the culture at large.

The dining room was another focal point. The wealthy had always used the dining room to show off their power and position, and other Americans adapted their model. The ritualistic evening meal became a bonding rite, a vehicle for forging intimate social relationships. Dining demanded proper behavior from the host family and the guests, particularly when the sexes mingled. Ceremony dictated the use of specialized utensils and decorations, such as damask tablecloths, fine china, silver, and floral centerpieces. A proper table setting featured separate forks for the fruit, the oysters, the fish, the meat course, the dessert, and even the pickles. The dining room became a place for family gatherings after harsh days away from home and a showcase for the artistic tastes of the housewife as consumer.

"Making Do"

Furnishing a beautiful home tested a family's financial, emotional, and aesthetic resources. Families negotiated expenditures as they faced the constant threat of unemployment, income stagnation, bankruptcy, and forced mobility. The aesthetic home, with its link to progress, served as a reminder of familial steadiness, determination, and improvement. Material comfort could be short-lived, sometimes lasting only until the next recession.

Yet Americans coveted consumer luxuries. Some objects testified to a family's participation in the mainstream, while other things showed its affinity with subcultures defined by income, occupation, gender, generation, or ethnicity. Mass retailers, the subject of Chapter Three, understood the segmented Victorian market, offering styles, decorations, and prices for nearly everyone. This elasticity made consumption appealing, empowering people to recast themselves into who they wanted to be through their possessions. The experiences of several real-life consumers demonstrate this point.

Frances James, the wife of a small-time lawyer and real-estate investor in St. Paul, Minnesota, typified the mainstream consumer. In 1888, Frances and her new husband, Henry, moved into a rambling house in the new suburban development of Newport Park, where they lived for eleven years. Henry left each day for his office, while Francis devoted her talent and energy to converting their house into a beautiful home.

Frances tackled projects one room at a time, soon discovering the challenges of creating her dream home. Shortly after moving in, she supervised a paint crew who scoffed at her choice of colors. With an iron fist in a velvet glove, she managed the truculent workers and emerged triumphant. "The parlor is lovely," she confided in a letter to her mother, "ceiling pale cream, frieze pale olive ending a foot from the ceiling, walls dull olive, woodwork natural pine which is a beautiful soft yellow." Frances asserted her aesthetic will over the male painters, who saw color choice as the prerogative of their craft. Her victory attested to the artisans' fading glory and to women's newfound command of aesthetics.

Over the next ten years, Frances repeatedly modified her interior decorations in the pursuit of perfection. She sometimes cut corners, recycling materials to "make do." Handicrafts were indispensable, enabling Frances to beautify on a budget. In 1888, for example, she built some furniture out of old boxes and fabric fragments. "We made some chairs; one I covered with dark green corduroy and it looks a handsome chair if one is not in [on] the secret," she wrote to her mother and sister. "I had a cheap pine music stand that the painter ebonized for me and with a green plush curtain and some pretty bits of china on it, it looks like a handsome thing." Frances's efforts paralleled those of other women whose desires outstripped their incomes. In countless homes across the nation, women decorated with whatever materials were available.

But Frances's beautification projects couldn't ward off the hardships wrought by the unstable economy. At the end of the long depression of the nineties, Henry's foundering businesses finally failed. His 1899 bankruptcy forced the family to sell their big suburban house and move into modest quarters in St. Paul. The move relieved Henry of financial burdens, but Frances lamented her family's spiraling fortunes and diminished social status. Nothing made her happier than decorating the Newport Park house, where the gorgeous interior spoke to her artistry and impressed the right guests. The "lovely dining room" served as a stage for the formal evening meals built around Frances's china, silver, and linens. Ritual and beauty, however, did not pay the bills. Bitterly, Frances blamed Henry for the loss of their "lovely home."

The experience of the James family, documented in Frances's letters, offers a rare glimpse at how cultural prescriptions, consumer practice, and economic realities intersected in one middle-class household. Anxious to promote her husband's career, Frances sized up other Newport Hill residents and tried to imitate them. She used her skills in interior decorating to interpret what she saw in magazines, books, and shopping expeditions, even if it meant making do. In the end, Frances's inability to keep up with the Joneses soured her temperament. She believed, following advice-book authors like Samuel B. Reed, that a home mirrored a family's position in the community.

Immigrants with modest incomes also partook of domestic consumerism, converting rooms in their cottages and flats into makeshift parlors. In their hands, household goods became instruments of ethnic distinction and group solidarity while symbolizing their hopes to join the middle class. Victorian photographs and parlor suites were treasured along with linens, lace curtains, holy pictures, and other ethnic or religious icons from the Old Country. Some objects, like the upright piano, bridged continents and classes. The wheels of change meshed, as fashion and tradition played out in the choices of immigrant consumers.

Catherine Dougherty Gibbons, the immigrant wife of a foreman at the du Pont gunpowder mills in Wilmington, Delaware, is a case in point. Born in Ireland in 1821, Catherine immigrated to America as a young woman, marrying Irish powder worker John Gibbons in 1842. When John became a boss in 1863, the couple moved into a six-room, company-owned dwelling adjacent to the powder yards. Over the next twenty years, Catherine outfitted the house with the accessories of a middle-class lifestyle, creating an upstairs parlor with walnut furniture, a dining table, and a linen cabinet. After John died in 1885, she moved into her own house in a nearby neighborhood, where she lived until her death ten years later.

Catherine and John Gibbons had "made it" in America, at least in the eyes of other workers in the powder yards. Certainly, John's blue work shirt set him apart from Mr. du Pont. Yet the Gibbons family perched on the upper rungs of the powder yard's social hierarchy, and they savored this position by endorsing the ideology of social betterment as expressed through consumerism. Catherine valued her upward mobility, taking care to "show off a little bit" by using fancy tablecloths. She also remembered her humble beginnings, treating each piece of Irish linen as a prized possession, much like the sacred altar coverings in Catholic churches. Catherine epitomized the "lace-curtain Irish," who judiciously used a few sumptuous goods to mark social achievement and respectability.

Elsewhere, recent immigrants echoed Gibbons's behavior, blending their desires to become American with Old World nostalgia and religious devotion. New York social worker Louise Bolard More documented the eclectic tastes she observed among newcomers. "The typical home of the wage-earners in this district is quite well furnished and fairly neat and clean," she wrote in her 1907 study, *Wage-Earners' Budgets*. The average parlor was "usually gaudy," sporting "plush furniture (sometimes covered with washable covers), carpet on the floor, cheap lace-curtains at the windows, crayon portraits of the family on the walls, and usually religious pictures of saints, the Virgin Mary, or 'The Sacred Heart,' sometimes a couch, and the ubiquitous folding bed." Other observers reported that Jewish families had prints of rabbis, photographs of family in the Old Country, and colorful, traditional birthday plaques. Catholics and Jews placed religious icons, personal memorabilia, and household goods side-by-side, in an effort to convert modest interiors into American homes.

In Victorian times as now, there were people who skirted the edges of middle-class respectability or lived outside the family unit. Single men could live in a homelike environment, if it suited them. Their living quarters varied, from rooms in private homes to boarding houses and apartment hotels. Landladies decorated their boarding houses with comfortable furniture and pictures. A nice sitting room would attract boarders seeking respite from hang-outs like barber shops and billiard rooms. Some immigrant men created their own "home away from home" by filling their rooms with personal memorabilia, statuary, and holy pictures.

For many on the margins, consumer goods often had dual significance, signaling an awareness of the dominant value system while denoting connections to a subculture. Mainstream culture and its advice-book authors, magazine writers, and newspaper editors gave meaning to objects that readers could follow or discard. People could decide for themselves what objects meant. Thus a piano could be an item of prestige, a courtship tool, or a symbol of Old Country traditions.

Toward Modern Simplicity:
The Bungalow and the Living Room

By the end of the century, the media began criticizing the cozy rituals at the heart of Victorian consumer culture. The discovery that germs cause disease provided a rationale for zealous urban reformers to rid cities of health hazards, such as sewer gas and uncollected garbage. The war against germs extended into the home, where it clashed with the mainstays of Victorian design. Reformers stressed cleanliness and efficiency, while new technologies enabled the development of a simpler look. This resulted in clean architectural styles and floor plans; it also contributed to the slow death of the cluttered and hard-to-dust look and the evolution of the "parlor" into the less-formal "living room."

The immense popularity of the traditional Victorian parlor among working-class Americans did much to fuel the reform impulse that reshaped household interiors along simpler lines. As more and more working-class people created parlors, better-off families started to look askance at the overuse of plush carpets and knickknacks. Xenophobia bred fear; recent immigrants were perceived as being unkempt, their tastes unrefined, and their homes dirty.

Tastemakers, and the middle-class consumers who read their opinions, started to reject Victorian designs in favor of more authentic "American" styles. They looked to the past for inspiration and found a gold mine of examples in rural life and colonial history. Colonial artifacts, like the spinning wheel and the fireplace, were re-invented as humble symbols of an uncomplicated time. This "colonial revival" stimulated new hobbies like antique collecting and created a market for architecture and furniture in the Colonial and Mission styles.

Back in 1876, the Centennial Exposition stirred interest in "Ye olden time" with a restaurant called the Old Log Cabin, or the New England Kitchen. While other displays celebrated progress, the New England Kitchen sold food to hungry fairgoers in a make-believe colonial house. The building had an open floor plan with a large stone fireplace or hearth. Its single large space or "keeping room" was furnished with candlesticks, spinning wheels, cradles, and other quaint "old-time" objects. The effect contrasted with Victorian coziness, momentarily transporting fairgoers to a bygone era. Clarence Cook invoked this imagery in *The House Beautiful* as he pitched a return to pre-industrial styles. Middle-class consumers didn't blindly follow Cook, but many who had seen the New England Kitchen gave serious thought to his critique of Victorian design.

By 1900, a dramatic new idea from the social sciences—the concept of "personality"—found its way into popular culture. It fed the interest in design reform and began to supplant the Victorian emphasis on "character." This shift had been underway for decades, starting when advice-givers sanctioned beautiful interiors as a form of feminine self-expression. Ingenuity was still encouraged, object lessons still mattered, but the tone changed. Middle-class consumers cast aside their mothers' Victorian preferences and bought furnishings in new and simpler styles.

Between the 1890s and the 1920s, the specialized layout of the Victorian home gave way to the open floor plan of the bungalow, the first truly national housing style. Scholars don't agree on the origins of this modest dwelling. The term *bungalow* originated in British colonial India, where it referred to a single-story house with a veranda. Joseph C. Bigott argues that the American bungalow has eclectic roots. His study of blue-collar bungalows in Chicago shows how these dwellings combined features from the traditional hall-and-parlor house, the workingman's cottage, and the new California casual home. The bungalow typically blended traditional carpentry techniques, factory-made woodwork, and new technological amenities like electricity and indoor plumbing. Victorian-style ornamentation like stained-glass windows and crystal door knobs were toned down to match the plainer aesthetic. Most likely, architects and carpenters borrowed from various sources as they designed the first American bungalows for people of modest means who wanted to live in convenient surroundings.

The bungalow was often an unpretentious small house, with one-and-a-half floors, a shaded porch, and a front door opening directly into a large living room. Through a series of archways, the living room led into the dining area and the kitchen. Visually, the layout created an open, airy feeling, suggesting continuity between the indoors and the outdoors. While there were regional variations on this format, one theme was consistent: Victorian preciousness yielded to Modern openness. The total emphasis on *light* gave the illusion of space, so even the most diminutive bungalows didn't feel claustrophobic. After 1900, women's magazines promoted the bungalow as the most up-to-date form of housing.

The living room may have seemed novel to bungalow owners, but this multipurpose space had historical roots in the colonial keeping room. Influenced by the New England Kitchen, early-twentieth-century builders revived older ideas about spatial versatility, updating the keeping room as the modern living room. It often featured a prominent fireplace, the ultimate symbol of "olden days." After 1900, most new residential construction, including single-family bungalows, residential hotels, and apartment buildings, featured the living room, making it into a cornerstone of the American home.

The bungalow owed its versatility and appeal to the technologies of electrification, standardized plumbing, and central heating. Electrification, which will be studied in Chapter Five, delivered reliable power around the clock. With electricity and central heating, homemakers no longer had to arrange the furniture to make the best use of gas wall sconces or parlor stoves. Fabrics once used to retain warmth became quaint reminders of Victorian times. Standardized indoor plumbing and bathroom fixtures made it easier to clean the house, wash clothes, and attend to bodily functions.

These breakthroughs occurred at the same time as population shifts that limited the supply of household servants. Between 1900 and 1920, the number of American households counted by the U.S. Census Bureau grew from 15.9 to 24.4 million, while domestic servants declined from 1.6 to 1.4 million. In 1900, there was 1 servant for every 9.9 households; by 1920, 1 for every 17.4 homes. Increasingly, young immigrant women took jobs in factories and offices, which paid more and allowed them to socialize with their peers. Although black women still worked as domestics, some white households refused to hire them or the new immigrants, due to racial and ethnic biases. Concurrently, service providers such as laundries, butchers, dairies, and seamstresses cut back on home deliveries to reduce prices and compete with mass retailers, which stocked the new brands of packaged soap and ready-made clothes.

These changes created, in the words of historian Ruth Schwartz Cowan, "more work for mother," reducing or eliminating the time available for handiwork projects. The artistic home of the 1880s had required the labor of at least two women: the homemaker along with her daughter or another female relative or a domestic servant. The extra help had freed the homemaker's time for leisure and artistic pursuits. A generation later, the servant shortage meant that the homemaker had to shoulder the burdens of child rearing and housework. Early-twentieth-century women swept the art craze under the rug and adopted simpler decorating styles.

Advice books and magazines instructed consumers on banishing Victorian clutter from middle-class life. Transparent lace curtains replaced heavy velvet draperies, while oriental scatter rugs ousted wall-to-wall ingrain carpets. Decorative accents came from the studied placement of a few treasured objects, such as an electric table lamp with a stained-glass shade or a pottery vase in a solid green glaze. The living room and the bathroom, brightly lit and filled with sparkling fixtures, showcased the homemaker's awareness of cleanliness and efficiency.

Dozens of new household experts appeared to help consumers understand these decorating styles and to manage their work load. One of the most influential, Christine Frederick (1883–1970) might be described as the Martha Stewart of her time. As a contributing editor to the *Ladies' Home Journal* from 1912 to 1919, Frederick preached "simple living" to millions of readers, while running a profitable business that tested products for manufacturers. She used her reputation as the nation's leading domestic expert to sell appliances, much like Martha Stewart engages the media to market her brand. In the *Journal*, Frederick described ways to simplify chores, encouraging women to apply the principles of scientific management to tasks like cleaning and cooking. She aimed to streamline homemaking, eliminate drudgery, and value women's household work, while turning domestic advisement into a profitable business.

The case of Helen James, the daughter of Henry and Frances James from Minnesota, shows how women responded to the new prescriptions for household management. In 1909, Helen married Harry Sommers, whose family were prosperous dry-goods wholesalers in St. Paul. While Helen inherited her mother's artistic sensibilities, she readily adapted to the conventions of the moment. Her tastes extended to the new Mission style, marketed by furniture factories as perfect for the open floor plan. In outfitting her new home, Helen picked out furnishings and accessories that she thought reflected her personality, but she consulted husband Harry before making her final decisions. She excitedly wrote to a friend: "Harry & I are working every thing out together—He is lovely about every thing. & adopts my ways without a protest, candles & bare table & all." While her mother took full responsibility for interior decoration, Helen expected her partner

to contribute his thoughts. While the older woman made do by mending cushions and re-dyeing curtains, Helen purchased new things. Her
experiences reflected evolving cultural patterns that included men in
household choices, valued a simplified look, and redefined consumption around shopping.

Middle-class women less confident than Sommers were sometimes
confused by the proliferation of new decorating styles. In September
1908, one such consumer, Mrs. Old Fashioned, asked *Good Housekeeping* for help. Writing to the magazine's Good Taste in Furniture
column, Mrs. Old Fashioned reported a dislike for both working-class
aesthetics *and* the cutting-edge look appreciated by Sommers. What
should a consumer do if she loathed the "very elaborate and over-
ornamented cheap things of the stores which sell on the installment
plan" and the "clumsy, heavy furniture of the mission style, which
. . . suggests a public library or a railroad depot?"

Good Housekeeping advised against mixing-and-matching,
which created visual pollution. "Mission furniture does not belong in
a room with wallpaper, lace curtains, white-painted mantels, flowered
carpets, [or] dainty bric-a-brac." It "needs an environment all its own
of burlap and subdued tones, an environment of broad oak doors, of
carbon prints, of brasses, coppers and pottery." For consumers who
disliked Mission's massiveness, Colonial Revival was an option. But
above all, a home decorator had to know her taste, understand how
to carry it through, and exert discipline when shopping. "The first
law is to be sincere," the editors explained. "The second law is to be
self-restrained."

While the Victorian interior had pivoted on the profusion of artifacts and social rituals, a plainer aesthetic grew among Modern tastemakers and middle-class consumers. The new Modern look co-existed
with older Victorian styles, which remained the favorite of immigrant
and working-class consumers well into the twentieth century. In mainstream taste, warmth was defined by simplicity rather than clutter or
formality. Victorian parlors kept up appearances and presented the right
image, while Modern interiors revealed the homemaker's inner self in
a more transparent way. Significantly, nineteenth-century tastemakers
had described the parlor as the "face" of the Victorian house, while

Emily Post, the leading etiquette columnist of the twentieth century, called the living room "the very heart of the American home."

Martha Stewart Revisited

Many of the ideas, practices, and styles introduced in Victorian America remain with us today. Martha Stewart's product ensemble is a re-interpretation of housekeeping basics promoted by Catherine Beecher in the 1860s and Christine Frederick in the 1910s. Martha's handicraft projects such as refinishing chairs would have been familiar to Victorian consumers like Frances James and Catherine Gibbons. The simplicity of Martha Stewart Everyday owes much to the Colonial Revival and Mission styles that generated open floor plans and living rooms. Frances's daughter, Helen Sommers, would have made the connection.

Our own experiences with Martha Stewart raise important questions about the relationship between prescription and practice. Millions of Americans regularly follow Stewart's daily television shows, web site, magazines, and buy her products at Kmart and Macy's, while millions more openly criticize Stewart and other contemporary style mavens. There's no right or wrong way to approach people like Martha Stewart, Catherine Beecher, and Christine Frederick — American consumers have always taken the suggestions of domestic advisors piecemeal, using their ideas to a greater or lesser extent.

Stewart, like her forerunners, knows that the home is expressive but conservative. Homemaking reflects national ideologies about class, gender, race, ethnicity, and consumerism. Those values, in turn, embody ideas developed in Victorian America, which was dominated by white Protestants. People's continued faith in the home shows that those values are still part of the mainstream. American women have borrowed from the Victorian formula as they see fit, sometimes wholeheartedly, sometimes only in part. Some have abandoned their ethnic, blue-collar roots, using consumerism to create entirely new identities.

Born in New Jersey to Polish-American working-class parents as Martha Kostyra, Stewart is a living example of the re-invention that she promotes. Those humble origins may have engendered in Stewart the appreciation for how ordinary women see themselves in relation to the mass media and how they envision the home as a stage for self-presentation and personal fulfillment. For most twenty-first-century women, however, beautification is a high-wire balancing act between home and work. Victorian women pioneered those practices, following cultural expectations for proper gender roles while bending society's rules to define themselves as consumers.

CHAPTER TWO

Dress Codes

Carrie Bradshaw, the heroine of *Sex and the City,* epitomizes the single woman of the New Millennium. When not writing her column or dating, Carrie spends time with her girlfriends in restaurants, bars, beauty salons, and stores. Her closets overflow with designer outfits and a hundred pairs of $400 shoes. She lives for glamour and fashion, never wearing the same outfit twice.

Carrie's fans identify with her freewheeling spirit, thirty-something lifestyle, and impeccable fashion sense. She seems so smart and up-to-date that it's hard to believe that she had a Victorian namesake: Carrie Meeber, the heroine in Theodore Dreiser's 1900 novel, *Sister Carrie.* While Bradshaw browses SoHo boutiques for designer labels, Sister Carrie lusts after the clothes in Chicago's bustling new department stores. Contemporary Carrie relishes designer chic. Meeber craved the jackets and skirts stocked by stores like Marshall Field's.

While *Sex and the City* is a lighthearted comedy about contemporary single women, *Sister Carrie* is a morality tale about a Victorian consumer succumbing to worldly temptation. Eventually, Carrie Bradshaw and her girlfriends find happiness, love, and security. Youthful indiscretions leave no scars. Wild days in the big city and the pursuit of fashion, are just their rites of passage. Sister Carrie, in contrast, becomes a fallen woman. She is the victim of her own poor judgment about men and the pleasures they can provide.

For both characters, self-presentation hinges on choosing the right fashions, in assembling outfits that tell onlookers who they are and where they belong in American society. The Carrie of our time dresses in outfits that reflect her personality. In contrast, the Victorian Carrie understands that clothing certifies social class. As she encounters new people, Sister Carrie draws inferences about them from their dress. She fantasizes that rich people spend their time "counting money, dressing magnificently, and riding in carriages" and becomes self-conscious when seeing "better dressed girls" on the street. Their outfits demonstrate to her her inadequacies, both social and sartorial.

Carrie Bradshaw exists in a world where designer labels matter. Satin shoes by Manolo Blahnik; handbags by Louis Vuitton; and *prêt-à-porter* (high-end ready-to-wear clothes) by Vivienne Westwood define her world. These international luxury brands signify quality, status, and distinction. Her girlfriends understand the code, as do *Sex and the City* devotees who pant after these brands every day.

In contrast, Sister Carrie doesn't know what a designer label is. In 1900, there were no such things as global luxury brands like Louis Vuitton, the Liz Claiborne empire, or subcultural styles like grunge. Carrie Meeber lives at a time when the women's ready-to-wear industry is just beginning to develop. Not surprisingly, Sister Carrie yearns after having some store-bought clothes, which symbolize an escape from the drudgery of rural America and the embarrassment of the homemade dress. The country bumpkin transforms herself into an urban fashionista, giving up her "worn shirt-waist of dotted blue percale" for a little tan jacket with large mother-of-pearl buttons that was all the rage that fall. She uses fashion as a tool in her quest for respectability.

Separated by a century, Carrie Bradshaw and Carrie Meeber experience consumer culture in different ways emblematic of very different eras. For Bradshaw, personality matters more than social position; for Meeber, the opposite is true. For both, however, fashionable clothing is crucial. Each tries to follow the dress codes of her time, using personal appearance to establish her identity as a woman, a consumer, and a person.

Fashion and Social Identity

People have always believed in the persuasive power of fashion, using it to convey information about themselves to others. In old Europe, fashionable dress marked the power of aristocrats, while coarser clothing gave common people a proper sense of humility. These societies, which used birth to determine a person's rank, had formal systems of attire that passed from generation to generation. The "uniform" that a person wore revealed his or her predetermined status in society.

In colonial America, everyone knew how to read these signs, sizing up each other by appearance. Wealthy people were the only ones who owned more than a few outfits, which they wore on different occasions to flaunt their riches and mark their status. Merchants and plantation owners emulated aristocrats by wearing powdered wigs, embroidered silk coats, and buckled shoes in colorful London styles. Priests and ministers wore ecclesiastical garb, craftsman sported leather britches and aprons, and so forth. Clothing was expensive, and most people had very little. Colonists wore the same thing, changing only on laundry day.

In Victorian America, this convention—dressing for a predetermined social role—began to fray. Fashion and aspiration started to supersede custom and tradition as drivers of consumer choice. In Europe, cities like London and Paris housed the prosperous *bourgeois* class of merchants, bankers, and manufacturers. The *bourgeoisie* (referring to a middle class whose wealth was not a birthright) wore fashions that set them apart from both royals and the riff-raff. Transatlantic trade brought European styles to the United States, to consumers hungry for fashion news. Women's magazines like *Godey's Lady's Book* and *Peterson's Magazine* published colorful engravings of the latest Paris styles. In major cities, stores sold fine European fabrics, shawls, and scarves; they imported Paris dresses to copy for their own "French salons." Men's tailors kept abreast of Bond Street news, to cut a stylish London fit. Nearly everyone in America at some time caught a glimpse of the new styles from Berlin, London, Paris, and Vienna.

European glamour mingled with relaxed American mobility and the democratic impulse to create a new way of "dressing the part." In the United States, clothes could literally make the man. Clothing showed an affinity with mainstream values, a deliberate divergence from them, or something in between. People new to the middle-class learned to dress like respectable men and women. Immigrants who wanted to be American copied local styles. Subcultural fads like bloomers were a political statement for suffragists; black velvet trousers, the mark of rebellion among artists and gays. The Old World convention of "dressing for the role assigned to you" became the American innovation: "dressing for the role you want."

Ready-to-Wear and the Democratization of Clothing

In 1895, one of America's major mail-order houses, Montgomery Ward, gave a fitting name to the affordable women's blouses and skirts in its catalog: ready-to-wear. This Chicago retailer didn't invent factory-made clothing, but its catalogs helped shoppers from Boston to Billings find it. Montgomery Ward's catchy phrase, ready to wear, stuck and assumed a life of its own. Today, ready-to-wear describes almost everything produced by the vast international apparel business: Carrie Bradshaw's prêt-à-porter, global brands sold at Macy's, jeans at The Gap, and baby clothes at Wal★Mart.

After the Civil War, the industrialization of clothing production put serviceable and fashionable clothes within the reach of more consumers. Until the mid-twentieth century, Europeans still wore items sewn by tailors, dressmakers, and seamstresses, and clothing continued to mark a person's rank in society. However, by the late nineteenth century, middle- and working-class Americans could buy some factory-made clothing, helping to blur social distinctions. From its nineteenth-century beginnings, the American ready-to-wear industry, based in New York and smaller centers, was the world's most advanced in terms of both production and merchandising.

Colonial American households acquired their clothing in two ways. First, women bought British textiles from local shopkeepers and stitched the family's simplest clothes by hand. Second, they paid dressmakers and tailors to make more complicated articles. Style trends dictated particular silhouettes, requiring the skills of trained professionals who knew how to cut fabric and fit garments to different body types. It was a challenge for eighteenth-century women to make a good dress or a man's coat. This was true for most people throughout the colonies. One exception was a mobile population at the lower end of colonial society. Sailors could buy cheap, ready-made, hand-sewn clothing from "slop shops" near the docks.

The U.S. clothing industry grew dramatically in the early nineteenth century, particularly in New York. The nascent ready-made industry, the slop shops that principally catered to men and boys, provided the model for expansion. In 1860, New York had 1,286 firms that made and retailed clothing. Other clothing centers included New Orleans with 982 firms, Philadelphia 560, Cincinnati 345, and San Francisco 271. Each served regional markets, catering to local needs. New Orleans, for example, produced clothes for the hot Southern climate, including cheap clothes for slaves.

The men's clothing trade rationalized and consolidated earlier than the women's apparel industry. The Civil War created a large demand for military uniforms and civilian garb, which encouraged small clothiers to consolidate production, purchase sewing machines, and expand their output. The Army compiled statistics on men's body measurements and shared this information with clothing contractors. Civil War uniforms were the first clothes made in standardized sizes.

In menswear, the sewing machine introduced high-speed production, which co-existed with hand-tailoring methods even in the largest factories. Relatively plain articles of men's clothing, such as nightshirts, underwear, work clothes, and sports attire, were among the first garments to be entirely machine sewn or machine-knitted. On the other hand, the familiar business suit blended machine sewing with a good deal of hand finishing. That's still true today.

Women's clothing was different. Fashionable ladies' attire was difficult to construct and was subject to sudden style changes. Clothing needed to be simpler before manufacturers could make it, and this wouldn't happen until the flapper styles of the 1920s. The transition from custom-sewn garments to ready-to-wear occurred in several phases. In the 1860s, cloaks and mantles (a loose coat worn over other outer garments) were among the few factory-made articles of women's clothing. By the 1870s, women's undergarments and simple housedresses were sold by stores and mail-order catalogs. In the ensuing decades, the garment industry began making basic washable outfits for women who worked in factories, offices, and stores. Tailored suits and separates, like the blouses and skirts in the Montgomery Ward catalog, gained popularity during the 1880s and 1890s, marking the real debut of women's ready-to-wear.

By 1900, consumers at the top and bottom of the social ladder could easily purchase *some* articles of ready-made clothing. Yet Victorian closets weren't as large and well-stocked as our own, nor did shopping revolve around designer labels, mass advertising, and suburban malls. Historical change occurred unevenly, in fits and starts, buffeted by the forces of Victorian fashion, personal identity, and consumer culture.

The Clothes Make the Man: Dark Suits and White Collars

Sex and the City heroine Carrie Bradshaw has a string of boyfriends, but one named Mr. Big makes her head spin again and again. The dashing Big spends his workday behind a large mahogany desk in a corner office of a Manhattan skyscraper. Fans never learn exactly what Big does, but they know he's loaded. His possessions provide the clues: uptown condo, chauffeured limousine, and exquisitely tailored suits.

Carrie and Big use fashion to make identity statements, and each follows the gendered dress codes inaugurated in the Victorian era. While Carrie dresses to accentuate her curves, Big wears a business suit that emphasizes his height and build. Carrie looks like a flower, her delicacy accented by Big's simple elegance. The interplay of styles, textures, and colors helps to define each character's age, class, and gender.

Gender presentation through fashion has a long history. For centuries in the West, men have worn trousers and women skirts, which stress the sexual dimorphism of the human race and the gender roles sanctioned by the culture. In the eighteenth century, wealthy men and women both wore bright colors and sported lace, ruffles, and embroidery. These visual elements spoke to his or her *rank* in society, more than his or her *gender*. By the nineteenth century, the reverse was the case. Middle-class males dressed to look like the ideal Victorian man, and females to match the Victorian epitome of womanhood. Today's casual unisex look didn't exist, even in bohemian or homoerotic subcultures.

In the 1890s, the contrast between women's and men's clothing was at its sharpest, reflecting idealized notions about character, sexuality, and gender. The masculine look conveyed solidity and uniformity to signal the white-collar breadwinner's steady earning power. The feminine hourglass shape emphasized the woman's fertility and her role as a caregiver and nurturer.

Masculine ambition in the Victorian era was tied to progress, the advancement of civilization through improved material conditions. During the early part of the century, the typical male hero in newspapers, novels, and magazines had been a religious, military, frontier, or political figure. By the 1870s, the businessman displaced these images, and the media praised "captains of industry" as pinnacles of manliness.

To succeed in his job, the Victorian breadwinner had to stay in shape and be alert, unsentimental, and healthy. Advice literature—self-help books, newspapers, and magazines—encouraged men to pursue their careers vigorously and exercise their bodies. This was the time when the masculine penchant for modern sports took its form. By the 1890s, men reveled in leisure activities like body building, tennis, golf, croquet, badminton, ping pong, and baseball, all of which used specialized equipment and clothing. Some activities even required that sports enthusiasts join the new urban athletic clubs that had tracks, gymnasiums, swimming pools, bowling alleys, and exercise machines.

Teddy Roosevelt was the role model for this strapping version of American manliness. His escapades as a Wild West cowboy, New York City police commissioner, and Spanish-American War Rough Rider made front-page news. Roosevelt's athletic body epitomized the masculine solidity that suggested trust and confidence in the business sphere. Men born with brawny builds were blessed with the ideal physique. Others tried to develop muscles through exercise, and still others could "fake it," presenting a massive, bulky silhouette by wearing the right clothes.

For Victorian men, the suit was the era's most important fashion development, an instrument that helped to blur social differences.

During the late eighteenth- and early nineteenth-centuries, the frilly aristocratic look—with delicate slippers, ornamental hose, tight britches, powdered wigs, ruffles, and jewelry—was replaced by a new sartorial idea: a simpler, dark, more conservative form of male dress. Dubbed "The Great Masculine Renunciation" by the psychologist J. C. Flugel in 1930, this radical shift in men's attire was inspired by the sociopolitical upheavals of the French Revolution, but also had roots in the English struggle for political and cultural power between aristocrats and the rising middle class, dating back to 1688. In Regency England, Beau Brummell introduced beautifully cut black waistcoats, white shirts, and silk cravats to his fellow dandies in London's West End, making black into a fashionable color for men's evening wear. The dark suit with matching trousers evolved over the next few decades. Long pants displaced knee britches. Standing collars gave men a crisp, clean appearance, and elaborately knotted neckties added an air of elegant formality.

As Americans experimented with the suit, the lower classes adopted wild colors and contrasting patterns, much like those worn by Butcher Bill and Boss Tweed in the 2002 movie, *Gangs of New York*. The upper classes played with fabric and cut, like the suits of editor Horace Greeley and financier-politician "Mr. Schermerhorn" in the same film. By the middle of the century, the black suit and white shirt had become symbolic of middle-class respectability. "Every sober mechanic has his one or two suits of broadcloth," wrote Greeley in 1853, "and, so far as mere clothes go, can make as good a display, when he chooses, as what are called the upper classes."

In the second half of the nineteenth century, the suit evolved into the form that came to dominate men's clothing, along with the etiquette dictating appropriate variations for different occasions, such as white linen suits for warm Sunday afternoons and tuxedoes or "tails" for formal evening events. Middle- and upper-class men wore suits in subdued tones and textures every day. As salaried office jobs came to dominate their lives, the suit came to express the seriousness of purpose associated with the business world. It inspired confidence, testifying to a man's status and good taste.

By the early 1900s, middle-class men saw the suit as their ideal uniform because it fit perfectly into business routines. Dark suits always looked polished and hid dirt created by the coal heating and kerosene lighting. Office workers looked presentable as they labored over daily tasks: bank clerks counting money, accountants writing in ledgers, and engineers drafting plans. When buttoned, the jacket provided a formal look for meetings with bosses and clients. In retail stores, clerks in suits looked clean, competent, and courteous. Managers adopted the suit because it allowed them to look professional while supervising workers or entertaining clients at restaurants. A well-equipped businessman's wardrobe consisted entirely of suits, which conveyed sobriety, frugality, and conservatism.

Along with the suit, the detachable white "collar" became an important symbol of the discerning male consumer. Introduced in the late 1820s, detachable collars remained part of the businessman's attire until the 1920s, when washable shirts with sewn-in collars became popular. In the mid-nineteenth century, the separate white linen collar gained favor as a low-cost solution to laundering, along with a matching "bosom" worn over the shirtfront and "cuffs" at the wrists. Few people bathed every day, so the neck accumulated perspiration and dirt, particularly in hot weather before the invention of air conditioning. Men could change collars, bosoms, and cuffs on a daily basis, presenting a clean, crisp appearance at work.

Detachable collars, made either from linen or celluloid, also shaped the wearer's body into the form of a respectable gentleman, who conveyed authority by holding his head high, thrusting his chest out, and sucking in his stomach. Low-ranking clerks had smaller collars that allowed them to bend over their writing desks. Supervisors donned high-standing collars that prevented the neck from easily bending. They literally had to "look down their noses" at their subordinates! Working men, who wore overalls, loose jackets, and blue shirts with attached collars, watched the businessmen's parade in amusement. In the 1880s, they coined the term "white-collar stiffs" to connote clerks who flaunted their positions by dressing like their employers. Later, the term "white collar" came to describe all men in office jobs.

The suit was a good match for the emerging men's clothing industry, which blended machine sewing and fine tailoring. While men gravitated towards a standard "look," they paid careful attention to the details of their clothes. They were fastidious shoppers who followed the London styles and demanded variation in design, quality in fabrics, and excellence in details.

Menswear shows that the transition to twentieth-century consumerism incorporated aspects of the old and the new. Men adopted business suits because they embodied the themes of progress, industriousness, expertise, and respectability while continuing to display facets of individualism and gentility. The uniform-like suit embodied emerging ideas about how the male physique should conform to a new athletic muscularity, while proving that there was no such thing as complete conformity.

Corsets and the Hourglass Shape

The shapely corseted figure of the Victorian woman was a contrast to this boxy masculine ideal. The "hourglass" shape was intentionally designed to look extravagant next to the man's suit. The voluptuous Victorian beauty, with large hips and breasts and a tiny waist, was first popularized as the coquette, Dolly Varden, the working-class heroine of Charles Dickens's *Barnaby Rudge* (1841), and later by Lillian Russell, the great star of American musical theater. Russell, "the American Beauty," didn't count calories, and exulted in her curvaceous dimensions. Others re-formed their bodies into the stylish shape, achieving the buxom look with leg-of-mutton sleeves, bell-shape skirts, and tight corsets.

While Victorian feminists, physicians, and social workers saw corsets as unhealthy and oppressive, journalists simply ridiculed the frivolity and frippery of women's fashion. Taking another view, historian Valerie Steele, author of *Fashion and Eroticism*, argues that the hourglass shape celebrated sexuality and sensuality. Full skirts proclaimed curvaceous opulence and hinted at erotic pleasures. A woman who lifted her skirts to step into a carriage might inadvertently (or deliberately!) provide passersby with a glimpse of her ankles or, with luck, lacy bloomers. The hourglass shape helped to construct an aesthetic that idealized women's physical attributes, simultaneously honoring their sexuality, fertility, creativity, and independence.

The corset was one of the consumer goods that played an important role in the Victorian construction of femininity. Today, there are many versions of womanly beauty. Carrie Bradshaw and her girlfriends spend hours at the gym striving for the lean, muscular bodies of fashion models. Other celebrities with different physiques, such as Jennifer Lopez, Dolly Parton, and Oprah Winfrey, advocate a Rubenesque balance of indulgence, diet, and exercise. The focus is on how the body can be molded into an individualized version of perfection. In earlier eras, women used corsets and padded undergarments to achieve the one vision of perfection.

By the Victorian period, women strapped themselves into corsets daily. Worn with layers of shifts, drawers, and petticoats, the corset pressed the Victorian woman into a beautiful shape and helped alleviate back pain caused by the weight of the clothing. Those who wanted more "assets" wore bust extenders and bustles, further exaggerating feminine curves.

The corset was one of the few ready-made articles of clothing available for women in the nineteenth century. The plain white color was associated with purity, making it appropriate for Victorian women's underclothing. Corsets got their shape from layers of stitched padding and stays (first whalebone and later steel), closed in the front with hooks-and-eyes, and laced up the back. Advertised in fashion magazines like *Harper's Bazar*, corsets could be purchased in local dry-goods stores, specialized corset shops, and mail-order catalogs. Factory production put corsets within reach of working-class women.

The Art of Dressmaking

In addition to the corset, there was a lot more to the shapely feminine look than met the eye. Dresses that fit "like wallpaper" were far beyond the skill of most home seamstresses. It was difficult for amateurs to construct a bodice that would lay flat across the shoulders when the wearer was standing up, sitting down, and walking. A dress that looked perfect over one corset might pull or snag over another. The professional dressmaker knew how to design, cut, and fit an outfit to her client's body.

Professional dressmakers were the heart of the world of women's fashion, their occupation rooted in fine craftsmanship and personal relationships. These custom clothiers sustained the individualized look into the early twentieth century, interpreting Paris fashions for American clients until ready-to-wear clothing put them out of business. The dressmaker's skill lay in her ability to generate creations that augmented her customer's complexion, shape, and personality. Craft embellishments distinguished one outfit from another. Trade secrets allowed dressmakers to accessorize the hourglass look in ways that enhanced each customer's best features.

Only wealthy- and upper-middle-class women could afford to order *all* of their clothes from dressmakers. Middle-class women with limited resources created their wardrobes through some combination of ready-made clothing, professionally fitted garments, and home-sewn items. When budgets allowed, they paid dressmakers to make outfits for special events: dances, parties, or weddings. Working-class women, including shop girls and mill hands, probably relied more heavily on store-bought clothes and did their own alterations and mending. This certainly was Sister Carrie's experience. These mix-and-match strategies resembled the Victorian approach to interior-decorating projects, for which middle- and working-class consumers often had to "make do."

The experience of Mary Swift Thoms, a Cincinnati socialite, shows how upper-class Americans dressed for their roles. Her family's wealth enabled Thoms in 1877–78 to visit Paris, where she was fitted for a dress by the house of Charles Frederick Worth, the father of *haute couture*. Clients like Thoms were among the most important customers for Parisian couture, which signified dignity, status, and refined taste. When she wore her Worth "afternoon dress"—a two-part outfit comprised of a matching skirt and bodice, or top—to entertain fellow Cincinnatians, those privileged to sit in her Mount Auburn parlor would certainly have been impressed.

Thoms's foray into high style didn't end in Paris. She bought extra yards of Worth's exquisite silk fabric, which she took home to her Irish immigrant dressmaker Selina Cadwallader. Cadwallader used the French silk to sew a sleeveless bodice, which turned the Worth afternoon dress into a gown suitable for dinner parties. Revered as a local "authority on fashion," Cadwallader catered to other wealthy customers, copying elements of Paris designs from fashion plates and using her own ideas to satisfy her clients' Midwestern tastes.

In Philadelphia, middle-class Susan McManus kept diaries for 1857–80, which recorded her sewing projects, shopping trips, and fashion choices. Married to a stockbroker, McManus strove to balance the realities of a limited household budget with her desire to be fashionable. She hired a dressmaker when family finances allowed, but often economized by sewing her own clothes. Dressmaking proved to be one of her greatest challenges.

Her experiences show how middle-class women tried to accommodate the conventions of Paris fashion. As she and husband Charles struggled to make ends meet, Susan had to sacrifice her regular visits to the dressmaker and combined strategies to create a wardrobe. Charles invested $55 in a home sewing machine, which Susan used for clothing projects. She altered her professionally made dresses to fit during pregnancies or to look more stylish, and used paper patterns to make new outfits with the help of her friends, mother, and servant. Susan discovered that sewing a dress from scratch was a daunting task. In spring 1877, she made a black silk dress and matching coat, an endeavor that entailed one pattern, twenty-five yards of fabric, and two full months!

McManus acquired her ideas about fashion from several sources. She modeled her dresses after those she had seen others wear, or created them from patterns that she traded with her friends. Susan loved *Harper's Bazar*, with its fold-out patterns and illustrated articles on Paris fashion. She learned much from local shopping trips, walking down Chestnut Street with her mother or going downtown with her husband.

These accounts of wardrobe building in Philadelphia sound luxurious compared to the experiences of women on the frontier. Army wives stationed on the plains described tedious sewing projects, frustrating visits to poorly stocked military stores, and hours daydreaming over *Harper's Bazar, Godey's Lady's Book, Demorest's,* and *Frank Leslie's Illustrated Newspaper*. Before her marriage, Elizabeth Bacon Custer, wife of George Armstrong Custer, the Civil War general and Indian fighter, had patronized dressmakers at home in Michigan. The bride started army life with few sewing skills, but out of necessity, she learned to make clothes for her entire family.

As George traveled from one remote post to another, Elizabeth spent her layovers on sewing projects, patching garments and remaking old clothes into new ones. She formed sewing bees with other military wives. Elizabeth described how, on one such occasion, "a roomful of busy women" cut, basted, and sewed "a passable" child's outfit and a lady's nightgown. Cognizant of professional dressmakers' standards, she described these garments as "cobbled-out woollen [sic] clothes" created by "ignorant fingers." At Fort Lincoln, North Dakota, Elizabeth helped a sewing circle prepare for a wedding. Without a sewing machine, the women started with a paper pattern and ended up with a hand-sewn satin bridal dress embroidered with silk orange blossoms. Such elaborate projects, using luxury materials, were unusual. More often, Elizabeth had to "make do" with inexpensive fabrics, using a good deal of ingenuity to sew simple calico and linsey-woolsey into "fashionable shapes."

Whether made by a *couturier*, dressmaker, or home seamstress, customized clothing embodied the Victorian culture of consumption. Ordering goods from the dressmaker or milliner fostered commercial culture on the local level, giving female entrepreneurs a chance at prosperity. At the same time, home sewing projects allowed women to create garments that demonstrated their creativity, while fulfilling their duties as wives and mothers. Women integrated elements of commercial culture, including sewing machines, paper patterns, and advice from magazines, into their experiences, mixing prescriptions from the broader culture with established work habits and taste preferences. It worked, because for women, clothing that was both individualized and fashionable embodied Victorian expectations of how they should look and spend their time.

The Easter Parade

Every Easter Sunday, wealthy New Yorkers put on their best clothes for one of the city's iconic extravaganzas. In the morning, the captains of industry, with their wives and daughters by their sides, attended services at the best churches; in the afternoon, high society promenaded on Fifth Avenue. The men marched in crisp, fresh suits; the women sported gay spring dresses and flirtatious Easter bonnets. In 1890, the *New York Times* reported: "It was the great Easter Sunday parade, which has become such an established institution in New-York that the curious flock to Fifth-avenue almost as numerously and enthusiastically as they do to see a circus." Gawkers from lower Manhattan, New Jersey, and Long Island came to be part of this occasion "to see and be seen" in new spring fashions.

The famous Fifth Avenue procession emerged as a fashion ritual during the 1870s. Victorian churches celebrated the holy day with stunning floral arrangements, while stores piqued shoppers' interest in Easter goods with thematic windows trimmed with rabbits, crucifixes, and lilies. Soon, fashions in Easter flowers and clothing styles influenced each other. Christ's resurrection had a corollary in material culture: the new set of spring clothes. Easter became the pre-eminent season for fabric purchases, as women selected dresses, millinery, and accessories that were certain to complement the season's blooms. In their glorious new outfits, wealthy women took center stage in the Easter parade. Looking like blossoms, they strutted between churches, creating dazzling displays of texture and color.

By the 1890s, the Easter parade was one among several spectacles feeding the American aristocracy's craving for celebrity and the public's curiosity about the super rich. Tabloid newspapers published by Joseph Pulitzer and William Randolph Hearst built huge circulations exploiting this impulse. Society women were targeted by the gossip columnists, who excitedly reported what the debutantes wore to balls, parties, weddings, the opera, and the Easter parade. Vivid descriptions of the belles' fashions thrilled readers, who crowded the sidewalks at the next big event to catch a glimpse of the good life.

People-watching wasn't the only impulse that attracted crowds to the Easter Parade. In Manhattan, the unusual spring costumes, seasonal rejoicing, and social competition appealed to the city's immigrants who flocked to watch the procession. All working-class New Yorkers relished the chance to watch the millionaires flaunt their wealth. Immigrants, though, also saw the Easter Parade as a venue for displaying *their* sartorial splendor: suits for men, skirts and shirtwaists for women. At the moment when the wealthy turned to Europe and the middle class to local dressmakers, those with humbler roots embraced the factory-made aesthetic. For immigrants, a new set of ready-made clothes provided important cultural clues, signaling to onlookers that the wearer was upwardly mobile, and more important, becoming an American.

The dominant Victorian culture formed a master definition of American-ness informed by Social Darwinism, a definition that depended on the unquestioned superiority of the Anglo-Saxon race. Immigrants from Southern and Eastern Europe were quick studies, and recognized that conforming to mainstream models would help their chances in society. It might take years to learn to speak English—and *sounding* American might take a generation to effect—but *looking* American was not nearly as difficult. The marketplace offered a cornucopia of goods that immigrants could use to remake themselves, and evidence of their stake in ready-made clothing abounds.

Single girls, who emigrated from Europe by themselves or with family and friends, quickly learned that American styles flattered their figures and helped them fit in. Having left Russia in 1894, Mary Antin in *The Promised Land,* her 1912 memoir of the Jewish immigrant experience, remembered the glorious moment when a social worker took her family uptown to a "dazzlingly beautiful palace called a 'department store.'" There, the family shed their "hateful homemade European costumes," which pointed them "out as 'greenhorns' to the children on the street, for real American machine-made garments." In 1919, social worker Louise C. Odencrantz, author of the Russell Sage Foundation's report on *Italian Women in Industry*, noted that immigrants usually brought "large quantities of clothing with them from Italy," often accumulated for a dowry. But soon after landing at Ellis Island, they began to "discard these Italian costumes for American clothing." While some older Italian women wore the Old Country clothes to work at the factory, younger women skimped and saved to get new clothes so they could "look American."

The Easter parade celebrated American consumer culture, with its abundance of goods, wide range of choices, and ever-changing styles. It was a tableau of American prosperity, showcasing the crucial role of fashion to the formation of new identities. It had a far-reaching impact, inspiring parallel events in major cities and smaller towns across the country. By the early twentieth century, seaside resorts, such as Coney Island, New York, and Atlantic City, New Jersey, sponsored Easter parades as tourist attractions. This annual fashion fête joined the variety of leisure activities that gave American consumer culture its distinctively public flavor. The Easter parade, band concerts in the park, movie "palaces," world's fairs, and dance halls provided consumers with some place to go—once they had gotten all dressed up.

Stepping Out with the Gibson Girl and Arrow Man

By the 1890s, the Victorian models of feminine beauty and behavior, although still entrenched among middle-class Americans, began to change. Challenges came from many places. At the top of society, Fifth Avenue socialites like Ava Astor, heir to a New York real-estate fortune, toned up their bodies on the Newport tennis courts. Working-class girls who earned their living in offices, stores, and factories developed freer standards of sensuality. On the margins of society, bohemians pressed for a new pleasure ethic, while feminists lobbied against the corset. These forces helped to redefine the consumer's relationship to clothing and had a profound influence on American popular culture.

Between the 1890s and World War I, the Gibson Girl and the chorus girl came to symbolize new attitudes toward women's attire and consumer culture. As the idealized aristocratic beauty, the Gibson Girl first appeared as a lithograph in *Life* magazine in 1890, making her one of the original "cover girls." Created by illustrator Charles Dana Gibson, she blended Victorian propriety with a Modern attitude, accounting for her appeal across age, class, gender, and geographic lines. Her tightly corseted hourglass figure, in a shirtwaist and skirt, was complemented by a charming face with Cupid lips. Although the fictional Gibson Girl played sports, looked self-reliant, and wore comfortable clothes like the "new woman," she exuded an air of modesty that upheld the status quo for romance, marriage, and femininity. By the mid 1890s, observers noted that all the women on the streets of America, from Main to Fifth Avenue, seemed to look like the Gibson Girl.

The chorus girl expressed another alternative to the voluptuous Victorian beauty and her restrained good manners. At the turn of the century, the feisty variety show dancer was the most popular type of actress, the comedic precursor to Goldie Hawn and Meg Ryan in the late twentieth century. Throughout the land, the popularity of musical theater among people of all ages, genders, and classes enhanced the chorus girl's status and visibility. Advances in photography, printing, and advertising allowed for the circulation of her image in publicity photos, trade cards, and tabloid newspapers. From the days of the

Swedish nightingale Jenny Lind, actresses had been setting fashion trends, but the demand for gossip about theatrical figures expanded with newspapers and magazines in the 1880s. "Celebrities created fans," notes historian Lois W. Banner in *American Beauty*, "who in turn created celebrities." As the female symbol of the rags-to-riches story, the chorus girl symbolized a better life to millions of young maids, clerks, typists, and mill hands who believed in the American promise of upward mobility.

After the turn of the century, the New York chorus girl captured the public imagination as a new type of beauty. As a theatrical type, she first appeared in the 1900 production of *Florodora* and became immortalized by the Ziegfeld Follies, a music hall review modeled after the Parisian Folies Bergère, in 1907. Vaudeville superstar Anna Held, brought to America from France by her future husband Florenz "Flo" Ziegfeld, Jr., in 1896, epitomized the chorus girl. A sultry singer with a petite, shapely figure, Held mounted one publicity stunt after another, scandalizing proper Victorians and inspiring a rebellion against prevailing social norms.

Images like the Gibson Girl and celebrities like Anna Held are important signs of cultural change. They showed women stepping out of the domestic sphere, working for a living, and wearing clothes that testified to their newfound independence. Not every woman emulated these role models, but the widespread circulation of their images legitimated the desire for change that many people felt. Popular pictures of the Gibson Girl and the chorus girl—disseminated by magazines, newspapers, theater posters, billboards, trade cards, and product packages—gained currency just as other crucial social developments were percolating.

Men continued to wear suits, but subtle changes in them were developing. In print culture, the iconic image of the Arrow Man, used by Cluett, Peabody & Company to advertise the Arrow Collar, reflected evolving notions about manliness and fashion. Created by Joseph Christian Leyendecker, whose illustrations appeared in the *Saturday Evening Post*, the immensely successful Arrow Collar Man graced advertising copy from 1907 to 1931. He was the male equivalent of the Gibson Girl, admired by woman and copied by competitors. He was created to sell changeable collars, but he came to symbolize changing notions of masculinity and appropriate male dress.

The Arrow Man captured the American imagination because Leyendecker's compelling iconography depicted a transitional world that meshed the past, present, and future, according to historian Carole Turbin. The Arrow Man blended the brawny muscularity of the 1890s with a softened, sophisticated refinement. He gazed at onlookers with a direct, reserved authority that had a sensuous edge. He appeared in cultured settings, such as the library or smoking room, reading a newspaper and contemplating serious masculine subjects. The Arrow Man was virile, refined, cool, and confident, with a hint of tough sexuality. The figure blurred distinctions between social classes, proffering a homogenized male persona that combined the old and the new. By meshing Victorian notions of progress and hierarchy with a hedonistic Modern thread, the Arrow Man suggested that elegance and respectability had been democratized.

The ascendance of the Gibson Girl and Arrow Man as visual icons paralleled other major cultural shifts. The ballroom dance craze, which swept across the country beginning in 1909, is worth examining for what it reveals about dress codes at the end of the Victorian era. While the middle class was using interior decoration and fashion to advance progress, excluded groups and subcultures were creating other ways of expressing *their* sense of distinctiveness. By the late 1800s, working-class tastes dominated mass commercial leisure; entertainment venues such as urban dance palaces, amusement parks, and sporting arenas depended primarily on these customers. At the same time, spectacles like the Easter parade and the media's fascination with celebrities stimulated cross fertilization between styles. Working girls who adopted the Gibson Girl's look as their daytime uniform emulated theatrical idols at night, wearing bright colors and costume jewelry to cafés, boardwalks, and dance halls. Among the middle class, matrons took a break from shopping expeditions to see vaudeville matinees. Young couples, with their new passion for exercise, took to the dance floors.

Dance halls, a longtime feature of Victorian working-class neighborhoods, gained respectability around 1900, throwing their doors open to anyone paying the price of admission. These late-night establishments provided working men and women with a place for partying with friends, meeting potential dates, and showing off their clothes. By 1912, other Americans embraced the passion for the frenzied ragtime dances that had originated on the dance hall floor and on the vaudeville stage. *Life* magazine reported that virtually all New Yorkers had gone dance mad, taking to late-night cabarets to learn the bunny hug, the turkey trot, the grizzly bear, and the tango.

Enthusiasm for ballroom dancing was inspired by showcase performers like Vernon and Irene Castle, a husband-and-wife team whose genteel style appealed to middle-class couples. This young Englishman and his American wife, backed by James Reese Europe's "Negro band," sanitized the wild ragtime repertoire for middle-class consumers, and toned down its sexuality while retaining its spirit and energy.

Irene Castle's impeccable fashion sense struck a chord with middle-class women who wanted to break out of the Victorian mold. The lithe dancer draped her petite body with loose, flowing dresses straight from Paris and London. Her style showed the influence of the couturier Paul Poiret, who had recently introduced the sheath dress to the Paris fashion scene. The lightweight silk fell gently around Castle's body, and the absence of tight undergarments permitted her to dance with ease and grace. Her bobbed hairstyle, light makeup, and comfortable shoes further pointed away from the curvaceous Victorian ideal. Castle and silent movie stars like Mary Pickford and Lillian Gish set a new standard for feminine beauty, based on girlish good looks. Ordinary women could emulate this style, buying dress patterns in the Castle mode from the *Delineator* and the *Ladies' Home Journal*. The simple designs lent themselves to home sewing, helping to create a new aesthetic that would be further popularized by the ready-to-wear industry in the 1920s.

Why Fashion Mattered

In 1896, Lillian Russell went on a diet when theater critics compared her to a white elephant, the voluptuous Victorian superstar a high-profile victim of the sudden shift in dress code. New fashion mandates affected men and women up and down the social ladder, most of whom adjusted their bodies, lifestyles, and clothing to "fit in." Those who decided not to make the transition were labeled "old-fashioned."

For Russell and others in the limelight, a fashionable appearance was essential to continued success. In the theater world, the dress code changed rapidly, dictated by the media's relentless quest for novelty and the widespread popularity of the latest European trends. But rapid style shifts also dominated the lower end of the ladies' garment trade, where working-class women like Sister Carrie relished flashy clothes. Where budgets permitted, a new Easter outfit was the rule, plus a new blouse, hat, and pair of gloves every fall and spring. Dress shops, dry goods stores, and five-and-tens were filled with tempting trimmings, buttons, and feathers, all of which enticed working-class girls to splurge on new ornaments that might spice up an old wardrobe. It was these female consumers—mill hands, shop girls, clerks, and farmer's daughters—who anxiously looked ahead to the Modern era, foreshadowing Carrie Bradshaw's fashion preferences by wearing ready-made clothing that added a touch of Parisian glamour to their otherwise humdrum lives.

Elsewhere in American culture, fashions moved at a glacial pace. Men's suits continued to look the same, changing only slowly over the course of decades. At first glance, suits appeared free of the whims of fashion, but such was an illusion. Like Big's look, the Victorian male silhouette commanded the onlooker's attention, the flirtatious glance of a female admirer, or the critical assessment of his business associates. Those who knew the rules could size up a man by the shape of his collar, the quality of his felt hat, and the tailoring of his suit. Even Sister Carrie knew how to distinguish a good suit from a cheap one. No wonder, then, that the suit continues to serve as the all-purpose male uniform.

Women's clothing continued to play off the masculine values of stability and solidity by constantly finding new ways to stress variety and difference. Into the early twentieth century, middle-class women continued to prefer highly individualized clothing, created through the collaboration between the dressmaker and her customer. In 1916, a researcher for the U.S. Bureau of Labor Statistics, reporting on *Dressmaking as a Trade for Women in Massachusetts*, noted that most consumers still insisted that "no two gowns shall be alike." This imperative meant that dressmakers had to adapt the "fashion, style, and material of a garment to the particular form and personal characteristics of the individual woman."

In some ways, Victorian clothing shared features with the Victorian home; both provided frameworks that consumers could adapt to their particular circumstances. The difference was that between private and public worlds. The home was primarily a private space, while clothing was both personal and public. Interior decoration reflected the homemaker's perception of her family's role in the social hierarchy, showcasing her aesthetic tastes and her husband's earning power. Primarily, the home was a stage for feminine talent, with men occasionally making artistic contributions as connoisseurs or collectors. In contrast, the Victorian dress code had an impact on both genders, as men and women used clothing to express their biological, social, cultural, and economic roles. Victorian dress not only marked the physical differences between the sexes but also told onlookers who the wearer wanted to be.

CHAPTER THREE

New Ways to Shop

Where did Victorian consumers buy the things that would make them comfortable and stylish? Throughout the era, Victorian merchants developed new ways for getting new goods to market. Some of today's famous merchandising names—Lord & Taylor, Macy's, Kmart, and Sears—trace their roots to the mid-to-late 1800s, when dry-goods emporiums, department stores, chain stores, and mail-order houses first appeared on the commercial scene. These mass merchandisers transformed shopping from an arduous daily chore into an exciting, pleasurable pastime.

During the first half of the nineteenth century, Americans purchased commodities from small shopkeepers, rural general merchants, and roadside peddlers. These local retailers acquired processed food and manufactured products from wholesalers who specialized in grain, textiles, crockery, or hardware. Wholesalers, in turn, were linked to factories, workshops, and mills by other middlemen, including commission merchants, exporters, auctioneers, factors, importers, and manufacturers' agents. Transactions between multiple parties added significantly to the retail price of particular items. Stores were small, their stock limited.

By the 1850s and 1860s, *some* retailing entrepreneurs recognized the advantages of cutting wholesalers out of the picture. Buying goods directly from the factory allowed stores to reduce transaction costs and lower prices. Cheaper prices meant that consumers from lower income brackets could afford amenities like bric-a-brac and ready-made clothing. Victorian retailers also introduced larger stores with more inventory, self-service, liberal return policies, free alterations, home delivery, charge cards, and on-site restaurants.

This "retailing revolution," so labeled by the late business historian Alfred D. Chandler, Jr., began in large cities like Boston, Chicago, New York, and Philadelphia. By the early twentieth century, there were dry-goods palaces, department stores, five-and-tens, and mail-order houses across the United States. Mid-sized cities like Rochester, New York; Dayton, Ohio; and Boulder, Colorado, all had prosperous commercial districts, connected to residential areas by streetcars or trolleys. Each downtown had family-run department stores, branches of national dime stores, and dozens of small specialty shops operated by local entrepreneurs. These Main Street retailers offered customers a new way to shop.

Dry-Goods Emporiums

Early in the retailing revolution, dry-goods emporiums emerged as America's first mass merchandisers. The term *dry goods* dates from the colonial era, when seaport stores run by merchant-importers sold rum and calico fabric, otherwise known as "wet" and "dry" goods, respectively. Between the 1850s and 1870s, a handful of large stores specializing in dry goods—fabrics, trimmings, thread, feathers, ribbons, and other sewing supplies—appeared in major Northeastern cities, ushering a new phase in merchandising.

In practice and scale, these wholesale-retail houses differed dramatically from the general stores and specialty shops that had dominated commerce for decades. Traditional dry-goods shops were small and had a limited selection. The new dry-goods superstores bought goods directly from manufacturers, sold them for cash at low prices, and served thousands of customers. They offered money-back, satisfaction-guaranteed policies. They paved the way for the department stores that dominated the retailing scene from the 1890s to the 1960s.

In the mid 1800s, dry-goods emporiums were the leading stores in major Eastern cities. In New York, merchants such as Alexander T. Stewart, Arnold Constable, Samuel Lord, and George Washington Taylor ran the first of these wholesale-retail stores, which carried extensive selections of fabrics, thread, and buttons used by dressmakers, milliners, and home seamstresses. Some dry-goods merchants, including Stewart (1803–76), started to produce clothing, making men's garments for the retail and wholesale trade.

Entrepreneurs like Stewart recognized that recent technological breakthroughs in the building trades might provide a competitive advantage in retailing. American foundries had perfected cast iron as a structural and ornamental material for large, showy buildings that looked like Venetian palaces. French glassworks had refined ways to make huge sheets of plate glass for floor-to-ceiling "show windows," replacing small window panes and mullions. These technologies enabled builders to erect well-lighted buildings with cavernous rooms suitable for extensive dry-goods counters and large, unobstructed, street-level windows for "showing" tempting displays.

Around the same time, retailers like Charles Lewis Tiffany proved that New York could sustain luxury stores. From 1837, Tiffany had run a fancy goods store on Broadway opposite City Hall, diversifying into diamonds after 1848 when world prices for precious gems fell. He ran a mail-order business, and opened a shop in Paris to augment his cultural capital. Most important, Tiffany & Company created a shopping environment that enveloped shoppers in complete luxury. By the 1860s, Tiffany & Company attracted the nation's elite, including Abraham Lincoln, who bought the fashion-conscious first lady, Mary Todd Lincoln, a gold-and-pearl necklace.

The idea of a showcase store captured Stewart's imagination. By the Civil War, his lucrative business had outgrown the Marble Dry Goods Palace on lower Broadway. In 1862, Stewart spent $2.75 million on a spectacular new uptown store, the Cast Iron Palace at Broadway and Tenth Street, which employed 2,000 workers to sell everything from baby blankets to "black goods," clothing for wakes and funerals.

Called "The Greatest Store in the World," the Cast Iron Palace was one of New York's major attractions. Its cast-iron facade was painted as faux marble, and it sported hundreds of plate-glass windows. Inside, there was a grand stairway, a central rotunda, and a domed skylight that impressed the most worldly of visitors. The spacious interior contrasted sharply with that of the traditional store, which was small, dark, and cluttered. On the fourth floor, a clothing factory made men's garments. Below, female shoppers browsed in the capacious rooms illuminated in the daytime by skylights and windows, at night with gas lamps.

Stewart's contribution to consumer society was his re-conceptualization of the store as a *social space*. The Cast Iron Palace celebrated the world of goods and provided a safe, comfortable shopping environment for women. It was a vastly different experience from the cutthroat environment of small stores, where shopkeepers expected everyone to buy something after haggling over the price. Stewart eliminated bargaining by selling goods at fixed prices. His store was friendlier than Tiffany's, which intimated ordinary people with its snobbish atmosphere. Women were encouraged to browse, linger, and socialize while listening to live organ music, which played continuously. This shoppers' paradise was a place to enjoy.

Department Stores as "Palaces of Consumption"

The first American department stores emerged when dry-goods merchants began to specialize and then diversify into household goods. These new stores expanded retail sales to the comfortable classes with entire "departments" for home furnishings and accessories. The term "department store" was not recorded until 1887, but its precedents included Stewart's Cast Iron Palace and stores like the Bon Marché and the Grand Magasin du Louvre in Paris, which sold a broad selection of merchandise on fixed prices by the mid-1800s.

With the emphasis on household goods, department stores helped to make women's work—the job of decorating the home—into a creative, leisure activity. The new "palaces of consumption" transformed shopping from a wifely duty into a mechanism by which women refined their tastes and expanded their visions of the good life. The department store facilitated a woman's transition from a homemaker to a consumer.

In the United States, these "new kind of stores" first appeared in New York City, which had a population of 1.3 million in 1870 and constituted the nation's largest urban market. During the 1870s and 1880s, dry goods merchants such as Abraham & Strauss, B. Altman & Company, Lord & Taylor, and R. H. Macy & Company opened department stores on Broadway between Eighth and Twenty-Third Streets. Here on the "Ladies' Mile," middle- and upper-class women promenaded from store to store, spending entire days browsing and socializing.

Department stores soon dominated the major retailing districts of cities and large towns. Chicago had three major department stores: Marshall Field's; Carson Pirie Scott & Company; and Mandel Brothers. In Philadelphia, Strawbridge & Clothier and John Wanamaker anchored the shopping district on Market Street. By the early 1900s, department stores appeared on the Main Streets of Buffalo and Roch- · ester, luring shoppers from towns in upstate New York. Throughout America, the story was much the same. Whether in Milwaukee, New Orleans, or San Francisco, cities witnessed the birth and growth of these suave stores, which transformed the downtowns and made shopping into a fashionable pursuit.

John Wanamaker's Luxury Department Store

Sizing up the future of American retailing, Stewart remarked that John Wanamaker was destined to become "the greatest merchant in America." He was right. Following a profitable Civil War venture in men's clothing, Wanamaker spent the next fifty years perfecting the *luxury department store*. His Philadelphia store, a high-end Macy's/Target/IKEA, was the world's largest department store and a major urban attraction.

Wanamaker understood Victorian domesticity, which idealized the woman and the home as the moral center of American life. His mission extended beyond turning a profit; it was to better the nation's homes. "The home makes or unmakes the character of each member of the family," Wanamaker told one customer, Mrs. T. J. Wallace, in 1895. "Whoever makes the homes of the people, makes the history of the nation."

To set his store apart from local competitors like Gimbel Brothers and Strawbridge & Clothier, Wanamaker positioned it as luxury central. His strategy focused on high-quality merchandise, newspaper advertising, and tempting bargains. The retail buyers, the store staff who selected each season's stock, traveled across the world in search of distinctive merchandise, from Italian pottery to French fashion.

Around 1880, Wanamaker became one of the first American department stores to open a Paris Bureau. Parisian buyers managed the store's purchases of European merchandise and kept up with fashion trends. They attended haute couture shows, studied how elegant women dressed, browsed Parisian boutiques, and shipped their chosen French goods back to America. The Wanamaker stores excitedly publicized the new arrivals with fashion extravaganzas. Wanamaker's fitted these French fashions to American bodies and created spinoffs of them for middle-class shoppers at lower prices. The French cachet appealed to wealthy Americans who had visited Europe, and stirred envy among middle-class consumers longing to make the trip. Wanamaker's extended this approach to other departments. Shoppers who coveted French couture would also appreciate imitation Louis XIV furniture. The emphasis on French taste and quality products helped to establish Wanamaker's as luxury central.

Between 1907 and 1911, Wanamaker completely remodeled his Philadelphia store and extended his empire to New York. On Manhattan's Ladies' Mile, the Wanamaker Store for Women, housed in the revamped Cast Iron Palace, was a shoppers' paradise with the newest Paris modes. Next door, the sixteen-story Wanamaker Building housed a Men's Store and the Galleries of Furnishing and Decoration, the world's largest retail space "devoted to the furnishing and decorating of the home." The main attraction was the "House Palatial," a fully appointed Fifth Avenue mansion, and more than hundred other model rooms showing "home-makers [how] to select proper furniture and house adornments, and to enable them to individualize their homes."

In Philadelphia, Wanamaker replaced his aging Grand Depot with an imposing skyscraper designed by the famed Chicago architect Daniel Burnham, who had just built a fabulous store for Marshall Field's. Wanamaker's new store comprised concert halls, specialty departments, fashion salons, fur vaults, and elegant dining rooms. The Grand Court, its stunning atrium, featured two impressive souvenirs from the 1904 Louisiana Purchase Exposition: the world's largest organ, played three times each day for customers, and a 2,500-pound bronze eagle. Parts of the store were organized like a museum of art and archeology—the Egyptian Hall, the Greek Hall, the Moorish Room, the Byzantine Chamber, and the Empire Salon—all carrying fashions and household goods for "the classes."

Five-and-Tens

If department stores were urban America's consumption palaces, dime stores, or five-and-tens, were its bazaars. At the five-and-ten, consumers mingled, looked, and bought into the American promise of abundance. Bargain shoppers went to Kresge, Kress, McCrory, Newberry, and Woolworth stores searching for a modicum of luxury. Until 1932, nothing at Woolworth's cost more than a dime, which encouraged frequent visits and repeat purchases. Today's big-box discounters and dollar stores are descendants of dime-stores like Woolworth's and Kresge's. Indeed, the K in Kmart refers to S. S. Kresge Company, the Detroit dime-store chain that founded these discount superstores in 1962.

Five-and-tens appeared in American cities just as the lower end of the American market dramatically expanded. Dime stores appealed to the "shawl trade," that is, European immigrants who had not yet been Americanized. Accustomed to pinching pennies, "shawl women"—so dubbed for the traditional peasant garb they wore—knew where to hunt for bargains. In the South, blacks lifting themselves out of slavery migrated to commercial centers like Richmond, Virginia, and Memphis, Tennessee. Immigrants and blacks formed a ready market for inexpensive products: china and glassware, ribbons and hair accessories, dolls and mechanical toys, and other novelties. To these marginalized groups, simple luxuries from the five-and-ten symbolized having accomplished something in the new social order.

To compete on price, five-and-tens borrowed some of the merchandising strategies developed by dry-goods emporiums and department stores: buying direct from factories, selling goods for cash, and earning profits through frequent stock turnover. They innovated by introducing self-service, replacing clerks who helped customers with counter girls who simply rang up and bagged the purchases. Most important, five-and-tens achieved efficiency by organizing themselves as chain stores. Chains are groups of stores owned and operated by a single company. A central office negotiates with manufacturers, using its bargaining power to buy huge quantities of goods at low prices. In turn, chains pass on these discounts to their customers, offering highly competitive retail prices.

Five-and-tens took the chain idea from the "tea store," a grocery retailer that appeared in New York during the mid-1800s. The Great Atlantic & Pacific Tea Company, later known as the A&P, pioneered the chain concept with a string of shops selling pantry staples. Tea stores eventually diversified to include packaged foods, meats, and vegetables, evolving into the first full-fledged grocery chains. By 1881, the A&P chain had a hundred stores; by 1901, nearly twice that number. A&P executives recognized branding as a means for gaining competitive advantage, developing a unique persona for the chain through the careful management of merchandise, service, and appearance. Whether in Boston or San Francisco, shoppers recognized the distinctive red-and-gold logo that decorated the front of every A&P, much as consumers recognize Wal★Mart's signature blue and gray colors today.

The entrepreneur who modified tea-store principles to create the first national chain of five-and-tens was Frank W. Woolworth (1852–1919), a dry-goods clerk with a talent for economy merchandising. As a young man working for a corner store in upstate New York, Woolworth created a bargain counter filled with "Yankee notions," such as tin pans, button hooks, and bright red napkins for 5¢. When shoppers cleared off his bargain shelves, Woolworth suspected that a store selling inexpensive merchandise might succeed. In 1879, he established a five-and-ten of his own in Lancaster, Pennsylvania, and over the next decade, opened a string of dime stores as the Woolworth "syndicate," or chain.

Recognizing the importance of location, Frank Woolworth initially set up stores in market towns, but he soon realized that cities were *the* place for five-and-tens. During the early 1890s, he read U.S. Census Bureau reports about growth markets in the Northeast, and he spent the next decade opening stores from New Hampshire to Virginia. By 1900, the Woolworth chain had fifty-nine stores, including several big-city locations. By 1913, overseas expansion and mergers with competitors gave Woolworth nearly 700 stores in the United States, Canada, and England.

Each Woolworth's, located on a highly trafficked street, was recognizable from its bright red sign, distinctive gold lettering, and large display windows. Like A&Ps, Woolworth's "red fronts" alerted penny-wise urban shoppers to the bargains that awaited them. Inside, the layout reiterated the store's ties to quantity production and mass consumption. Early five-and-tens had limited frontage but stretched back from the street, much like a townhouse. Store managers made the most out of the space by using open counters instead of glass display cases. Tidy stacks of merchandise stretched as far as the eye could see. The visual impact was stunning and seductive, encouraging customers to wander around and touch the goods. Self-service was a welcome change for shoppers who couldn't speak English well, disliked face-to-face encounters, or simply took pleasure from browsing. Woolworth literally put the goods at the consumer's fingertips.

In New York City, Woolworth's main office set the standards for the chain. Frank Woolworth expected each store to turn over its stock five times per year and to make a 20 percent net profit. Woolworth also had high expectations for the store's cleanliness, the clerks' demeanor, and corporate confidentiality. These details shaped Woolworth's into a retailer that shawl women recognized as trustworthy, reliable, and affordable.

Finally, Woolworth's close attention to retail buying contributed to its success as the people's bazaar. Woolworth's retail buyers, each specializing in different merchandise, wielded enormous purchasing power and made important choices that affected millions of people. Their impact on consumer society and consumer products can't be overemphasized. By 1913, the chain's nineteen buyers bought merchandise that produced $66.2 million in sales and $6.4 million in profits. Woolworth's sold 27.5 million pairs of hosiery, 1.4 million tin toys, and 20.7 million bars of soap.

Dime-store buyers had to understand the wants of this vast, segmented market. In the volume business, selecting the wrong merchandise could bring disaster. At Woolworth's Manhattan headquarters, the buyers developed strategies for getting in touch with the desires of dime-store customers. They studied local sales reports, trying to learn which products met favor and where. They corresponded with store managers, who described local taste preferences, and visited the stores to observe. Buyers watched women browse and make choices on the selling floor, discerning important clues about a shopper's ethnicity, income, and taste from her bearing, clothing, accent, and purchases. These visual cues complemented statistical data, augmenting the buyer's knowledge of the Woolworth shopper and her tastes.

Woolworth buyers used this information to select merchandise for the chain from American and European factories. The mantra, "good goods and plenty of them at fair prices," underpinned their choices. When one jewelry buyer found a golden ring that he liked, he told the manufacturer that Woolworth's wanted to retail the item for a dime. The jeweler scoffed, boasting that he could sell 5,400 rings per year for 50¢ each. The Woolworth buyer explained why the jeweler should lower prices and sell to him. For starters, Woolworth's would order 750,000 rings! A deal was struck, and the chain store sold 6 million of the new 10¢ rings in 1916 alone.

Window Shopping

By 1900, cities were among the nation's great attractions, luring curiosity seekers and potential residents from far and wide. People visited big cities to see lavish theaters, capacious parks, and enormous luxury hotels, complete with running water and indoor plumbing. Downtown shopping districts, with their specialty shops, chain stores, and department stores, were also big draws. To imagine what it was like for rural Americans seeing a big city for the first time, we only need to hark back to Theodore Dreiser's novel, *Sister Carrie*, which describes the awestruck heroine wandering through downtown Chicago in 1900.

In Carrie Meeber's Chicago, the luxury department store was the jewel in the metropolitan crown, a major cultural amenity. Everyone, from wealthy city dwellers to country folk, made pilgrimages to these palaces of consumption to see the latest goods. Those who couldn't afford to buy anything, browsed to their hearts' content. Carrie belonged to the latter group; during her visits to the city's great department stores, she ogled the latest fashions and envied the customers.

In the 1880s, luxury department stores adopted flamboyant display techniques to make their stock "come alive." As factories produced larger pieces of plate glass, department stores used them to perfect the art of window displays. In 1883, window dressers at Jordan Marsh in Boston creatively arranged silk fabrics in different windows to create a springtime garden, a game of lawn tennis, and the interior of a French palace. By the late 1890s, throngs regularly crowded the sidewalk in front of Marshall Field's in Chicago to witness the unveiling of the store's thematic windows, stupendous exhibits of light, color, and texture, especially at Christmas.

As twenty-first century consumers, it's difficult to understand the excitement surrounding department-store windows. Today, Americans drive to malls and shop at warehouse stores that stock familiar brands, or surf the web to find what they want. Shopping is simply another chore as opposed to an aesthetic experience. Nineteenth-century Americans loved to walk for exercise and fun. After work, young men and women put on their best outfits, took to the streets or trolleys, and headed downtown. Stores kept evening hours to accommodate crowds shopping before the shows, clubs, and dance halls opened. Besides looking at others, people gawked at the displays and prepared their wish lists.

Specialty stores had long catered to foot traffic with attractive window displays. Created for eye-level viewing, window displays encouraged pedestrians to stop, look, study the products, and go inside. Five-and-tens had also mastered the art of window trimming, mounting artistic exhibits that emphasized abundance and accessibility. A Woolworth's window of stationery might feature envelopes arranged in interesting shapes, surrounded by colorful paper trim keyed in to a holiday theme. Frank Woolworth understood the market value of visual novelty, and he directed store managers to change their windows frequently, at least twice a week!

Department stores built on these traditions, adding a new dimension to window dressing with elaborate holiday exhibits. We can find vestiges of this tradition at the world's few remaining luxury department stores: Bon Marché, Galleries Lafayette, and Printemps in Paris; Harrod's and Harvey Nichols in London; and Barney's and Macy's in New York. The first Christmas windows at Macy's, mounted in the mid-1870s, presented a spectacle of Parisian dolls in the latest French fashions, ice skating on a pond. New seasons, religious days, and secular celebrations provided other themes. For Easter, there were bunnies and eggs; for Valentine's Day, cupids and hearts. Mother's Day, a holiday invented by John Wanamaker, featured sentimental floral displays. By the 1890s, window trimmers took advantage of technological developments in dyeing, glassmaking, and lighting, illuminating colorful windows with electric lights to create exhibits that could be seen from a distance. Department stores transformed the display window into a merchandising tool that delighted the eye and stimulated the senses.

Consumers from all walks of life took pleasure from these show windows, describing the thrill to family and friends. Visiting her mother in Detroit, Wisconsin homemaker Miriam Andrews often went downtown to see the windows and browse through the stores. She excitedly described her experience in letters to her husband James. The stores "are full of such beautiful things. . . . you can imagine me standing in front of the windows, (which are arranged differently nearly every day) until I take everything in, and then I go in and stand, and look and look, and then when I come home try to remember all I saw."

For housewives like Andrews, department store displays provided a "real-life glimpse" of the glamour illustrated in mass-circulation magazines, advertisements, advice books, and mail-order catalogs. By window shopping, Andrews experienced the sumptuousness that consumer society held out to all. When returning home, she shared her visual and tactile experience with family, friends, and neighbors. Andrews had actually *touched* some of the new household devices, including the mechanical carpet sweeper, which her friends had only seen in pictures. To many, Andrews's stories about her Detroit shopping adventure "brought alive" the illustrations in Victorian America's virtual department store: the Sears, Roebuck catalog.

Mail-Order Catalogs

Mail-order houses targeted rural and small-town Americans, a significant market in its own right. In the mid-1800s, dry-goods emporiums, clothing manufacturers, and department stores all had profitable mail-order branches that sold goods to small-time merchants who wanted to cut retail prices by navigating around wholesalers. By the 1880s, these East Coast stores were publishing mail-order catalogs for consumers. J. N. Collins's *Fashion Catalogue* for fall-winter 1883–84 showed the "the very latest and best goods in the market," including imported apparel from Europe and New York merchandise made under its supervision. Collins offered reassurance to those unfamiliar with how mail order worked: "The following pages are so carefully arranged that you can do your shopping with us without leaving home, with the same accuracy, and with as efficient results as though purchasing in person." By promoting style and service, these pioneers helped to establish mail order as a quality way to shop.

With the completion of the transcontinental railroad in 1869, a transportation network of trains and telegraphs stretched across the land, with Chicago as the great metropolitan hub connecting the industrial Northeast and Midwest to the agricultural hinterland. Chicago had a symbiotic relationship with the communities of rural and frontier America. Dozens of mail-order houses sprang up, benefiting from the advantageous rates on freight trains going to and from Iowa hog farms and Texas cattle ranches. Among these, Montgomery Ward and Sears, Roebuck and Company were the most long-lived and successful.

Until 1920, most Americans lived on farms and in villages remote from bustling cities. As agriculture mechanized, millions of former farmhands migrated to the cities, but the rural population still continued to grow. By 1920, 52 million of the nation's 106 million people still lived in the countryside. Farmers, sharecroppers, cattlemen, miners, and small townspeople counted for 49 percent of the population, constituting a great market.

Like city dwellers, rural Americans grew more attuned to consumer society through innovations in education, communications, and transportation. Starting in the mid-1800s, the federal government took measures to improve the quality of rural life. Through agricultural colleges and country fairs, the U.S. Department of Agriculture encouraged country households to modernize by adopting new technologies and consumer goods. With the expansion of the agricultural press, subscription journals like *Progressive Farmer* campaigned against rural isolation, published lifestyle articles, and advertised products to enhance comfort and convenience.

Economic factors contributed to farmers' new desires for consumer comforts. Between 1900 and World War I, rising discretionary incomes put more purchasing power in the hands of rural householders. In the decade between 1910 and 1920, farm income rose by 47 percent in the upper South, buoyed by the demands of World War I. Some families channeled their extra dollars into agricultural equipment, buying tractors, automobiles, reapers, and cream separators. To rural men, these new technologies were symbols of success, hallmarks that the family farm was modernizing. Other farm families also bought products that improved domestic life: kitchen appliances, home furnishings, carpets, toys, bicycles, and cameras.

Fewer entrepreneurs understood the consumption habits of rural Americans better than Aaron Montgomery Ward (1844–1913) and Richard W. Sears (1863–1914), founders of Chicago's most important mail-order businesses. During the 1860s, rural Americans had bought what they needed from itinerant peddlers or made credit purchases at general stores, paying at harvest time. General stores secured their stock from traveling salesman like Ward, who started out selling dry goods for a wholesaler. Noting the high prices charged by rural merchants, Ward realized that he could win the country trade by underselling these general stores. In 1872, he established a retail catalog house, which expanded the shopping options available in rural America.

Ward pioneered a number of practices that competitors copied. Like large department stores and five-and-tens, Ward's mail-order house cut costs by eliminating middlemen and purchasing goods directly from manufacturers. Ward advertised the items in a catalog, took prepaid cash orders from consumers by mail, and shipped merchandise from a Chicago warehouse. Precedents for this existed in the mail-order branches of major dry-goods emporiums and department stores, but those operations catered primarily to merchants. Ward's 1872 retail catalog was a modest one-page circular, listing goods and prices. Within a few years, he was publishing a 72-page book describing practical, enticing, and inexpensive goods, from horse harnesses to ladies' parasols. As the exclusive distributor for the Grange (a farmers' cooperative formally group known as the Patrons of Husbandry), Ward secured the trust of rural Americans. He bolstered customers' confidence by paying all shipping charges and providing a "Satisfaction Guaranteed or Your Money Back" warranty. By the 1880s, Ward's 240-page catalog featured more than 10,000 products, and the breadth of Ward's inventory distinguished his catalog from the books published by New York stores.

Ward encountered a serious rival when Richard W. Sears, a flashy and aggressive salesman, joined forces with Alvah Curtis Roebuck, a quiet watch repairer, to form Sears, Roebuck and Company. The men had been partners since 1887, selling watches, jewelry, and diamonds through a retail catalog. In 1893, Sears, Roebuck expanded its mail-order business, publishing a 196-page catalog featuring ready-made men's clothing, bicycles, sewing machines, furniture, and other consumer products. The next year, the company made a conscious effort to associate itself with the new consumption-oriented society by labeling its semiannual catalog, the "consumers' guide."

The 1890s were good years for mail-order retailing. By then, Victorian America's communications and transportation systems — the telegraph, the postal system, and the railroads — were largely in place, making it possible to ship catalogs and packages across the country. Nonetheless, three-quarters of Americans still had to pick up their mail and freight at the post office or the general store, necessitating long and arduous trips by horseback, carriage, or wagon. In 1896, a new federal government policy removed this cumbersome aspect of the mail-order business.

That year, the U.S. Post Office initiated rural free delivery (RFD), which enabled mail-order retailers to expand their markets. Proposed in 1891, RFD was the brainchild of John Wanamaker, then serving as postmaster general under President Benjamin Harrison. In addition to everything else, Wanamaker's department store operated a mail-order business. With RFD, postal carriers delivered the mail directly to letter boxes on country roads, making it possible for consumers to receive catalogs at home. Shoppers could now browse through the catalog in privacy, fill out an order blank, and entrust the postman with the money. In turn, the carrier converted the cash into a money order at the post office, put it in the envelope, and mailed the whole thing.

As a result of the creation of RFD, the nation's mail-order business skyrocketed. At Sears, sales grew from $746,000 in 1895 to $10 million in 1900 and $41 million in 1908. By 1916, Sears was well established as America's largest retailer, with $137 million in sales. That year, Woolworth sales totaled $87 million; Montgomery Ward, $62 million; and Macy's, $22 million. Like Wal★Mart today, Sears had enormous leverage among manufacturers, securing unbelievably low prices because it purchased such immense quantities. It was so successful at undercutting the competition that rural Americans began to associate the name Sears with bargains.

Richard Sears prided himself on low prices and sensational promotions, like the sewing-machine deals that became the stuff of legend. Few household items meant as much to rural women as their sewing machine, which lessened the burden of making and repairing the household's linens, curtains, and clothing. Yet, for rural women, the sewing machine did more than save eyesight, labor, and time; it symbolized participation in consumer society and the promise of a middle-class lifestyle. Fittingly, women proudly displayed their sewing machines in the parlor or front room for everyone to see. In 1867, Nevada diarist Rachel Haskell wrote a loving description of her cozy sitting room, filled with laughing children; collections of shells, minerals, and books; a sofa, easy chair, and piano; and a sewing machine. Richard Sears fully understood the sewing machine's role as a domestic status symbol. The store's 1897 catalog encouraged consumers to invest in a cabinet sewing machine, which could double as parlor furniture, as "a center table, library stand or writing desk."

The retail catalog was the premier vehicle for educating rural Americans about changing consumer habits. Known as "the big book," the Sears catalog was said to be the only printed volume besides the Bible in many a rural home. It served to mitigate the loneliness of country life and brought a bit of showmanship to the dreary existence experienced by thousands of isolated farm families. Like world's fair exhibits and department-store displays, the mail-order catalog was an advertisement for the fruits of abundance.

A promotional wizard who "could sell a breath of air," Sears publicized his mail-order catalog by advertising in mass-circulation magazines. Often, those advertisements featured "loss leaders," products priced at little or no profit to stimulate interest in other lines. In 1898, consumers reading *Harper's Weekly* saw a beautiful ladies' velvet cape with fur trim for a mere $4.95. The next year, men flipping through *Munsey's* saw nice dress pants for only $1.95. *Youth's Companion* featured the Sears advertisements for pianos, bicycles, boy's suits, and the Edison Graphophone, an early "talking machine" that recorded sounds and played music on cylinders. In *Cosmopolitan* (then a family magazine), Sears offered sewing machines for $15, some $25 to $40 less than the competition. This ad proved so successful that during the late 1890s, the factory fell three weeks behind in production of the sewing machines.

For a short period, Sears sold catalogs for 15 to 50¢, while sending a free book to every customer who spent $50. By 1904, mail-order houses began to realize that free catalogs encouraged sales, and they started giving them away. That year, Sears inaugurated an "Iowaization" scheme, asking loyal customers in Iowa to distribute twenty-five catalogs to people in their communities. As a reward, the distributors received prizes based on the value of the orders received. When Iowa sales soared, Sears tried the plan elsewhere. The circulation of the Sears catalog doubled, from 541,000 in fall 1903 to 1.1 million in spring 1904. Four years later, the company gave away nearly 6.5 million catalogs. Between 1902 and 1908, it circulated more than 24 million catalogs, or one for every three to four people in America. In rural areas, this meant that there was one Sears catalog for every two people.

Another federal government initiative, the U.S. Post Office's parcel post service, gave an additional boost to the mail-order business. Ceremoniously, John Wanamaker mailed the first parcel post package in 1913. With parcel post, delivery men would deliver packages weighing up to eleven pounds to the addressee's door. By 1920, the weight limit was raised to fifty pounds. Although parcel post infuriated express companies and general storekeepers, the innovation helped the mail-order business. From 1913 to 1920, the annual sales at Sears, Roebuck increased from $91 million to $245 million; those at Montgomery Ward soared from $39 to $101 million.

Victorian consumers nicknamed mail-order catalogs in ways that described their contents and linked them to broader social trends. Titles and slogans like "a department store in a book," "a consumers' guide," "a city shopping district at your fingertips," and the "world's largest country store" testified to role of the catalog in bringing mass consumption to the countryside. Flipping through the pages of a Sears catalog was comparable to browsing through Gimbel Brothers, Philadelphia's department store for budget shoppers, who looked up the social ladder for models to emulate. Sears offered rural consumers the products that marked status: parlor sets consisting of a couch and matching chairs for him and her; ladies' ready-made shirtwaists and skirts in the Gibson Girl style; sewing machines in different prices and models; and the new leisure products such as the bicycle, phonograph, and player piano. After 1900, the Sears catalog featured a department devoted to "Modern Homes," which listed building materials and, eventually, prefabricated houses. Like Wanamaker's, Sears encouraged consumers to link the home and consumption with their personal identity, playing a seminal role in extending new beliefs and behaviors to rural Americans.

Old-Fashioned Retailers

Victorian America's commercial landscape was remarkably diverse and vibrant. Big cities like Philadelphia had major downtown shopping districts. The Wanamaker department store dominated the center, but there were other department stores, chain stores, and plenty of small specialty retailers nearby. Residential neighborhoods on the urban periphery had their own shopping districts dominated by family businesses. On a smaller scale, midsized cities from Rochester, New York, to Kansas City, Missouri, followed a similar pattern.

A brief look at Philadelphia's South Street in 1880 reiterates the point about the persistence of traditional retailing. Today, South Street is a hipster magnet, with urban stores, sex shops, and tattoo parlors. In the Victorian period, this commercial center, a thirty-minute walk from Wanamaker's Grand Depot, catered to local needs. Workshops and factories sold carpets, cigars, guns, and soap. Food vendors included bakers, confectioners, and oyster dealers, selling shellfish from the Delaware Bay. Residents depended on South Street's barbers, boardinghouses, cobblers, dressmakers, druggists, milliners, pawn brokers, plumbers, tailors, and upholsterers. Notably, several dressmakers and milliners had set up shop, taking advantage of a nearby enclave of dry-goods stores. Most important, South Street shoppers found a wide variety of consumer goods, including household products. Specialty stores sold china, clothing, dry goods, furniture, hardware, jewelry, liquor, and tobacco, while variety stores functioned as the precursors to convenience stores.

Although Wanamaker, Woolworth, and Sears pioneered new methods, it's important to remember that their institutional innovations—the department store, the five-and-ten, and the mail-order catalog—coexisted with traditional commercial forms and practices. Neighborhood businesses carried many everyday necessities. At the high end of the market, Tiffany & Company and its competitors, like Bailey Banks and Biddle, sold precious jewelry, bronze statuary, and stained-glass lamps to wealthy shoppers. In nearly every neighborhood, the Mom-and-Pop store—the corner grocery run by a family—remained an icon and a reality well into the twentieth century when it morphed into the local Express Mart. While the retailing revolution had a lasting influence, the rise of mass merchandisers didn't eliminate traditional retailers and their suppliers, the wholesalers. These businesses continued to provide many of the products that Americans used to define themselves as consumers.

Tiffany Tastes and a Woolworth's Pocketbook

The vibrant commercial scene of Victorian cities, with luxury department stores and old-fashioned specialty shops, opened the doors to the wide, wide world. Shoppers wandered, browsed, and dreamed. Retailers were still inventing ways to operate their massive stores at a profit. They experimented with the stock, the store layout, the sales staff, and the customers they attracted. The variety of goods and the sheer novelty of shopping was astounding.

But although everyone could look, not everyone could buy. The ragged street urchin stared at the luxurious goods in the plate-glass window, lamenting, "Ain't it hell to be poor?" While she longed for a Tiffany necklace, the gamin could barely afford a Woolworth's bracelet. Initially, much of the new retailing targeted the middle-class market, but as merchants raised people's expectations for a higher standard of living, the boundaries of the middle class expanded. So did the merchants' profits.

Victorian retailers like Marshall Field and F. W. Woolworth created the model for mass merchandising, which would take off in the Modern era. The department store was the urban superstar until the post–World War II era, when malls eroded its profits. The dime store's business model proved to be most elastic and adaptable. By the 1920s, chain stores appeared on Main Streets from coast to coast, pushing old-fashioned retailers out of business. Innovations like centralized buying and distribution allowed new chains like Lerner Stores, a ready-to-wear retailer now called New York & Company, to introduce big-city styles across America at competitive prices. Local communities saw the chains as a double-edged sword that cut the profits of neighborhood stores but introduced a taste of urban sophistication to Main Street.

In the twentieth century, the retailing formats developed in Victorian times struggled with each other, vying for commercial dominance. Ultimately, merchants would find a way to make money selling fine feathered hats to that raggedy street urchin. John Wanamaker is now part of Macy's Inc., the world's largest department store. F. W. Woolworth and other dime stores provided the model for Wal★Mart. Mail-order merchandising has been reinvented by the internet. Mass merchandisers learned that the vast American market had Tiffany tastes and a Woolworth's pocketbook.

Top: The Centennial Exposition celebrated consumer society with displays of the newest products. Central aisle of Main Building, from James Dabney McCabe, *The Illustrated History of the Centennial Exhibition* (Cincinnati: Jones Brothers, [1876]), 6. *Courtesy of Hagley Museum and Library.*

Bottom: A typical display from the Centennial Exposition. Bronze bric-a-brac made by Nicholas Muller's Sons, from Frank H. Norton, *Illustrated Historical Register of the Centennial Exhibition, Philadelphia, 1876* (New York: American News Co., 1879): 106. *Courtesy of Hagley Museum and Library.*

Top: Relaxing by the piano, 1880s. This musician poses with her instruments in the family parlor on a hot summer day, surrounded by bric-a-brac. *Author's collection.*

Bottom: Chicago boardinghouse, ca. 1915. Dressed in his best clothes, a Lithuanian immigrant sits in his room alongside some prized possessions: holy pictures, doilies, statues, candles, newspaper clippings, photographs, and an alarm clock. *Courtesy, Chicago Historical Society.*

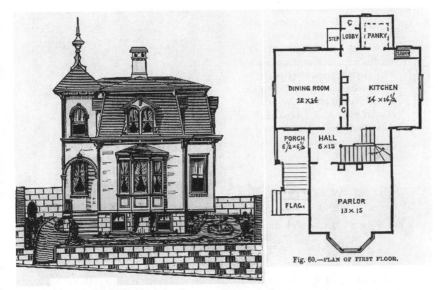

Fig. 60.—PLAN OF FIRST FLOOR.

Top: The Victorian home as imagined by tastemakers had small, cozy rooms and an elaborate exterior. From S. B. Reed, *House-plans for Everybody* (New York: Orange Judd Company, 1878): 82, 84. *Courtesy of Hagley Museum and Library.*

Bottom: The bungalow, America's favorite housing style. Mail-order millwork companies marketed bungalow plans and construction materials to carpenters across the nation. *Millwork and Building Material that Satisfy: Catalog No. 375* (Chicago: Chicago Millwork Supply Company, Aug. 1929), 77. *Author's collection.*

A Model of Convenience

Read our FREE PLAN Offer on page 72

Design 158C—Size 24x42 feet, not including porch or bay

For $1315.00

we agree to furnish all material to build this house consisting of lumber, lath, shingles, flooring, building paper, millwork, guttering, tinwork, hardware, paints—everything but labor, plaster, masonry, plumbing and heating.

The cost of labor and masonry varies in different localities. With the aid of our complete plans any local builder can readily give you the cost of erecting this building.

FLOOR PLAN

By the early 1900s, low-end retailers like Hartman Furniture offered Mission-style furniture, as shown by the Fumed Oak Spanish Imperial Library Set. Budget-conscious shoppers with Victorian tastes could buy more traditional styles, such as the dining-room set with a china cabinet. *Hartman's Holiday Bargains,* (Chicago: Hartman Furniture & Carpet Co., 1913): cover, 6, 9. *Author's collection.*

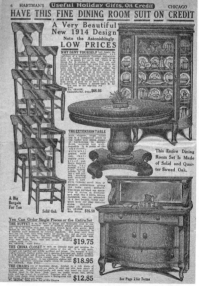

A CHANGED MAN.

This Man by his Wife's advice,
Bought one of our Suits so nice.

Reader his advice to you,
Is "Walk in and do so too."

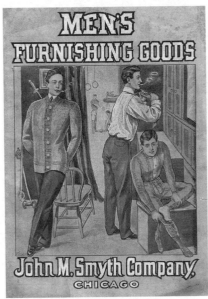

Top: A Changed Man, 1880. This Currier and Ives chromolithograph suggests the transformative power of clothing. *Courtesy, Henry T. Peters Collection, Museum of the City of New York.*

Bottom: Three young men dress in warm clothing after working out at a sports club. *Men's Furnishing Goods* (Chicago: John M. Smyth Company, [1900-5]). *Author's collection.*

Top: Tailors encouraged men to wear suits that reflected their personalities, ambitions, and social class. Here, a well-heeled businessman consults with the sales staff as he selects fabrics. Puritan Tailors, *Spring and Summer 1910* (Chicago, 1910), cover. *Author's collection.*

Bottom: The Arrow Collar Man, created by illustrator J. C. Leyendecker, was a model of youthful sophistication. Cluett, Peabody & Company, advertisement from *Literary Digest,* c. 1915. *Author's collection.*

Top: Paris set the pace in women's fashions. A La Coquette, Paris, trade card, ca. 1895. *Author's collection.*

Bottom: "Walking Down Broadway." Americans copied Parisian styles, but poked fun at the French. Union Package Dye Co., trade card, 1880. *Author's collection.*

Top: American beauty Lillian Russell. Wearing a custom-made gown by the English couturier John Redfern, Russell endorsed fibre chamois, a warm lining for winter clothes. Flock & Wade, Hackettstown, N.J., trade card, 1895. *Author's collection.*

Bottom: Corsets molded the female body into the hourglass shape. Boston Store, *Woman's Reference and Receipt Book, No. 46, Fall and Winter 1894-95* (Chicago, 1894), 30. *Author's collection.*

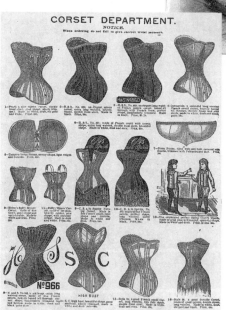

Irene Castle designed a ready-to-wear line in the loose, flowing style she popularized as a dancer. Philipsborn's, advertisement from *People's Home Journal* (Sept. 1920): 21. *Author's collection.*

Top: Main Street, USA. A typical small-town commercial street lined with small stores run by local merchants, ca. 1900. Postcard of Clinton Street, looking east from Main Street in Frankfort, Indiana, published by the Indiana News Company, Indianapolis. *Author's collection.*

Bottom: Store interior, showing the hodgepodge of toys, household goods, and ready-to-wear, Michigan, ca. 1905. *Author's collection.*

Top: Local shopkeepers tempted passersby with sidewalk displays of merchandise. People's China House, ca. 1890, neg. no. 87-13977. *National Museum of American History, Smithsonian Institution, Behring Center.*

Bottom: In large cities, skyscraper department stores stretched across entire blocks. Stern Brothers, *Book of Authoritative Fashions, Spring and Summer, 1911* (NY, 1911), back cover. *Author's collection.*

Top: Urban department stores sometimes had separate buildings for men and women. Marshall Field, Store for Men, postcard, 1914. *Author's collection.*

Bottom: "Meet me at the eagle." John Wanamaker's luxury department store had two attractions from the 1904 Louisiana Purchase Exposition: the world's largest organ and the famous bronze eagle, which became a rendezvous point for shoppers. Postcard, early 1900s. *Author's collection.*

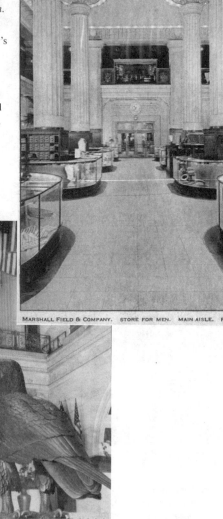

MARSHALL FIELD & COMPANY.   STORE FOR MEN.   MAIN AISLE.   FIRST FLOOR

More Buying Power for the Small Coins of the World

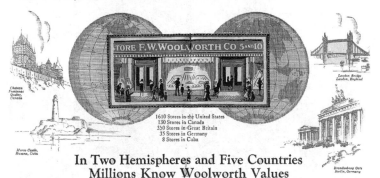

1610 Stores in the United States
130 Stores in Canada
350 Stores in Great Britain
35 Stores in Germany
8 Stores in Cuba

In Two Hemispheres and Five Countries
Millions Know Woolworth Values

Wise buyers know that they save money at the Woolworth stores. They know, too, that Woolworth service goes beyond the saving of money. There is a conserving of the shopper's time and energy and the happy convenience of buying easily and quickly on open counters a thousand and one indispensables of living. And the store locations are central and easily reached.

Men, women and children from Maine to California, from Canada to Cuba and from the British Isles to Germany now know that buying at Woolworths is not only a matter of economy but a matter of intelligent shopping in a well-ordered store thoughtfully planned to give every shopper the most for the minimum expenditure of time, effort and money.

Top: Five and tens expanded globally by catering to working-class consumers. *Fifty Years of Woolworth, 1879-1929* (NY: F. W. Woolworth Co., 1929), [24-25]. *Author's collection.*

Bottom: Sears depicted America as the land of plenty, juxtaposing the allegorical figure of Columbia and an overflowing cornucopia against billowing factories and prosperous farms. *Sears, Roebuck & Company, Catalogue No. 107* (Chicago, 1897), cover, neg. no. 94-2030. Warshaw Collection of Business Americana–Dry Goods, *Archives Center, National Museum of American History, Behring Center, Smithsonian Institution.*

Top: Some shoppers overindulged, as did this Philadelphia dandy burdened with packages from Strawbridge and Clothier. Trade card, 1880s. *Author's collection.*

Bottom: Window shopping. Sometimes poor consumers coveted fashions they couldn't afford. Postcard, 1880s. *Author's collection.*

PART TWO

Modern America, 1900–1945

What made Modern Americans modern? What separated consumers who lived between 1900 and World War II from their Victorian counterparts? In November 1924, journalist Samuel Strauss grappled with these questions in the *Atlantic Monthly* and ended up with a laundry list of new things. "The American citizen," he mused, "has more comforts and conveniences than kings had two hundred years ago." Those luxuries included "a stream of automobiles and radios, buildings and bathrooms, furs and furniture, [ocean] liners, hotels, bridges, vacuum cleaners, cameras, bus lines, electric toasters, moving-pictures, railway cars, package foods, telephones, pianos, novels, [and] comic supplements." Consumption for the masses, a mere twinkle in the Victorian eye, grew into an exuberant and sometimes cranky toddler in Modern times.

But was Modern American consumption simply a matter of having more and better things? While Strauss described the proliferation of new goods, what really mattered was how these new things intersected with older goods, established patterns of behavior, and newer social relationships. Products of the new technologies like cars, radios, vacuum cleaners, cameras, and toasters didn't simply "impact" society. People bought these new goods and then integrated them into existing routines, traditions, communities, and ways of self-understanding. The mixture of the old and the new created the Modern consumer culture, and it left Modern Americans living vastly different lives than had the Victorians.

The nation's sheer size, ethnic diversity, and urbanity were important factors in the change. Between 1890 and 1920, the United States population nearly doubled, from 63 to 120 million. Fifteen million immigrants from Southern and Eastern Europe arrived in America between 1900 and 1915, and half a million blacks moved to Northern cities during World War I. By 1920, most Americans—51 percent—lived in urban centers. The vast majority of them resided in the Smokestack belt that sprawled from the Atlantic Ocean to the Mississippi River above the old Mason-Dixon Line. Large metropolises like New York, Philadelphia, and Chicago were home to millions, but the average city was much smaller. Dozens of mid-sized cities, from Lowell, Massachusetts, to Dayton, Ohio, had populations of around 100,000; and dozens more were of modest size, like Muncie, Indiana, with around 40,000.

Over the previous decades, American industry laid the cornerstone of the mass-production economy. The United States went from being a major manufacturing nation, similar to England and Germany, into the world's leading economic power. This transition was not smooth. During World War I, the United States had assumed Great Britain's premier role in international finance and banking. It would emerge from World War II with unscathed factories, superior armed forces, and a terrible new weapon: the atomic bomb. In between the wars, Americans enjoyed a spurt of economic growth, endured thirteen years of Prohibition, and suffered the worst economic depression in their history. These massive upheavals created a new world order and left an indelible mark on consumer society.

The New Tempo

Economic developments paralleled the major cultural changes that defined Modernity. Where the Victorians had valued consistency, their early-twentieth-century counterparts lived in a state of constant flux. Commodities that were the result of wondrous new technologies, such as automobiles, electricity, movies, and radio, altered people's sense of space, speed, and time. Distances became truncated, attention spans shortened, and more goods and experiences found their way into the consumer identity kit. The concept of "personality," which came from the new disciplines of psychology and psychiatry, encouraged people to expand their worldview.

Modernity and *Modern* were terms used to describe an emerging mainstream culture that was fast-paced, technologically savvy, and always changing. This new culture featured a seemingly endless parade of new attitudes, ideas, and things. And it was geared toward immediate, if not yet instant, satisfaction. Modern culture also provoked and embodied great conflict. Americans didn't simply absorb the new attitudes, values, and experiences like sponges, just as new technology didn't immediately alter everyday life. Some people rejected the rapid changes, as shown by the revival of the Ku Klux Klan, the Scopes "monkey" trial, film censorship, the nascent consumer movement, and the rise of two iconic figures, the Madison Avenue executive and the Detroit automaker, epitomized by Henry Ford, which we will examine later.

The late historian Roland Marchand described the Madison Avenue executive as "the most modern of men." Admen were well-paid and well-educated, seeing themselves as the arbiters of a new order. They yearned for change but were reluctant to surrender their own privileged social status. Blinders often prevented them from seeing "others"—for instance, blacks, immigrants, and farmers—as real people with feelings, needs, and ideas. They wanted to know the female consumer, but their conventional ideas about gender led them to believe she was fickle, incurious, and easily manipulated.

Art historian Terry Smith has identified a real person, Henry Ford, the father of the Model T, as another archetype of Modernity. Ford venerated and loathed the speed-driven world that his assembly line helped to create. As he democratized car ownership, Ford amassed a vast collection of old buildings and artifacts into Greenfield Village, an idyllic museum that preserved an imagined rural American past. Whether adman or automaker, both types speak to the contradictions of Modernity. Both rushed headlong into the future, tripped on their heels, tumbled to the ground, and looked back, dazed.

Victorian sensibilities didn't entirely disappear overnight but were integral to the evolving culture. As shown in Part I, earlier consumers had been guided by rules: the concept of "character," prescriptions for "good manners," and the belief that "civilized" people were superior to the "savages" of nonindustrial nations. The class rules had started to break down, but some were still in force. Many Modern consumers still arranged their lives around Victorian conventions and found in the "middle class" their comfort zone. However, generational differences rendered a cleft between the Victorian version of middle-class respectability and the Modern ideal.

In tune with the new faster tempo, some younger people turned to self-discovery, making it part of the middle-class experience. The yearning for self-expression had motivated Victorian consumers who decorated their homes, wore fashionable dress, and went pleasure shopping, but that tenor changed in the Modern era. Frugality and thrift didn't evaporate, but now they existed in conflict with spending and gratification. New behaviors joined the Victorian values of sincerity and consistency and began to eat away at them. Most important, people started to manage their emotions in new ways. For one, feelings that had been intensely private became very public. Romance, passion, and courtship dominated magazines, movies, and popular music. For another, feelings themselves became commodities in the new world of branded goods and their emotionally charged advertisements.

This emotional upheaval had important ramifications for Modern consumer society. It became more acceptable to *envy* one's neighbors and *covet* their possessions, as suggested by the phrase "keeping up with the Joneses," introduced by a 1916 *New York World* comic strip about social climbers. Some people rejected the old straight-laced conventions for exciting urban experiences such as going to dance halls and movie palaces and buying mass-produced objects such as clothes, cars, records, and radios. Where Victorians corseted themselves to conform to a sensuous ideal, Moderns felt freer to feel desire for its own sake. Hedonism was by no means rampant, but hedonistic cravings were becoming more common. Pleasure-seeking, an aspect of the Protestant ethic that had fueled consumer demand during the British industrial revolution in the 1700s, assumed an even more vital role as a stimulant to consumers and the economy.

More than before, subcultures originated new cultural forms that entered popular experience and reshaped middle-class life. Groups on the fringes of the mainstream—such as artists and musicians, homosexuals, recent immigrants, and working-class men and women—incubated new ways of thinking and doing. In creative circles, avant-garde artists and writers challenged academic practices. Impressionist painters like Mary Cassatt and Lost Generation novelists like Ernest Hemingway and John Dos Passos found new ways of telling stories. In Detroit, Mexican artist Diego Rivera painted murals that captured the dignity of men who worked at Ford's dehumanizing factories. The subject matter—the nobility of sweating factory workers in their shirt-sleeves—was new, different, emotionally charged, and distinctively Modern. Jazz originated among black musicians who played in New Orleans brothels (a topic covered in Chapter Five), while the daily use of lipstick and rouge was first popularized by men and women on the edges of respectability: prostitutes, transvestites, actors, and other performers. Immigrants introduced old world craftsmanship and epicurean novelties, such as Jewish fine men's tailoring and Italian pizza and spaghetti to the mainstream.

Guided by the concept of personality, Modern consumers came to see reinvention, individual expression, and subcultural influences as an expected part of their lives. After Israel Zangwill's 1908 play *The Melting Pot* popularized the concept of assimilation, some people placed less value on their ethnic roots and more on going with the flow. The happy-go-lucky symbol of the Jazz Age—a dancing flapper drinking a forbidden cocktail and smoking a cigarette, perhaps in a holder—is based on these new attitudes. Americans, in constant search of the perfect self, expanded their vision of how possessions and experiences could enhance personal pleasure. Certainly, the persistence of old social hierarchies meant that some people remained relegated to the margins of society or entirely left out, due to ethnic bias, racial prejudice, geography, or inadequate income. Not everyone was Modern, wanted to be, or could be. Like Henry Ford, some people embraced parts of the Modern tempo yet hesitated to let go of the comfy Victorian past. Nonetheless, people increasingly came to see convenience and speed, envy and desire, and mutability and change as parts of consumer society.

From the Standard of Living to the American Dream

A new group of professions emerged to study Modern life and, more important, to manage its consequences. For the first time, college-educated "experts" in fields like engineering, home economics, and sociology used scientific methods to identify and categorize people as consumers and to analyze their needs. Passionate about democracy, many observers criticized the monopolistic practices of big business, blamed corporations for skyrocketing inflation between 1900 and 1920, and advocated the redistribution of wealth. They re-crafted the Victorian notion of progress into the Modern concept of "progressive," a social and political philosophy that advocated social betterment and stressed material comfort for all.

In 1902, progressive reformers studying living conditions among industrial workers coined the term *standard of living*. This phrase referred to the minimum assortment of goods and services required to attain good health and decency, as determined by the experts. Early social workers used this concept as a yardstick to determine if wages and prices allowed working families to enjoy an adequate level of comfort and happiness. The accepted standard of living was also a powerful explanatory tool for convincing charities, employers, and governments to support higher wages and social welfare programs.

The new focus on living standards helped to shift some of the federal government's attention to consumer needs. In Victorian America, state and local authorities had protected public health by prohibiting the sale of rotten meat and sour dairy products. In contrast, federal economic policy had focused on international trade, with the tariff being the major issue in presidential elections and congressional debates. Progressive reformers lobbied local, state, and federal governments for fairer tax policies, public ownership of utilities, and consumer protection legislation. They achieved a landmark victory in 1906 when Congress passed the first federal laws that protected consumers from exploitation. The Pure Food and Drugs Act and the Meat Inspection Act authorized federal authorities to ban the sale of tainted products and led to the famous "USDA Approved" stamp on meats.

Initially, the standard of living referred to a *minimum* bundle of goods and conveniences, but it soon expanded to include what middle-class people found acceptable for themselves. Middle-class Americans saw the standard of living as a cultural goal, an objective to which they could strive. They applied what they saw in advertising, stores, and advice books to upgrade their own measure. In the Victorian era, there was an implicit understanding about how the members of the middle class should live. In the Modern era, there was an attempt to codify how *everyone* should live.

Before World War I, mainstream Americans came to see certain types of goods as necessities for all families who aspired to the middle class: matching sets of silverware, indoor plumbing and white bathroom fixtures, and the airy Modern bungalow. The standard later extended to the landscape, where the new practice of zoning separated real-estate parcels into industrial, commercial, and residential lots. The impulse to collect, compartmentalize, and categorize was a spillover from Victorian times, but the idea that things and space could be *managed* to enhance appearance and comfort was distinctly Modern.

By the 1920s, Modern ideas about efficiency and standards began to intrigue business professionals. The prospect of applying the standardization idea to consumer goods tantalized businesspeople versed in the theories of Frederick Winslow Taylor, the father of scientific management. Some Modern industries had used Taylor's theories about rationalization and efficiency to build and run high-tech facilities. These new factories were so efficient that they could produce more goods than the market could absorb. It seemed possible, however, that the creation of new standards in product quality might help businesses cope with the great puzzle of how to reconcile oversupply with current demand.

Experts in advertising, home economics, marketing, merchandising, and product design began to focus less on the abstract "market" and more on "the consumer." These corporate experts, who by the 1930s sometimes called themselves "consumption engineers," borrowed methods from the social sciences in an effort to unravel the mysteries of desire and stimulate sales. While their answers weren't always correct, they did steer businesses in new directions and help give consumer society a distinctly Modern twist. Chapter Four will show how advertising agencies pioneered market research and visual strategies for tapping into people's desires and fears. National advertising became an important corporate vehicle for selling the standard product as well as the managed ideal. Chapter Six spotlights the work of consumption engineers who made aesthetic decisions for the largest U.S. industry: the automotive industry in Detroit.

By the late 1920s, the standard of living was firmly embedded in mainstream thought and middle-class consumption synonymous with the *American dream*. This phrase was coined by Pulitzer Prize–winning historian James Truslow Adams, who articulated the basic premise in his 1932 book, *The Epic of America*. Adams wrote about the "dream of a land in which life should be better and richer and fuller for every man, according to his ability or achievement." The clothes that people wore, the cars they drove, their houses, hats, pets, and other possessions were part of that dream.

Middletown, U.S.A.: Average America

The Modern penchant for social analysis and the need to decipher desire inspired a new generation of experts to look for the "Average American." In the mid-1920s, sociologists Robert S. and Helen Merrell Lynd, a husband-and-wife research team from Columbia University, determined to find out how the Average American lived and how Modernity was eroding traditions. Their 1929 best seller, *Middletown*, kept people talking for decades. Around the time anthropologist Margaret Mead submersed herself in Samoan culture, the Lynds and their research team lived among the people of Muncie, Indiana. Putting this Midwestern city under the microscope, the experts discovered a hometown of consumers who embodied the contradictions of Modernity. Middletowners were intently focused on local matters and took pride in this parochialism. At the same time, many of them had come to buy into national standards that shaped their aspirations.

Selected for its "middle-of-the-road quality," Muncie was a county seat with a diversified economy based on government, manufacturing, and agriculture. The population was relatively homogeneous: 85 percent white, 6 percent black, and 2 percent immigrant. Within the social structure, families were ranked by factors like wealth, income, inheritance, occupation, and race. The workforce had either white- or blue-collar jobs, with people describing themselves as either "business class" (29 percent) or "working class" (71 percent). The power elite, who owned and managed the large glassmaking plant and other local businesses, exerted a stultifying control over the city, setting the bar for which goods and leisure activities were acceptable. Business owners enjoyed comfortable incomes, lived on the outskirts of town, and were confident in their social roles, while other white-collar workers looked up to and tried to emulate them. On the other side of the tracks, factory workers evolved their own sense of self and community.

Two things about Middletown stood out: the robust pace of work and the frenetic rate of consumption. The typical Middletowner of the 1890s had received psychological satisfaction from a job well done. Community activities, such as a person's role as a citizen, churchgoer, neighbor, fraternal brother, or trade unionist, had given texture to daily life. Back then, people had "lived on a series of plateaus as regards standard of living," explained the Lynds. A family would achieve a certain degree of accomplishment, and stay within that range. By the 1920s, "the edges of the plateaus" had been "shaved off." Everyone in Muncie had lived "on a slope from any point of which desirable things belonging to people all the way to the top" could be glimpsed. Envy kicked in, and consumers wanted what they saw. They now had "urgent occasions for spending money." Breadwinners put in long hours at the office, store, or factory, working five-and-a-half days per week to increase their family's discretionary income. People valued being able to enjoy a high standard of living, and defined themselves primarily as consumers. Echoing the *Atlantic Monthly*, one Muncie newspaper put it succinctly: "The American citizen's first importance to his country is no longer that of citizen but that of consumer. Consumption is a new necessity."

The Modern Identity Kit

The Lynds explored how Middletowners defined themselves as consumers and how they evaluated each other by looking through the prism of possessions. Most Muncie families still observed a sharp division of labor by gender, following the Victorian ideal that categorized men and women almost as different species. The husband brought home the bacon, while the wife kept house, raised the children, orchestrated the social activities, and managed the family's status.

In part, the objects that made a difference in people's lives resembled the ones that had meaning in Victorian times. Although no one used the term *consumer identity kit*, this metaphor is useful for understanding what types of goods people used to identify themselves and their class. One's home was the major item in the Middletown identity kit, but the ensemble of durable goods had been revamped and expanded in essential ways. The concept of middle-class standards figured into this change.

The home and its contents still said much about a family's place in the community. Middetown had 9,200 homes, 86 percent of which were single-family dwellings with yards. Most people still rented, but home ownership was on the rise. In 1900, 65 percent of Muncie's homes had been rented; by 1920, the figure was down to 54 percent. The Lynds saw this "deep-rooted sentiment" for home ownership as a "mark of independence, of respectability, or belonging." The granting of credit to individuals was a new phenomenon, and it extended the possibility of home ownership to a wider range of men. Families occupied different types of dwellings, clustered in neighborhoods by occupation: cluttered shacks for the poor, comparatively roomy bungalows or cottages for prosperous factory workers, and Dutch colonials or rambling Victorian houses for business owners and upper management. Interior decorations varied by income and taste, but certain trends marked people as members of specific groups. Executives had a passion for antique Chinese vases and grand pianos, while blue-collar workers were most likely to own radio sets, a new technology discussed in Chapter Five.

New technology played a prominent role in consumer identity. Blue-collar workers had always learned about middle-class ways by scrutinizing their social betters, but now they had ready access to object lessons offered them by mass culture. By the 1920s, national advertising, phonograph records, weekly magazines, radio sets, and movies exposed mainstream Americans to the goings on in style centers like New York City and Los Angeles. People in the heartland saw versions of the good life as conceived by advertising agencies, industrial designers, and movie producers, and these glamourous images began to recast their perceptions about what was desirable, comfortable, and beautiful. As Chapter Five explains, mass culture also took consumer beyond the parochialism of hometowns in the heartland, exposing them to the sights and sounds of big-city neighborhoods, immigrant life, and African American culture.

Also during this time, high-tech items themselves became objects of desire. Families now judged their neighbors and the strangers they encountered by their taste in cars, phonograph sets, records, and radios. "The kind of car they drive, and similar externals," reported the Lynds, said much about people's place in Muncie. During the 1920s, the radio and the car (the subjects of Chapters Five and Six), joined the single-family home in the ensemble of objects that symbolized the middle-class standard. Chapter Six will also discuss the expansion of consumer credit—increased personal lending by local banks, credit agencies, retail stores, and automakers—that made much of this acquisition possible.

Resetting the Stage, Hollywood Style

"Like the automobile," the Lynds reported, "the motion picture is more to Middletown than simply a new way of doing an old thing." In the 1890s, Muncie residents occasionally went to the Opera House to hear performances, but by the 1920s, they preferred to see movies. Movie-going was almost a total experience—"talkie" technology was not yet developed, that would come in 1927—that appealed to the senses and stirred basic desires. Consumers relished sitting in the dark hushed theaters, ogling the stars of the "silver screen" with their stylish clothes, slick cars, and defiant attitudes toward drinking and partying in the midst of Prohibition.

By the mid-1920s, the major Hollywood studios each produced from forty to eighty pictures per year, for a total output of nearly 700. In 1927, the United States had more than 17,000 movie theaters. Nearly every town had at least one, and larger cities boasted entire theater districts, with several movie palaces side-by-side. Going to the movies became a major attraction for middle-class Americans, displacing older pastimes like singing in the parlor and promenading through the park.

Movies amused people on multiple levels. For starters, the architecture and interior decoration of these early "picture palaces" were stunning. The largest Hollywood studios owned their own theaters, lavish structures that enhanced their prestige while catering to the public yearning for a place to escape, to experience, even if only for a few hours, exoticism and beauty. Elaborate big-city palaces had exotic names, Moorish and Oriental decorations, and the first air-condition-ing systems. Neighborhood movie theaters offered a taste of luxury on a smaller scale. The theaters themselves enveloped consumers in extravagance, submerging them in a fantasy experience that was a world apart from their boring jobs and tedious household chores.

Second, the movies showed Americans how others lived, expos-ing consumers to new outlooks and lifestyles. Theaters changed their matinee billings several times a week to lure housewives and high-school students. Typically, moviegoers expected a series of amuse-ments: vaudeville acts, live orchestras, a newsreel, a short travelogue, and, finally, the feature film. It was in the Modern era that Hollywood established a standard repertoire of crime stories, westerns, historical dramas, melodramas, and romances. Movies expanded middle-class horizons by showcasing the lifestyles of the rich and famous, lives of adventure, glamour, and sexual innuendo.

Finally, the movies created a new type of celebrity culture focused on Hollywood stars rather than on vaudeville or theater performers. The 1910s and 1920s were the heyday of silent black-and-white films. The "silver screen" favored expressive actors who could convey a universe of emotions without uttering a word. Success stories included wholesome figures like Charlie Chaplin, a British comedian whose endearing character, The Tramp, poked fun at the poor, and Mary Pickford, nicknamed America's sweetheart for her girlish charm and mastery of romantic comedy. Pickford's second husband, Douglas Fairbanks, became Hollywood's biggest male star by perfecting ath-letic action roles. In the 1920s, the couple joined Chaplin and director D. W. Griffith to form the United Artists studio, making them mil-lionaires several times over in a real-life Horatio Alger story.

Twenties cinema thrived on the ingénue and the ladies' man. The decade's biggest female attraction, Clara Bow, made twenty-five films in two years, as the self-confident flapper with short dresses and bobbed hair who "spoke" her mind. America called Bow the "It Girl," *it* being a synonym for sex appeal. Italian-born dancer Rudolph Valentino became the most popular male matinee idol after he tangoed across the screen as a Mediterranean lover in *The Sheik* (1921). Female audiences swooned over Valentino's graceful dance moves and erotic allure. Bow and Valentino personified an exoticism and sensuality missing from ordinary life, captivating audiences who began to dream about transcending the humdrum.

When the Lynds did their field work in 1923–24, Middletown had five movie theaters that were open seven days a week. Admission was 10¢ to 30¢, and attendance peaked in December, when the theaters sold 4.5 tickets a week for every person, dropping in July to 3 per resident. Middletown tastes echoed national trends, favoring Wild West, slapstick comedy, romance, and high-society stories. Movies with a burning "heart interest" packed the theaters. Much can be inferred from titles, posters, and newspaper ads. James W. Horne's now-forgotten *Alimony* (1924) featured "brilliant men, beautiful jazz babies, champagne baths, midnight revels, petting parties at purple dawn, all ending in one terrific smashing climax that makes you gasp." Couples on dates flocked to see *Flaming Youth*, a 1923 film that practically defined the Roaring Twenties; it featured "neckers, petters, white kisses, red kisses, pleasure-mad daughters, sensations-craving mothers, [written] by an author who didn't dare sign his name; the truth bold, naked, sensational." Exciting pictures like these were a world apart from the Victorian parlor, with its sentimental sheet music and piano-playing.

Although the Lynds couldn't quantify the effect of Hollywood on the residents of Muncie, they did draw inferences about the Average Americans they studied. By the 1920s, consumers read about city life in baseball magazines like *Sporting News*, which followed the exploits of superstar players like Babe Ruth, and in family magazines like the *Saturday Evening Post,* which had plenty of features and testimonial ads showing New York socialites. But photographs of The Babe in his raccoon coat or Eleanor Roosevelt in her pearls were static images that paled in comparison to the movies, which made luxury *come alive*. Every week, Middletowner moviegoers stepped into "Fifth Avenue drawing rooms and English country houses" and watched "the habitual activities of a different cultural level." The Hollywood star system created out-of-this-world standards, which fans gobbled up. A stenographer might go to a dreamy matinee when she got off work on Saturday and spend every lunch break poring over *Motion Picture Magazine*. Exposure to the lifestyles of the rich and famous made the office worker painfully aware of her unpolished nails and the bare spot in her living-room rug. The films, the stars, and the magazines focused consumers' attention on glamour and helped them to imagine how their own lives might become more luxurious.

Down and Out

The wild excesses of the Roaring Twenties contrasted sharply with the restraint and deprivation of the depression decade (1929–41). The Great Depression was an international catastrophe that shook the major European nations, but it devastated the U.S. economy because of its sheer size. While scholars still debate what caused the Great Depression, many believe that underconsumption in the 1920s stuck a stick in the spokes of the mass-production economy. At the root lay an inadequate distribution of income and wealth, which economists and standard-of-living advocates had decried decades earlier.

While mainstream culture celebrated mass consumption, in reality the 1920s had been a decade of the haves, the have nots, and the have somes. The gap between the rich and poor increased. By 1929, the top 0.1 percent of American households had an aggregate income equal to that of the entire bottom 42 percent. Between 1920 and 1929, the per capita income of all Americans rose by 9 percent, but for the top 1 percent it increased by 75 percent! Savings reflected similar inequalities. Nearly 80 percent of U.S. households didn't have money in the bank, while the top 0.1 percent controlled 34 percent of savings nationwide.

This grossly unequal allocation of resources had an adverse effect on consumption, even during the Roaring Twenties. In time, the capacity of American factories to produce exceeded the collective ability of the vast majority of consumers to buy. Average Americans like those in Middletown spent nearly every penny they had on durable goods like cars and houses, necessities like food and clothing, and mass entertainments such as the movies. All of their earnings, plus the money they borrowed for big-ticket purchases like houses, went into the consumer economy. The poor washer woman, shoe-factory worker, and corner barber spent, too, but many simply struggled just to get by. While elites purchased their share of luxury goods, they soon ran out of things to buy. The rich could only own so many fur coats, tuxedos, luxury cars, racehorses, yachts, and mansions. Much of their money was tied up in stocks, bonds, and other investments that had funded the industrial buildup. This scenario was a recipe for disaster, and the whole thing collapsed after the Stock Market Crash of October 1929. Prices, employment, and wages fell sharply for 43 months, and although there was an upswing after that, the Great Depression really lasted until the outbreak of World War II. It was the longest downswing in the economy since the 1873–78 downturn, which had lasted for 65 months.

The industrial and agriculture sectors were hardest hit. Construction, devastated by falling birth rates, declining migration, rising interest rates, and reduced creditworthiness, suffered the most. The curtailment in building had a negative impact on cement- and brick-making, which declined by 63 and 83 percent, respectively. Automobile sales declined by 65 percent, with similar reverberations in the glass, textiles, and rubber industries. Between 1929 and 1933, unemployment rose from 1.5 to 12.3 million, from 3 to 25 percent of the civilian workforce. The dramatic collapse of agricultural prices affected nearly all farmers, particularly after a prolonged drought created the Dust Bowl and destroyed the crops. Countless farmers were dragged down by debt and foreclosure.

Amidst the catastrophe, high-tech industries like chemicals, aircraft, radio, and electricity continued to be profitable in part due to government spending, and kept thousands employed. Consumers still needed new shoes and clothes, so the footwear and textile industries declined only slightly. People with jobs watched their wallets, but they still went out dancing, smoked cigarettes, bought gasoline, and did what they could to keep their cars running. The film industry slumped, at least for a few years, but radio was a big winner. Radio was a godsend, a new form of "free" indoor entertainment for people who couldn't afford gas or the price of admission to the movie theater.

In 1935, the Lynds returned to Muncie to see how the Average American had fared during the depression and reported their findings two years later in *Middletown in Transition*. Between 1926 and 1935,

Muncie's population swelled from 37,000 to 47,000, due to an influx of rural job seekers, an expanded service sector, and local public works projects. However, annual retail sales had dropped from $27 to $12 million, as consumers spent less on food, radios and music, apparel, jewelry, and automobiles. Blue-collar workers were most likely to tighten their belts because Muncie's economy was heavily dependent on the automotive industry. Between 1929 and 1933, the city's industrial output declined by 57 percent, factory wages by 67 percent.

Yet the Lynds did discover cultural continuities and material novelties in Muncie. They ascribed the persistence of certain traditions to cultural lag, to "the thick blubber of custom that envelops the city's life." "Here in these big and little, clean and cluttered houses in their green yards," they sensed that middle-class life had "gone on unaltered." On closer inspection, they found subtle changes—modernizing influences—such as an "occasional shiny new filling station" that stood out "like a gold tooth." While some neighborhoods looked "a bit dingy"—"the iron lions in the front yards less challenging"—others had "new bungalows scattered among the weathered cottages and boxlike two-story houses." Everywhere, "the blare of radios was more pervasive than in 1925." Even down-and-out factory workers held on to "their great symbol of advancement—the automobile." For many, "car ownership" was a "large share of the American dream," an emblem of self-respect. Everywhere, Middletowners still believed in the "rising standard of living offered them . . . on the installment plan."

The American dream didn't wither after the 1929 Stock Market Crash. Certainly, some people suggested that poverty built character, as did director Frank Capra in his 1934 film *It Happened One Night*. Its protagonists, the penniless lovers Claudette Colbert and Clark Gable, hitchhike around and sleep in cheap roadside tourist cabins, content to wear the same clothes everyday as long as they can enjoy each other's company. Many people in positions of power, however, believed that since underconsumption was to blame for the sick economy, the solution was to stimulate desire. Manufacturers cut back on national advertising but didn't eliminate it, thinking seductive imagery might coax Americans back into being loyal customers. For his part, President Herbert Hoover advised Americans to help jumpstart the economy by spending rather than saving. Economists like Simon N. Patten and

Edwin R. A. Seligman concurred, and encouraged consumers to use credit. Walter Pitkin's 1932 best-selling self-help book, *Life Begins at Forty*, urged people to live for the moment, spending their money to buy happiness.

Purchasing Power and the New Deal

The concept of "purchasing power," which had evolved from standard-of-living debates, captured wider attention beginning in 1933 with the New Deal, President Franklin Delano Roosevelt's initiative to get the economy back on track and restore prosperity. Many Americans in the 1930s, from reformers and policymakers to ordinary folks, not only believed that consumption was the "new necessity," but they also began to see "the consumer" as an interest group equal to labor and business. Roosevelt summarized this perspective in a 1932 campaign speech: "I believe we are at the threshold of a fundamental change in our popular economic thought, [and] that in the future we are going to think less about the producer and more about the consumer."

As president, Roosevelt gave substance to his prediction in two important ways. First, he involved consumers in New Deal programs and agencies. During the early 1930s, the federal budget was small, leading the president to organize the First [phase of the] New Deal around the private-public partnership endorsed by his predecessor, Herbert Hoover. This guided the National Industrial Recovery Act (NIRA), the keystone of Roosevelt's early economic recovery program. Through the National Recovery Administration (NRA), volunteer roundtables of management, labor, and government representatives set production codes, wage rates, and price controls for various industries. The aim was to set standard practices that boosted wages, limited production, and stabilized prices, so as to increase consumer spending and revive business. The NRA's Consumer Advisory Board tried to mobilize ordinary citizens into grassroots councils, which were to serve as community watchdogs that conveyed the concerns of real people to Washington policymakers. Although these councils proved ineffective, they legitimated consumer activism and raised consumers' consciousness. Robert Lynd credited the New Deal for introducing the "word 'consumer'. . . into popular language." Once the NIRA was declared unconstitutional in 1935, other New Deal bureaucracies, such as the Rural Electrification Administration and the Federal Housing Administration, sought consumer support and feedback in one way or another.

Second, the Roosevelt administration made purchasing power—the question of what consumers could afford—a central concern of the federal government, particularly when a brief recession in 1937–38 adversely affected morale and business confidence. From 1933 to 1940, prices rose steadily, as did the gross domestic product (GDP). But the problem of adequate wages—how much people earned affected what and how much they could buy—remained a concern. It was the driving force behind one of the most important pieces of New Deal legislation, the National Labor Relations Act of 1935. This law permitted labor unions to organize and engage in collective bargaining without the fear of retaliation by employers, effectively giving blue-collar workers a voice in determining the size of their paychecks. The later phases of the New Deal also created laws that mandated quality standards for some consumer products, regulated prices in chain stores, broke up monopolies that kept prices high, created the eight-hour day, and established the minimum wage.

These public policies had important cultural ramifications. The triumph of purchasing power at the federal level helped to overturn lingering Victorian conventions. From the Civil War through the 1920s, producers had been revered as the architects of economic growth. Now, leading economists, backed by the authority of Washington, said that this responsibility belonged to consumers. In a 1939 government report, *The Structure of the American Economy,* Gardiner Means summed it up: "American consumers, if they had sufficient money income, would constitute a market sufficient to absorb all the production which American industry has the resources to turn out." New Dealers like Means designed federal policies aimed to increase the Average American's buying power and guarantee the country's prosperity. In doing so, they harnessed the weight of the national government to dethrone thriftiness as a virtue and to legitimate mass consumption as a right and obligation of citizenship.

Patriotic Consumers at War

Like nothing before in the nation's history, the massive economic stimulus created by World War II (1939–45) gave the Modern American the chance to be a patriotic consumer. It offered some people their first real taste of affluence and prosperity, while across the nation, people learned that consumption and community cooperation were good for they, themselves, and the country.

As the Axis war machine tore through Europe, Roosevelt framed the need to rearm and aid brave democracies in the context of consumption and citizenship. In his January 1941 State of the Union Address, famously nicknamed the Four Freedoms, the president described the role of "a strong and healthy democracy." A nation's principal responsibility was to ensure that its people could enjoy "the fruits of scientific progress in a wider and constantly rising standard of living." This was the Victorian technological promise dramatically updated by a progressive thinker for a poignant Modern moment.

War production revitalized the economy and washed out the last taste of depression. The United States was already on its way to creating a war economy before the Japanese attack on Pearl Harbor in December 1941. After Pearl Harbor, full-scale mobilization and military conscription virtually eliminated unemployment. Cities grew as millions of jobseekers flocked to factories retooled to make aircraft, bullets and bombs, and uniforms. As 11 million people, mostly men, joined the armed services, employers tackled the "manpower" shortage by hiring women, teenagers, and the elderly to work in factories, steel mills, and shipyards. For the first time, many African Americans and Mexican Americans secured decent wages in industrial jobs, wages they could only have dreamt of before the war. These people had to eat, buy clothing, and find places to live, creating even more jobs. Between 1940 and 1945, the GDP more than doubled, from $100 to $212 billion.

The U.S. government spent $321 billion on the war, financed by heavy borrowing and taxation. Patriotic home-front consumers paid for 60 percent of these costs by purchasing U.S. savings bonds through payroll deduction plans and bond drives. Taxes paid for the remaining 40 percent of the war's costs. In 1943, the U.S. Treasury

Department initiated the practice of withholding income taxes from workers' wages. A revision to the tax code raised the rates for wealthy citizens and corporate profits.

The war reduced the gap between rich and poor and enlarged the middle class. With steady wages, bank accounts, and war bonds, the average American had more money than he or she had before the Stock Market Crash. In the workplace, tensions arose as blacks and whites vied for jobs, and newly organized labor began to demand better wages and working conditions, threatening wildcat strikes if denied. Most Americans, however, greatly appreciated their wartime paychecks. One Kentucky woman who worked in a war plant with her mother and sister remembered, "We made the fabulous sum of $32 a week. To us it was just an absolute miracle. Before that, we made nothing."

As the economy boomed, the government faced a distinctively new problem: demand now outstripped supply. The war economy was a hungry giant gobbling up enormous resources. Its appetite for certain raw materials seemed insatiable. But after years of hardship, the consumer impulse was alive and well, and people were ready to spend, spend, spend.

To prevent runaway inflation and the hoarding of food and other necessities, the federal government enlisted consumers in a patriotic home-front campaign for victory. For the public, rationing, short-ages, and price controls became facts of life. Government propaganda, designed by advertising experts for various war agencies, bombarded consumers with messages on how they could "fight for freedom" at home. Eye-catching graphics and snappy slogans such as "Save Your Cans" and "Use It Up—Wear It Out—Make Do!" appeared in newspapers, in magazines, and on posters. The government sponsored recycling drives to save paper and cardboard. It urged consumers to plant Victory Gardens to raise and then can their own vegetables. In 1944, 44 percent of the country's fresh vegetables were grown by ordinary people in 20 million Victory Gardens. These efforts conserved the commerically grown food required to feed the troops and packaging materials, like steel, needed to make bombers, tanks, and shells.

Consumers came to appreciate rationing, which prevented greedy or wealthy people from hoarding. At first, rationing was limited to tires, automobiles, and sugar. Gradually, the list of rationed commodities expanded to include coffee, gasoline, and milk. Some manufactured goods like washing machines, automobiles, and nylon stockings, became virtually impossible to buy. Consumers even learned to live without chocolate bars, sacrificing them for the boys on the front.

The war gave American corporations the chance to show how mass-production know-how might serve as a springboard to prosperity. Corporate leaders went to Washington to apply their managerial skills as "dollar a year men." William Knudsen from General Motors Corporation and Donald M. Nelson from Sears, Roebuck and Company headed government agencies. As chief of the War Production Board (WPB), Nelson helped big businesses in major industries, including steel, rubber, automobiles, glass, textiles, pharmaceuticals, and so forth, convert to military production. After the long depression, some industries hesitated to tool up for war, relishing the profits they were making in the civilian market. It took a combination of federal authority and executive decisiveness to turn things around. In January 1942, Nelson clenched his fist, shutting down the civilian automobile industry and ordering Detroit to start making military trucks, tanks, and aircraft.

The government realized that consumption was good for morale, and it permitted certain products and services to flow into the civilian economy. Apparel wasn't subject to rationing, but new styles were patriotically designed to save fabric, leather, metal, and plastic. Skirts got shorter and narrower, wooden buttons replaced zippers, and shoulder pads were eliminated. The output of clothing, textiles, processed foods, and alcoholic beverages expanded. Juke boxes, crooners like Frank Sinatra, and big bands grew in popularity, as the music industry, with so many young men abroad, catered to young working women. Department stores profited, as did Hollywood. As wages soared, thousands of Rosie the Riveters splurged on Saturday matinees, lipstick, and rhinestone pins, or saved up for stylish fur coats. Luxuries, large and small, rewarded Americans for their sacrifices, satisfied their yearnings to consume, and prepared them for a peacetime burst of mass consumption.

•••

Modern times were hard, with the Panic of 1907, World War I, the recession of 1920–21, the Great Depression, and World War II taking the economy on a wild roller coaster ride. Despite these disruptions, the consumer society continued to gain momentum. In a period of global turmoil, geographic isolation protected the mainland United States from enemy attack. As Europeans fought bloody battles on their native soil, Americans built farms and factories, ships and automobiles, armaments and artillery. They also cultivated an enlarged vision of consumer society. The progressive dream of the redistribution of wealth morphed into the drive for American standards and eventually turned "purchasing power" into a national mantra.

In the process, a power struggle arose between two major players: the federal government and private enterprise. The government became a mediator between producers and consumers, ultimately putting spending power at the center of national economic policy. Big business used the Great Depression and World War II as a platform for selling its version of consumerism, as Chapter Four shows, using iconic advertising imagery and forceful public-relations campaigns.

Historian Marina Moskowitz, author of *Standard of Living*, reminds us that the Modern consumer culture was forged at the consumption junction, from the give-and-take among multiple actors. "Neither producers nor consumers alone could create the standard of living," she writes. "It was a by-product of the marketplace itself." Mass producers had the capacity, while advertising, marketing, and popular entertainment stimulated desire. Government stepped in as the umpire. In the next three chapters, we will examine New York advertising agencies, global record companies, and Detroit automobile factories to see how these imperatives and interventions dovetailed with the changing values and tastes of consumers.

CHAPTER FOUR

Mr. Advertiser Meets Mrs. Consumer

In the Victorian period, American manufacturers and retailers had just begun to imagine their primary consumers. Intuitively, they understood that the principal purchaser of household goods was a woman. This visceral feeling, based on decades of observation and guesswork, would be verified, measured, and codified in the Modern era. Pioneer marketer Paul T. Cherington, research director for America's largest advertising agency, was instrumental in this process. His 1913 book, *Advertising as a Business Force*, popularized "Mr. Advertiser" and "Mrs. Consumer" as commercial parlance. These gendered categories, based on Victorian conventions about men as breadwinners and women as homemakers, dominated marketing for decades. In 1929, the trade journal *Printers' Ink* summed it up: "The proper study of mankind is *man*, but the proper study of markets is *woman*."

National Magazines, National Brands

Between the 1890s and 1930s, magazines became one of the institutional pillars of consumer society. In 1900, more than 90 percent of the 76 million people in the United States were literate, and some 3,500 magazines catered to their voracious appetite as readers. Folks spent their evenings reading, and magazines offered something for nearly every taste and pocketbook. The most popular magazines—*Century, Collier's, Cosmopolitan, Delineator, Harper's, Ladies' Home Journal, McCall's, McClure's, Munsey's, Saturday Evening Post, Scribner's,* and *Woman's Home Companion*—published fiction, biography, and editorials, along with tips on fashion, cooking, and child care. Others catered to special interests: *Atlantic Monthly* to college graduates; *Vogue* to socialites; *Farmer's Wife* to rural women, and so forth.

National magazines became *the* hot new advertising medium for brands like Maxwell House Coffee, Coca-Cola, Sherwin Williams paints, and Johnson & Johnson health care products. Today, consumers take national brands in stride, and corporate branding seems "natural." If Tide and Wisk didn't have different names and packages, how else would shoppers tell them apart as they rushed through the laundry aisle at the supermarket? Few consumers stop and think about the origins of brands, which emerged in the trial-and-error quest for national markets during the late 1800s. When packaged soap, bottled ketchup, and personal cameras were new, manufacturers like Procter & Gamble, Heinz, and Eastman Kodak needed ways to build trust in their names among consumers. They introduced corporate logos, eye-catching packages, and memorable slogans like "When it rains, it pours" and "You know Uneeda biscuit?" Advertising "characters" like the friendly Quaker Oats Man, Aunt Jemima, and the little Morton Salt Girl gave a human face to the brand as they replaced the shopkeeper as an intermediary between the producer and the consumer.

Once brands were established, national magazines provided a venue for advertising them to consumers. National magazines needed national brands and vice versa. Whereas Victorian magazines had relied on subscription revenues, Modern publishers developed a new business model based on advertising income. They substantially increased their circulations by reducing the subscription price and redesigning their content around middle-class aspirations. In turn, they expanded their advertising space—from small ads in the back to full-page ads in the front—and sold brand manufacturers on the new format. With the help of advertising agencies and professional illustrators, brand manufacturers filled these pages with stunning, full-color ads showing how Jell-O gelatin and Kodak cameras improved daily life. By 1918, national magazines generated $58 million, or two-thirds of their revenue, from advertising. By 1920, these earnings had more than doubled, to $129 million; by 1929, to $200 million.

National magazines co-existed with hundreds of local newspapers that flourished in cities and towns across the land. The 2,000 daily and

13,000 weekly newspapers were the favorite advertising medium for local retailers, who used them to publicize new merchandise they'd selected for the customers, relying heavily on text to describe their bargains and new products, styles, and prices.

Ladies' Home Journal, the Bible of the American Home

Women's magazines had special appeal to brand advertisers because they reached the majority of middle-class shoppers, an infinite number of Mrs. Consumers across the nation. By 1900, six major titles were advertisers' favorites: *Ladies' Home Journal, Woman's Home Companion, Good Housekeeping, Delineator, McCall's,* and *Pictorial Review.* These Big Six, which coexisted with countless small magazines geared to regional tastes, grew in tandem with national advertising.

Demographics help explain the enormous success of women's magazines. Between 1890 and 1920, the U.S. population jumped from 63 to 105.7 million, and the female population increased by two-thirds, from 30.7 to 51.8 million. These women read more magazines, and they liked the romantic fiction, decorating tips, recipes, needlework patterns, and fashion news offered them. As women flipped through magazines in their kitchens, advertisers gained an entrée into consumers' private worlds, and by 1897, women's magazines had already become, in the words of one adman, "Gateways to the Home Circle."

They also advanced the creation of Mrs. Consumer, a process begun when Victorian advice books pried open the front door of the cozy cottage. Women's magazines were bolder, stepping into the Modern living room and plopping down in a comfortable chair, much like Martha Stewart does today. By 1900, women relied on magazines for expert guidance on cooking, child rearing, clothing, interior decoration, and shopping, while advertisements told readers about the value of national brands. Women took this advice and weighed it against personal experience to decide whether or not to purchase these brands and which ones to get.

America's largest women's magazine, the *Ladies' Home Journal,* set high standards for content, advertising, and marketing. The "Bible of the American home," the *Journal* was owned by the Philadelphia-based Curtis Publishing Company, whose weekly the *Saturday Evening Post* was the leading family magazine. Curtis made the *Journal* into the first American magazine to reach a circulation of 1 million by offering the right mix of feminine content, high-grade advertising, and a new cover illustration every month. At 25¢ per issue, the *Journal* greatly undersold other fashion magazines that cost $2 or more. Anxious to know more about Mrs. Consumer, the *Journal's* editor Edward Bok developed a market-research project that employed knocking on readers' doors and a correspondence department that analyzed their letters. This led to the 1911 creation of Curtis's Commercial Research Division, which compiled economic and demographic data on subscribers. The pioneering Curtis model was soon emulated by other American publishers.

Market research served the *Ladies' Home Journal* well. By 1915, the *Journal* had a clearer picture of its audience, which Bok shared with corporate advertisers. The *Journal's* principal readers were middle-class women in households with an annual income of $1,200 to $2,500; wealthier families making $3,000 to $5,000 comprised an important supplemental audience. Mrs. Consumer was coming into focus.

In 1912, Bok hired Christine Frederick to tickle Mrs. Consumer's fancies. In 1929, Frederick would publish *Selling Mrs. Consumer*, a business best seller that advised manufacturers on how to get in touch with shoppers. On her book tour, Frederick identified herself as the archetype, as the consumer surrogate. "I am the most important woman in your lives," she told audiences. "I am Mrs. Consumer." If Beecher was the nineteenth-century Martha Stewart, Frederick was her early-twentieth-century counterpart.

At the moment when more women entered the workplace and suffragists battled for voting rights, the ultraconservative *Journal* believed that women should eschew the public realm to pursue the "simple life" of homemakers. Frederick's ideas about housework, which drew on the principles of scientific management, made her the ideal consumption coach. Her articles explained how new electrical appliances like the vacuum cleaner would make dusting, sweeping, and other chores less onerous, leaving more time for mothering and shopping. Frederick's efficiency program resonated among Bok's readers, raising the circulation figures and attracting even more advertising revenue. By 1917, Curtis's magazines took in more than half of the advertising dollars spent in the United States. The next year, the *Ladies' Home Journal* reaped 37 percent of the total revenues earned by all women's magazines.

When Bok retired in 1919, he left the *Ladies' Home Journal* on solid financial footing. Under his leadership, the *Journal* helped to legitimate consumption as an extension of women's "traditional" responsibilities. Bok associated frivolous consumption with moral corruption and tried to elevate getting and spending to a higher plane. The lasting influence of his approach, which established national brands as corollaries to simple living, is seen in contemporary figures such as Oprah Winfrey, *Real Simple* magazine, and House and Garden TV.

Selling Soap, or Selling Sex?

National magazines, brands, and advertising agencies expanded together. In the Victorian era, advertising agencies had been space buyers, but with the rise of mass-circulation magazines, they displaced printers as the primary creators of copy, layout, and illustrations. Although very few professional ad agencies existed in the 1880s, they handled 95 percent of national advertising by 1917.

Advertising agencies like J. Walter Thompson became the principal mediators between manufacturers and publishers and between advertisers and consumers. In the 1910s, Thompson grew into one of the first "full-service agencies," helping clients with copywriting, illustration, photography, layout, and market research. In 1916, Stanley Resor bought the Cincinnati-based agency from its aging founder and ran it with his wife Helen, a talented copywriter. The couple transformed it into the nation's leading agency by focusing on Mrs. Consumer. In 1924, Helen Resor explained: "The success of the J. Walter Thompson Company has been in large measure due to the fact that we have concentrated and specialized upon products sold to women."

Like Christine Frederick, Helen Resor built her career as an expert on the "woman's viewpoint." She created the Women's Editorial Department at Thompson's New York office, where an all-female staff collected information about shoppers' preferences and used it to produce copy with girl appeal and garner more than 50 percent of the agency's billings.

Helen Resor cut her teeth on the Woodbury's Facial Soap advertising and the memorable tag line, "A Skin You Love to Touch." The Woodbury campaign was the first "sex appeal" series in American advertising, the basis for today's television ads for L'Oreal and other beauty products. Earlier advertisers had featured pretty Gibson Girls, but Woodbury was the first to show a man and a woman in a romantic embrace. The artist's rendition of a courting couple looks restrained to twenty-first-century eyes, but it was sensuous, alluring, and more than slightly shocking in 1911. Rather than promoting soap, "A Skin You Love to Touch" sold, in the agency's words, "masculine admiration and feminine envy."

The Woodbury campaign shows how the "look" and "feel" of national advertising changed between 1900 and 1920. In 1911, Thompson secured the Woodbury account from the Andrew Jergens Company, the world's largest manufacturer of toilet soaps. Between 1901 and 1910, this Cincinnati soapmaker had tried unsuccessfully to invigorate the foundering Woodbury brand with ads touting its medicinal benefits. In 1910, the soapmaker had spent $44,000 on Woodbury ads, reaping a mere $108,000 in sales! Bars of this soap languished on drugstore shelves, with one competitor outselling the brand by twenty to one. "Woodbury's became known to the trade as dead," recalled a 1926 Thompson précis of the account, "and its manufacturers admitted that it was almost hopeless."

Jergens engaged Thompson as a last-ditch effort to reinvigorate the soap, giving the agency a modest $25,000 for the first year. Under Helen Resor's direction, the Women's Editorial Department compiled data from door-to-door interviews, watched shoppers in stores, researched the medical journals, did a laboratory analysis of the soap, and consulted with dermatologists. Between 1911 and 1922, Thompson used this research to revamp the brand's image with remarkable results. Woodbury sales grew from $122,000 in 1911 to a peak of more than $2 million in 1922. Thompson documented total market penetration by 1926, when 50,000 drug stores nationwide carried the brand.

Artwork for the Woodbury campaign shows the transition from "reason-why" advertising, popular before World War I, to a newer "atmospheric" mode that stirred the emotions. Original Woodbury ads described the medicinal benefits of the Woodbury Treatment, a method of scrubbing the face in soap, hot water, and ice to get rid of conspicuous pores. In the mid-teens, Thompson introduced emotional appeals, addressing women as sensual creatures yearning for romance and glamour. The memorable phrase, "A Skin You Love to Touch," written by Helen Resor for retail window displays, became the backbone of the new campaign. Thompson's artists paired this tag line with colorful illustrations of a handsome couple, sometimes dressed in evening attire, sometimes in sportswear, always touching, always caressing. Over the years, the Woodbury couple came to signify the allure of modern romance.

"A Skin You Love to Touch" touched nearly every American. "The phrase sings itself into your memory," reported the *Atlantic Monthly* in 1919. "The pictures of this famous series have probably been seen by more people at one time than any other ever painted." Each month, magazines like the *Ladies' Home Journal* published a new Woodbury ad illustrated by a famous artist. Coupon clippers could send in for a soap sample and a collectible print of the Woodbury couple. Newspaper coverage complemented the national campaign. In 1912, Thompson placed Woodbury ads in 23 national magazines and 12 local newspapers; by 1920, 18 magazines and 382 newspapers.

By introducing romantic love and sex appeal into soap buying, the Woodbury campaign broke away from Victorian propriety, and it established J. Walter Thompson as an agency attuned to the beat of the twentieth century. Helen Resor had set out to find a theme that would resonate with women and ended up using a psychological approach. By the 1900s, the Victorian tradition of arranged marriages started to dissolve in favor of romantic love. The prospects for a love match transformed the outlook of young middle-class men and women searching for a mate. New social pastimes, such as ballroom dancing, gave courting couples an appropriate public venue; as mentioned, the showcase dancers Vernon and Irene Castle, genteel models for Modern romance. In the competition for suitors, feminine good looks became a cultural fetish, and the cosmetics, personal-care, and ready-to-wear industries enjoyed a boom.

Thompson's ads for Odorono deodorant, Pond's cold cream, and Jergens hand lotion also incorporated the themes of fear, sex, and social emulation. The Woodbury's campaign had tapped into women's fears of not having the beautiful complexion that would attract a mate. Pond's and Jergens also capitalized on these fears, while Odorono added perspiration to the equation, turning "body odor" into a liability that could be overcome by using the right deodorant. This process kept repeating itself, as Thompson and other agencies fed on women's unspoken longings, converting mundane convenience products like soap, hand lotion, and perfume into tools for self-transformation.

The Colonel's Lady and Judy O'Grady

During the twenties, the advertising trade consolidated in New York, with major offices on Park, Lexington, and Madison Avenues. By 1923, the term *Madison Avenue* was shorthand for the advertising industry, reflecting the concentrated expertise in midtown Manhattan. Firms like N. W. Ayer & Son; Batten, Barton, Durstine & Osborn (BBDO); and J. Walter Thompson established national reputations.

The vision of Mrs. Consumer crafted by the *Ladies' Home Journal* permeated print culture. In some respects, retailers, publishers, and advertisers, working in a rarefied white-collar world, had imagined Mrs. Consumer in their own image. She lived in the city or suburbs, came from Protestant stock, and had a husband with a professional job. Her family was prosperous but not wealthy or elite. They owned a single-family home, perhaps a staid Victorian cottage, a colonial-style house, or a spiffy new bungalow. The woman of the house had a high-school degree, subscribed to the *Ladies' Home Journal* and the *Saturday Evening Post* and dreamed about Paris fashion. In other words, this white, Anglo Saxon Protestant was a member of the solid middle class.

In reality, this picture of Mrs. Consumer described but a small portion of the vast American market, which was divided into many segments. By the 1920s, big businesses like General Motors and Procter & Gamble had started to assemble more specific demographic data about their customers. J. Walter Thompson was one of the first agencies to analyze the class structure of the buying public. That firm's staff now included superstars like Paul T. Cherington, the father of market research, and John B. Watson, a pioneer behavioral psychologist. Edward Steichen, a photographer famous for his Tonalist pictures of New York's Flat Iron Building, presided over the art department. Thompson was well positioned to research the American audience and design advertising campaigns in virtually any mood or style, depending on what the client, the product, and the budget needed.

Thompson's research department, directed by Cherington, developed a system for analyzing Mrs. Consumers across the social spectrum. With a specific client or product in mind, surveyors went door-to-door and questioned women about their preferences in brands, designs, and prices. Cherington created an ABCD typology that divided households by income, occupation, and education. Class A referred to elite homes with live-in servants and $10,000-plus incomes; Class B, middle-class families "personally directed by intelligent women"; Class C, the "industrial classes," including mechanics, mill operators, and tradesmen; and Class D, unskilled laborers, immigrants, and blacks earning less than $2,000 a year. Cherington called A the "class" market, the wealthy segment that could afford luxury goods. He combined B and C into the "mass" market, the majority audience for most national brands.

Watson pioneered new methods for psychological advertising. Based on studies of rats, he theorized that the social environment, rather than genes or heredity, conditioned animals to make choices. His theories had startling implications. The agency that understood human psychology could manipulate the innate emotions—fear, hate, love—that motivated consumers to buy. Thompson had dabbled in amateur psychology with Woodbury's, but Watson, the professional behaviorist, helped the Resors understand *why* sex sold soap.

Market research and behavioral psychology became the bedrock of Modern ad agency practice. Hard data on "class" and "mass" markets gave substance to the industry's favorite Rudyard Kipling phrase, "the Colonel's Lady and Judy O'Grady," shorthand for the refined socialite and her Irish maid. Initially, advertising agencies tried to understand both classes of consumers, but by the late 1920s and 1930s, some looked down their noses at the "masses." Behavioral research, buttressed by gender stereotypes, fostered the belief that Judy O'Grady read pulp magazines like *True Story* and tabloids like the *Daily News*, had the intelligence of a twelve-year-old, and was capricious, irrational, passive, and conformist. Gender stereotypes extended to the Colonel's Lady, who although better educated, was seen as just as susceptible to feminine irrationality. The presence of Helen Resor did much to overcome these prejudices at Thompson, but major industry publications perpetuated them.

As researchers extrapolated meaningful patterns about the "class" and "mass" markets, account executives figured out how to apply their findings to advertising problems. Door-to-door research helped the agencies understand women's preferences for durable goods like Simmons mattresses and Pyrex Ovenware. After years of national advertising and flagging sales, Thompson advised the manufacturer of Pyrex that glass baking ware would never reach the "masses" until its price got lower. Watson's psychological theories applied to convenience goods like Jergens hand lotion and Pond's face cream. Campaigns for these products targeted the feminine fear of social inadequacy and promised to make women beautiful. Durable goods like Pyrex glassware and disposable goods like Woodbury's soap were seen as flip sides of a coin. The Colonel's Lady *invested* in Simmons mattresses and Pyrex Ovenware, but she and Judy O'Grady *splurged* on Woodbury's Facial Soap, Cutex nail polish, and Pond's face cream.

Thompson's skill in codifying those differences validated the function of Mr. Advertiser as a mediator to Mrs. Consumer. This approach did well for Thompson in the Great Depression, when the firm passed longtime competitors Lord & Thomas and N. W. Ayer & Son to become the industry leader, enjoying global dominance until the 1970s.

Images of the Good Life

As they perfected the format for magazine advertising, agencies experimented with graphic design, borrowing from theatrical posters and wartime propaganda, the Art Nouveau and Art Deco movements, Pictorial and Realist photography, and even comic books. Before big-format magazines like the *Saturday Evening Post* and the *Ladies' Home Journal*, no one had ever produced large full-page ads with illustrations. Agencies had to figure out how to create them, what they should say, and how they should look. They hired professional graphic artists and photographers, whose work demonstrated that the "look" of an ad was just as important as the copy.

In the teens, the Chicago agency Calkins & Holden had given advertising graphics a Modern facelift, introducing eye-catching ads that caught the reader's attention and temporarily stopped him (or her) from turning the page. Ernest Elmo Calkins hired illustrator Joseph Christian Leyendecker, a cover artist for the *Saturday Evening Post*, to create a menswear icon for Cluett, Peabody & Company. Leyendecker's famous Arrow Man, always elegantly attired beyond his means, became a model for college men; they too could "dress the part." The Arrow campaign was an example of "soft-sell," relying on an artistically rendered "atmosphere" to stimulate desire for the product. Other agencies followed Calkins's example by hiring famous illustrators: N. C. Wyatt painted ads for Cream of Wheat; Maxfield Parrish for Community Silverplate; Normal Rockwell for Grape Nuts; and Rosie O'Neill for Jell-O.

During World War I, illustrators had demonstrated that graphic design could be an effective sales tool. Countless artists rallied to the clarion call of Gibson Girl creator Charles Dana Gibson, who spearheaded an illustrators' initiative at a federal propaganda agency. Hundreds of professional artists went to Washington, creating posters that recruited soldiers, sold war bonds, and promoted civic duty, including Wheatless Wednesdays and Porkless Saturdays. Most famously, James Montgomery Flagg's Uncle Sam poster pointed at the viewer: "I Want YOU for the U.S. Army." Wartime propaganda accustomed people to seeing high-quality imagery almost everywhere.

Advertising in the 1920s focused on lifestyle choices, urging consumers to buy the "right" bread or car. As discussed, many businesses had the capacity to produce more than the market could absorb, and advertising was seen as a means for stimulating sales. Graphic designers portrayed an idyllic dream world, full of handsome men and slim women who used and relied on glamourous products. The "right" products had the power to transport Mrs. Consumer beyond her humdrum worries like preparing grocery lists and cleaning the kitchen floor. Ads suggested that Mrs. Consumer should look and smell a certain way, scrub her pots and pans with Bon Ami, and "Reach for a Lucky [cigarette] instead of a sweet" in order to keep her svelte flapper figure.

Graphic designers targeting the Colonel's Lady, the "class" market, sometimes used Art Deco motifs to convey an upscale ambiance of stylish Modernity. After the 1925 world's fair, the Exposition Internationale des Arts Décoratifs et Industriels Modernes in Paris, some manufacturers and retailers adopted Art Deco as their signature style. Luxury goods like Atwater-Kent radio consoles, Standard bathroom fixtures, and Victrola phonographs were redesigned or repackaged in Art Deco designs. Graphic artists used the iconography of upper-class life to flatter prospective purchasers, situating smart-looking console radios in lavish penthouse apartments to convey a sense of impeccable taste and craftsmanship. Few people lived in such luxury.

Advertisements geared toward Judy O'Grady, the "mass" market, borrowed dramatic realism from the tabloids, confessional magazines, and radio soap operas. Tabloids titillated readers with exposés on gruesome murders and sex scandals, while confessional magazines like *True Story* published fiction on love triangles and broken hearts. Agencies captured this sensationalism in ads for personal-care products. The Chicago agency Williams & Cunnyngham invented "halitosis" and wrote a fear-ridden tagline—"Often a bridesmaid but never a bride"—to sell Listerine as a "breath deodorant." Tabloid-style imagery often used black-and-white photographs and extra-large headlines to capture the attention of the *True Story* reader.

The Great Depression put pressure on the advertising industry and eventually affected the look of the ads. Costly color artwork, which appeared in the *Post* and the *Journal* in the twenties, didn't disappear but was used sparingly. The tabloid-style ads dominated, as agencies focused on the economic plight of consumers. Emotional appeals, louder headlines, hard-sell copy, and coupon-clipping gave some ads a bargain-basement look. Advertisements for Lifebuoy and Rinso soaps created mini-dramas on the page, using comic-book techniques like cartoon panels and speech balloons. In comparison with their Jazz Age counterparts, ads from the Great Depression definitely looked down-and-out.

Discovering Boys and Girls

Farsighted marketers began to see Mrs. Consumer as an analytical concept that didn't reflect demographic reality. It would be some time before the mainstream fully acknowledged American diversity, but some eyes began to open as early as the 1920s.

Immigrants and blacks, who skirted the edges of consumer society, fascinated a handful of prescient marketers. In 1924, Cherington put the "American market under the microscope," pointing to the diverse tastes of the nation's many ethnic groups. New York City alone, he told the trade journal *Advertising and Selling*, had "more Irish people than in Dublin, more Jews than in Jerusalem, and more Italians than in Rome." While Cherington pondered the pocketbooks of Italian Americans, others pointed to the promising "Negro market." In 1928, *Forbes* reported that chain stores were assembling data on the "living and buying habits of Negroes," and two years later, *Advertising and Selling* identified urban blacks, who had migrated to northern and western cities, as potential customers for phonograph records, radio sets, and musical instruments. In reality, the majority of African Americans, constrained by racial prejudice, were at the bottom of the wage hierarchy. Nonetheless, advertisers' widening perspectives broke with convention, paving the way for a deeper understanding of the multicultural market.

One new market segment, the child consumer, garnered substantial attention from some national advertisers. The Victorians had considered childhood as a sheltered moment in the life cycle, and the Moderns endowed kids with a sense of entitlement. As the middle-class household became smaller, the hierarchy of the large Victorian family was replaced by Modern democratic relationships and a new child-centeredness. Men were encouraged to be playmates to their children, rather than aloof grownups. In the 1920s and 1930s, way before Benjamin Spock suggested that parenting could be fun, permissive child rearing gained a foothold. Children were given allowances, greater freedom from adult supervision, and a voice in some family purchases. This development proved to be a commercial goldmine.

Victorian advertisers had already conceived of children as consumers-in-training, the buyers of tomorrow. The use of trade cards built customer loyalty, creating in children a lasting impression of brands in the hope of future sales. If a boy collected trade cards from Arbuckle Coffee, he might drink this brand when he grew up. If a girl cut up A&P cards and pasted the bits in her scrapbook, she might shop at this grocery chain when the time came to buy food for her own family.

By the early 1900s, advertisers began to imagine the child as a consumer with more *immediate* desires, as a customer in the short term. They saw children as critical allies who could badger their parents, loosen adult purse strings, and stimulate sales of national brands. Modern ads taught children to recognize brand names and distrust those products not found in the magazines. Advertisements for Shredded Wheat and Cream of Wheat showed boys and girls spelling out the name of their favorite cereal on the blackboard. Jell-O ads pictured kids running errands for their mothers, asking the grocer for this national brand. These wholesome images encouraged children to identify with the kids in the picture and to believe that the right cereal would make them picture perfect, too. To parents, images of innocence suggested that brands were free from worldly corruption and, as such, appropriate additions to the wholesome middle-class pantry.

In the 1920s, childcentric advertising changed in scope and tone, targeting kids as consumers in their own right. Popular periodicals such as *American Boy, American Girl, Boy's Life, St. Nicholas,* and *Youth's Companion* catered to juvenile readers from both "class" and "mass" households. In 1928, J. Walter Thompson told its clients that magazine advertising reached 2 million kids, from ages ten to twenty, each year.

The precocious young boy, an avid consumer with a bit of spending money of his own, stood at the center of a big juvenile advertising push. As portrayed by advertisers, the boy consumer bridged the Victorian and Modern worlds, displaying the older virtues of industriousness and entrepreneurship alongside the newer traits of middle-class manhood: adaptability, enthusiasm, loyalty, and salesmanship. *American Boy,* the favorite magazine for middle-class boys, portrayed this consumer as an authority figure, due to his mechanical flair and mastery of technical change. Further, the objects of his desire—automobiles, radios, record players, and other mechanical devices—were symbols of progress. Fathers were shown consulting their sons about technological purchases, helping them with masculine hobbies, and yielding to their recommendations on batteries, cameras, cars, and radios. A love of technological innovation separated the boy consumer from the feminine longings of girls and women. The items in his consumer identity kit testified to masculine vitality.

Many historians have identified the Boomer era as the pivotal moment in the emergence of the child consumer, given the influence of Dr. Spock's wildly successful 1946 book, *Baby and Child Care*. But, market segmentation by age was well underway in Modern era. It was already part of advertisers' efforts to imagine the consumer and inculcate Americans with a wider brand consciousness.

The Power of Marketing

The J. Walter Thompson Company set the standard for other advertising agencies to become "full-service" providers during the 1930s. The depression encouraged agencies like McCann-Erikson, Mac Martin, Federal Advertising, and McManus to offer marketing services.

In 1931, adman Kenneth Groesbeck, writing in *Printers' Ink Monthly*, told Madison Avenue why his firm, McCann-Erikson, had adopted Thompson's techniques. While scads of observers blamed poor sales on the hard times, Groesbeck looked at producers, exhorting them to make informed decisions. Did their product meet consumer needs? How well did it work? How did consumers use it? Producers had to consider "the product itself . . . in relation to competing products" and analyze the price, packaging, size, color, smell, and ease of use. A manufacturer had to know the product's "consumer appeal, and whether the consumer [was] a mother of a family or a foreman of a foundry." The best way to get this information was to put on the shoes of the man on the street, "listening to the product's public through trade ears and by direct contact."

Another marketing-oriented agency was Benton & Bowles, founded in 1929 by Yale college buddies Bill Benton and Chester Bowles. The partners cut their teeth doing market research for General Foods, which struggled with flagging sales of Hellmann's mayonnaise. Playing the man on the street, Benton followed Hellmann's delivery trucks around Brooklyn, studied how delivery drivers interacted with retailers, and recommended a new approach to distribution. Benton & Bowles thus supplied General Foods with traditional advertising services — artwork, copywriting, and buying space in newspapers and magazines — and new marketing services: business advice on getting the goods to stores and shoppers.

The emphasis on marketing helped Benton & Bowles prosper during the 1930s. Within a few years, General Foods asked the agency for marketing studies on brands such as Baker's Chocolate, Post Toasties, Jell-O, and Maxwell House Coffee. In 1932–33, General Foods adopted a Benton & Bowles marketing plan for Maxwell House Coffee, completely revamping the product's packaging, pricing, and advertising. Previously, Thompson had the account for this prestigious Southern brand, popularized by a Nashville hotel in the 1870s. The Maxwell House Hotel, once a favorite dining spot for presidents Andrew Jackson, Grover Cleveland, and William McKinley, had the patina of the Old South. Another visitor, the young Teddy Roosevelt, had pronounced Maxwell House Coffee "good to the last drop," coining the phrase that provided the basis for later advertising slogans. Benton & Bowles updated the Maxwell House ad campaign with "Showboat," a radio variety show that capitalized on the brand's Southern roots. Produced in New York, "Showboat," which recreated the atmosphere of a real Mississippi River extravaganza, became one of the most popular radio programs of the 1930s. Between 1932 and late 1933, Maxwell House Coffee enjoyed an 81 percent increase in sales. By 1941, it had become America's leading brand of coffee; sales had increased 350 percent since 1932. Similarly, Benton & Bowles helped Colgate-Palmolive-Peet Company rethink its approach to soap. Marketing catapulted Benton & Bowles to success on Madison Avenue. By 1936, the firm had billings of $9.3 million, making it one of America's most prominent advertising agencies.

Trade journals like *Advertising and Selling* and *Printers' Ink* brimmed with articles exhorting manufacturers and agencies to get in touch with the average American. Still, not every agency wanted to go into marketing — or even approved of it. Some well-established firms, including Calkins & Holden, Lord & Thomas (later Foote, Cone & Belding), Young & Rubicam, and N. W. Ayer & Son, didn't immediately add marketing to their roster of client services. Lord & Thomas scoffed at marketing, thinking this function lay outside the proper scope of the advertising profession.

Advertising Overload

By the mid-1920s, a small group of concerned consumers launched a full-scale attack on Modern advertising. Earlier reformers had spearheaded legislation on food safety, demanding "truth in advertising." The new generation of consumer activists lobbied for national laws to regulate "business propaganda" and warned the public about advertisements that preyed on human weaknesses. Madison Avenue was under siege.

Consumer advocates believed that rather than giving purchasers the facts they needed to make informed choices, advertisers manipulated people's fears and insecurities. They criticized market research that probed the customer's mind and advertising images that pandered to personal insecurities and sexual longings. Fraudulent advertisements in the food, drug, and cosmetics industries were of special concern. Economist Stuart Chase's 1925 book, *The Tragedy of Waste*, lashed out against national advertisers and their manipulative tactics. A few years later, Chase teamed up with the engineer Frederick Schlink to co-author *Your Money's Worth,* a Book-of-the-Month Club selection that adjured the federal government to test products on consumers' behalf. Schlink's 1933 follow-up book, *100,000,000 Guinea Pigs*, described "the dangers in everyday foods, drugs, and cosmetics." This was the progressive critique of capitalism, recast for the era of unbridled boom and bust.

The consumer movement gained momentum during the Great Depression, when Chase and Schlink co-founded Consumers' Research, a nonprofit organization that tested products, published a newsletter, and lobbied Congress to regulate advertisers. In 1936, a spin-off group, Consumers Union, introduced the famous magazine, *Consumer Reports*, which offered advice on everything from cereals to cars. When consumer groups brought their concerns to Congress, New Deal legislators responded. In 1933, the National Recovery Administration formed a Consumer Advisory Board, acknowledging consumer interests at the federal level. The next year, Congress expanded the powers of the Food and Drug Administration to adjudicate on advertising matters. In 1938, the Wheeler-Lea Amendment to the Federal Trade Commission Act tightened the label requirements on food, drugs, and cosmetics.

Forging the American Way

Depression-era corporations enlisted national advertising to re-establish public confidence in the business system, creating the "American Way of Life" as a blueprint for economic rejuvenation and growth. This set of ideas, promulgated in print and radio advertising, redefined the American dream around the triad of corporate progress, individual freedom, and mass consumption. It held that Modern materialism—an endless flow of cars and kitchen gadgets, coffee and toothpaste—was the birthright of every American. It was the job of "free enterprise" to facilitate spending, and the responsibility of patriotic Americans to buy things and make the economy run.

The American Way was a concerted business effort to revitalize the economy and combat the criticisms levied by the consumer movement, labor unions, and the New Deal. This set of ideas built on the Victorian notion of technological progress, promoting the concept of Modern business as *the* rightful architect of prosperity. The underlying premise of the American Way had gestated for decades, going back to the time when progressive companies set up model factories, retirement plans, and other welfare benefits. In 1914, automaker Henry Ford had initiated the Five Dollar Day, paying blue-collar workers a high-enough wage to enable them to save up to buy cars, appliances, and houses. The dream that bosses and workers could happily co-exist enjoyed a brief heyday under the Republican administrations of the 1920s. But the New Deal's activist approach to economic recovery outraged some business leaders who believed that private enterprise, not the federal government, should distribute wealth and resources.

In the mid-1930s, some big businesses argued that free enterprise was the only proper solution to the depression, the American Way the only mechanism that could eradicate social inequality. The American Way promised mass consumption for everyone: if managers and workers could put aside their differences, they would be able to maximize national output, creating full employment and abundance for all. Big business, the target of a Congressional review of war profiteering, became a prime mover behind the American Way. Firms like U.S. Steel Corporation and American Telephone & Telegraph asked advertising agencies to refashion their public image, from monopoly power to gentle giants with the nation's best interests at heart. The DuPont

Company, a chemical powerhouse, enlisted adman Bruce Barton to remake its image, from war profiteer into scientific super-marvel committed to "better things for better living."

Some strands of 1930s advertising portrayed producers and consumers in new ways, using nationalist images and historical motifs. These ads personified big business as the friendly neighbor, the concerned guy next door who wanted to help out in a time of need. Increasingly, some national advertisers depicted the consumer as the Average American, a member of the typical American family, a resident of an imaginary version of Middletown, U.S.A. In early 1940, that bastion of middle-class domesticity, the *Ladies' Home Journal*, embarked on a year-long series entitled "How America Lives," accompanied by matching advertisements. The *Journal* focused on real people, "warm and American as pumpkin pie straight out of the oven," who defined themselves by what they ate, drank, wore, and drove, which magazines they read, and radio programs they enjoyed. Laboring under the auspices of the American Way, Mr. Advertiser had abandoned sex appeal and seduction, along with the "classes" and the "masses." Mr. Advertiser had replaced Mrs. Consumer with Mr. and Mrs. Average America.

The American Way moved full steam ahead during World War II, when freedom from fascism was equated with freedom of consumer choice. Advertisers cautioned consumers to be patriotic, squirrel away their earnings, and help win the war by rationing and recycling. Propagandistic films like Frank Capra's *Why We Fight,* a seven-part series (1942–45) portrayed the war as a battle to defend and preserve the American Way, which hinged on everyone's access to a certain level of comfort. In exchange for wartime sacrifices, big business held out the carrot of postwar affluence, meshing the obligations of citizenship with people's expectations for a payoff as consumers. Even war bond advertising implied that helping the government pay for bullets and bayonets now would pave the way for a future of material comfort.

As generals anticipated the war's end, the architects of the American Way geared up for prosperity. In 1944, the National Association of Manufacturers, a conservative business association, published *How America Can Earn More, Buy More, Have More: A Practical Guide to Postwar Prosperity*, a pamphlet about the American Way's "sound program" to increase "opportunities for all to *earn*" and "to *buy*." The Association believed that the principal responsibility of business was to "*put on the market the finest products that can be made at the lowest prices for which they can be sold.*" In exchange for their labor, blue-collar workers would receive record-high wages, allowing them to buy new products and join the middle class.

In depression and war, Madison Avenue used visual culture to depict a blissful future of suburban cottages and streamlined kitchens, a tomorrowland in which everyone would have access to better living. The American Way promised to make the American dream a reality as factories converted World War II facilities into peacetime plants that made newfangled products, benefiting Mr. and Mrs. Average American, the people as consumers.

•••

Victorian producers had inched toward marketing practice, but they didn't see the need to codify patterns of consumption. John Wanamaker knew that shoppers had different tastes, but he never devised a formal method for coordinating what he knew with design, advertising, and sales. Much of what he did was intuitive. Frank Woolworth and Richard Sears learned to compile and analyze enormous quantities of data, but they focused only on the dime-store or mail-order shopper. In contrast, modern marketers like Edward Bok, Paul T. Cherington, and Bruce Barton learned to generalize from one product or account to another, devising a theory of practice. The "simple life," "mass versus class," "better living," and the "American Way" were all about image-making. These concepts wrapped a product in an idea and then marketed the idea.

Advertisers inherited Victorian conventions about men and women that assigned the role of the consumer to the female. Many advertising professionals imagined Mrs. Consumer in their self-image, as a privileged customer with an Ivy League degree, a passion for French fashion, and a discerning eye for things in "good taste." Market research demonstrated the follies of these assumptions, pushing ad men and women to think more expansively. Concepts like "mass versus class," the "Negro market," and "the juvenile market" rattled old marketing tenets. However, the powerful need for national unity during the depression and World War II shut the door, temporarily, on more nuanced discussions of multiculturalism. Mrs. Consumer yielded to the Average American, another monolithic social construct, this one designed to build consensus among men and women during a time of national emergency.

Modern advertising reshaped the visual iconography of American consumer society. Consumers who grew up with trade cards and newspapers marveled at the stunning new magazines and their gorgeous advertisements. Ads altered to deliver a dramatically different message. Brands like Woodbury's Soap and Arrow Collars helped consumers fantasize about who they wished to be, and offered prescriptions for designing a new self. For the first time, consumers identified with national brands rather than styles of furniture or the cut of a suit. And for the first time, those brands promised to uplift a person's circumstances, helping the consumer to fit into the middle class.

CHAPTER FIVE

Sensing a Wider World

Between the 1890s and the 1930s, Americans began their love affair with technologies that altered time, sound, light, and distance. Technology allowed people to join a wider community while simultaneously creating their own personal space. People "connected" to popular national radio shows, songs, and movies; at the same time they had access to locally produced media choices that seemed highly individual. They could tune in to *Amos'n'Andy*, the most successful radio show in broadcasting history, and then listen to their cousin's band play "Who Stole the Kishka?" on their hometown's Polish-language station. Other Americans were doing the same thing, adjusting their radio dials to create their own personal soundscape by meshing national and local broadcasts. Some Modern technologies promised to help people save time while doing household chores; other items, like the Kodak camera, helped consumers preserve their most evanescent experiences. Time no longer just "slipped away"; it became manageable, memorable, and malleable.

Bicycles, Cameras, and the Great Outdoors

The bicycle was one of the first new-tech products marketed to consumers in newspapers and mass-circulation magazines. A precursor to the car, it provided people with cheap private transportation for work and play. In 1887, the Boston entrepreneur Albert A. Pope promoted his bicycle as an appropriate mode of transportation for everyone: girls, boys, men, and women. The cycling fad during the next decade more than doubled bicycle production to 1.1 million in 1899.

Women saw the bicycle as an emancipator, a vehicle that expanded their horizons by carrying them beyond the local neighborhood. Frances E. Willard, a noted temperance advocate and the most famous bicyclist of her time, began cycling at age fifty-three to set an example that might "help women to a wider world." Indeed, for thousands of women, cycling made vigorous outdoor activity acceptable, and it spawned liberating forms of clothing like divided skirts, or culottes.

Men embraced bicycling in the early 1890s, along with other newly popular masculine sports such as golf, baseball, and football. Cycling clubs sponsored races and rides in the countryside. Men's cycling was so widespread that the high-wheeler became a visual motif of the Gay Nineties, a symbol of male athleticism to match the iconic Gibson Girl. The cycling craze fed on the decade's passion for healthy living, as exemplified by Teddy Roosevelt's outdoor exploits and the 1896 revival of the Olympic Games.

Americans' growing fascination with physical fitness and their purchases of sports equipment turned into one of the great marketing sensations of the 1890s. Manufacturers of everything from breakfast cereal to cameras capitalized on the theme of sports and the great outdoors. The Eastman Dry Plate and Film Company, later called the Eastman Kodak Company, was no exception. In 1888, it launched a national advertising campaign for its simple new personal camera, designed to make photography as "convenient as a pencil." Previously, people who wanted photographs of themselves had to hire professional photographers who used clunky box cameras and glass negatives. Subjects had to sit still during the long exposure times, only to be disappointed to see how stiff and unnatural they looked in the prints.

George Eastman changed all of this with the 1888 introduction of the "Kodak," a $25 ($529 in 2005 dollars) portable camera that used film loaded by the factory. This easy-to-use camera fit into a coat pocket and, as it was refined over the years, launched a snapshot revolution. The memorable advertising slogan, "You press the button, we do the rest," stressed the camera's ease of use. With the simple

"Kodak System," consumers became their own photographers. After taking a hundred snapshots, amateur photographers shipped their cameras to the Eastman Kodak facility in Rochester, New York, which processed the film, printed the pictures, and sent everything back. The Kodak System made picture-taking into a fun-filled hobby and altered consumer's notions about convenience, space, time, and memory.

Together, the bicycling craze and the camera fad turned American consumers on to something exciting. Although consumer culture still glorified self-expression in the home and dress, it inched toward a new model. Outdoor hobbies expanded consumers' horizons, allowing men and women to mingle in social situations, just as they did in dance halls. Bicycling, tennis, and lawn croquet fine-tuned the body, just as sketching and photography refined the artistic eye. These pastimes encouraged a new type of Do-It-Yourself culture emphasizing physical improvement, while honing consumers' technological prowess. The bicycle shortened distances, while the camera turned ephemeral experiences into memorabilia. They allowed consumers to feel comfortable with mechanical devices as personal possessions.

Giving a Human Face to Electricity

Today, electricity is universal and daily life without it unimaginable. In the early twentieth century, however, there was virtually no residential demand for electric lighting, heat, or appliances. From the 1880s through the 1910s, electricity was used mostly in commerce, industry, and transportation. It illuminated stores, offices, and streets, and powered elevators, trolleys, and factories. World's fairs, from the Columbian Exposition in 1893 (Chicago) to the Panama Pacific Exhibition of 1915 (San Francisco), celebrated the new energy source as white magic and predicted an electrical utopia.

But residential use of electricity and electrical appliances remained limited. Wealthy Americans showed off their status by bringing electric service to their homes, but the Average American balked at the high cost of wiring a residence, buying new electric appliances, and then paying the monthly utility bills. Some people were even afraid of electricity, associating it with explosions, fires, and accidental electrocution.

After 1910, the electrical industry took several steps to make electrification accessible to consumers. The makers of electrical equipment adopted alternating current, or "AC," as the national standard. This meant that an iron, lamp, or coffee pot made to specification could plug into any AC outlet across the country. Utility companies found ways to generate cheaper energy, and they took measures to demystify electricity in the public mind. They discovered that personal interactions between company representatives and homemakers could alleviate customers' anxieties, pique curiosity, and sell products. Popular interest in electricity started to grow. In 1910, only one in seven American homes was wired, but by 1930, seven in ten had electricity.

One utility company that put a smile on the concept of residential electricity was the Denver Gas & Electric Company in Denver, Colorado, whose friendly sales force explained its advantages in a focused, disciplined fashion. Salespeople went door to door, putting householders at ease. A salesman pitched the new appliances, while a female home-service agent demonstrated an electric toaster. Between 1907 and 1909, Denver Gas & Electric used newspaper advertising, personalized sales pitches, and home demonstrations to promote a $5 electric iron. After two years, the utility company had sold 9,000 new irons to nearly half the households in Denver! Elsewhere, urban power companies adopted similar merchandising tactics, giving electricity a human face.

The Phonograph in the Parlor

The phonograph, or "talking machine," whose glory years ran from around 1900 to the mid-1920s, further piqued consumers' interest in personal technology. These mechanical devices expanded people's musical options, bringing popular song, orchestra, opera, jazz, sacred, and ethnic recordings to the home. In Victorian times, live music had been a vital aspect of domestic life, with instruments, sheet music, and feminine performance the focal point of cloistered evenings in the parlor. The phonograph changed this. With phonographs, home entertainment became more varied, sophisticated, and exciting for everyone. Americans put aside their sheet music and stopped *playing* in order to *listen*. The act of listening provided the opportunity to experience previously unimaginable cultures.

Recorded sound didn't begin life for application as a household appliance. It originated with Thomas A. Edison's 1877–78 invention of a talking machine that was eventually used for office dictation. Variations on Edison's acoustic device entered consumer culture through two channels: first, as music machines in public arcades or "phonograph parlors," and, second, as spring-operated phonographs for the home.

By the 1890s, consumers could pay to listen to early sound recordings and watch the first moving pictures in public arcades. These arcades had phonograph parlors and picture shows, or nickelodeons. They were located in cities, close to public transportation hubs. In phonograph parlors, travelers spent time listening to different sound machines, spending 10¢ to 25¢ per visit to hear a variety of recorded music, much as kids loiter in video-game arcades today.

Manufacturers responded to consumers' passion for phonograph parlors by introducing phonographs and recordings for home use. Three major firms—Edison, Columbia, and Victor—dominated the industry. In 1896, the first home phonograph appeared on the market: Edison's Standard, made by his National Phonograph Company, played music recorded on cylinders and retailed for $20 (equivalent to $479 in 2005). Next year came the Columbia Phonograph Company's Eagle, which sold for only $10 ($242 in 2005). Established in 1901, the Victor Talking Machine Company of Camden, New Jersey, perfected flat-disc technology and established a reputation for high-quality records and phonographs. Called the Big Three, these multinational firms did millions of dollars of business annually, holding nearly every important patent in the industry. Their European offices sold American-made machines and records abroad, their employees scouring the Continent for new recording talent. Smaller concerns competed vigorously in the lower end of the market.

Victor, the largest of the phonograph firms, dominated the industry from 1901 to 1926, when radio eroded its market. Under the leadership of Eldridge Johnson, Victor lifted the phonograph up from the gritty street arcade and transformed it into a respected cultural icon, one suitable to grace American living rooms. A testament to the firm's success is that its brand name, "Victrola," became a household synonym for any type of phonograph.

Records were one of the keys to Victor's success. Victor had two record labels, Red Seal and Black Seal, which together catered to nearly every musical taste. Introduced in 1903, the Red Seal label featured recordings by classically trained singers, instrumentalists, and symphony orchestras. Red Seal pioneered the concept of the "celebrity record," signing the world's leading musical figures and marketing their recordings as Victor "exclusives." Its most successful performer was the Italian opera star Enrico Caruso, discovered by a Victor talent scout in Milan. Caruso's extraordinary voice, known for its power and richness of tone, was ideal for early acoustic recording methods, and his popularity helped to establish the record industry. Red Seal sold middle Americans on the prestige of recorded classical music, celebrity singers, and artistic exclusivity.

The other Victor label, Black Seal, catered to popular tastes with dance music, songs, vaudeville vocalists, and ethnic comedy. America's most popular recording artist of the 1900s and 1910s was Billy Murray, an Irish American music hall star who had a contract with Victor. His most famous songs on Victor included "Meet Me in St. Louis, Louis" (1904), "In My Merry Oldsmobile" (1905), "Grand Old Rag" (1906), "By the Light of the Silvery Moon" (1910), "They Start the Victrola (and Go Dancing Around the Floor)" (1914), and "K-K-K-Katie" (1918). Black Seal also capitalized on the ballroom dance craze of the 1910s by recording bands that played in big-city hotels and cabarets. Victor gave the first record contract to an African American band, James Reese Europe's Society Orchestra, which accompanied the celebrity dance instructors Vernon and Irene Castle.

Victor's Black Seal label launched the Jazz Age in 1917 when the Original Dixieland Jazz Band's first record made the African American music of New Orleans brothels and bars available to a wider public. Black Seal reached its peak with hotel orchestra leader Paul Whiteman, who put a respectable face on this bawdy black sound, known as jazz. In the early 1920s, Victor billed Whiteman as the "King of Jazz." "Whispering," a 1920 instrumental recording that sold more than 1.25 million copies, was typical of Whiteman's style, which mixed jazz, dance music, and symphonic arrangements. A more sophisticated example was Whiteman's 1924 commission and première of George Gershwin's "Rhapsody in Blue." Black Seal, with artists like Whiteman, exposed middle-class listeners to a tempered version of African American music that was sufficiently refined for the parlor.

Victor developed other tactics for domesticating the phonograph and building customer loyalty. Foremost, Victor used styling to transform the record player into a desirable piece of furniture that replaced the piano as the home's entertainment center. The early phonograph was a tabletop device with an exposed turntable, an external crank, and a protruding, trumpet-shaped horn. After the novelty of the purchase had worn off, homemakers grew frustrated by this unsightly device and the stacks of records they accumulated. The Victrola, introduced in 1906, was a thing of beauty as well as a technical marvel. Built from solid mahogany, the Victrola was a piece of cabinet furniture that hid the horn, motor, turntable, and storage shelves from view. The Victrola's popularity led other manufacturers to put their phonographs in wooden cabinets and disguise them as living-room furniture.

Victor poured more money into national advertising than did any other American phonograph maker. In 1912, Victor's annual advertising budget surpassed $1.5 million; in contrast, the Andrew Jergens Company, as you might recall, spent a mere $25,000 on advertising Woodbury's soap. Victor's color ads in the *Saturday Evening Post* showed attentive high-class listeners, in an effort to make the talking machine into a must-have. Victrola ads always showed the manufacturer's trademark: a white fox terrier named Nipper listening to a phonograph playing "His Master's Voice." An enduring symbol of fidelity, the dog's attentiveness implied the accuracy of Victor's recordings and invoked consumer loyalty to the brand.

By the late 1910s, Victor's strategies had helped create a place for the phonograph in American consumer society. Between 1909 and 1919, total U.S. sales of phonographs grew dramatically, from 345,000 to 2.2 million.

Who, you might ask, bought all these phonographs and records? In 1919, *Talking Machine World* reported that women made the final decision in phonograph purchases nearly 80 percent of the time. Men saw the phonograph as "an article of furniture" and believed that "the wife" should look after "those things." Department stores added special phonograph displays in model rooms to show how the Victrolas looked in proximity to other furniture, rugs, and drapes. Customers could listen to records in soundproof booths, deciding which ones they wished to buy. Female clerks waited on shoppers and helped them feel comfortable with operating the strange machines.

Women dominated the lively market for phonograph records, affordably priced for middle-class budgets. Some phonograph enthusiasts assembled extensive record collections and avidly read about their favorite bandleaders, musicians, singers, and songwriters. In 1917, *Talking Machine World* explained that women, rather than men, developed "more of a fan spirit." Female fans helped to create new musical stars and a new type of celebrity watching.

Some men also became avid record collectors. Historians know little about men's use of the phonograph, but anecdotal evidence provides a glimpse of their enthusiasm. In Spokane, Washington, a young bookkeeper, Harry Crosby came home to his family one evening in 1906 with a huge box. Beaming, Crosby unpacked an Edison cylinder phonograph and recordings of "The Stars and Stripes Forever" and "The Merry Widow Waltz." The Crosby family was the first in their neighborhood to own a talking machine, and they played it constantly. Even though his salary at the local brewery was modest, Harry vigorously pursued his musical hobby. He eventually upgraded to a disc phonograph and assembled an impressive record collection. Favorite recordings included the Peerless Quartet, *The Mikado*, and singers like John McCormack and Al Jolson. Years later, Harry's son recalled having listened to these as a boy and being especially impressed by the sincerity of the Irish tenor and the intensity of the Jewish black-faced minstrel. Recordings by McCormack and Jolson inspired him to become a singer. That extraordinary son, Bing Crosby (1903–77), became America's number one crooner in the radio era. His father Harry was far more typical, perhaps an archetype of the male phonograph lover whose full history has yet to be written.

During World War I, the sound recording industry went on hold, as companies like Victor turned to military work. After the war, the pent-up demand for popular music gave a boost to the industry. Americans bought 106 million records in 1921, spending more on this form of entertainment than on any other. But these remarkable figures masked the dark cloud that hung over the vanguard of the sound recording industry. The new technology of radio was about to disrupt the phonograph industry.

Radio, the Electronic Hearth

Radio was the first *electronic* device to enter domestic life, making way for the home electronics boom of the late-twentieth century. In the 1920s, the radio displaced the phonograph as the "music box" of choice, much as the Victrola had pushed the organ and the piano aside. With broadcast radio, people could listen to music by the country's finest bands, orchestras, and singers without investing in a phonograph or record collection. Radio delivered quality performances with an immediacy and fidelity not possible with records. Taking their cues from the Victrola, radio manufacturers introduced console models that looked like furniture as well as compact "midgets" that consumers could move from room to room.

As radio prices fell, more Americans could afford to buy them. In 1924, only 11 percent of American homes had a radio; by 1940, more than 81 percent owned one. Only the poorest households — the urban working class without jobs and rural people living from hand-to-mouth — didn't have enough money to buy some type of radio. Some country folk lived too far from town to receive radio broadcasts, so rural sales were more limited than were urban sales.

Radio's early history was tied to the commercial need for a reliable way to communicate over long distances not served by the wired technologies of the time, the telegraph or telephone. The first successful transatlantic "wireless" message was transmitted from England to Canada in 1901, using an enormous antenna designed by the Italian inventor Guglielmo Marconi. The first practical application of Marconi's wireless was for ship-to-shore communications, allowing vessels to improve the safety of navigation in dangerous waters and bad weather. The military proved to be another large market for early radio apparatus.

Over the next two decades, independent inventors and corporate research laboratories improved radio technology. Lee de Forest invented the audion, a glass vacuum tube that amplified sound and made it possible for radios to receive a weak signal, while Edward Armstrong refined the audion's amplification abilities and used it to transmit signals. Although these developments laid the foundation for modern electronics, independent inventors lacked the resources necessary to commercialize radio. During the 1910s, two corporations with sophisticated industrial research labs—American Telephone & Telegraph Company (AT&T) and General Electric (GE)—invested heavily in radio and improved its operating characteristics.

Some visionaries imagined how radio could reshape communications and entertainment in consumer markets. In a 1904 issue of *Electrical World*, the inventor Nicola Tesla envisioned a "world system of communications," made possible through radio broadcasting. This system would "prove very efficient in enlightening the masses, particularly in still uncivilized countries and less accessible regions," explained Tesla. "A cheap and simple device, which might be carried in one's pocket, may then be set up anywhere on sea or land, and will record the world's news or special messages. . . . Thus the entire earth will be converted into a huge brain," he continued, "capable of response in every one of its parts." Tesla's expansive vision wouldn't materialize until the twenty-first century, when the web, the personal computer, and the telephone converged to produce the iPhone.

In 1916, David Sarnoff, a young manager at American Marconi, sketched out a more realistic plan for a "radio music box," which would reach consumers' hands in the next decade. Sarnoff outlined "a plan of development which would make radio a 'household utility' in the same sense as the piano or phonograph. The idea is to bring music into the house by wireless. . . . The box can be placed on a table in the parlor or living room, the switch set accordingly, and the transmitted music received. . . . This proposition would be especially interesting to farmers and others living in outlying districts removed from cities. By the purchase of a 'Radio Music Box' they could enjoy concerts, lectures, music, recitals, etc., which may be going on in the nearest city within their radius."

Tesla's and Sarnoff's proposals for connecting people across the globe via radio took cues from consumers' enthusiasm for the new technology. In 1910, nobody could walk into a store and buy a tabletop or console radio that had been assembled at the factory, like a Victrola. People interested in technology had to buy electronic parts made for commercial or military use and put together their own radio sets at home. As technical journals and popular magazines publicized the wireless, middle-class people who liked to tinker discovered the fun of home electronics. These hobbyists—mostly schoolboys, but some men and women, too—bought electronic parts, assembled their own receivers, and spent countless hours sending messages to each other. Radio buffs were well-educated Do-It-Yourself types, the first "nerds." They used large portable radios that ran on batteries, and they wore ear tubes or headsets to hear the sounds collected by large antennae. These early radios weren't things of beauty but consisted of glass vacuum tubes, black boxes, and plastic knobs connected by wires. Twisting the knobs to find the right frequency was a fine art, often mastered by the young people in the family who relished the challenge.

Radio's popularity among these amateur transmitters, later nicknamed "hams," paved the way for its entry into the home as a major entertainment vehicle. Radio is one of the best examples of a consumer-driven innovation, with enthusiastic users pushing business in a new direction.

The growth of ham radio was sensational. By 1908, the wireless hobby had its own magazine, *Modern Electrics*; and by 1910, there was a national club with 10,000 members. The Radio Act of 1912, passed to monitor the airwaves, dedicated higher frequencies to amateurs, while reserving band widths with greater geographical reach for commercial and military applications. The Radio Act also required amateurs who planned to transmit sounds to be licensed. By 1917, there were more than 13,000 licensed wireless buffs. During World War I, some ham operators joined the armed forces, bringing their technical skills to the military. On the home front, the government prohibited ham transmissions, which could interfere with military signals. Afterwards, radio buffs began anew with improved equipment designed during the war. Better vacuum tubes transmitted flawless waves, and receivers operated more efficiently.

In 1919, the major patent holders, including American Marconi, AT&T, GE, and United Fruit Company, pooled their resources to form a new company: the Radio Corporation of America (RCA). Westinghouse joined in 1921. RCA used its radio patents to develop new equipment for commercial, industrial, and military markets. At the beginning, consumers weren't on RCA's radar screen. In the 1920s, David Sarnoff, who moved from American Marconi to RCA, would change this, expanding the firm's role in consumer markets and broadcasting. Before this, Westinghouse was the first big business that woke up to consumers' bubbling interest in broadcasting and home radio sets.

In 1920, Pittsburgh radio buffs were listening to occasional broadcasts by Frank Conrad, a local ham operator with a day job as a Westinghouse engineer. For several evenings each week, Conrad tinkered with his transmitter, playing records and broadcasting live piano and saxophone concerts from his station, 8XK. Word spread about Conrad's wireless concerts, and more ham operators tuned in. In September, the city's leading department store, Joseph Horne, advertised preassembled radio sets in the *Pittsburgh Sun*. For a $10 investment, people who didn't like to tinker or didn't have the time to build their own radios could now listen in! When a Westinghouse executive saw Horne's ad for ready-made radios, he realized that radio sets had great potential as a consumer product.

Westinghouse invited Conrad to build a more powerful radio station at its Pittsburgh facility. KDKA's first broadcast—the election returns from the 1920 presidential election—attracted hundreds of local listeners, who in turn used their ham radios to publicize KDKA. Soon, hundreds of companies—department stores, major newspapers, and other electronics firms like GE and AT&T—were setting up radio stations. By 1923, there were more than 500 stations, and the market for ready-made radio sets exploded. Westinghouse had stumbled into a receptive consumer market, catalyzing the broadcasting boom of the 1920s.

The Jazz Age Radio Craze

In the 1920s, radio makers realized that families who wanted wholesome leisure activities *and* a connection to the wider world were a large untapped market. Hams who assembled their own sets and constantly upgraded their components simply didn't buy enough electronics to justify the corporate expansion of broadcasting. Families were really the force behind the radio boom. In the 1920s, people still played their pianos and used their Victrolas, but they began to embrace the radio as the home entertainment technology of choice.

Through radio, music became more fully integrated into the American consumer experience. Radio sets provided a common ground, reaching more people than either movies or magazines.

Sheet music and records had spread songs throughout the land, but "on" the radio, a new tune could reach millions and become a hit in a matter of weeks. Radio obliterated distance, shortened time horizons, and expanded personal perspectives. As it became ubiquitous, consumers incorporated radio into their daily rituals. They could listen attentively, dance to the music, or simply treat it as background noise while performing tasks.

In the 1920s, consumers saw the new world of radio unfolding. Information about radio sets and programs was easy to find. More than a dozen new magazines, such as *Radio Age*, *Radio Broadcast*, and *Radio News*, collectively reached more than a million readers. Newspapers and magazines also promoted radio, ensuring that nearly every segment of society, from the upper crust to farm families, read about it. Radio shops opened in cities and good-sized towns.

Electronics manufacturers helped radio find a permanent place in the consumer's personal identity kit by making it easy to use. Companies like Atwater Kent and RCA revamped the radio, both inside and out. They eliminated the heavy, cumbersome batteries that had powered makeshift sets, creating "all electric" units that one could plug in. By 1927, one-knob tuning became standard, putting radio within everyone's touch: young children just learning and grandparents with arthritic hands. Tuning the radio—a job once relegated to the family geek—became easy. By 1928, the unsightly horn-shaped speaker disappeared, replaced by an internal cone speaker that reproduced a wider range of musical notes with greater fidelity. Emulating the Victrola, major radio makers produced console units that matched contemporary interior decorating styles.

Improvements in the design of radios paralleled major shifts in programming. Stations experimented with different program formats, most broadcasts featuring some type of live talent. Early radio technology, which faithfully conveyed certain sounds but mangled others, influenced the selection. Stations started broadcasting live "salon music" from local hotels. This type of broadcast featured a live soprano or contralto, backed by a pianist, delivering popular tunes such as "After the Ball Is Over." Stations alternated these "singers programs" with live solo instrumentalists, including pianists playing Beethoven, Chopin, Liszt, and Rachmaninoff.

Consumers soon challenged this conservative repertoire. By the early 1920s, listeners had grown accustomed to musical variety by listening to the offerings of record labels like Victor's Black Seal and the popular new sounds of nightclubs and speakeasies. They lined up on the streets to buy the latest jazz and blues releases, or what became known as "race records." In 1920, urban blacks made Mamie Smith's recording of "Crazy Blues" into a smash hit that sold 8,000 records per week. Blacks and whites alike began to think about "race music" as a distinctively American sound. Those who bought Paul Whiteman's records appreciated his mixture of melodies, what some called "sweet jazz." Consumers wanted radio to reflect the sounds of the Jazz Age, writing letters to stations adjuring them to expand the repertoire.

By the mid-1920s, radio stations responded to consumers' demands by moving away from salon music to a variety of live and recorded musical genres, including symphonic, jazz, blues, and hillbilly. Although radio disseminated a patchwork of sounds, jazz began to dominate the airwaves. In October 1924, the *Outlook* noted, "You can scarcely listen in on the radio, especially in the evening, without hearing jazz."

Paul Whiteman still reigned as the "King of Jazz," but the demand for variety created space for black performers. This was a surprising development in the 1920s, when racial prejudice ran high. In 1921, black musicians first appeared on KDKA, and by mid decade, listeners clamored for more jazzy sounds. By 1927, African American band leaders Duke Ellington and Cab Calloway became international stars when the CBS network featured their live performances from Harlem's famous night spot, the Cotton Club. Such "colored" bands, as they were called at the time, adopted the polite manners and formal dress code expected by white audiences. Bandleaders like Whiteman, Ellington, Calloway, and Louis Armstrong each developed a unique style, but all of them capitalized on the idea that black and white music could comingle to entertain a paying mainstream America.

Conservative critics denounced the spread of jazz, lashing out against it and condemning popular dances like the Charleston, the fox trot, and the shimmy as "lewd" and uncivilized behavior. The most hysterical among the critics feared that jazz—which as a word in black slang referred to sexual intercourse—would encourage licentiousness among young fans.

But even as critics assailed jazz as decadent, record buyers and radio listeners made this cutting-edge sound into America's most popular music. In the 1920s, some consumers rejected the trappings of Victorian life, which seemed stifling in a fast-paced world. They updated consumer culture, making jazz a focal point of Modernity. Jazz and blues encouraged people to transcend the perceived hypocrisy of religion, the horrors of World War I, and the repression of racism. Jazz performers seemed to address universal truths, while assuring radio listeners that commercial broadcasting could be elevating, soulful, and redeeming. From its origins in the Storyville brothel district of New Orleans, jazz invited listeners to experience the underbelly of America, to visit safely places that were "off limits," or at least less formal, more spontaneous, and more rebellious than Main Street.

Through the radio, jazz inverted the gender roles Victorians had established in regard to musical production and consumption. The radio extended music appreciation to men. Jazz played an especially important role in turning music listening into a male hobby. In 1924, *Outlook* noted that the new sound had "seized hold of the great mass of American young men." The iconoclastic, improvisational style of jazz was culturally defined as a masculine purview, as were the rough-hewn, distinctly unpretty hillbilly styles also popular in the 1920s. This stood in contrast to the safe, staid conventions of feminine parlor music. As Susan Douglas writes in *Listening In*, radio provided a "trapdoor for men into new realms of gender pleasure" just as it opened a "trapdoor between the races" to reshape desire, behavior, and self-image.

Women also embraced new musical options through the radio. By 1929, American radio had its first romantic matinee idol, singer Rudy Vallee. As broadcasting's answer to Hollywood's Rudolph Valentino, Vallee attracted the attention of millions of women, who swooned over his commercially sponsored radio show, *The Fleischmann Hour*, and at his personal appearances. Using the newly invented microphone to good advantage, Vallee evolved the seductive singing style known as crooning. Like Clara Bow, Vallee had "it," and American women took note.

Changes in musical tastes evolved in conjunction with the transformation of radio operations, financing, and management. In 1927, Washington lawmakers created the Federal Radio Commission, predecessor to the Federal Communications Commission, to manage the airwaves and allocate frequencies. Around this time, the public demand for immediate news about sporting events like the World Series, the Kentucky Derby, and champion boxing matches provided a major impetus for the creation of the first national broadcast networks, NBC and CBS. These networks had local affiliates, which made simultaneous broadcasts across the country of shows like Vallee's *Fleischmann Hour,* introducing immediacy and uniformity to programs. In short order, shows produced in New York and paid for by commercials began to supplement local programming.

National radio broadcasting brought new voices to American living rooms, exposing Midwesterners to people and music from the South, farm families to the big city, and symphony fans to hillbilly sounds. Radio built on the phonograph's immediacy and personalized the experience of listening. By tuning in to jazz radio in their leisure time, men tried to escape the routine aspects of office jobs or the dehumanizing elements of factory work. But whether male or female, consumers took pleasure from sitting back, closing their eyes, and imagining that the voice coming through the ether was talking or singing directly to them. In this sense, radio was a strangely empowering, personal force in an increasingly impersonal age.

The Electric Twenties

As radio took off, Americans also embraced electrification with vigor. By 1930, 68 percent of homes were wired. Some places, including Middletown, U.S.A., exceeded the national average; the Lynds' research team found electrification in 96 percent of Muncie's homes by 1926. But other places lagged behind. In 1920, only 1.6 percent of farm households had electrical service; ten years later, the number had grown to only 10.4 percent. Rural electrification accelerated with New Deal programs in the 1930s, but farmers would not catch up to city folks until major hydroelectric dam construction in the 1950s.

While the power grid grew in the 1920s, the electrical industry looked to household consumers as a new market for energy and small appliances. An appliance boom hit after World War I, when the growth of suburbia created a fresh market for residential electric service. Older urban houses were difficult to retrofit with electrical wiring, but new ones in adjacent areas were wired for electric light and power during construction. Small electrical appliances—irons, coffee pots, roasting pans, curling irons, toasters, and the like—soon found their ways into these homes, giving the decade one of its many nicknames, the "electric twenties."

The economics of the power system determined the timing of electricity's dissemination. Electricity can't be stored for long periods so must be used soon after it's generated. To maximize their investments in generating plants and transmission systems, utility companies needed to deepen the demand for electricity and spread their costs over a wider clientele. Urban households provided the ideal complement to commercial customers and industrial users. As they did the chores, women plugged in electrical appliances like irons at midday, which coincided with the time when the demand from electric streetcars ebbed. The smart utility seeking a balanced load recognized that a brisk appliance trade would increase kilowatt sales to household consumers, allowing the company to sell electricity that would otherwise go to waste.

To expand the market for household appliances and power, the electrical industry—which consisted of equipment manufacturers and utility companies—developed extensive promotions at the national and local levels. Appliance manufacturer General Electric invested heavily in national advertising, increasing its budget from $2 million in 1922 to $12 million in 1930. The firm's Madison Avenue agency, BBDO, generated nearly 200 GE advertisements annually, designed to awaken America's "electrical consciousness." Local utilities expanded the power grid and promoted the use of household electric appliances at the community level, using many of the techniques pioneered by the Denver Gas & Electric Company. They also created luxurious utility showrooms staffed by home economists who targeted prospective middle-class buyers of appliances.

The Golden Age of Radio

Popular culture has inscribed a powerful image of the 1930s on the imagination. The Average American family sits around the radio in the evening, attentively listening to President Franklin Delano Roosevelt give one of his twenty-eight "fireside chats." This snug image of the radio in the parlor celebrates family ties and national solidarity during troubled times. Less apparent but just as potent, this nostalgic vision of radio listeners also symbolizes the importance of technological networks in creating intimacy and familiarity, linking the people to their political leader, and connecting the local to the national.

A good deal of historical truth underpins this cozy picture of domestic harmony and culture shared over the airwaves. During the 1930s, radio was one of the most important forces knitting the nation together, fostering a one-on-one intimacy between the radio performer and the listener. The expansion of network broadcasting in this decade gave birth to the "golden age of radio," which introduced a slate of standardized programs across the nation. Radio fans of the 1930s not only listened to jazz programs and FDR's fireside chats, but they also heard baseball games, soap operas, radio plays, and the *Make Believe Ballroom*. The selection of programs was new, different, and culturally invigorating. For the first time, Americans from Philadelphia to Seattle could simultaneously be part of the same listening audience.

The triumph of network radio during the Great Depression did not signal the demise of individuality or the mass homogenization of taste. People listened to a mixture of local and national programming, just as they wore clothes acquired at different times and in different ways. Modern consumers put together highly individualized outfits by mixing and matching homemade items and hand-me-downs with the new ready-to-wear. This same practice characterized radio listening. While thirties radio didn't offer the limitless variety available on the twenty-first century web, it began moving entertainment in this direction.

During radio's golden age, listeners also learned about the wider world and different ethnic groups through a new type of program: the syndicated serial. The first and most popular syndicated show, *Amos'n'Andy*, was a slapstick comedy that aired for fifteen minutes every weekday evening at 7 o'clock. This comedy show documented the exploits of Amos Jones and Andy Brown, two black men who left rural Georgia to search for opportunity in the North, first in Chicago and then in Harlem. The show was created by two white comedians working in the blackface minstrel tradition, Charles J. Correll and Freeman Fisher Gosden, who had broadcast a skit, *Sam 'n' Harry,* from a Chicago station beginning in 1926. By 1929, Correll and Gosden had moved to the NBC network, where they created *Amos 'n' Andy,* which became a national favorite. They recorded their routines on phonograph discs that were distributed to stations across the country, who in turn broadcast the programs to local listeners.

Amos 'n' Andy became the longest-lived program in broadcast radio history, exposing many white Americans to a version of black culture dramatically different from their own. Migrating between NBC and CBS, the show played until 1960. Listeners across the land reveled in the exploits of Amos and Andy as they ran the Fresh Air Taxi Company, Incorpulated, and their socializing at the fraternal lodge, Mystic Knights of the Sea. Love interests were introduced through Amos's courtship and marriage to Ruby Taylor and Andy's romance with Harlem beautician Madame Queen. During the depression, *Amos 'n' Andy* reached an estimated 40 million listeners, one-third of the national population. The show became, in Susan Douglas's words, a "national addiction." During its 7 PM time slot, the country stood still. Taxis parked at their stands, and telephones didn't ring, as people sat glued to their radio sets.

Although the program exploited racial stereotypes, it sympathetically poked fun at everyday experiences with a type of humor that resonated with Americans who had grown up with vestiges of the minstrel tradition. Many prejudiced white listeners may have laughed at the misadventures of Amos and Andy because these goofy characters fit their stereotypes of "the Negroes," but many others may have simply chuckled at the exploits of Amos and Andy as backwoods folk groping their way around the big city. Questions of racism aside, *Amos 'n' Andy* got consumers into the habit of listening to their favorite program on a regular basis, while encouraging them to arrange their leisure time around commercial broadcasting.

The commercial investment in radio advertising grew by leaps and bounds during the 1930s. *Amos 'n' Andy* and other popular shows relied heavily on business sponsors. Anxious to grow their customer base during the depression, manufacturers purchased advertising airtime from the networks and created the first "commercials," setting a pattern that became universal in radio, television, and cable operation. Selling airtime for commercials became the standard way for stations and networks to finance operations and programs. Americans came to associate their favorite programs with sponsors such as Fleischmann's Yeast and King Biscuit Flour. Over its long history, *Amos 'n' Andy* had a series of corporate sponsors: Pepsodent toothpaste, Campbell's soup, Rinso detergent, and Columbia television sets.

By the late 1930s, radio listening was the nation's favorite pastime, surpassing movie-going and reading as popular entertainments. In 1938, *Fortune*'s editors estimated that on a typical winter evening, 40 percent of America's homes tuned in to the radio. Low-income families especially appreciated the radio as a money-saving alternative to movies and magazine and book purchases. A year later in 1939, *Fortune* reported that Americans relied on the radio as their primary source of news, with 58 percent believing it was more accurate than the daily paper.

As the listening audience expanded, networks had to develop programs that appealed to different interests and tastes. The phonograph and the radio brought something unique to American consumer culture. The power of these media lay in their ability to cross cultural boundaries. They were the conduits through which popular tastes bubbled up and circulated in the wider culture. As the soulful sounds of Louis Armstrong *and* the patrician accent of FDR poured in to American homes, the listeners heard "the masses" and "the classes." The mixture produced mainstream American culture: vibrant and exciting, sometimes crass, but never homogeneous.

Creating Unity amid Diversity

Modern technology had important consequences for middle-class consumers. Primarily, phonographs, radio, and electricity were entirely new kinds of cultural artifacts, opening consumers' eyes, minds, and ears to a wider world. Telephones, radios, and appliances differed from bicycles and cameras because they were part of complex technological systems. Appliances had to be *connected* to a service provider; radios needed to receive signals from independent stations and network broadcasters.

In Modern America, the people as consumers were inexorably linked to high-tech systems. Some of these technologies, including records and radio, fostered a national culture where there had been none. In the 1930s, Americans around the country heard the same music and recognized hit songs; later, they would nostalgically be transported back in time when they heard those tunes. This phenomenon, which is so common today that we don't think twice about it, was dramatically new in the 1930s. As the century progressed, this pattern would repeat, paving the way for communications media like broadcast TV, cable, and the web to proliferate and assume central roles in consumer society.

While Modern technologies fostered a national culture of consumption, they also helped Americans to retain their individuality and their ties to local communities and meaningful subcultures. Although changing, the family was still the social bedrock, and the home a refuge from the hard world. Social groups defined by gender, ethnicity, and race found new means for connecting. Fan clubs, cooking classes, record shopping, and nightclubbing were social activities created by technological change. Musical appreciation lost any gender affiliation and opened new doors for women and especially men. Most important, audio technologies expanded consumers' perceptions of themselves, helping many to understand that the United States was "a nation of nations," and that diverse elements didn't completely melt away in the "melting pot." Racism, prejudice, and indifference still marred the landscape, but the many different voices and sounds disseminated by the new technologies had started to open eyes and bring Americans together.

•••

During the Modern era, millions of ordinary Americans embraced a new way of defining themselves through the use of high-tech goods. The technologies had transformed their sensations and perceptions, time and space, and had helped to introduce new ideas and values. Yet these items were not the only meaningful artifacts in the Modern consumer's identity kit. If we follow the money to find out what consumers valued, we find that while people may have lavished millions of dollars on cameras, phonographs, radios, and kitchen appliances, they spent far more on their automobiles. That quintessential American artifact—the personal automobile—is the subject of the next chapter.

CHAPTER SIX

Designing the Automobile Age

"Why on earth do you need to study what's changing in this country?" In 1923, a longtime resident of Muncie asked the Lynds this question as they researched *Middletown*. "I can tell you what's happening in just four letters: A-U-T-O!" Two out of three families in Muncie owned an automobile. The wife of an unemployed factory worker exclaimed: "I'll never cut on gas! I'd go without a meal before I'd cut down on using the car!" Another told why she preferred a car to indoor plumbing—"You can't go to town in a bathtub!"

Middletown residents were fully aware of the social effects of the car, which pushed Muncie out of the Victorian era into Modern times. For example, the automobile made a big impact on family gatherings, such as the evening meal and the midday Sunday dinner. Before the 1920s, middle-class sociability had revolved around leisurely Sunday afternoons in the dining room, enjoying the roast ham, the gossip, and the heirloom cut glass, Irish linen, and wedding china. The auto age rendered this ritual obsolete. One butcher put it plainly, "Folks today want to eat in a hurry and get out in the car."

In Middletown, "automobility"—a popular word used in the 1920s to describe the car's impact on personal mobility—widened people's experience, much as had the *Saturday Evening Post*, Victor's Black Seal label, and Rudy Vallee's *Fleischmann Hour* on the radio. Like other Americans, Middletowners used their cars to go to the grocery store, commute to work, and take Sunday drives. Parents even admitted that a car could improve a kid's status among his peers, and some bought cars "to help their children's social standing in high school." People were learning to love the car, putting it at the center of their experience as consumers.

Automobility and the Pursuit of Pleasure

The twenties were a peak time in automobile ownership, unsurpassed until after World War II. In 1910, only 1 percent of American households owned cars, but by 1920 this number had ballooned to 26 percent of America's 24.5 million households. By 1930, this figure had more than doubled, with 60 percent of America's 30 million households owning automobiles. Although the depression dampened purchases, 55 percent of households had personal vehicles in the 1930s.

Government spending helped to launch the auto age. Under Presidents Woodrow Wilson and Warren G. Harding, the federal government invested in road improvement, paving dirt turnpikes to make them friendlier to cars. In 1928, the government built the first cloverleaf highway intersection in Woodbridge, New Jersey. Federal spending on roads continued during the depression, when New Deal agencies like the Works Progress Administration hired the unemployed to build parkways, put up bridges, and upgrade older byways.

The auto age paved the way for the first supermarkets, which started in the California suburbs during the 1920s. Within a few years, they spread to the East Coast and the first King Kullen opened in Queens, New York. A large self-service store with free parking, the supermarket stocked a wide selection of fresh food, canned goods, and pantry staples. Consumers learned to pick out groceries for themselves, rather than depending on clerks to fill their orders. They also learned to take their purchases home themselves, rather than going to the store in the morning and waiting for an afternoon delivery of groceries. The automobile, the supermarket, and the electric refrigerator ended the hassle of daily food shopping for many people, except in dense urban neighborhoods that still had meat markets, produce stands, bakeries, and variety stores nearby.

The automobile changed the American relationship to food in other ways, inaugurating the era of roadside restaurants. Between 1910 and 1927, the country experienced a restaurant boom, with the number of public eateries increasing by 40 percent. Many of these new restaurants were oriented around the car. In 1921, Royce Hailey opened the world's first drive-in restaurant, Hailey's Pig Stand in Dallas, Texas. A few years later in Massachusetts, Howard D. Johnson opened a beachfront drug store with a soda fountain that sold homemade ice cream. In a short time, Johnson was running a chain of restaurants serving family-style meals to motorists. By 1939, there were more than a hundred Howard Johnson restaurants sporting their signature orange roofs along East Coast highways. When the New Jersey and Ohio turnpikes were built in the 1940s and 1950s, HoJo's negotiated for the exclusive right to sell food at the service stops. In step with fast cars, "fast food" became a part of the American lifestyle.

America's love affair with the car didn't escape the notice of the nation's artists and writers. Americans started composing songs about automobiles soon after they appeared. In 1905, Victor artist Billy Murray recorded a catchy tune that sold millions of records and kept his fans happy for decades. "In My Merry Oldsmobile" captured the spirit of Modern America, an era of heightened mobility and changing morals. In the song, Johnnie Steele courts his sweetheart Lucille in an Oldsmobile, teaching her to drive while whispering sweet nothings in her ear. Steele promises Lucille wedding bells, a fabulous honeymoon, and wedded bliss, but meanwhile the two "spark in the dark old park as they go flying along." The snappy song is filled with double entendres like "You can go as far as you like with me in my merry Oldsmobile." Other songs, like Charles Johnson's "The Auto Man" (1906) and Hal Burton's and Billie J. Morrissey's "Come Take a Trip in My Automobile" (1912), added to the image of the car as a forum for sexual liberties.

By the twenties, many middle-class Americans, particularly men, often considered the car as a pleasure vehicle, a means to adventure, romance—and sex. Conservative observers, like the editors of *House Beautiful* magazine, claimed that the car was eroding the morals of young Americans. Where dating couples once "sparked" on the front porch, they now sought the privacy of the car and the intimacies of the back seat. In contrast, Hollywood glamourized the car as a symbol of sexual liberation. In 1927, *The Jazz Age*, the first commercially successful film that featured sound—a "talkie"—showed young people joyriding in their cars.

Novelists also found much material in the automobile age. In 1922, Sinclair Lewis published *Babbitt*, which satirized the lives of middle Americans in the fictional Midwestern town of Zenith, Ohio. The lead character, a real-estate agent named George F. Babbitt, treasured his car as a prized possession. The motor vehicle spiced up Babbitt's dreary routine, carrying him away from an irksome family into the arms of his mistress. Through his automobile, Babbitt experienced a fuller life, enjoying "poetry and tragedy, love and heroism." Babbitt was not alone among fictional characters changed by the car. In 1926, novelist F. Scott Fitzgerald put Jay Gatsby, the tragic millionaire protagonist of *The Great Gatsby*, into an ornate mansion, a pink suit, and a yellow Rolls-Royce with green upholstery. Readers who were attuned to the imagery of the auto age appreciated the symbolism. Gatsby's expensive Rolls-Royce, embellished in gold and green, the colors of money, was a potent emblem of his upscale lifestyle, ambition, and greed.

"The Proper Thing for a Man of Wealth": Motor Racing and Car Collecting

Although automobiles had been established as middle-class symbols of consumption by the 1920s, the process took several decades. The first motor vehicles powered by a gasoline engine appeared in Germany in the 1880s. Manufacturers in Europe and the United States were soon making cars, using carriage-building techniques to assemble them by hand. In 1905, the retail price of a new motor vehicle ranged from $600 to $7,500, but the annual income in the United States was only $450 per year. (In 2005 dollars, this translated into $14,000 to $172,000 for the car and $10,000 for the average income). These prices made the first cars into luxury goods for the super rich. Wealthy men became the first automobile collectors, establishing the car as a masculine object.

Multimillionaire William K. Vanderbilt II, president of the New York Central Railroad, was a sportsman who loved traveling, yachting, and car racing. In 1902, he set a world record by driving his Mercedes from Monte Carlo to Paris in seventeen hours; later, he held the distinction of driving the fastest mile. Vanderbilt amassed an extensive car collection, mostly handcrafted European vehicles, on his Long Island estate. Every weekday, a hired driver took him into New York City in one of the cars, making Vanderbilt one the first automobile commuters.

Wealthy collectors like Vanderbilt used their vehicles for transportation, pleasure, and to display their status. In October 1905, the *New York Times* reported that "a stable of cars is coming to be recognized as the proper thing for a man of wealth, just as his private yacht, his box at the Opera, and his town and country houses." Accustomed to having household staffs, wealthy men hired chauffeurs to drive their cars and keep them in good repair. Prominent New Yorkers formed the Automobile Club of America, the activities of which were followed by the press. Newspaper accounts of the club's races at Newport and the annual car show at Madison Square Garden stirred public interest in the automobile.

Between 1905 and World War I, U.S. car production increased dramatically, and automobile ownership started to trickle down the social ladder. As vehicle prices fell, men in the professions—accountants, attorneys, engineers, physicians, and real-estate agents—could indulge in the luxury of car ownership. Where the Vanderbilts had French, German, and Italian vehicles, middle-class motor enthusiasts purchased American models, many of which have long since disappeared from the scene. Today, only classic car buffs recognize the names that once lay on the tip of every middle-class man's lips: Studebaker, Hupmobile, and Packard. "The machine" became a favorite hobby shared by father and son, driving a skill passed from mature adults to young men. As fathers taught their sons to take the wheel, they fortified the car's status as a manly artifact. While it remained a hobby for "the classes," the automobile joined spectator sports, saloons and barbershops, three-piece suits, and jazz music as one of the objects that defined modern masculinity.

Ford's Model T, The Car for the Common Man

In 1908, the Ford Motor Company introduced the affordable Model T, the best-selling car of the early-twentieth century. Produced until 1927, the Model T redefined the American motor vehicle market, shifting the emphasis from "class" to "mass" by creating "basic transportation" made expressly for "the common man."

The Model T became a "universal car" because Henry Ford transformed the way in which automobiles were made. Before Ford, carmakers employed skilled craftsmen to machine-make parts and assemble them into an automobile. A team of workers labored over a single vehicle from start to finish. These craft practices, inherited from the wooden carriage industry, added substantially to the price of the finished product. In 1910, Ford built a new factory in the Highland Park section of Detroit; three years later, he equipped it with the automobile industry's first moving assembly line. Ford had reduced the time required to assemble a chassis from 12 hours to 1½ hours!

Mass production had a big impact on the look of the automobile. In the relentless drive to cut costs, Ford focused on engineering rather than aesthetics. In 1915, he standardized the most expensive part of the bodywork, the finishing process, by switching from carriage paints to black enamel. Colorful carriage paints looked nice, but they were expensive to apply and took a long time to dry. Black enamel could be baked on in a fraction of the time. When queried about the lack of color options, Ford was reported to have quipped, famously: "Any customer can have a car painted any color he wants as long as it is black."

Ford's pragmatic approach to manufacturing greatly lowered the price of the automobile. Between 1908 and 1913, the retail price of a Model T touring car fell from $850 to $550; by 1916, the price had reached further down to $360. With these reductions, the Model T came within the grasp of the average American. Sales of Model Ts skyrocketed: nearly 6,000 units in 1908 to 183,000 in 1913 and 580,000 in 1916. In 1920, half of the automobiles in the world were Model

Ts. Ford rode on the general prosperity of the early-to-mid-twenties and contributed to it. By 1924, the Model T touring car retailed at a mere $290.

The typical Model T owner was a man. Without an electric starter, the Model T had to be cranked by hand, a task that required exceptional physical strength. Early versions were also difficult to steer and shift and, although reliable, still needed tinkering. With rutted dirt roads and primitive rubber tires, punctures were a constant headache. Additionally, the gas tank, located under the front seat, exuded noxious smells that many women found distasteful. Finally, like most early cars, the Model T was an "open" vehicle, without a hard roof or windows, making driving unpleasant in inclement weather. When suffragists started driving as a form of social liberation, many turned to specially designed "ladies' cars," electric vehicles with self-starters. World War I would dramatically change the roadside, as more women learned to drive and fix cars like the Model T. In the decades that followed, women became an important force with which automakers had to reckon, but in the beginning, most drivers were men.

Rural men looking for dependable transportation were the Model T's biggest customers. A no-frills kind of guy, Henry Ford grew up on a farm, and he envisioned the Model T customer in his own image: a self-reliant man who needed basic transportation. For the country doctor or farmer, the Model T was the ideal substitute for the wagon pulled by Lizzie, the horse. The former was durable, easy-to-fix for the mechanically minded, and relatively inexpensive. It was more appealing than Lizzie, who needed to eat, got tired after a few hours, and deposited manure everywhere. A horse, whether alone or part of a team, could be skittish and hard to control; a motor vehicle was more maneuverable and dependable. The Model T was soon nicknamed the "Tin Lizzie," perhaps by enthusiasts who saw it as a surrogate horse.

Farmers viewed the Model T as a godsend that helped to alleviate the isolation of rural life. With the car, farm families could get to town faster, and they started going on a regular basis. The Saturday drive into town became a feature of rural life. Once in town, farmers not only sold their products but also went shopping and visited friends. Like RFD, parcel post, mail-order houses, and radio, the availability of the low-priced Model T helped to bring rural Americans into the

Modern age. Across the land, Ford dealers courted Mr. Farmer, building confidence in the Tin Lizzie with newspaper ads like "Your Harvest Is Incomplete without a Ford."

Another type of Model T customer was the industrial worker, whose ranks grew in the early 1900s. Henry Ford encouraged his own workforce to save up for a car with the Five Dollar Day. Soon, the notion of the Model T as the workingman's car spread across America. Like farmers, factory workers loved cars and made sacrifices to buy them.

Car ownership did, however, vary by region and race. From 1910 to 1929, California led the nation in car registrations as a percentage of the population. During the 1920s, registrations were highest in the Pacific and Great Lakes states, lowest in the South. Blue-collar workers in small communities were more likely to purchase cars than were their urban counterparts, who lived close to the plant and walked to work. White Americans were more likely to own cars than were blacks, but regardless of race, the poor couldn't afford cars. The poorest Americans walked, rode the streetcars and trolleys, and, in rural areas, depended on old Lizzie rather than Tin Lizzie.

As basic transportation, the Model T rolled off the assembly line with few amenities. To keep the retail price low, Ford even curtailed national advertising after 1917. The car lacked many features that we now take for granted: electric starters, fuel gauges, headlights, heaters, turn signals, windshield wipers, side windows, and a hard roof. Customers came to expect they would modify their Model Ts, giving birth to a lively aftermarket business of parts and accessories. Writer E. B. White recalled the Model T's early years: "When you bought a Ford, you figured you had a start—a vibrant spirited framework to which could be screwed an almost limitless assortment of decorative and functional hardware. Driving away from the agency . . . you were already full of creative worry."

Creative worriers shopped for Model T accessories at local garages or repair shops, in the Sears catalog, five-and-tens like Woolworth, and new specialty chains, such as Western Auto. Pep Boys, the national automotive chain, was founded in 1920 to cater to car jockeys who wanted to fix up their vehicles. The most imaginative enjoyed designing novel equipment for their cars, including luggage racks and collapsible beds for the new family hobbies of motor touring and car camping.

By the 1920s, these consumer-tinkerers, mostly men, were sending countless letters to Ford, suggesting how to improve the Model T. Some hoped to profit from their inventions. In 1924, J. C. Long, a building contractor in Charleston, South Carolina, wrote Ford about his patented device for operating the car's horn from a button on the clutch pedal. In 1926, M. A. Zielinksi, a tailor from Trenton, New Jersey, offered Ford his patented gasoline gauge, an idea inspired when he ran out of fuel while driving his Model T on a dark, deserted road. Other Ford customers focused on the car's appearance. Richard A. Slaughter, Jr.'s 1926 letter suggested how to beautify the Model T and included a sketch of how it would look with a two-tone paint job in blue and yellow. In 1927, Maybelle H. McKee also stressed the importance of a pleasing palette when she asked Ford to design a "Ladies Car."

The flurry of consumer letters spoke to an attitude change. By 1925, the American market for new cars was saturated; almost every household that could afford a vehicle already had one. The features that had made the Model T into a mass-market favorite now seemed stodgy and old-fashioned. Jazz Age consumers demanded "price-plus," a phrase that denoted a combination of winning features: competitive prices, installment financing, trade-ins, stylish interiors, fashion colors, side windows, hard roofs, and annual model changes.

The automobile industry—the largest industry in the United States—had to adjust to changing demand, and many firms fell by the wayside. In 1908, the year Ford introduced the Model T, the United States had 253 automakers; by 1921, the number had fallen to 88. In the interim, automaking had been transformed from a highly competitive, diversified industry to an *oligopoly* dominated by a few very large firms. In 1921, 88 American automakers produced 1.47 million cars. By 1929, there were only 20 U.S. car manufacturers; collectively they made 4.4 million vehicles.

The Ford Motor Company resisted the customers' growing interest in comfort, convenience, and styling but lost its position as America's largest automaker as a result. The company's market share slipped from 55 percent in 1921 to 32 percent in 1929. Ford survived by virtue of its size, primarily making inexpensive cars. "Fordism," the system of mass production that handed automobility to "the masses," proved to be a dead end. Fordism generated basic transportation but, like farmer-mechanic Henry Ford, could not accommodate fashion. Although it remained one of America's largest automakers, Ford soon surrendered the top slot to General Motors, a firm that had mastered marketing.

GM and the "Car for Every Purse and Purpose"

During the 1920s, General Motors (GM) became Ford's greatest rival and a powerful force in the American automobile business. GM revolutionized the industry by introducing "a car for every purse and purpose"—a product range that catered to the "mass-class" market. This strategy was the brainchild of GM executive Alfred P. Sloan, Jr., who first articulated the idea in the early 1920s and spent the next three decades expanding and refining it.

Sloan's plans for enhancing the GM product line in part revolved around the notion that cars, like clothes, should have style. This reorientation coincided with the growing corporate awareness of Mrs. Consumer. In 1917, automaker Edward S. Jordon had observed in *Motor Age* that "while men buy cars, women choose them." By 1923, *Automotive Industries* and *Motor* chattered about the new female driver and what she wanted in terms of color, fabrics, and accessories. "The automobile has become fashion merchandise," noted *Harper's Bazaar* in 1929. "Fashion, and its interpretation, is largely a matter of the women concerned."

Women were one of the new consumer groups discovered by GM. Sloan also recognized that auto consumers were divided by income. Where Ford courted the budget-minded customer, GM developed a range of cars that appealed to a wider spectrum of consumers. Sloan organized GM into seven corporate divisions that produced different brands for different market segments. Chevrolet competed with the Model T at the bottom, while the Pontiac, Oldsmobile, Buick, and Oakland divisions catered to middle- and upper-middle class consumers. Finally, the Cadillac and LaSalle targeted the luxury trade.

In 1923, Sloan first experimented with a better-looking car when he asked Chevrolet to update body designs, hoping that a beautified economy vehicle—including a closed model with a roof—might appeal to the Model T devotee. When customers voted for the 1924 Chevy with their pocketbooks, Sloan made a big commitment to design innovation. The next year's model combined reliable engineering with new embellishments that looked really spiffy. The 1925 Chevrolet had a colorful paint job, a one-piece windshield, automatic windshield wipers, a dome light, and a horn. The Model T, still bulky and black, offered none of these amenities. In 1926, Chevrolet sales nearly doubled, while the Model T's dropped by 25 percent. From 1926 to 1927, GM's retail sales grew from nearly 900,000 to 1.2 million; Ford's sales fell from 1.1 million to around 400,000.

Under Sloan's leadership, GM evolved the model change, a practice that gave all new cars a distinctive look. Between the mid-1920s and the early 1930s, GM experimented by making cosmetic changes to each model every year or so. This approach, called "flexible mass production" or "Sloanism," combined Ford's dedication to volume production with aesthetic practices common in the style industries. When a pottery made dishes for Woolworth's or Marshall Field's, it customized the orders by decorating basic shapes with different enamels, decals, and trim. Shoppers knew that Woolworth dishes looked different and cost less than those for sale at Marshall Field's. In automobiles, GM achieved variation in a similar way. It standardized the car's mechanical elements and shared interchangeable parts among the divisions, reducing the costs of the chassis, body, and drive train. It made accessories like horns, turn signals, and headlights into standard features and glamourized the body shape, paint color, chrome trim, and upholstery fabrics. The stylistic changes were superficial and had no effect on the vehicle's operation.

With this approach, Sloan hoped to encourage Americans to buy new cars, even though their old ones—with a life expectancy of seven years—hadn't worn out. Many of GM's competitors weren't ready, willing, or able to compete on the basis of frequent model changes. During the early 1920s, Henry Ford balked at the prospect of the car as a fashion accessory. But as *Motor* reported in August 1927, the Model T was a car for the first-time buyer, who was fast becoming an endangered species. The return customer had grown tired of basic transportation and wanted a vehicle with more power and style. The annual model change signaled GM's acceptance that consumers used the automobile as a personal statement, much as they did with clothing and household furnishings. This move set GM apart from the other mass-production automakers before the end of the 1920s.

Design Wars

GM institutionalized its commitment to styling by establishing an Art and Colour Section to oversee product design. The division was headed by the impressive Harley J. Earl, a 6'4" giant destined to become the world's most famous auto designer. A native Californian, Earl had spent the early 1920s working for his dad's custom auto shop in Los Angeles, building cars for Hollywood celebrities. In 1925, Cadillac's division chief, Lawrence P. Fisher, met Earl at a Hollywood party. With characteristic flamboyance, Earl bragged that he could "make a car for you, like your Chevrolet, to look like a Cadillac." Fisher thought the proposal audacious but promising.

The chance meeting between Fisher and Earl coincided with an escalation of the GM-Ford rivalry. By mid-decade, Henry Ford knew the Model T was in trouble. As a first-aid measure, he authorized cosmetic changes, but the measure failed to stimulate sales. Ford's market share plummeted.

In May 1927, Henry Ford officially announced the end of Model T production and the introduction of the new Model A, a vehicle "superior in design and performance to any low-priced, light car." While Henry Ford oversaw the engineering components of the new car, his artistic son Edsel, who understood consumer culture, worked on the design of the body, upholstery, and accessories. "Women are a greater influence in the automobile buying field than ever before," Edsel Ford told the *New York Times* in early 1924. In a company memo that same year, he identified "a very large field of Ford prospects among the middle class in which women are usually an important factor." These customers, he continued, "are able to pay more for a car and pride, vanity, a desire for something more impressive, etc., enter very strongly into the sale." Edsel helped to design the Model A, which sported rounded corners, fuller fenders, and multicolored paint jobs. It was available as a roadster with a soft convertible roof, and in several body types with a closed roof, such as the sedan or town car.

On December 1, 1927, a million people rushed to see the Ford Model A unveiled in showrooms throughout the world. The changeover to the Model A had taken six months, cost $18 million, and enabled Ford to regain some share of the budget market. The Model A won popular acclaim, with one song writer declaring, "Henry's made a lady out of Lizzie!" But Henry Ford saw things differently. Backhandedly, he nodded to fashion, carping about the high costs of retooling and advertising the Model A. "We are no longer in the automobile" industry, Ford quipped, "but in the millinery business."

But the Model A didn't enjoy its reign as the sole beauty queen for long, not with GM and Harley Earl in the picture. Earl's design for the 1927 Cadillac La Salle brought the look of an expensive classic to the mass market. The La Salle evoked Hollywood glamour, a theme fortified in its national advertising. The upscale car was long-and-low with rounded corners, emulating the look of luxury cars long favored by the rich and famous. It suggested a star-studded world far removed from the monotonous workday of the office or factory. These features were rooted in Earl's belief that consumers saw automobiles as entertainment and escapism. "People like something new and exciting in an automobile as well as in a Broadway show," Earl reflected in a 1957 interview, "they like visual excitement and that's what we stylists give them." In contrast to the La Salle, the Model A looked boxy, stodgy, and old-fashioned.

Styling helped Ford, GM, and a third major automaker, Chrysler, to consolidate their power, and it provided them with a new tool for stimulating desire. Sloan called this tactic the "constant upgrading of product." In his 1928 book, *American Prosperity,* economist Paul M. Mazur described upgrading as deliberate obsolescence. "Wear alone made replacement too slow for the needs of American industry," wrote Mazur. "Business elected a new god to take its place along with—or even before—the other household gods. Obsolescence was made supreme."

Buy Now, Pay Later

Although style mattered, good looks alone couldn't ensure GM's rise to the top. During the late 1910s and early 1920s, most car dealers had "cash only" purchase policies. Even in prosperous times, the consumer who wanted to buy a new vehicle often had trouble pulling together enough money. A Model T from the dealer's showroom cost one-fourth of a male factory worker's annual wages. Maintenance—tires, oil, gasoline, tune-ups—was a continuous expense. Credit helped people navigate around these financial obstacles and extended automobile ownership to "the masses." The installment plan, perfected by a GM subsidiary, made it possible for people living on small or seasonal incomes to buy cars "on time," much as they do now.

In the Victorian era, consumers of limited means had bought into the middle-class lifestyle by purchasing items "on time." In 1895, newlyweds Walter and Lillie Post, living on his modest salary as a railroad clerk, purchased furniture, carpets, and a stove on credit from a St. Paul department store. For decades, consumer credit had been associated with people like the Posts, who lived from payday to payday and were always strapped for cash. Thrift and sobriety had governed mainstream culture, discouraging credit as an indulgence. Borrowing to buy household goods was seen as an unnecessary evil, a sign of profligacy and a lack of self-discipline. By the 1920s, these prejudices started to fade as middle-class consumers who wanted phonographs and electric appliances reconsidered time-payment plans. The recession of 1920–21 spurred a wave of credit financing, as retailers—department stores, hardware shops, appliance dealers, and furniture dealers—competed for customers. When middle-class consumers joined the credit economy, the term "buy now, pay later" lost its stigma.

In the automobile industry, consumer credit didn't become common until after World War I. Early credit plans were created to benefit dealers, who themselves needed to borrow money in order to buy new cars to put in their showrooms. For the most part, consumers were expected to pay cash for a car, and this limited the market. Installment plans democratized automobile ownership and further expanded the credit economy.

In the mid-1910s, automaker John Willys created a finance company that helped dealers to sell Willys-Knight and Overland cars. The Guaranty Securities Corporation (GSC) lent money to dealers who in turn lent it consumers. This company, which had Alfred P. Sloan, Jr., on its board, was financing "time sales" of twenty-one different makes, including GM, Dodge, Ford, Hudson, Maxwell, REO, and Studebaker, by 1916. GSC advertised in the local newspapers to educate the middle class on the benefits of the installment plan. It also advertised in the *Saturday Evening Post*, the great entrée to the family circle.

Taking cues from this success, Alfred Sloan designed a credit plan that targeted GM customers. In March 1919, he created the General Motors Acceptance Corporation (GMAC) to help dealers and consumers pay for GM cars. GMAC was unusual because it extended credit directly to consumers. Borrowers had to put down a third of the price and repay the balance, with interest, within twelve months. But they could trade in their old cars for better models, upgrading from economy to luxury as they climbed the ladder of consumption. The trade-in was an important marketing concept that gave GM a competitive edge.

The Ford Motor Company also joined the credit economy, albeit over a period of ten years. In 1919, 65 percent of Ford cars were sold on installment by Ford dealers, aided by local finance companies. The company kept this a secret from founder Henry Ford, who loathed moneylending. But in 1923, the company inched into Modern times by introducing the Ford Weekly Purchasing Plan, modeled after local banks' Christmas Clubs. Now a customer could drive away with his new Ford after having paid for it by making weekly deposits at a local savings bank. The Ford plan emphasized delayed gratification and reinforced the older values of thrift and discipline. Ultimately, however, Ford Motors bowed to the cultural imperatives of getting and spending. In March 1928, it established the Universal Credit Corporation, which offered credit directly to Model A customers. Ford's reluctance inadvertently assisted its competitors, encouraging budget customers to shift their allegiance to GM's Chevrolet.

Consumer credit extended automobility to large segments of the American population. In 1917, a dozen companies lent money to consumers for vehicle purchases; by 1922, a thousand firms were in this business. Three years later, in 1925, 1,700 companies were financing vehicles, and the majority of automobiles were purchased on time. In 1920, one-third of the purchasers bought cars on credit; by 1925, about three-fourths did so.

Automobiles were not the only items sold on time. In 1910, the amount of retail installment credit had totaled less than $1 billion; by 1929, it had grown to $7 billion. The U.S. Department of Commerce reported that, in 1928–30 only 9.2 percent of retail purchases were made on time, but this figure masks the real impact on installment sales. By the late 1920s, the installment plan provided consumers with a way to buy many new durable goods. Between 60 and 70 percent of automobiles were bought on time; 80 to 90 percent of furniture, 75 percent of washing machines, 65 percent of vacuum cleaners, 75 percent of radios, and 80 percent of phonographs. Installment sales promoted the adoption and use of high-tech goods.

The installment plan, which achieved its fullest expression in the automotive market, empowered more Americans to define themselves as consumers. By the mid 1930s, the National Bureau of Economic Research, a private think tank, found that installment purchasing was widely accepted among the middle class. More people were willing to pledge future earnings to lenders if they could have immediate gratification.

The Paradox of the Auto Boom

During the twenties, the automobile became an essential item in the consumer identity kit; the industry, the backbone of the American economy. By 1929, the United States had 26.7 million registered vehicles, or 1 car for every 4.5 people. Advertising fueled consumers' longings for a car, while installment credit made car ownership possible.

Amidst the Coolidge-era prosperity, some observers felt a chill, sensing the economic dangers that lay ahead. In 1925, automaker Charles W. Nash, head of Nash Motors, warned car dealers that a saturation point had been reached and urged fellow executives to reduce production. Signs of instability abounded: Detroit's unyielding pursuit of mass production; the rise of deliberate obsolescence; the relentless pressure on dealers to sell, sell, sell; and the glut of used cars created by trade-ins. Dealers began to wonder about how they would fill monthly sales quotas and whether they would make ends meet.

The injudicious expansion of the automobile industry and installment credit played a role in creating the Great Depression. After a certain point, business tools like advertising, salesmanship, and installment plans could no longer stimulate sales. Nearly everyone who could afford a car already had one. The economy that the automobile helped to create was, ironically, the economy that it helped to topple.

Streamlining the Great Depression

The American love affair with the car continued during the depression. The car was a means by which consumers forgot their woes; it provided escapism, much like movies, records, and radio. It also allowed people to look for work in places where the streetcar didn't go. Consumers kept their old cars and spent what little spare cash they had on gasoline, maintenance, and repairs.

Hard times hastened the trend to oligopoly, solidifying the positions of GM, Ford, and Chrysler, which became known as the "Big Three." After the stock market crash, new car sales plummeted, from 4.5 million in 1929 to 1.1 million in 1932. Ford, especially, struggled. From 1929 to 1932, Ford's car production dropped from 1.5 million to a mere 232,000; between 1931 and 1933, the company lost more than $12 million. Chrysler reduced capacity, and kept its head above water. GM did the best, partially due to the statistical controls and strategic planning that Alfred Sloan had put into place. By the late 1920s, Sloan began to suspect that an economic slump lay ahead, allowing him to make adjustments in advance. In 1932, the worst year of the depression, GM made a modest profit, and by 1937, it had more fully recovered than had Ford and Chrysler. Smaller auto firms didn't fare well; luxury brands like Peerless and Moon vanished from the roads, relegated to the realm of nostalgia and collectibles.

The Big Three tried to re-instill confidence in the American dream, promoting themselves as harbingers of technological progress. Designers like Harley Earl advocated the judicious use of aesthetics as a tool for uplifting the public spirit and reinvigorating consumer desire. Art departments went into high gear, applying the principles of consumption engineering to new models. GM led the pack; but by the mid-1930s, even Ford, the bulwark of conservatism, had a styling department.

Streamlining was the promising new aesthetic of the decade. Originally based on aerodynamic principles, it soon became a cosmetic element. To save costs while offering something new, automakers used older designs for the power train and chassis, focusing on changes to the passenger area and the steel exterior. Year after model year they hid older mechanisms under a sleek new skin, creating a car that looked like the embodiment of technological progress. In reality, the car's beauty was but skin deep.

Streamlining debuted at the National Automobile Show in New York, with the Chrysler Airflow 1934. The Airflow appealed to connoisseurs but didn't resonate with the general public and was not a commercial success. The new streamlined aesthetic was more widely disseminated when Harley Earl applied it to the entire GM lineup. Between 1934 and 1941, he developed the flamboyance that became GM's signature look and distinguished its cars through the 1950s. Earl's version of streamlining fed public fantasies about consumption, modernity, and progress. His cars were big and bulky with lots of chrome; they were longer, lower, and wider than the offerings of the competition. The designs equated size with value, conveying the idea that GM customers were getting more for their dollar.

Imagining the Future

The 1939 New York World's Fair at Flushing Meadows focused on the theme, "Building the World of Tomorrow." Designed as a futurist spectacle, the fair updated the idea of progress for the mid-twentieth century. Technology, which had fascinated the Victorians back in 1876, was given a new suit of clothes: streamlining.

All the major automakers erected pavilions, but a major attraction was GM's "Highways and Horizons" building, which featured the "Futurama" by consultant designer Norman Bel Geddes. Its centerpiece was a diorama depicting the imagined City of 1960, a hybrid urban-suburban space filled with sanitized skyscrapers, spaghetti-strand superhighways, and plenty of room for all the cars.

The GM exhibit highlighted the social benefits of widespread ownership of the automobile and speculated on what changes it might bring. As the United States exited the depression and stood on the brink of war, Mr. and Mrs. Average American visited the fair and pondered the pluses and minuses of the technological present and the utopian tomorrow. The Futurama said nothing about depression-era poverty and decay, bread lines and labor strife, but instead stressed the purity of form associated with streamlined design. It equated GM, the sponsor, with social betterment and the unhampered evolution of a better future. This was not only streamlining, but the embodiment of the American Way of Life, which GM and the National Association of Manufacturers had introduced in a folksy guise back in the mid-1930s.

The Futurama was a public relations tool designed to rebuild public confidence in automakers after a period of economic stagnation. It pressed headlong into an imagined future, much as the auto industry had been catapulted into the boom of the 1910s and 1920s. Over the past forty years, automakers had revolutionized transportation and the personal expectations of the Average American. Not every consumer had a car, but nearly every consumer saw the car as a major symbol of the American dream.

The automobile was one of the great consumer technologies of Modern America. Weekly magazines had stirred the visual imagination, while records and radio had introduced new sound experiences. All of those innovations brought the wider world into the parlor and living room. The automobile was different because it put mobility—automobility—in people's hands. The car was also a consumer good that crossed gender boundaries. Men, who flitted around the borders of consumer society, enjoyed full participation when it came to cars. Women, who were prohibited from driving early on, eventually took the wheel and pointed automotive design in new directions. Few technologies have transformed personal experience so dramatically and inclusively. Few have changed the landscape and the environment so thoroughly.

The Futurama pointed to the late twentieth century in ways that GM and Bel Geddes might have found eerie. Looking at pictures, the

Futurama bears an uncanny resemblance to new technoburbs created on the urban outskirts by the car beginning in the 1970s. It's to these car-driven suburbs, the Edge Cities, that we'll turn in the final chapters.

Big businesses and their advertising agencies developed the "Better Living" and "American Way" themes during the Great Depression and used them to boost worker morale and productivity during World War II. Westinghouse Home Economics Institute, *For Better Living in the American Way,* pamphlet, early 1940s. *Author's collection; courtesy, Westinghouse Electric Corporation.*

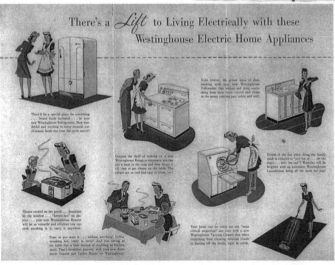

Right: Turn-of-the-century magazine advertisements: small, wordy, and cluttered. *Christian Herald and Signs of Our Times* (24 Aug. 1898). *Author's collection.*

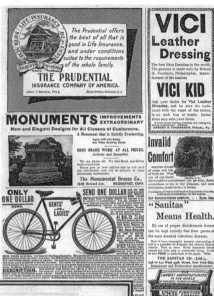

Left: Some advertisers used ethnic stereotypes to promote their brands. This ad shows an Irish maid and an African-American cook known as Rastus serving cereal at a time when middle-class households were strapped for servants. Cream of Wheat Co., advertisement in *Youth's Companion* (19 Sept. 1901): 464. *Author's collection.*

The easy-to-use Kodak camera revolutionized photography and introduced consumers to personal technology. Eastman Kodak Co., advertisement in the *World's Work* (Dec. 1903. *Author's collection.*

Top: Mrs. Consumer appreciated the Victrola as a reliable music box and an attractive piece of furniture. Victor Talking Machine Company, advertisement, 1913. *Author's collection.*

Bottom: The new hobby of record collecting exposed middle-class consumers to a range of sounds: classical music, black-faced minstrel singers, and jazz orchestras. Columbia Graphophone Co., advertisement in the *Ladies' Home Journal* (March 1920): 64. *Author's collection.*

It is easy to identify Victrola instruments

You can tell them the moment you raise the lid and see the trademark "Victrola." You will also see other Victor trademarks, as the picture and the phrase "His Master's Voice."

Be sure to get a Victrola instrument, for it is the chosen instrument of the greatest artists and specially made to play their Victor records.

The Victor trademarks besides being your means of identification are also your guarantees of quality. Victrola instruments are built to give a lifetime of service. Look under the lid for the Victor trademarks—"Victrola," the picture and the phrase "His Master's Voice" ... lasting satisfaction.

... 5 to $1500.

"HIS MASTER'S VOICE"
REG. U.S. PAT. OFF
This trademark and the trademarked word "Victrola" identify all our products. Look under the lid! Look on the label!
VICTOR TALKING MACHINE CO.
Camden, N.J.

...hine Company, Camden, N.J.

Columbia Grafonola

Exclusive Columbia Artists in the Latest Song Hits

Who kids them along in the latest song on Columbia Records only?—*Al Jolson!*
Who raises the roof with melodious mirth on Columbia Records only?—*Nora Bayes!*
Who knows how to mix song with laughter and tricks on Columbia Records only?—*Van & Schenck!*
Who jazzes the house by just opening his mouth on Columbia Records only?—*Harry Fox!*

Who starts on the quiet and ends in a riot on Columbia Records only?—*Bert Williams!*
Where first do you find the newest of song hits by all the most popular artists?—*On their exclusive Columbia Records!*
Where best will you hear these Columbia Records played?—*On the Columbia Grafonola!*

COLUMBIA GRAPHOPHONE COMPANY, NEW YORK

Top: Budget retailers offered working-class consumers easy credit. Spiegel, May, Stern Co., advertisement for Congoleum Gold Seal Art Rug, *True Story Magazine*, 1923. *Author's collection.*

Bottom: Householders without central heating systems could buy coal-fired parlor stoves to warm their living rooms. Straus & Schram, *Annual Cold Weather Sale: When Dreams Come True* (Chicago, 1914), cover. *Author's collection.*

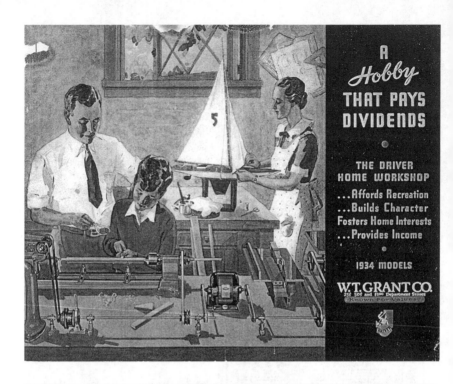

Opposite Top: Depression-era businesses advertised stay-at-home hobbies that encouraged family togetherness. This brochure for Driver Power Tools, retailed by W. T. Grant Co., stressed the gender divide and privileged the father-son relationship. *A Hobby that Pays Dividends* (Plainfield, NJ: Waker-Turner Co., 1933), cover. *Author's collection.*

Opposite Bottom: The BBDO agency helped General Electric promote appliances by advertising them as surrogate servants. General Electric Company, advertisement in the *Saturday Evening Post* (14 Oct. 1933): 78-79. *Author's collection; courtesy, General Electric Company.*

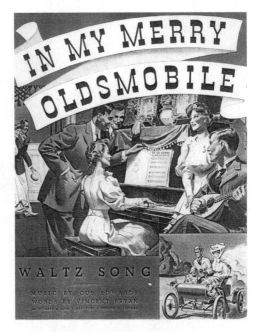

Top: Young people—dressed in the Gibson Girl and Arrow Man styles—loved cars and made songs about them into hits. Vincent Ryan and Gus Edwards, *In My Merry Oldsmobile* (NY: M. Witmark & Cons, 1905), cover of sheet music. *Author's collection.*

Bottom: With cars, people drove to the beach rather than take the train. Automobile lineup at a Cape May, New Jersey, band concert. Postcard by Tichnor Quality Views, 1920s; *Author's collection.*

Top: Hard times: boarded up houses, dilapidated cars, and vegetables from a pushcart, 1936. Orange Street, Cleveland, Ohio. *Courtesy, Cleveland Public Library Photograph Collection.*

Bottom: Automakers advertised streamlined cars as stylish goods akin to Marshall Field's fashions and jazz music. Chrysler Motor Co., advertisement in *Collier's* (20 May 1939). Author's collection. *Courtesy of Chrysler LLC.*

The 1939 World's Fair predicted a high-tech future of streamlined buildings, superhighways, and consumer goods. *The General Motors Exhibit Building: 1939 New York World's Fair, Highways and Horizons* (Detroit, 1939). *Author's collection; courtesy, General Motors Corporation.*

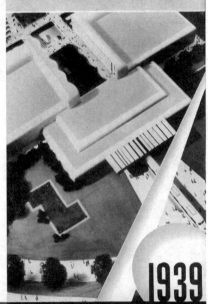

THE
GENERAL MOTORS
EXHIBIT BUILDING

1939
New York World's Fair
HIGHWAYS AND HORIZONS

A 4,000 horsepower, streamlined Diesel passenger locomotive, 140 feet in length, marks one of the entrances to the Highways and Horizons building.

Long ramps lead you into this lobby, where a 110 foot animated map of the United States tells the story of highway progress in years to come.

Nine glass pillars contain the exhibit of GM's Overseas Operations in the "Department Store." Inside are Frigidaire, Delco and Research exhibits.

THE CITY
OF THE FUTURE

IMAGINE being suddenly transported twenty years into the future! . . . to the heart of a great city! . . . in the year 1960! This seems to happen to you as you stand in the City of the Future, heart of the General Motors exhibit building, Highways and Horizons. It IS 1960—broad elevated sidewalks extend a full block in two directions, while below the city streets are filled with motor vehicles. On all sides buildings of tomorrow tower skyward—here an "Apartment House," there an Automobile Display Salon, across the way an Auditorium, and there a "Department Store"—all designed and executed in the mode of days to come, sheathed in gleaming copper, glass and aluminum. Broad expanses of glistening glass line the walkways of this City of the Future, inviting you to step within and see the many wonders of science and industry there displayed— wonders not of tomorrow, but of the world today.

This copper and glass building houses the Automobile Display Salon where cut-away chassis and engines explain details of automotive construction.

This "Apartment House" occupies one corner of the City of the Future. Here are displays of General Motors parts and accessory divisions.

Climaxing the "Futurama" ride, visitors alight from their moving chairs on this platform overlooking the heart of the City of the Future.

Moonlight becomes You

THE BREATHLESS NIGHT. The moon turning on its billion-watt radiance. Multiplying mystery, quickening the pulse. Stirring up a sudden sweet tumult. Heady stuff, this. To look into his eyes and know that you were never lovelier. To hear him say the words that match the music in your heart.

The guardian of your beauty ... a Woodbury Facial Cocktail, gentlest of cleansing care with Woodbury, the soap made for the skin alone. A beauty treatment in cake form ... its formula finer than when it sold for a dollar a cake. Now yours for a few pennies ... to soften, smooth and clear your complexion for the moonglow look of romance.

FOR THE SKIN
YOU LOVE
TO TOUCH

10¢

This 1944 advertisement for Woodbury's Facial Soap used the "Skin You Love to Touch" theme developed by J. Walter Thompson before World War I. Andrew Jergens, magazine advertisement, 1944. *Author's collection.*

PART THREE

Boomer America, 1945–2005

On October 24, 2005, the headline for *Business Week*'s cover story declared "Love Those Boomers!" For the past sixty years, the massive population cohort born between 1946 and 1964 had been reshaping marketers' expectations and assumptions. Weaned on postwar prosperity, America's Baby Boomers matured along with the mass market, their media experience framed by the rise (and decline) of network television and the revolution of cyberspace. As children, Boomers regularly tuned in to TV programs like *The Howdy Doody Show, Gilligan's Island,* and *The Brady Bunch*; as teenagers, they made early rock and rollers like Elvis, The Beatles, and The Rolling Stones into superstars. Growing up, these consumers — 77 million strong in 2005 — cast aside traditional concepts about brands, body identity, work, and aging. In middle age, they shook convention by staying physically and mentally fit and active. Baby Boomers broke all the rules: they were the largest consumer group in history, and their constant redefinition of what goods were meaningful befuddled marketers.

The Boomers represented a new type of consumer: an affluent customer with heterogeneous tastes. Boomers shared the generational experiences of postwar prosperity, Reaganomics, and the dawn of the electronic age, but their sheer numbers wreaked havoc with marketing theories. For the first time, marketers had to deal with a substantial demographic group that divided according to variables *other than* gender, income, geography, race, and social class. Born at a time of restrictive immigration, most Boomers grew up with a clear sense of what it meant to be American. They spent their childhood in neighborhoods where most people looked just like them. But they came of age during the turbulent 1960s and 1970s, with the civil rights, feminist, and gay rights movements that made them uncomfortable with conformity and intrigued by diversity. They had significant disposable income and leisure time, which they filled with structured entertainment, from Little League to cable television. Finally, Boomers demanded constant novelty—in fashion, music, sports, and other goods and services.

The Boomers redefined what it meant to be middle class, leaving an indelible mark on consumer culture. In earlier eras, American consumer society privileged middle-class values and lifestyles. The Victorians made the house into a cozy home and a site of entertainment, accumulation, and display. The Moderns developed important new technologies, institutions, and professions, providing the foundation for the explosion of affluence. They also enlarged the consumer identity kit, adding radios, phonographs, and cars. But the political economy in these earlier periods—the absence of a social safety net, economic panics and depressions, trade protectionism, racial segregation, gender discrimination, and two horrific world wars—limited the spread of mass consumption. Many Americans longed for the good life but were prohibited from participating in it.

After World War II, much of this changed. As the United States became the world's most affluent society, the artifacts that delineated consumer identity—the home and its furnishings, private cars, personal music, and nice clothing—became accessible to more and more Americans. But getting there was not always easy since social injustices kept poor, rural, and uneducated Americans on the outside. Nonetheless, students of consumer society need to think in relative terms and keep their eyes fixed on the *tangible* prize: *the artifact*. By 2000, 89 percent of American households owned a vehicle, compared to only 26 percent in 1920. Nearly everyone had electricity, running water, indoor toilets, and refrigerators. These amenities are now so pervasive that consumers don't give them much, if any, thought, and forget that they were technological marvels and luxuries for the wealthy-only less than a century ago. The fact is that *most* Americans born after World War II have enjoyed what President Franklin Delano Roosevelt in 1941 famously called the "freedom from want."

Populuxe Push-Button Technology

The American economy grew at an astonishing rate between 1945 and 1960, when the gross national product (GNP) expanded by 250 percent. According to economist Walt Rostow, the nation entered the "high mass consumption" phase of growth. By the mid-1950s, nearly 60 percent of American households earned enough money to enjoy a middle-class standard of living. This was a big leap from the late 1920s, when many Americans aspired to those comforts but only 31 percent had a middle-class income. Reflecting on this, economic historian Harold G. Vatter identified 1960 as marking a "great divide" in human history, separating an era of relative scarcity from the new era of relative abundance.

The United States was the only world power that hadn't suffered huge civilian casualties and widespread bombing during World War II. The "arsenal of democracy" had built new factories, remodeled antiquated ones, and enlarged its airstrips and ports. In the Northeast and Midwest, war production revitalized depressed industries; it also created new manufacturing districts in the South and Southwest. Federally funded research and development (R&D) generated important innovations in atomic energy, chemistry, medicine, navigation, plastics, and telecommunications. The reconversion to civilian production had some ups and downs, but it occurred swiftly. As Europe and Asia struggled to rebuild their cities, ports, and factories, the healthy American economy accounted for nearly half of the world's output. Agriculture and industry were robust.

The Cold War—the U.S. effort to contain communism within the Soviet Bloc—fed a "military-industrial-academic complex" that used scientific insights to develop equipment for national defense. The armed services pushed for federal sponsorship of laboratory research by government agencies, corporations, and universities.

Federal contracts for fighter planes, thermonuclear devices, chemical weapons, satellites, and moon rockets made technology into a major growth sector. Private industry also invested its own funds in R&D, contributing to the high-tech takeoff.

Many new consumer technologies originated in military research or benefited from its insights. Breakthroughs in electronics, metallurgy, petrochemicals, plastics, and physics had ramifications for better living. By the 1940s and 1950s, the consumer electronics sector was commercializing novelties like television and the transistor radio. Over the next half century, a flurry of spin-off products hit the market: the cassette tape player in the 1960s, the personal computer and portable CD player in the 1980s, and the DVD and iPod in the 1990s and 2000s. Chapter Nine considers how consumers used these technologies first as instruments of sociability and then as mechanisms for creating personal space.

As the population grew from 133 to 180 million between 1945 and 1960, the United States moved from being an *industrial* economy to being a *service* economy. Factories still employed millions, but the most promising jobs revolved around "brain work" rather than "hand work." Scientists and engineers comprised the new technocratic elite. Big businesses like General Motors and Dow Chemical Company hired layers of managers to devise strategy, supervise laboratory scientists, and handle customer relations. Thousands of other service jobs grew: salesmen in automobile and appliance showrooms, operators and repairmen at public utilities, tellers and bookkeepers in banks, programmers and data-entry clerks for computers, and account executives and graphic artists in advertising agencies. The year 1965 was a watershed: white-collar workers outnumbered blue-collar workers for the first time.

The GI Generation—people born in the interwar years who lived through World War II—invested in marriage and the nuclear family more than any generation before or since, becoming the most prolific newlyweds in history. The number of annual births climbed steadily, from 2.8 million in 1945 to 4.2 million in 1961, giving rise to the term "Baby Boom." Improved prenatal care, medicine, and nutrition meant that greater numbers of babies survived the traumas that had once led to high rates of infant and child mortality. Birth rates were highest among blue-collar and upper-class families, who particularly valued home, family, and community and who, for religious reasons, might have been less likely to use birth control.

In popular culture, the life of the white-collar man—the manager, engineer, accountant, or salesman in a large corporation—became a potent symbol of the status quo. Movies, television shows, and advertisements exploited his routine. Movies like *Mr. Blandings Builds His Dream House* (1948) and *How to Succeed in Business without Really Trying* (1967) satirized his conservative suit, daily commute on the train, and office politics. Squeaky-clean movies like Doris Day's *Please Don't Eat the Daisies* (1960) and happy-go-lucky sitcoms like *The Donna Reed Show* (1958–66) and *Father Knows Best* (1954–63) showed homemaking and nest-building as ideal female pursuits. Many advertisements in *Better Homes and Gardens*, the *Ladies' Home Journal, Life, Look,* and *Time* depicted a new age of innocence and celebrated motherhood, housekeeping, child rearing, and familial togetherness.

The mass-market wedding industry also encouraged this "homeward bound" direction. Starting in the 1920s, businesses identified brides-to-be as a market segment, but the lavish wedding ritual as we know it—with magazines like *Bride's*, the gift registry and the bridal shower, the white dress and the bridal salon, and the double-ring ceremony—first appeared in the 1930s and was more fully commercialized in the Boomer era. During the 1950s, various types of self-described bridal experts, such as jewelers, department stores, and publishers, invented the "traditional wedding" and connected it to the period's renewed emphasis on domesticity. Advertisers also encouraged single women to plan for their wifely futures, choosing their china pattern and investing in linens. One furniture maker, the Lane Company, built its reputation on the Hope Chest, a moth-proof cedar box for hopeful brides-to-be to store new tablecloths, towels, and sheets until they married and set up housekeeping.

GI families went on a high-tech shopping spree, splurging on Ranch Houses, Formica dinette sets, and big white GE refrigerators. The material culture of the 1950s and 1960s evolved a distinctive aesthetic that catered to the craving for "popular luxury." Consumer goods in the style called "populuxe" by journalist Thomas Hine included pink Buicks with tailfins and Magnavox TVs disguised as Early American furniture. Postwar designers saw populuxe as the embodiment of comfort and style, industrial might, and national achievement.

In the midst of this buying spree, *U.S. News and World Report* contemplated the prospects of continued growth. In 1957, this conservative business magazine described the annual "crop of 4 million babies" as "the customers of the future," who would be "in the market for goods and services over an average span of seventy years." While some critics warned that the population explosion would strain the world's resources and erode living standards, the editors saw the Baby Boom as a guarantee of endless prosperity. Agriculture and industry had a bright future, because Boomers would demand "clothing, furniture, appliances, automobiles, and everything else that goes to make up the high standard of American living." During their lifetimes, the millions of Americans born *in 1957 alone* would purchase more than 1 billion pairs of shoes, 6.3 million refrigerators, 62.8 million suits of clothes, and 10.8 million new cars!

Keeping *Away* from the Joneses

Some social critics sized up postwar affluence and saw a dark side to it. Harvard economist John Kenneth Galbraith chastised consumer society and wondered if so much stuff was really necessary. In a 1960 best seller, *The Waste Makers*, journalist Vance Packard examined Detroit's frequent model changes and populuxe features like tail fins, chrome trim, and pink paint. This type of "planned obsolescence," Packard famously wrote, added up to the egregious misapplication of manpower and materials. Books and movies like *The Man in the Grey Flannel Suit* (1956), *The Feminine Mystique* (1963), and *The Stepford Wives* (1972) contemplated the rat race, gender discrimination, and the mind-numbing monotony of suburbia.

Other observers marveled over the cultural creativity and countered that high mass consumption had *not* translated into profligacy or cookie-cutter behavior. Marketers were among the first to make the case for a rising tide of personalized taste, shifting away from the Modern "one best way." When experts had first codified data on consumers, Mrs. Consumer and then the Average American were the focal points, with other groups coming into the field of vision only on the periphery. In 1935, the NAACP's *Crisis* reported that Standard Oil of New Jersey, which ran Esso gas stations, was conducting "research and promotion work in the Negro market." Elsewhere, immigrant entrepreneurs served niche markets, their own ethnic groups. In 1936, Prudencio Unanue opened a food warehouse in lower Manhattan, sold ingredients for "authentic Spanish cuisine" to *bodegas*, and launched the company that would become Goya Foods. These efforts, however, were overshadowed by mainstream marketing ideas about the "mass market" and the "melting pot."

In Boomer America, a new group of corporate consultants started to imagine the consumer in ways that were more sensitive to human psychology, attuned to material culture, and aware of cultural diversity. Motivational research, a new discipline rooted in Freudian psychology, tried to learn exactly what people believed about certain types of products, why they bought them or why not, and how they felt about those purchases. Ernest Dichter, the leading expert in this field, believed that consumers valued the material world and affixed meanings to objects based on a variety of factors: private experiences, family traditions, peer-group pressure, neighborhood trends, workplace interactions, and popular culture.

In 1958, Dichter explained how major demographic shifts had already reshaped mainstream taste. No one could actually get inside the shopper's head, and consumers themselves sometimes couldn't articulate the reasons for their choices. But Dichter believed that the newly mobile "upper lower class"—factory workers with union wages, and countless clerks, salesmen, middle managers, and other people in white-collar jobs—had ushered in a new era. Unsure of their toehold on the ladder of acquisition, these people yearned to buy "not merely products but roots in the middle class." They shopped "not as members of the anonymous masses" but "as individual human beings" who *finally* had enough buying power to "follow their own tastes." "The American market," Dichter wrote in 1963, "relies more and more on psychological segmentations." While the Woolworth shawl woman could only long for a Tiffany brooch, and the envious Modern shopper could try to emulate Mrs. Vassar-Yale, this new consumer was far more self-confident in her social position, more comfortable with her tastes, and better able to buy.

People now identified less with their next-door neighbors, and more with their bowling club, favorite beat poet, or most admired recording artist. As shown in Chapters Seven and Eight, they turned look-alike suburban Ranch Houses into individualized homes and, rejecting the Victorian notion of clothing as a middle-class uniform, began to see casual style as a form of self expression. The "suits" who commuted into the city every day weren't necessarily conformist in their private lives. A fair number of men cast aside staid office attire for casual weekend wear, became the first readers of *Playboy,* and made Do-It-Yourself hobbies, from carpentry to consumer electronics, into a national pastime. Additionally, many wives broke the Donna Reed stay-at-home mold by taking jobs as typists, secretaries, teachers, salesgirls, and candy stripers. Gender biases kept many women in low-paying "pink-collar" jobs, but a few pioneers, like Tupperware vice president Brownie Wise, climbed the corporate ladder and in the process became role models.

Madison Avenue executive E. B. Weiss echoed Dichter when he called these trends the "rise of *independent* taste." A creative director at the Doyle Dane Bernbach agency and a columnist for *Advertising Age,* Weiss alerted fellow marketers to the vast "consumer rebellion against enforced conformity." The "new American consumer," he wrote in 1963, aspired "less to keep up *with* the Joneses" and "more to keep *away* from the Joneses."

Plastics Triumphant

Nothing embodied the populuxe style more than did plastic, a material developed by the Victorian inventor John Wesley Hyatt as a substitute for ivory. Plastics enjoyed popularity in early-twentieth-century consumer products like records, hair brushes, tobacco pipes, lampshades, radio cabinets, and cellophane. After World War II, a new family of plastics and a new fabrication technique called injection molding created unprecedented opportunities for industrial designers to create a slew of populuxe novelties. Commercial spaces and domestic interiors got a facelift, as store fixtures, office furniture, and consumer goods were recast in plastic. As testimony to the material's central place in Boomer culture, Benjamin Braddock, the main character in the 1967 movie *The Graduate*, was advised: "There's a great future in plastics."

Plastics replaced conventional materials, such as wood, metal, and glass, in everything from milk bottles to automobile bumpers. Consumers grew accustomed to eating from plastic plates, cups, and dishes, which didn't break when dropped, and to drinking takeout coffee from Styrofoam cups, which retained heat better than did paper cups. Saran Wrap, Tupperware food containers, and Ivory dish soap in squeezable polyethylene bottles became common in the kitchen. AT&T hired a professional colorist to update the telephone, which was previously cast in black resin, in fashion hues available in the new injection-molded plastics. Children's dolls and toy cars, once made from wood or metal, were created in colored plastic, eliminating the need for paint that could flake off. The 1957 Hula-Hoop craze taxed the capacity of the extrusion industry, speaking to plastic's popularity among kids. The roadside got a facelift when painted signs, which weathered poorly, were replaced with illuminated Plexiglas advertisements for gas stations, stores, and restaurants. Some plastic road signs became cultural icons: Texaco's Star of the American Road and, most famously, McDonald's Golden Arches.

Boomer plastics were made from resins derived from gas and oil feed stocks and owed much to the expanding petrochemical industry. Some plastics, such as Tupperware kitchen containers, were marketed as "investments" for the homemaker, treasures to be used again and again over the years, much like Victorian china, glass, and silverware. But for the most part, plastic's growing ubiquity and disposability introduced the idea that consumer goods—once valued as family keepsakes—could be discarded and replaced. In the years after World War II, people believed that oil resources were plentiful, along with spin-off products such as gasoline, plastic, and nylon fibers. Plastic thus made living more convenient, while laying the foundation of a throwaway culture.

Fallout of Affluence

In the 1970s and 1980s, America was jolted by the fallout from affluence, the rise of nonconformist values, and shifts in the political economy. Populuxe prosperity yielded to economic uncertainty, as the nation and the world realigned and set the stage for a new global order. The federal government initiated some of these changes, and grappled with the consequences.

America's role in the Allied victory in World War II engendered policymakers with heightened awareness of the United States as a bastion of freedom and opportunity. Democratic presidents Harry S. Truman, John F. Kennedy, and Lyndon Baines Johnson sustained the New Deal tradition, making the federal government an agent of reform. From Truman's desegregation of the military to Johnson's Great Society, this "New Deal order" extended equal rights and the promise of the American dream to unrepresented groups. Civil Rights legislation outlawed Jim Crow, opening the door of equality to African Americans. New immigration laws, implemented from the 1960s to the 1980s, reversed quotas and restrictions that had been put in place during Victorian and Modern times. Government initiatives both inspired and took their cues from grassroots movements and the individualist tide. Civil Rights activism, the black power movement, and the arrival of new ethnic groups encouraged other marginal factions, such as women, gays, and senior citizens, to celebrate their own uniqueness.

Federal spending and private investment fueled a major shift in economic geography, giving rise to the Sunbelt. Military procurement channeled a large percentage of federal research money into universities, think tanks, and high-tech industries in the South, the Southwest, and the Pacific Coast. Cities like Atlanta, Houston, and Phoenix became high-tech magnets. Companies in the military-industrial complex, from Boeing and Lockheed-Martin to Dow and DuPont, expanded production in California and Washington, Georgia and Texas. To stay competitive, other types of manufacturers, including textile mills, closed aging Smokestack plants and opened new Sunbelt facilities.

Government initiatives encouraged population shifts, changes in the commercial landscape, and new consumer experiences. The federal government built the interstate highways that made high-speed automobile travel possible, giving material expression to the five-lane roads dreamed about in the 1939 Futurama. Federal tax policies encouraged businesses to move out of older commercial centers to the suburbs, creating the strip malls, shopping centers, and office parks discussed in

Chapter Seven. While municipalities funded airport expansion, federal deregulation of the airline industry led to airfare price wars that turned jet travel from an occasional splurge into an everyday necessity. The salesman who took the train from Cleveland to Miami in 1960 now drastically cut his travel time by flying. People not only zipped around in their cars but started to feel at ease with jetting around.

The Sunbelt's rise cast a dark shadow over parts of the Northeast and Midwest, hastening the Rust Belt's deterioration—with some exceptions. To be sure, some older industries weathered the macroeconomic shifts of the 1970s and 1980s, and some reinvented themselves. New York's garment industry survived, emerged as a centerpiece of the city's creative industries, and retained its crown as a world leader in mass-market fashion. The chemical industry buckled under the oil crises of the 1970s, but it continued to grow afterwards. Electronic equipment and electronic materials, often associated with Silicon Valley, were also growth industries in the Northeast.

Suckled on affluence, many Boomers who came of age in the industrial heartland confronted a bleak job market. *Stagflation*, a macroeconomic term coined in 1960s Britain to describe a *stag*nant economy crippled by runaway in*flation*, paralyzed the United States from the Nixon years through the early Reagan years. Inflation that in part stemmed from the Vietnam War and two oil crises eroded spending power, while double-digit mortgage rates pushed home ownership beyond the reach of many. A great number of consumers had to rely on the new bank-issued credit cards like Visa and MasterCard to carry them from month to month. Just as the GI Generation had moved to the suburbs, many Boomers scattered across the land in search of opportunity, while those who stayed behind struggled to get by.

Rediscovering Diversity

By the 1970s, a new generation of corporate marketers, who had grown up keeping away from the Joneses, became frustrated with the touchy-feely nature of motivational research and conventional market surveys because neither captured the nuances of America's highly mobile, patchwork society. Some consultants started showing big business how to think "outside the box."

John H. Johnson, publisher of *Ebony* and *Jet*, shared his expertise on African Americans, while the lesser-known Cuban immigrants Alicia and Rafael Conill ran a New York advertising agency that advised Pepsi, Coca-Cola, Greyhound Lines, Scott Paper, and McDonald's on how to "Think Spanish!" In the 1970s, Conill Advertising helped Campbell's Soup develop Spanish-language television commercials that touted family values, wholesome ingredients, and supermarket visits as special events. Like earlier immigrants who loved the five-and-ten, Hispanic newcomers appreciated well-stocked supermarkets that symbolized their version of the American dream. Ethnic marketers explained these key points to corporate clients.

While this approach built on older ways of dividing consumers by sex, race, and income, a dramatic new methodology appeared with geodemographics, which used computers to probe the fractured marketplace. In the 1970s, a computer-whiz turned marketing entrepreneur, Jonathan Robbin, devised a popular "target-market" system that matched zip codes, census data, and survey research. Robbin's computer programs sorted the nation's 36,000 zip codes into forty "lifestyle clusters" to produce a detailed portrait of any given neighborhood in America. In effect, he meshed the national with the local. By the next decade, this "King of the Zip Codes" and his Claritas Corporation were helping clients like *Time*, General Motors, and American Express tailor their products and promotions to lifestyle clusters.

By the late 1980s, marketers readily acknowledged the diversity of preferences, which divided consumers into different lifestyle segments. "Anyone who's traveled this country outside its metropolitan sprawl," wrote lifestyle expert Michael J. Weiss in *The Clustering of America* (1988), would soon discover a nation "too full of local charms and contradictions to be reduced to a single pale village." That same year, Regis McKenna, chairman of a Palo Alto marketing company with high-tech clients, put it differently. "When we see wealthy people driving Volkswagens and pickup trucks, it becomes clear that this is a society where individual tastes are no longer predictable," he wrote in the *Harvard Business Review*. Marketers agreed on diversity, but disagreed as to whether or not differences could be anticipated, quantified, and measured.

The Global Village of Goods

The eruptions of the 1970s and 1980s, and the woes they brought to millions of ordinary Boomers, were signs of a worldwide transformation. These tremors forecasted an earthquake called "globalization," a change in production, distribution, and consumption that now inexorably links producers and consumers from Denver to Dubai.

Today, most scholars agree that multinational corporations, backed by powerful financial institutions, are the driving force behind the global economy: companies headquartered in Midland and Mumbai; stock markets in New York and Tokyo; and banks in Geneva and London. But looking back, a combination of private interests and public policy set the stage for globalization, making Toyota Corollas, Nokia cell phones, IKEA kitchens, and H&M kids' clothes into indispensable components in the consumer identity kit.

Transnational trade has existed for centuries, shaping the choices of colonial shoppers and, to some extent, their nineteenth-century descendants. Victorian-era protectionism kept out most imports, while World War I, the Great Depression, World War II, and reconstruction reduced trade to a trickle. The Arrow shirts and flappers' frocks of the twenties and the populuxe ensemble of the fifties were mostly homegrown, made in factories from New York to Chicago.

When Allied policymakers convened in 1944 to craft the postwar economy, they set the stage for global integration. Heeding the lessons of the interwar years, the architects of the postwar economy set up mechanisms to prevent history from repeating itself, guarding against another round of crippling reparations, another tariff war, and another collapse of trade. The Bretton Woods Agreement set up institutions to regulate the monetary system, including the World Bank and the International Monetary Fund. In several stages between 1947 and 1994, the General Agreement on Tariffs and Trade, a treaty born of Bretton Woods, opened trade between Europe, the Americas, and Asia. Its successor, the World Trade Organization, has crafted the terms for international commerce since 1995. Another treaty, the North American Free Trade Agreement, initiated in 1994, greatly eases trade between Mexico, Canada, and the United States. Even though some of the Bretton Woods initiatives didn't last, many of the fundamental principles underlying the original concepts of integration and cooperation have continued to frame globalization.

The architects of "free trade" extolled the likely benefits of global commerce to U.S. consumers. Speaking to the National Industrial Conference Board in 1968, one American executive explained how trade liberalization would work. "As tariffs are gradually lowered over the next five years, there will be greater opportunity and incentive for each country to transfer resources from less productive to more productive uses." Each nation would stick to its knitting, focusing on its strengths and expanding exports of those items. The end result would be "greater world specialization in production, greater efficiency, and a faster rise in world standards of living."

Globalization proved to be a doubled-edged sword, cutting the price of basic necessities while deepening the wounds of de-industrialization. Without a tariff wall, American factories, which paid the "living wage" or a higher union rate, were undercut by cheap imports. Goods once made in the Northeast, the Midwest, and then the South were manufactured overseas, first in Latin America and then in Asia. One by one, ready-to-wear, automobiles, and electronics buckled under competition from the Third World, where raw materials, wages, and overhead were low and government regulations nonexistent.

While imports devastated what was left of Smokestack America, the introduction of containerized shipping eliminated thousands of jobs on the docks. The giant "box boats" that docked at newly created deepwater ports like Long Beach, Miami, and Elizabeth were poignant symbols of change. In the 1954 film *On the Waterfront*, longshoreman Terry Malloy (Marlon Brando) takes on the union, only to get beaten up by the racketeers and see the necks of his beloved roof-top pigeons broken by street toughs. The high wages, the long hours spent unpacking and repacking barrels, and the rampant corruption of the industry explains why the mechanized "container revolution," launched two years later, caught on. The box-boat modular system replaced longshoremen with computerized cranes that lifted standardized containers from ship to tractor-trailer in a matter of minutes. By the new century, dockworkers like Malloy were a thing of the past; "crate and barrel" no longer meant merchandise on the docks, but was the name of a big-box retailer of imported, inexpensive—and readily replaceable—home goods.

In 2005, much of the merchandise sold by major retailers like Wal★Mart, Sears, and Macy's was made in Southeast Asia, China, or Eastern Europe. American companies provided much of the brainwork that went into product design, development, and packaging, while the muscle and some of the raw materials were supplied by the developing country. The end result was a Sony HDTV bearing a Japanese brand name, made from components designed by U.S. engineers, assembled by Asian workers, packaged in biodegradable recycled plastics, and transported to a California port by Danish containerships. In contrast, the black-and-white Magnavox television watched by Boomers in 1955 originated almost entirely in the United States.

Brands as Experience

Globalization altered the consumer identity kit in other significant ways, encouraging a shift from collecting "hard goods" to enjoying "experiences" that began with dance halls and nickelodeons, magazines and movies, and records and radio. In 2005, students shopping for clothes were just as likely to visit H&M, a Swedish store, or The Gap, an American chain. In either place, they shopped in an "experiential" environment and bought a new type of product: the global brand.

Brands emerged more than a hundred years ago, but in Boomer America a new way of branding superseded cuddly icons like the Michelin Man (tires) and Buster Brown (shoes). Madison Avenue promoted the idea that a company, rather than a product, should have an identity, much like General Motors, the good neighbor, or DuPont, the gentle science giant. This identity would "humanize" the firm and build goodwill, which in turn would build "brand equity" and sales. Firms like Coke, Pepsi, McDonald's, Burger King, and especially Disney, understood this concept early on, becoming "pals" with the customers who bought soft drinks, cheeseburgers, and the family-friendly world of make-believe.

Companies like Benetton and Calvin Klein, IKEA and The Body Shop, The Gap, and Starbucks gave a big boost to image branding.

Like Disney, these firms created "experiences" around themselves and their products. Calvin Klein didn't really sell jeans, underwear, or perfume; his gigantic billboards sold the alluring presence of Brooke Shields, Kate Moss, Mark Wahlberg, and Kristy Turlington with sexy taglines like, "You know what comes between me and my Calvins? Nothing." Retailers like The Body Shop, The Gap, Banana Republic, and Benetton immersed consumers in a total retail environment. Shopping at their stores was all about experiencing the brand.

For example, Starbucks became a grand master of the brand, transcending the ambíance of the hole-in-the-wall coffee shop and replacing it with a hip destination. Starbucks stores didn't look like retail stores, but like cozy cafes filled with books, soothing-yet-stimulating music, wall art, and Mission furniture. Starbucks made an impact on the culture as a whole, creating what its managers called a "third space," or a space that was neither home nor work. People didn't line up just to buy their coffee, but to buy a Kenyan latte with soymilk and a shot of sugar-free hazelnut syrup, and to sip this concoction while listening to electro-Brazilian pop chanteuse CéU in a comfy chair.

Master branders like Starbucks took lifestyle marketing to new limits. They not only wrapped the product in an idea, but they also wrapped themselves in an idea, and sold the whole kit and caboodle, along with a virtual airline ticket to a faraway place, to consumers looking for something beyond the humdrum. People hurrying to work got coffee and donuts at Dunkin' Donuts which offered speedy service and mild shot of caffeine. The modern multitasker surfed the web and talked on his cell phone, while sipping that "skinny" latte at Starbucks, part of the hip, urban atmosphere of Portland, Oregon, or Paris, France.

The New Mainstream

By 2005, a new consumer had emerged, a worldly shopper with omnivorous tastes and habits. To varying degrees, the GI Generation, Baby Boomers, Generation X, and Generation Y had lived with decades of multiculturalism, networking technologies, and globalization. These trends brought people closer together, while teaching them to accept difference as a reality.

As the U.S. population went from 200 to 300 million between 1970 and 2006, the middle class swelled with newcomers: African Americans, Latinos, Asians, gays, singles, and senior citizens. Most people recognized that America wasn't a "melting pot" but a "salad bowl" of gigantic proportions. Although Boomers grew up with people like themselves, their children—Gen X and Gen Y—were likely to have gone to grade school with kids from different races, ethnic groups, or countries. By the time multiracial actress Halle Berry won her Oscar in 2002, salsa was the new ketchup, and there was nothing exotic about hip-hop culture, Latin music, or country and western.

In the millennial marketplace, the factors that earlier marketers thought were important—gender, social class, "race," and income—now mattered less than how different tastes fused into the eclectic mix that anthropologists called "bricolage." This expression comes from the French verb *bricoler*, which means to fiddle, tinker, or make creative use of the materials at hand. American consumers have always mixed and matched different styles, artifacts, and influences to create their own personal looks. By the New Millennium, however, this decades-old practice was shaping the design, marketing, and branding functions at *Fortune* 500 global corporations like Nike, Ford, and Apple.

Journalist Guy Garcia, an astute observer of contemporary culture, has predicted that the twenty-first-century American marketplace will be dominated by the multicultural, multiethnic consumer. That speculation, which seems intuitively correct, is nonetheless a conjecture, particularly because Garcia's analysis focuses on how households have changed as a result of ethnic stimuli but not from a demographic perspective.

In 2000, the U.S. Census reported a demographic trend that startled marketers and has kept them talking ever since. The primary household unit in America was the single person, followed by the two-adult household. Single people included older widows, gays, and singles by choice. The two-adult household included empty nesters, the childfree by choice, those delaying having children, and gay couples. The traditional family with two parents and children was now a distant third. If a real-life *Leave It to Beaver* family had ever existed, its majority was gone by the New Millennium.

•••

This book has shown that broad patterns of historical change occur as consumers, institutions, and governments haggled over their best interests and that innovation came from unexpected places. The consumer history of the past hundred years, from the strivers who wanted to keep up with the Joneses in the 1910s to the individual-ists who ran away from the Joneses in the 1950s, highlights cultural tendencies that may play out as Garcia suggests, or may play out in very different ways. The historian has a clouded crystal ball and is far from an adept futurist.

Nevertheless, the bricolage effect that characterized Garcia's new mainstream culture had deep historical roots, beginning when the first Woolworth's shawl woman bought something pretty to decorate her parlor. It bloomed more fully when blue collarites new to the middle class insisted on bringing flashy Cadillacs and Early American furni-ture to the postwar suburbs. They initiated a tidal wave of bricolage that swept across Boomer America, playing out in Ranch Homes and Edge Cities, in casual fashion choices, and in consumer electronics.

CHAPTER SEVEN

Destination Suburbia

The 1947 film *Miracle on 34th Street*, a poignant story about a little girl who didn't believe in Santa Claus, is a perennial Christmas favorite on cable TV. The film tells the story of nine-year-old Susan Walker, whose mother Doris works as the public-relations director for R. H. Macy & Company's flagship store in New York City. This divorced working mom has raised her daughter to be skeptical of Santa's promises to provide for her material well-being. The story pivots on the realization that the hired Macy's Santa is the real Kris Kringle who lives in the North Pole. In the end, Susan tells Santa that she wants to live in a house rather than a small New York apartment. The girl gets her wish when her mother marries Fred Gailey, the lawyer next door, and the family moves into a modest house in the suburbs.

Miracle on 34th Street showcases important themes in the postwar consumer culture: the department store as a major commercial destination, suburbia as the ideal place to live, and shopping as the means to wish fulfillment. When *Miracle* ran in theaters, the nation had endured the Great Depression, World War II, the reconversion to the civilian economy, which brought skyrocketing prices. During the war, department stores like Macy's had prospered, providing a glimpse of the good life to consumers tired of rationing, recycling, and worn-out cars and appliances. A small family like the Walkers had to live on a budget, accustomed to want. Their remarkable postwar transformation—from skeptics to believers, frugal to free-wheeling, apartment dwellers to suburbanites—epitomized the hopes of countless consumers. The Modern ambition had been to democratize consumption, but troubles had derailed that agenda. In the late 1940s and 1950s, "normalcy" resumed in fits and starts, ultimately achieving the comfort and convenience revolution ignited in Victorian and Modern times.

America Moves from City to Suburb

In the postwar decade, suburbia—developments on the outskirts of large cities or towns—became the principal site of American consumption, the place where the majority of young families lived, worked, played, and shopped. Earlier flights from the inner city outward paled by comparison to the post–World War II migration, and the Boomer era's love of shopping and driving made Victorian collecting and the Modern auto age look quaint. Between 1946 and 1970, the national output of goods and services quadrupled, and a vast majority of American consumers enjoyed comforts unparalleled anywhere in the world.

Suburbanization owed much to changes in the political economy, buoyed by federal initiatives that put full employment and mass consumption at the center of national growth. Millions of new houses were needed for returning soldiers—nicknamed GIs during the war after their "government issue" uniforms—and their young families. Federal aid to mass consumption came in many forms, but one of the most important was the low-interest government-insured mortgage.

During the twentieth century, financing still presented problems for aspiring homeowners, as mortgages required hefty down payments and rigid payback schedules. According to the U.S. Department of Housing and Urban Development, only 40 percent of householders had owned their homes in 1934. The banking crisis of the Great Depression worsened this situation. Most home loans were short-term balloon mortgages; the borrower needed a large down payment and had to pay back the balance in a lump sum after three to fifteen years. Factory workers, drought-plagued farmers, and white-collars clerks couldn't meet their obligations and tried to renew their mortgages, but the instability of the banking system worked against them. Cash-strapped lenders called in mortgages when they were due, and borrowers couldn't find new loans, so banks foreclosed on the property. John Steinbeck's 1939 novel, *The Grapes of Wrath*, winner of the Pulitzer and Nobel Prizes, portrays the way foreclosures affected ordinary Americans. After drought and dust storms destroy the crops, Tom Joad's family defaults on their mortgage, and the bank repossesses the farm, forcing them to leave Oklahoma for California.

In 1934, the New Deal created the National Housing Act, which encouraged residential construction, promoted housing standards, and laid the foundation for a solid mortgage system. Its Federal Housing Administration (FHA) insured mortgages issued by private institutions, creating a safety net for lenders and buyers. In 1944, the last piece of New Deal legislation, the Servicemen's Readjustment Act, popularly known as the "GI Bill of Rights," awarded substantial benefits to World War II combat veterans, who most often came from working-class backgrounds. The Veterans Administration (VA), which oversaw the implementation of the bill, provided returning soldiers with hospital care, living allowances, college tuition, and low-interest FHA mortgages. Similar veterans' benefits were awarded to Korean War veterans beginning in 1952; to Vietnam vets in 1966.

The GI Bill's mortgage provision backed nearly 2.4 million home loans between 1944 and 1952. Eligible veterans received a low-interest, 30-year loan with no down payment. While the VA tended to veterans, the FHA extended its reach to ever more homeowners in the 1960s, 1970s, and 1980s. The FHA and the GI Bill, combined with the more recent liberalization of qualification requirements by private lenders, increased the national home ownership rate to 62 percent in 1960 and to almost 69 percent in 2005.

The sudden availability of mortgages put home ownership—the ultimate symbol of middle-class status—within the grasp of millions. The expansion of consumer credit also fueled the purchase of automobiles and appliances. Between 1941 and 1961, the annual consumer expenditure for housing and automobiles tripled, growing from $713 to $2,513 per household. Much, but not all, of this money was spent in the suburbs, where investor-builders like William J. Levitt put up expansive new developments that housed thousands of young families.

"We Got a Piece of the American Dream": Levittown, New York

In early 1947, the construction firm of Levitt & Sons—a family business run by William J. Levitt, his brother Alfred, and father Abraham—broke ground for a suburban development in Nassau County, Long Island. Built on former potato fields, Levittown lay just outside of Hempstead, a commercial center that had branches of major department stores, and Minneola, the county seat. An army air base and several defense plants were close by. Within commuting distance of Manhattan by train and an easy drive to defense jobs, Levittown became a magnet for returning GIs who wanted affordable, family-friendly housing. Before the war, these folks had rented apartments in or near the cities. Levittown provided them with entry into the middle class; home ownership signaled that they were achieving the American dream.

During World War II, William J. Levitt had built emergency housing—tiny, four-room concrete buildings—for defense workers in Norfolk, Virginia, while his brother Alfred had learned speedy construction techniques working for the Navy Seabees. Later, the firm's three Levittowns—one on Long Island, a second north of Philadelphia near a U.S. Steel plant, and a third in Willingboro, New Jersey—and its lesser-known developments used many of the low-cost techniques perfected for defense housing. Created from prefabricated materials, Levitt houses delivered on the assurances of the 1939 World's Fair, where the "Home of Tomorrow" had promised affordable dwellings to nearly everyone. Levitt & Sons, nicknamed the "General Motors of the housing industry" by *Time* in July 1950, was one of the home builders that made the Everyman's House a reality.

Levittown began as a rental community for the families of young veterans, and the first house designs—Cape Cod models—embodied Alfred Levitt's ideas for basic shelter. These 800-square-foot starter homes were modeled after turn-of-the-century bungalows, but the name Cape Cod implied New England and Yankee origins. Each house had four main rooms—a kitchen, a living room, and two bedrooms—plus a full bathroom, kitchen appliances, a paved driveway, and a lawn. The floor plan reduced the standard middle-class home to a minimalist state. The Cape Cod was a training ground for lower-income people who were just entering the middle class. Levittown's spacious green lawns and curvilinear streets, mandated by the FHA for federally subsidized developments, offered inhabitants a pleasant respite from the pavement and noise of the city.

Levitt & Sons, like other developers, didn't stay landlords for long. When Congress extended rent control—one of President Truman's Fair Deal measures designed to combat postwar inflation—developers divested themselves of rental properties. In 1947, Levitt & Sons put each of its 6,000 Cape Cod houses on the market for $7,600, targeting buyers who earned up to $3,750 and qualified for FHA financing under the GI Bill.

That same year, Levitt & Sons launched an ambitious plan to build more owner-occupied homes, using Alfred's designs for the Ranch House. Slightly larger than the Cape Cod, the Ranch had four main rooms—a kitchen, a living room, and two bedrooms—plus a bathroom, and two new features: an attic and a covered carport. The carport, an incipient garage, was a distinctively male space, a corollary to the frilly, feminized domestic interior. Men used these covered areas for their automobile repairs and carpentry projects. Finished in 1951, Levittown had 17,500 four-room houses, seven shopping areas, nine swimming pools, and a community hall.

Levittown was America's most famous blue-collar suburb, but it wasn't the only one. Park Forest, Illinois, and Lakewood, California, housed 30,000 and 80,000 people, respectively. Park Forest combined multifamily structures, duplexes, and single-family homes, arranged in courtyards off curved streets. Just outside Los Angeles, Lakewood was laid out on a grid plan, lined by lots of 50 by 100 feet, each of which held an 1,100-square-foot stucco house. From New Jersey to California, GI Towns appeared where there had once been apple orchards and cattle ranches.

Many residents of these subdivisions were first-time home owners, and very few of them knew how to be suburban. As blue-collar consumers grew comfortable in places like Levittown, many realized that prefabricated Capes and Ranches didn't really fit their lifestyles. Among immigrant groups, the large, welcoming kitchen had always been the center of family life, the hearth and heart of the home. The family gathered around the kitchen table, sharing news and food. In Levittown's Cape Cods, the living room was the designated center of activity, following the model of the middle-class parlor. By the late 1950s, people began to modify the layouts of their homes, adjusting the standardized floor plans to fit their social needs and aesthetic tastes. People added dens, covered their carports and made them into extra bedrooms, and planted trees and shrubs. The impulse to personalize the prefabricated designs fed a Do-It-Yourself fad, sowing the seeds for Home Depot and Lowe's. The "cookie-cutter suburb" became instead a *tabula rasa* on which consumers chose to write their own cultural history.

GI Towns weren't the only housing options available after World War II. Before the Civil Rights era, many blacks were prohibited from moving into the new suburbs by the FHA, which, unfortunately, supported racial covenants that banned racially mixed communities. They were forced to stay in urban areas, while a fair number of young blue-collar couples chose to remain in cities all across the nation. In 1950s Baltimore, die-hard city dwellers remained committed to the old ethnic communities that clustered around churches, social clubs, and taverns, arguing that they were more convenient and friendly than the suburbs. Many invested in the old neighborhoods, proudly scrubbing their white marble steps spotless, updating rowhouse façades with Formstone, and renovating basements into "club cellars," the urban equivalent of a den or recreation room. Within greater Baltimore, conflict arose over which lifestyle was superior, and the lawn became either a symbol of success or a point of defiance. In 1973, city dweller Barbara Mikulski lamented to a *Baltimore Sun* reporter: "It became a status thing to get enough money to move 'out the road' to those three inches of grass." Mikulski decided to stay behind. Many urbanites preferred the pavement and declared war on grass, as did the man who in 1968 covered the "yard" in front of his house with green concrete.

For many people, however, the suburbs seemed like an improvement over decrepit urban neighborhoods, depression scarcities, and wartime overcrowding. People didn't have to endure their neighbors' arguments through common walls, sweep the sidewalks and streets because of a lack of city services, or worry about encroaching crime. They relished the higher standard of living, exemplified by the open air, green grass, and detached houses. One Levitt–home owner, interviewed by historian Barbara M. Kelly in 1988, put it plainly. "The war was over, and we were living in one room in my parents' apartment ... with *two* children.... Then, Mr. Levitt turned all these little potato farms into Levittown, and we got a piece of the American Dream.... It was—at least to us—a Paradise."

Blue-Collar Aesthetics, Appliances, and Automobiles

Today, consumers take the accessories of "better living" for granted: single-family homes, lawns and decks, new cars, and glistening appliances. Postwar Americans saw colorful refrigerators, barbeque grills, and two-toned cars with chrome fins as emblems of the good life—artifacts to be valued much as the Victorians treasured their parlors and china cabinets.

Nothing more famously summarizes America's fascination with these new durable goods than the "kitchen debate" between Vice President Richard M. Nixon and Soviet Premier Nikita S. Khrushchev, which took place at the American National Exhibition in Moscow in July 1959. Two years before, in October 1957, the Russians had launched *Sputnik*, the world's first manmade satellite, and earlier in 1959, had mounted an exhibit of Soviet achievements in New York City. At the apex of the Cold War, the U.S. government was determined not to be outdone. The U.S. Information Agency, the State Department's propaganda arm, mounted a $5 million display in Moscow, showing the products of 800 companies. The exhibit included "Split-nik," a $14,000 luxury Ranch House furnished with $5,000 in the latest high-tech gear, including a built-in clothes washer, a color television, and a Do-It-Yourself workshop. Nixon and Khrushchev toured the show and bantered about the standard of living in their two countries. Nixon boasted that Split-nik, outfitted with electric appliances, demonstrated the superior lifestyle enjoyed by average Americans.

Kitchen appliances were among the most coveted of consumer goods, must-haves for every postwar family's identity kit. In 1930, only 8 percent of U.S. households had refrigerators; by 1960, that number had skyrocketed to 90 percent. Similarly, households with washing machines increased from 24 to 73 percent; and vacuums, from 30 to 73 percent.

While Nixon and Khrushchev debated living standards, tastemakers and consumers negotiated the *style* of kitchen appliances. Blue-collar Americans new to the middle class craved designs that proved they had arrived. Rather than simply emulate their upscale neighbors, they shopped for appliances that fit *their* ideal definition of what it meant to be successful. They wanted refrigerators, stoves, and kitchen cabinets that looked big, powerful, and flashy. Their purchasing power was so great that it redefined "average" taste.

This "more is better" aesthetic extended to other consumer goods. Whether in Levittown or Baltimore, young families needed furniture, carpets, drapes, swing sets, and a multitude of other items. In home furnishings, the wives of professors, attorneys, and physicians gobbled up imported Danish Modern furniture, which embodied high-style simplicity. But in GI Towns and the old urban neighborhoods, blue-collar consumers preferred Early American furniture, along with linoleum flooring, braided rugs, and frilly café curtains. The names Early American and Colonial not only suggested the values of freedom and patriotism that GIs had defended during the war, but the furniture's bulbous wooden forms and overstuffed cushions delivered the abundance that blue-collar consumers wanted: more bang for the buck.

While women took pride in their appliances, men indulged their consumer desires and demonstrated their prowess with their cars. In January 1959, George Walker, vice president in charge of styling at Ford, elaborated on masculine desires in *Popular Mechanics*. "The American public is aggressive, it's moving upward all the time . . . and that means bigness. When the American workingman gets a little money he wants a bigger house and he wants a bigger car." Annual automobile purchases increased from 70,000 vehicles in 1945 to 10 million in 1973. Consumers doubled their expenditures on automobiles—loan payments, gasoline, oil, tires, and regular maintenance—to $60 billion per year, which amounted to about 10 percent of the GNP.

Detroit's design rivalries reached a feverish pitch. With a 94 percent market share, the Big Three automakers—General Motors, Ford, and Chrysler—poured resources into their styling divisions, giving designers free rein. Auto designers created "dream machines" that fed consumer fantasies of luxury and power. For the populuxe market, they introduced models with more horsepower, longer wheelbases, and flashier accessories. These designs insulated the driver from the sensations of the newly built interstates, allowing men to imagine themselves as fighter pilots soaring through the wild blue yonder. In pursuit of the American dream, blue-collar car owners coveted all the comforts and accessories that had once been the exclusive prerogative of the rich. The two-tone Chevy with a car radio, glittery upholstery, and wide girth symbolized that a factory worker was successful.

By the 1960s, the automotive market changed again as Baby Boomers came of age and the two-car family emerged. In 1950, only 7 percent of American households owned more than one car. By 1960, the number had grown to 15 percent; by 1970, to 29 percent. While the primary car was an all-purpose vehicle that showed the family's place in the world, the second car fit the needs of the driver. Station wagons, the forerunner to the soccer mom's minivan, were created for suburban mothers to haul children and groceries around.

As the early Boomers matured, Detroit introduced the first vehicles designed around youthful exuberance and rebelliousness. GM's 1964 Pontiac GTO sports coupe imitated the hot rod, a blue-collar favorite since the 1940s. The 1965 Ford Mustang targeted the growing market segment of 16- to 24-year olds, who were young, style-conscious, and had spending money. The car's rugged good looks meshed Western cowboy styles with the populuxe preference for bold, flashy designs. By the 1960s, blue-collar aesthetics had become synonymous with the mainstream, and manufacturers had to keep up.

Mall Culture

The shopping mall was a new commercial community created around suburbia, climate control, and automobility. Businesses experimented with new types of retail spaces, and the ones that met with public approval became models for further development. The result was the great commercial shift of retailing from the city to the suburbs, and the rise of the regional shopping mall as the new palace of consumption.

In 1950, retailing was still located in the center of the city or town, with smaller commercial strips in outlying neighborhoods. By the time British pop star Petula Clark's "Downtown" was released as a record in the United States in 1965, most Americans had turned their backs on city centers. While a sufficient number of Americans loved downtown enough to make Clark's tune into a Top Forty hit, many shoppers believed that "the lights" were "much brighter" in suburban malls.

The shift from urban to suburban shopping began before World War II, but the change was most dramatic in the postwar years. Early *strip malls* appeared on busy suburban roads along with car dealerships, diners, bowling alleys, furniture stores, and low-end department stores. At these open-air centers, consumers walked from their cars to stores connected by a sidewalk and a canopy. Strip malls paid little attention to consumers' comfort apart from their need to hunt for a parking space.

Next came the *shopping mall*, a self-contained, inward-looking, pedestrian-friendly space. The layout of the first of these new malls, including Shopper's World in Framingham outside of Boston, emulated the colonial village green, suggesting an alternative to crowded downtowns and unsightly commercial strips. But the weather remained an issue. As they darted from store to store, shoppers still sweltered in the summer, got wet in the rain, and, in places like Massachusetts, shivered in the winter.

Substantial changes came with the introduction of the *regional shopping mall*, introduced in 1956 and dominant by the 1970s. Architect Victor Gruen, the "father of the shopping mall," designed these commercial spaces as completely self-contained environments. His first enclosed mall, the Southdale Shopping Center in Edina, Minnesota, offered ample parking and was disconnected from the highway. Its large blocky buildings with plain facades looked like a cohesive whole only from the air. Automobile use determined the size, layout, and placement of the stores. Gruen had to provide easy access from everywhere in the parking lot, with the aim of ushering consumers into the temperature-controlled environment as quickly as possible.

The regional shopping mall became one of the most familiar types of retailing space in America. A typical regional mall housed a hierarchy of stores. National powerhouses like J. C. Penney's and Sears, Roebuck and Company, or regional department stores like Dayton's, the Minneapolis retailer that built Southdale, were dubbed "anchors," while chains of specialty stores, movie theaters, restaurants, and food courts composed the rest of the retail businesses one could find under the same roof. Opening and closing at designated hours, the regional shopping mall was clean, well-lighted, and climate-controlled.

Finally, the most impressive retailing space was the *super-regional shopping mall*. By 2005, the largest of these American shopping destinations—the King of Prussia Mall west of Philadelphia (1962) and the Mall of America outside of Minneapolis–St. Paul (1995)—were national tourist attractions and models for mega-malls in Europe and Asia. Both comprised several major department stores and hundreds of chain stores, luxury boutiques, and restaurants. The Mall of America has family-friendly amenities, including a seven-acre amusement park.

Suburban shopping centers and malls developed in response to the declining fortunes of the central business district and the cultural desire for better living. By the 1950s, the great downtown department stores, from John Wanamaker's to Marshall Field's, faced rapidly declining profits. Suburban strips were stealing customers from these palatial stores, whose emphasis on customer service, quality, and high style seemed outmoded. Postwar consumers—young families in the new suburbs, older folks who wanted to spruce up their surroundings, and people getting by on tight budgets—valued low prices, self service, and locations accessible by car. They also appreciated shopping in an environment free from the crime and dirt of decaying inner cities.

Another important development at the low end of this market was the discount store, a large self-service merchandiser that resembled a variety chain on steroids. Frank Woolworth had created the dime store for blue-collar shoppers, but suburbanization and deindustrialization eroded this customer base in older sections of the country. Signs of change first appeared in New England, where mill closings depressed the economy and killed the old downtowns. In the 1950s, discount chains such as Ann and Hope, Turnstyle, Marshall's, Zayre, and Ames moved into old factories or built stores on the outskirts, luring those Woolworth shoppers who had cars. These "soft goods supermarkets" provided free parking, familiar dime-store amenities such as lunch counters, and a wide selection of everyday necessities at rock-bottom prices. By 1962, discount retailing was a $4.25 billion business with 1,500 stores; fourteen top chains led the pack with $1 billion in sales.

Among those 1,500 stores were the brand-new Kmart, Wal★Mart, and Target, destined to become the three dominant merchants in the discount market. S. S. Kresge Company, a five-and-ten based in Detroit, opened eighteen Kmarts on commercial strips in 1962. Kmart targeted blue-collar shoppers but offered more merchandise, supermarket-style checkouts, and free parking. In the same year, Arkansas entrepreneur Sam Walton launched a discount chain for Southern tastes: Wal★Mart Discount City. The maverick among these discount babies was Target, founded by the family who ran Dayton's, a luxury department store in Minneapolis. Building on this heritage, Target, also established in 1962, positioned itself as an upscale discounter.

Back in 1937, New Deal fair-trade laws had mandated that retailers sell trademarked or branded items at prices set by the manufacturer. These fair trade laws had been created to protect small retailers against early chain stores. By the 1950s, however, discount stores were blatantly ignoring the fair trade laws to undersell the competition. Shoppers voted for lower prices when they deserted traditional retailers and patronized discounters that sold nationally advertised brands or private labels for less. Consumers who once strolled down Main Street to browse through the department stores, five-and-tens, and appliance shops began driving to Wal★Mart to fill up their shopping carts.

Department stores, which had competed on service and style, were decimated as their profit margins sank to levels below those of the Great Depression. Many wrestled with their declining fortunes by following the money to the suburbs where they helped build regional malls. A department store like Strawbridge & Clothier, a major Philadelphia retailer, could collaborate with an architect like Victor Gruen and a developer like James Rouse to create a total commercial environment such as Cherry Hill Mall in New Jersey. Professional mall managers determined which tenants were "in" and which were "out." This tactic allowed the anchor to design a sales mix that complemented its stock and attracted consumers from certain socioeconomic groups.

Because operating costs—taxes, wages, and utilities—were lower outside the city, the mall kept longer hours than did center-city stores, making evenings and weekends into important shopping times.

Although enclosed malls have never comprised more than 5 percent of the total number of shopping destinations, their enormous popularity has made them into cultural icons. By the 1980s, the regional mall was the major hangout spot for teenagers, replacing the dance hall, bowling alley, and hamburger joint as the leisure destination of choice. The 1983 movie *Valley Girl* shows the stereotypical Southern California blonde, Julie Richman, frequenting the local San Fernando galleria with her girlfriends. The girls enjoyed themselves in the mall, shopping at "the really great shoe stores" and boutiques for "the neatest mini-skirts" and, of course, meeting boys

In 2005, the International Council of Shopping Centers, a trade association for all types of malls, published statistics on the growth of suburban retailing. In 1945, the United States had a few hundred shopping centers; by 1963, the number had grown to 7,100. In 1980, there were 22,000. By 2005, the United States had 49,000 shopping centers, which attracted 191 million adults—nearly two-thirds of the population—each month!

Making Ends Meet

By the late 1960s, major weaknesses in the political economy, especially overspending for the Great Society and the Vietnam War, produced a recession that suggested calamity lay ahead. In the next two decades, Baby Boomers in their twenties and thirties, who had rarely known hardship, suddenly confronted harsh economic realities: oil and gasoline shortages, job losses and a high rate of unemployment, dislocation, and stagflation. For the first time, Boomers had to watch their wallets and pocketbooks, pinching pennies as had their grandparents in the Great Depression.

This economic stress, combined with the value shifts of the 1960s, led Americans to think about goods less as identity markers and more as commodities. The important props of the postwar suburbs—Frigidaire refrigerators, Wonder Bread, Wash-and-Wear clothes, and Chevy convertibles—lost a good deal of their appeal. The GI Generation had valued their stoves and station wagons, much as the physician or engineer of the 1920s took pride in his Oakland sedan; but for Baby Boomers in the 1970s, appliances and automobiles were no longer novel. Newcomers to abundance, such as recent immigrants or poor Americans, may have thrilled in owning a washer-dryer, but for consumers who grew up in GI Towns, swooning over a stove was merely comedic material for cartoons, sitcoms, and commercials. In the 1970s, the 25-year-old Boomer, who spent her girlhood in Levittown, focused less on accumulation and more on making ends meet.

This psychic shift pushed appliances and automobiles into another stage in the product life cycle. By the 1970s, consumers saw cars as commodities, possessions that every American expected to have. The simplified designs of the era reflected these utilitarian values. In 1971, the *Wall Street Journal* summarized the new attitude, which eerily harked back to the days of the Model T. "Where once they viewed their cars as fun and something special to own, they currently are frustrated or bored with their cars," the *Journal* explained. "The novelty and status of car ownership are long gone. So they look at their auto as an appliance—to get them economically from place to place and to be replaced when it wears out."

Edge Cities and Big-Box Retailers

In the 1970s and 1980s, suburbia entered another stage in its evolution, paralleling the movement of industry and commerce. As businesses migrated to even more remote locales, the suburb, once a bedroom community, morphed into a new type of city in its own right. Shopping malls drew department stores, while colleges, universities, and hospitals established suburban branches. People now lived and died in these new landscapes, in oversized luxury homes called McMansions and rowhouses reinvented as townhomes. Historian Robert Fishman called these places "techno-burbs," while the *Washington Post*'s Joel Garreau coined the memorable term "Edge Cities."

The Edge City originated in the postwar boom, when the real-estate industry recognized that commercial development could provide extraordinary investment returns. In the 1954 Internal Revenue Code, Congress introduced "accelerated depreciation," an antirecession move to stimulate speculative building. Real-estate developers had a field day, putting up buildings along strips quickly and cheaply. Small roadside businesses, such as motels and diners, yielded to chains and franchises that could take advantage of the tax write-offs: Holiday Inn, McDonald's, and, eventually, discounters like Kmart and Wal★Mart. The bonanza lasted for more than thirty years, until Ronald Reagan's Tax Reform Act of 1986 ended the spree. Meanwhile, commercial strips had cropped up on the far outskirts of major cities, creating offices and stores for suburbanites who never, ever ventured into the center city. The new downtowns included Tyson's Corner, Virginia; Scottsdale, Arizona; and San Jose, California, to name a few. Americans no longer commuted from suburb to city, but used the beltways and highways to zip around the periphery, from node to node.

Urban retailing buckled under the pressure. Geared to middle- and upper-class shoppers, downtown department stores watched the last of their traditional customers disappear and their fortunes decline. Discounters like Kmart did well because their cut-rate prices and no-frills merchandising appealed to consumers forced into frugality. After 1975, discounters blossomed, benefiting from the Consumer Goods Pricing Act, which repealed the New Deal fair-trade laws. "The best way to ensure that consumers are paying the most reasonable price for consumer products," President Gerald R. Ford explained after signing the law, "is to restore competition in the marketplace."

The balance of power in retailing shifted to big suburban discounters. Smaller family-owned retailers that prided themselves in personalized service shut their doors, unable to compete with these large warehouse stores. In discount stores, colorful packages replaced human beings who had once advised customers on their purchases. The discounter's stock-in-trade consisted of national brands, which manufacturers promoted through aggressive television and magazine advertising. Cost-cutting measures included computer-controlled inventory, active supply-chain management, bulk deals with manufacturers, part-time labor without benefits, and a heavy reliance on cheap imports.

Bitten by stagflation, many middle-class Americans could no longer afford to shop at Sears or Macy's for their needs. Like blue-collar shoppers, they got in their cars and drove to discount stores, where everything seemed to be a few pennies cheaper. Kmart became famous for its "blue-light specials," markdowns for budget-conscious shoppers. The "bigger bang for your buck" theme took on new meaning as the dollar weakened. Average Americans shopped, not for flashy luxuries, but for deals on toothpaste, T-shirts, and toys.

In the long run, discount stores like Kmart, Wal★Mart, and Target changed the way consumers shopped through the relentless pursuit of standardization and endless cost reductions. Kmart's story illustrates the consolidation that changed the face of retailing over the past four decades. In 1966, Kresge's sales topped $1 billion for the first time. By 1977, however, Kresge had changed its name to Kmart to reflect the 94.5 percent of its U.S. sales that came from the discounter. By 1981, Kmart had more than 2,000 stores in the United States and Canada, and in 1987, it dumped its remaining five-and-tens. Kmart went upmarket by hiring Martha Stewart as its lifestyle consultant. But, by 2002, competition with Wal★Mart and Target had eroded Kmart's position, and it filed for bankruptcy. A year later, the retailer re-emerged as Kmart Holding Corporation and in 2005 was combined with Sears, Roebuck and Company to form Sears Holdings Corporation. Kmart's history makes heads spin, but it shows the instability of retailing in Boomer America.

During the 1990s, yet another format emerged: the big-box retailer. Wal★Mart established itself as the indisputable leader in this category, developing warehouse stores and super-centers that put groceries, tires, and general merchandise under one roof, with gasoline pumps in the parking lot. When Kmart was the dominant discounter in the 1980s, Wal★Mart was still an upstart regional retailer with 1,000 stores and 84 warehouse "clubs" in twenty states. In the 1990s, Wal★Mart grew dramatically by developing super-centers and aggressively pursuing international expansion. By 2005, the Arkansas-based discounter topped the global *Fortune* 500 list.

These changes had important consequences for consumer society. The downtown department store, the Victorian palace of consumption, spiraled into its final decline. Between the 1970s and the 2000s, many local and regional stores—such as Wanamaker's, Strawbridge's, Gimbel Brothers, Lit Brothers, and Snellenburg's in Philadelphia—shut their doors or were bought by other retailers and eventually absorbed by Macy's Inc. Discounters accounted for 27 percent of general retail sales in 1987; they controlled 41 percent in 1996. Department stores lost their share of retail sales, slipping from 20 percent in 1987 to 14 percent in 1996. Some consumers welcomed the rise of big-box retailers like Wal★Mart, whose warehouse prices allowed people of modest means to enjoy a middle-class lifestyle. For others, the demise of department stores and traditional shops and the commercial "death" of downtown—in small towns, cities big and small, and even some suburbs—signaled the erosion of product differentiation, which had always been vital to personal expression, as well as any uniqueness their hometown had offered.

•••

What did Americans expect from consumer society during the whirlwind 1970s, 1980s, and 1990s? How did the relentless quest to drive down costs affect consumer choices, the store-bought products people put in their identity kits? What role did new technologies like television and the digital revolution play in reforming people's ideas about goods? These major questions drive this book to its conclusion. Let's take a closer look at two important categories of consumer products—apparel and electronics—to see how tastes have evolved since World War II, and how generational shifts, market segmentation, retail consolidation, and globalization have influenced the types of things Americans defined as meaningful.

CHAPTER EIGHT

Casual Style

In her 1999 book, *The End of Fashion*, journalist Teri Agins, the *Wall Street Journal*'s senior fashion reporter, puzzled over one of the great conundrums of recent consumer history. Why did so many Americans—the most affluent consumers on earth—often dress down in jeans, T-shirts and athletic shoes? Less than a hundred years ago, the average American aspired to the beauty of the Gibson Girl and the Arrow Man. By the New Millennium, people wore casual clothes to work, church, and when stepping out. Where did dressing down originate, and why is it now synonymous with American style?

The Mamie Look

After World War II, Parisian glamour and American casual vied for dominance of women's fashion. The French style bumped into the new American phenomena: suburbanization, the materials revolution, the populuxe effect, and market segmentation.

When the *couture* salons reopened after the war, the sensation of 1947 was Christian Dior's fall collection, including the Corolla line, a romantic Victorian silhouette. Nicknamed the "New Look" by *Harper's Bazaar* editor Carmel Snow, Dior's dresses emphasized feminine curves, unlike the boyish flapper of the 1920s or the boxy sophisticate style. Modern foundations—the bra and girdle—molded women's bodies of the early 1940s into an hourglass shape accentuated by the New Look's tight, round-shouldered bodice, wasp waist, and billowy gathered skirt. The designs used yards and yards of fabric and miracle materials like nylon, as if to celebrate the return of productivity, affluence, and abundance.

First lady Mamie Eisenhower, an ardent clotheshorse, strongly favored the new French style. While President Dwight D. Eisenhower crafted another kind of New Look in national security policy, the first lady Americanized Dior's romanticism. The couple lived in Paris between 1950 and 1952, when Ike commanded NATO forces in Europe, and Mamie cultivated fashionable friends such as hairstylist Elizabeth Arden. Like other well-to-do American women, Mamie frequented the couture salons, but she was often proud to return home empty handed. A coupon clipper, she liked to search out fashion bargains and to mix and match designs. She also loved to "buy American," shopping at the Dallas-based Neiman Marcus department store and ordering outfits from her favorite designers on Seventh Avenue in New York. The media christened her unique style as the "Mamie Look."

The Mamie Look was a pretty, ladylike style that permitted freedom of movement and was highly personalized. Throughout her life, Mamie chose up-to-date clothes that reflected the "saucy" personality that had caught the young Ike's eye. Becoming first lady as a 51-year-old grandmother, Mamie knew that she looked best in plain outfits carefully cut from luxury fabrics. "I hate old lady clothes," she told *Collier's* in 1952. "And I shall never wear them."

With a busy social schedule, the first lady welcomed retailers and designers, who brought iridescent shirtdresses and fitted wool suits to the White House. She added a populuxe flair by wearing her trademark Elizabeth Arden hairdo with bangs, space-age hats, mink stoles, colored stockings, and charm bracelets—when many Washington wives, including Pat Nixon, sported Republican cloth coats. Her stunning inaugural gown, ordered from Neiman Marcus and made by New York designer Nettie Rosenstein, said it all. Sewn in pale pink chiffon, the dress was covered with 2,000 sequins, had a deep V-neck that fell off the shoulders, and a gigantic bell-shaped skirt. The total effect, writes art historian Karal Ann Marling, was a brassy, bold celebration of American acquisitiveness.

The Dior-Mamie Look influenced the American ready-to-wear industry, recreating the romantic silhouette for ordinary shoppers. Postwar prosperity fueled New York's garment trade, now located on and around Seventh Avenue near Macy's and Gimbel's. Seventh Avenue adapted the hourglass shape to affordable suits and shirtdresses, which consumers saw in stores, in magazines, and on TV-sitcom moms like June Cleaver. Advertisers capitalized on the new feminine style when promoting completely unrelated products. In 1955, American Motors posed well-dressed women, à la Mamie, with its new Rambler station wagon. The Mamie Look was self-presentation in the American Way: bold, sassy, individualistic, but normal and comfortable.

Rebels, Teens, and Beatniks

The affluent 1950s divided Americans into near-infinite interest groups, each seeking to express, in the words of adman E. B. Weiss, "*independent* taste." Consumers not only personalized their Levittown houses, but, like Mamie Eisenhower, reveled in making individualized fashion choices. While the Mamie Look staked out a middle ground between Paris and Levittown, Hollywood stars James Dean and Marlon Brando, and a smitten Swarthmore couple, took fashion inspiration from the Dust Bowl, the docks, and Greenwich Village.

Men's clothing combined the old and the new. Dress-wise, two 1956 best sellers, *The Man in the Grey Flannel Suit* and *The Organization Man*, stereotyped the junior executive, but in reality, people had more options of what to wear. For office jobs, the subdued suit, paired with a white shirt and plain tie, certainly continued to be standard attire. New synthetic fibers, including Dacron polyester, were blended into menswear fabrics to impart greater durability and wrinkle resistance. College students wore jackets or military uniforms to class, always with a tie or bow tie. Blue-collar workers wore work shirts and work pants, sometimes uniforms.

Casual menswear began to challenge conventions, encouraging men to select comfortable, expressive clothing for vacations and weekends. Before the war, a small menswear industry on the West Coast had introduced California casual, an informal style influenced by practical ranch clothes and Hollywood flamboyance. *Esquire* magazine, founded in the 1930s, had encouraged men to enjoy shopping, but in the 1950s, Hugh Heffner's *Playboy* offered organization men an escapist subculture of buxom bunnies and three-martini lunches. Dressed in tight jeans, white T-shirts, and black leather jackets, movie stars James Dean and Marlon Brando played blue-collar rebels who defied grey-flannel conventions. Few organization men abandoned their families to live rebellious lives, but many indulged their consumerist fantasies with sports cars and sportswear.

In 1944, the word *teenager* was coined to describe 13- to 19-year olds, who became a market segment in their own right with fads like the "sweater girl." When pinups like Jayne Mansfield and Marilyn Monroe showed off their "assets" in tight sweaters, teen girls competed as to who could look the most voluptuous in cashmere or acrylic. They collected sweaters in various styles and colors, to be worn with different skirts, jackets, hairstyles, and accessories. Between 1952 and 1959, sweater sales doubled to 100 million, with high-school girls and college women making nearly 50 percent of these purchases.

The sweater girls were one of the burgeoning teen subcultures that used fashion to express a collective identity. These wannabe pinups, constrained by mainstream values and gender definitions, limited their choice in dress to "feminine" tops and skirts, bras and girdles, saddle shoes and loafers. They didn't rebel by emulating country singer Kitty Wells's cowgirl affectations, or the Beat Generation's black turtlenecks and Levi jeans. The sweater girls played it safe, fusing the buxom allure of Jayne Mansfield with the conservative sassiness of Mamie Eisenhower, who, in turn, had borrowed their charm bracelets.

Consumers who did admire the Beat Generation's fashion choices included war babies like Nina de Angeli, a French literature major at Swarthmore College, outside Philadelphia, from 1958 to 1962. Her favorite outfit for classes combined beatnik and traditional styles: a white Oxford shirt, a baggy red sweater, work jeans, and loafers or ballet flats. "I felt very liberated in the jeans," because "in high school, we had to wear skirts" and could only wear dungarees at home. In October 1958, Nina "got a new green wool sheath dress for special occasions, just below knee length. That seemed like a radical departure from the long mid-calf length I always had before." Like other co-eds, Nina watched her pennies when shopping downtown at Wanamaker's.

Then as now, opposites attract, and that was the case when 17-year-old Nina began dating 26-year-old Bill Walls, a commuter student. The son of an assistant foreman in the Electrical Department of the Sun Shipbuilding Company in Chester, Bill entered college in 1950. After two years, he joined the Air Force to avoid being drafted into the Army during the Korean War and was stationed in Colorado. Returning to Swarthmore in 1957, Bill wasn't the average student; he lived at home in Chester and bought his work clothes from the Sears store on his aunt's employee discount. On dates, Bill dressed in a navy suit, white shirt, and tie; for class, he put on plain gray work pants and gray cotton shirts. Bill "had the engineer's slide rule always handily strapped on his belt," recalled Nina. "I doubt he ever gave a thought to fashion!"

Still, Bill had looked very up-to-date driving his vintage 1941 Buick around Pike's Peak in 1955, wearing form-fitting jeans and a nylon sports shirt with the sleeves rolled up, à la James Dean. "I don't believe I knew of James Dean at that time," Bill said, "but the rolled-up sleeves were the off-duty fashion norm of the day." He bought the nylon shirt, which "lasted a long time and was very easy to wash and dry," at the Air Force base exchange store in Biloxi, Mississippi, in 1953. Even consumers oblivious to fashion trends could put together a casual look that told others who they were.

In 1958, fashion played the role of matchmaker in Nina and Bill's romance. Waiting for a bus, Nina wore her green sheath dress, which attracted Bill's eye as he passed by. The former Air Force sergeant was "immediately and forever smitten" by Nina's "apparent happy disposition" and "obviously very high intelligence." Bill vividly recalled "the short pixie carefree haircut; no nail polish; no makeup on a comely face; really great legs and shapely figure which was clearly highlighted by the skimpy green dress."

Youth Quake

In the 1960s and 1970s, Baby Boomers gave full expression to the phrase, "there is power in numbers." In November 1957, *Cosmopolitan*, still a family weekly, published a special issue: "Are Teenagers

Taking Over?" Tongue-in-cheek, it conjured the image of "a vast, determined band of blue-jeaned storm troopers forcing us to do exactly as they dictate." Boomer dollars and tastes inflected what Diana Vreeland, editor of *Vogue* from 1962 to 1971, famously dubbed the "youth quake."

Boomers were not the only consumers in the 1960s, but their numbers and their attitudes attracted marketers. As teenagers, Boomers used their considerable spending money to buy the symbols of affluence. They were the first Americans to grow up with such conveniences as matching kitchen appliances, blue jeans and loafers, and portable phonographs. These things were novelties to people born before World War II, but many war babies and Boomers grew up thinking they were part of every American's birthright. By virtue of size, wealth, and timing, Boomers demanded new patterns of consumption and interjected energetic, youthful styles into the marketplace.

The icons for high-end youthful style were 43-year-old President John F. Kennedy and his wife, Jacqueline. He brandished a suave preppy look, alternating between impeccably tailored suits and sportswear with a casual California edge. The new first lady took a turn towards simplicity, offering an expression of young elegance. The "Jackie Look"—sheath dresses, pillbox hats, and ultra-plain suits—became fashionable among the wives of politicians and businessmen, and career women who wanted professional polish. The photogenic couple's understated glamour was popular with newspapers, magazines, and television. Stores like Brooks Brothers in New York offered JFK preppy wear, including chinos, knit tops, and button-down shirts in Oxford cloth.

At the same time, European fashion trends drove the casual impulse in new directions. Italian knitwear, Alpine ski clothes, and British mod designs all had a significant impact among fashionable young people. The youth quake devoured these styles, which coexisted alongside traditional modes.

The British invasion of music and fashion infiltrated the American teen scene, rendering hat-and-glove formality obsolete. The swinger influence started with The Beatles's February 1964 performance on *The Ed Sullivan Show*, the most popular variety hour on television. British Top Forty hits and concert tours followed, as The Rolling

Stones, The Animals, The Kinks, The Dave Clark Five, and Herman's Hermits continued the assault. In the early to mid-1960s, London became a global fashion center, bombarding the world with mod styles. The outrageous creations and relaxed boutiques of Carnaby Street made this Soho shopping district into a one-stop fashion destination for young clotheshorses. The Kinks celebrated "Carnabetian" style with their 1966 hit song, "Dedicated Follower of Fashion," about a young man who loved "frilly nylon panties" and shirts with stripes and polka-dots.

Esquire journalist George Frazier coined the term "peacock revolution" to describe how fashionable young men dressed. Novel menswear styles included flowered shirts, paisley scarves, striped bell bottoms, and pointy boots with chunky heels. In 1960, Paris designer Pierre Cardin introduced tight suits that gave men a slender neo-Edwardian silhouette. Cardin's elegant two-button suits found favor among diplomats and executives before younger men adopted them. Along with the immense popularity of jeans, these trends led to the acceptance of body-hugging clothes. Men's longer hairstyles prompted stares on the street and snide remarks in the press. By 1964, the lines between the sexes became so blurred that the *London Sunday Times* queried, "Is that a boy, or is it a girl?"

In women's fashion, British mod style was promulgated by designers like Mary Quant and the first ultra-thin model, Lesley Hornby, better known as Twiggy. Quant, who sought to liberate British women from frumpy woolens, offered vinyl hipster belts, crocheted tops, and most famously, the miniskirt. As the old New Look ran its course and hemlines inched up, pantyhose replaced girdles, garter belts, and stockings. By the late 1960s, the miniskirt, best with slim thighs and tights, was a worldwide phenomenon.

British pop music, rock idols, and fashion icons like Twiggy entranced the American media, which in turn spread the excitement. High-school girls in minis made good copy, as did the photographs of American boys in long hair, Beatle boots, and tight pants that appeared on the cover of *Life* in May 1966. Below the headline declaring a "Revolution in Male Clothes," four American high-school students posed before Chicago's towering skyline in the "new mod gear," sporting "the rakish, thin-shanked, high-heel booted, broad-belted, narrow-hipped and epauleted variations of attire" that were transforming "the fashion habits of the U.S. male."

Mod dress was worn to work, school, and play by people of all ages, who danced to rock and roll. In "The Sound of the Sixties," the May 21, 1965, issue of *Newsweek* reported that 5,000 discothèques were playing rock-and-roll records to which Boomers and their parents danced the twist, the watusi, the frug, the mashed potato, and the locomotion. New York City alone had twenty-one discothèques, including the world-famous Peppermint Lounge, frequented by luminaries like ballet dancer Rudolf Nureyev, Rat Pack singer Sammy Davis Jr., and the Kennedy clan. When the widowed first lady Jacqueline Kennedy put on a miniskirt and danced her "sedate version of the frug," this signaled the widespread acceptance of mod and, of course, nothing with widespread acceptance could be considered cutting edge.

Mod was already being replaced by the hippie psychedelic style. This counterculture social movement, started by idealistic students in San Francisco, New York, and Boston, criticized American capitalism, the Vietnam War, and racism; it also explored alternative lifestyles and mind-altering drugs. Hippies decried the "establishment" of the American Way, condemning hometown suburbs like Levittown as sterile wastelands. As consumers, they ignored mass-market retailers like Sears and the A&P in favor of boutiques, head shops, craft stores, and co-ops. Not everyone, however, followed the counterculture. In 1968, a Yankelovich Poll for *Fortune* suggested that 60 percent of college students—about one-third of Baby Boomers—still wore Kennedy-style chinos and listened to The Beach Boys.

This evolving hippie antifashion stance had an enduring influence on mainstream styles. The hippie look mixed clothes from boutiques, army surplus stores, Western shops, and the Goodwill. Blue jeans were indispensable to hippie taste, which helped to popularize slim-fitted clothes and the unisex look. Men and women wore hip-hugger bell bottoms, bright polyester or tie-dyed tops, necklaces, and Western boots or Indian moccasins. Women sometimes purchased men's Levis, taking them in to fit. Foreshadowing the tattoo and body piercing craze of our time, the hippie look parodied mainstream taste by taunting the clean-cut JFK preppy style.

The Me Generation

Raised to "keep *away* from the Joneses," Boomers matured into fiercely independent consumers. In the 1970s, the self-absorption and buying power of the "Me Generation" mixed into a heady combination expressed in the pop culture symbols of the era: polyester, disco, and fitness.

Mainstream fashion continued to evolve casual alternatives to the grey flannel suit for men and the sheath dress for women. The new designs were often sewn in man-made miracle fabrics. Synthetics entered American style with rayon and acetate in the 1920s and 1930s, and spread rapidly with nylon, acrylic, polyester, and spandex in the postwar years. By the 1970s, apparel manufacturers constructed garments from materials that could be easily washed and dried by machine. Permanent Press and Wash and Wear cut down on dry-cleaning bills, clotheslines, and hours spent with an iron in hand. For the first time, people could "just throw it in the machine."

Miracle fabrics, which could be dyed in brilliant colors, provided creative opportunities for apparel designers. Menswear manufacturers fused California casual, the slim European silhouette, and Western cowboy styling into an easy-care look. America's largest retailer, Sears, Roebuck and Company, collaborated with clothing manufacturers to bring counterculture styles to middle-class America. In 1970, the Sears catalog stocked conventional blazers, slacks, and shirts, along with a hipper Kings Road Collection that fused mod, Western, Italian, and ethnic fads. Five years later, the Kings Road Collection steered away from these trends toward cowboy styling in easy-care synthetics. For Sears' shoppers, American casual now meant Western-style clothes and leisure suits.

Polyester fashions also appealed to entertainers and celebrities, who liked the low maintenance, bright colors, and flashy cuts. For rock-and-roll heartthrobs like Elvis Presley and Mick Jagger, a one-piece stretch playsuit studded with rhinestones was perfect performance gear, hugging the body and showing off their physique. Early "blaxploitation" films like *Shaft* (1971) put well-built leads like Richard Roundtree in tight turtlenecks and double-knit polyester pants. As polyester prices fell, clothing companies increasingly used the versatile fiber to make wrinkle-free menswear. The brightly colored leisure suit, with a loose Western-style jacket, became a favorite among blue-collar workers, small-town business leaders, traveling salesmen, and retirees.

Polyester was perfect for the disco, a reborn discothèque that emerged from the gay underground in lower Manhattan before going straight in the mid-1970s. Features of mainstream discothèques included pulsating strobe lamps and the mirrored disco ball, which revolved to reflect light in a glittery update of Art Deco glamour. Disco created pop superstars that appealed to blue-collar and middle-class America. The Bee Gees, a fading 1960s pop group, reinvented themselves as disco's leading singers, draped in polyester. At the peak of the disco era, a white polyester suit made John Travolta into a sex symbol as he boogied to The Bee Gees's beat in the 1978 film *Saturday Night Fever*. Disco introduced sexy clothing styles to young Americans who had grown up on JFK preppy, the British invasion, and hippie antifashion. Women twirled around in sheer, flowing dresses, made from synthetics like Qiana, a washable nylon fabric that looked like silk. Imitating Travolta, blue-collar men wore bright polyester shirts with long pointed collars, open at the neck under a light-colored double-knit jacket.

Disco dancing and fashions represented the apotheosis of the populuxe Boomers' youthful dreams. Disco synthesized diverse musical styles—black rhythms, pop harmonies, Latin beats, and electronic mixing—into a hedonistic, yet commercial style. It tapped into African American, Latin, gay, and Broadway cultures to create a mass audience, becoming the decade's dominant pop music. As historian Bruce J. Schulman notes in *The Seventies*, disco's "intermingling of musical and cultural styles" produced a hybrid form that "acknowledged dancers' solidarity across racial and cultural lines," holding out the possibility of assimilation. "Like Woodstock," disco "fostered the gathering of a community." Yet, in fashion, disco was a world apart from anti-establishment hippiedom. The emphasis on ceremonial group dancing belies disco's most potent influence on consumer society: the personal celebration of bodily perfection.

Disco led to the fitness craze that swept across the United States in the late 1970s. Americans have long loved outdoor activities—camping, hiking, and cycling—but in the postwar years, few connected exercise and bodily perfection. Hula-Hoops were for kids; the frug for 1960s swingers. The counterculture, with its fascination for eastern religions and whole foods like granola and bean sprouts, revitalized the age-old idea of the body as the "temple of the soul." In 1960, only 24 percent of Americans exercised; by 1981, a record 70 million Americans—nearly half the adult population—pursued some form of physical activity. For the Me Generation, getting into shape became a national pastime, with a sweeping impact on casual fashion.

By 1981, middle-class Boomers who wanted to get in shape made fitness into $30 billion industry. That year, the market for sports shoes alone totaled $1 billion; active wear and equipment, $8 billion. Academy Award–winning actress Jane Fonda transformed herself from an antiwar activist into a hot fitness babe when she commercialized aerobic dancing, invented in 1968 by Air Force exercise instructor Jacki Sorenson. The *Jane Fonda Workout Book* (1981) and companion videotapes created a nation of aerobic fanatics. Other celebrities, including pop singer Olivia Newton-John, who had co-starred with John Travolta in the 1979 movie *Grease*, and TV star Victoria Principal, from the *Dallas* series, used their marquee value to help Americans "get physical." According to *Sporting Goods Dealer*, America had 22.7 million aerobic dancers by 1984. More than twenty new magazines, with names like *Shape*, *New Body*, and *Fit*, strove to sate the thirst for information about sweating and stretching. Sexy fitness queens like Fonda and Principal did wonders for sales of stylish workout gear—sweatbands, legwarmers, and Lycra leotards.

The fitness craze meant big business for health clubs, sporting goods stores, and sneaker manufacturers. In 1969, a small Oregon sneaker company, Blue Ribbon Sports, made $300,000 selling athletic shoes; by 1978, the firm, now known as Nike, Inc., had revenues of $71 million. The founders expected their company to do a decent business selling special waffle-soled shoes to athletes, but they were astounded when running became a national obsession. When Boomers weren't jogging around the track, they wore their athletic shoes, mostly Nikes with the "swoosh" logo, to congratulate themselves. In 1979, Nike's sales totaled $150 million; in 1980, $270 million. *Inc.* magazine reported in August 1981 that jogging shoes had become "fashion chic."

The enthusiasm for disco and fitness was tied into Boomers' growing awareness of their own immortality, the darker side of youth culture. As they climbed the career ladder, Boomers learned that a trim physique could be an asset in the corporate office. Putting aside Frye boots and floppy hats, career women adopted a comfortable office uniform modeled after menswear. The new dress code included below-the-knee skirts and matching blazers, or polished pantsuits that exuded authority. Men's office wear also turned away from the peacock revolution toward more staid, traditional styles.

Celebrity Style, Yuppie Tastes

Against the backdrop of the conservative Reagan presidency in the 1980s, some aspects of American style took on a glitzy, overblown character, symbolized by big hair and shoulder pads. In the White House, Ronald and Nancy Reagan surrounded themselves with glamourous diplomats, aristocrats, politicians and older stars of TV shows like *Dallas* and *Dynasty*, role models for middle-aged and senior consumers. The most popular style mavens for Boomer women were polar opposites: the elegant couture wardrobe of Diana, Princess of Wales, and the trashy underwear-as-outerwear chic of pop singer Madonna. For Boomer men, trendsetters included *Miami Vice* actors Don Johnson and Philip Michael Thomas, rock star Prince, and basketball superstar Michael Jordan.

These style icons had one thing in common: they were, above all else, world-famous celebrities. The massive growth of international media — stimulated by corporate consolidations, rapid global communication technology, and new outlets like 24-hour cable channels — fed the rabid public hunger for celebrity "news."

Stylish, multicultural masculinity dominated the popular NBC-TV cop show *Miami Vice* during its run from 1984 to 1989. Filmed in Miami's South Beach, the series popularized Caribbean culture and made the vintage pastels found on Art Deco hotels and fifties neon signs into fashionable menswear colors. The two handsome leads — Johnson's Vietnam vet and former football star, and Thomas's black-Hispanic refugee from the NYPD — introduced fans to Italian designers Giorgio Armani and Gianni Versace, who built global fashion empires around men's demands for practical, stylish attire. When Johnson's character,

Sonny Crockett, wore silk T-shirts under Armani sports jackets, this flagrantly sexual look, accompanied by a five o'clock shadow, set a new standard for dressing down.

Cable's MTV established a powerful link between visual style and pop music sensibilities. Launched in 1981, it revitalized Michael Jackson's career and made pop stars out of Madonna and Cindy Lauper, whose titillating stage presence stirred the loins of adolescent girls and boys alike. Madonna broke taboos by wearing little more than lacy corsets, bullet bras, and fishnet stockings, as she danced and sang "Like a Virgin" and "Material Girl." MTV popularized rap music and hip-hop style, showcasing early artists like Run-DMC and Grandmaster Flash. When Run-DMC rapped about Adidas sneakers in 1986, they scored a $1 million endorsement contract from the manufacturer. Bruce Springsteen's shaggy hair, white T-shirt, and blue-jean clad butt on the *Born in the USA* album and video turned the James Dean rebel without a cause into a blue-collar, patriotic icon. Retailers from Macy's to Footlocker marketed sexy Madonna fashions for "her," and oversized homeboy garb for "him." Subcultural aesthetics, from new wave to hip-hop to working-class patriot, found their way into American households through the youth culture.

But the prize segment of the market was the Young Urban Professional, the *crème de la crème* of vanguard Boomers who made too much money and spent it conspicuously. Yuppies sat atop the largest, richest, and best-educated generation ever born in America, and by virtue of their economic muscle, directed the economy and the culture. *Newsweek* dubbed 1984 "The Year of the Yuppie" and dedicated its year-end issue to this market segment. The *average* Boomer was married, lived in a suburban apartment, had 1.5 kids and 1.5 cars, and choked on stagflation. The *yuppie* was a Columbia student protester of 1968 who now had an M.B.A., worked in corporate America, and refused to rush into parenthood and suburbia. Yuppies rejected preppy privilege, the idea of hereditary social privilege. Only a select few could go to boarding school, but any desk jockey with an American Express card could vacation in Maine. Yuppies tossed aside the hippies' anti-capitalist stance, while domesticating the counterculture's love of healthy and exotic foods, natural fabrics, and liberating the inner self. They were the first consumers to drive BMWs and Volvos, renovate urban rowhouses, use video dating services, and eat goat cheese and sun-dried tomatoes. Even those who didn't meet all the statistical requirements found themselves following the yuppie consumption trends they could afford.

Marketers found yuppies to be maddeningly fickle because they put such a high value on independent thinking, but there were some predictable things about them. Weaned on a diet of TV and Cheerios, they appreciated lots of information and nationally advertised brands. A desire for instant gratification gave a boost to specialty mail-order houses like L.L. Bean, who set up 24 hour, toll-free order numbers. Yuppie drivers rejected flashy chrome for agile performance and European styling. The Saab, with its technical sophistication and understated design, became the yuppie-mobile of choice. In clothing, yuppies appreciated quality, particularly when it came with the credentials of "good designer labels."

Polo Meets Hip-Hop

Between the 1970s and 1990s, mainstream fashion became less about upscale affectations and more about image-making and identity politics. A new wave of Seventh Avenue fashion houses, who described themselves as "designer labels" instead of garment manufacturers, capitalized on Boomer demands. Anne Klein, Liz Claiborne, Perry Ellis, and Donna Karan became favorites of department-store shoppers who needed practical clothes for the office. Other designers borrowed Madison Avenue techniques, repackaged clothing as a lifestyle choice, and created Seventh Avenue's first megabrands.

Two of these pioneer image-makers were Ralph Lauren and Tommy Hilfiger, whose menswear empires capitalized on the fragmentation of America. Each designer reworked the JFK preppy basics—khakis, blazers, shirts, and sweaters—into a global brand. Every year, they reissued the same unisex designs in new colors and textures, cleverly repackaged to resonate among their target audiences, who wanted to be American in very different ways. They succeeded by being *out* of fashion and *in* marketing.

Ralph Lauren's Polo brand introduced "lifestyle merchandising" to major department stores, creating the idea of one-stop designer shopping. Polo boutiques displayed basic preppy attire in a thematic space reminiscent of an upscale gentleman's club. The aim was to stir dreams of upward mobility; men would select a shirt and matching trousers to help them look like JFK. Lauren's costume designs for *The Great Gatsby* (1974) and *Annie Hall* (1977) put his vintage Ivy League look in the public eye, as did his lavish advertising spreads in *Vanity Fair* and *New York Times Magazine*. Born Ralph Lifshitz, Lauren targeted consumers like himself and Martha Stewart, the children of immigrants who dreamed about riding with the horsy set rather than cleaning their stables. He fancied himself as a Jewish American Gatsby, often appearing in his own ads. Yuppies who wore the Polo brand, those ads implied, would transcend their ethnic roots to become American aristocrats.

Hilfiger plowed furrows in Polo's field. Hilfiger topped Lauren at his own game, selling Polo spin-offs at popular prices, before turning to the antithesis of preppy-yuppie: hip-hop culture. In the 1980s, Nike had discovered multiculturalism and hired basketball star Michael Jordan as the spokesman for Air Jordan footwear. A series of real-life "sneaker killings"—in which inner-city kids murdered their neighbors over designer footwear—were tragic, but pointed to the importance of logos and athletic gear among urban youth. To build a hip-hop brand, Hilfiger courted rappers Snoop Doggy Dogg and Grand Puba, who wore his logo shirts and oversized jackets on MTV videos and CD covers. Once Hilfiger became the favorite among superstar homeboys, both inner-city blacks and suburban white wannabe homies flocked to his label. The Hilfiger brand, a pastiche of prison styles and classic preppy, shouted that the wearer was cool, slick, and sexy.

Ralph Lauren and Tommy Hilfiger helped to reinvent Seventh Avenue as a creative center of multicultural fashion. They turned this mass-market fashion center into the capital of lifestyle branding, and along with Italian brands like Armani, Gucci, and Versace, did much to transform men's fashion. Tommy Hilfiger hired marketing people immersed in the newest subcultures, young African Americans, Latinos, and Asians who were in touch with tastes of the MTV generation. The old top-down way of producing fashion dissipated, replaced by a new version of the melting-pot ideal.

•••

In the New Millennium, clothing styles oozed up from city streets to suburban malls, making distressed denim into the new "uniform" of the Average American. The Gap, Lucky Jeans, and Wal★Mart profited from the preference for dressing down. Casual Friday pummeled the vestiges of the Victorian dress code. High fashion, antifashion, yuppie fashion, designer fashion, retro fashion, no fashion, and fast fashion combined to make Fashion itself nearly irrelevant. It was all about "doing your own thing."

The global economy, which grew exponentially in the nineties, dramatically reduced manufacturing costs, allowing The Gap and Wal★Mart to sell clothes as if they were mere commodities. People on the economic margins, who might have grown up with one pair of jeans and one good dress, could now own multiple outfits. Consumers on the lower rungs of the social ladder not only could afford to dress like middle-class Americans, but their tastes also helped define how middle-class Americans dressed.

Multinational corporations equipped with powerful marketing departments and cheap labor, backed by the fashion press, displaced Paris designers and super-celebrities as the arbiters of taste, sweeping the streets for trends and remaking them as global brands. Consumers who valued logos now shopped for their favorite brands in outlet malls or department stores, which had entirely rearranged their layouts around designer labels and boutiques. The Polo model triumphed, while the couture elegance of Mamie Eisenhower, Jackie Kennedy, and Nancy Reagan vanished. In a sense, Princess Diana's untimely death in 1997 symbolized the end of an era.

Terri Agins sees this great transformation as being consumer-driven. "We decide what we want to wear," she wrote in *The End of Fashion*, "when we buy it, and how much we pay for it." One African American fashion executive, Myorr Janha of Phat Farm, places it in a broader cultural context. "The Nu American Dream means to have high aspirations in life," he told *Business Week* in 2003. "Classic American Flava means we want to be accepted by all without forgetting we're born out of hip-hop." Fashion had become the embodiment of people's social origins, their perception of where they fit into the middle class, and an expression of who they wanted to become. It was less about following trendsetters, and more about dressing for who you were, are, and wish to be. As in the Victorian era, clothing again recalls class—but it is a class that is self-identified rather than one assigned at birth.

The transition from Christian Dior to The Gap, from the rue de la Paix to Mall USA, started with Mamie and Marlon, two decidedly different icons of American individualism. Identity politics, the fitness craze, and multiculturalism infused the marketplace with greater diversity. Baby Boomers and their kids, Generations X and Y, segmented into affinity groups, making it increasingly difficult for marketers to imagine an Average American. Boomers hoped to stay forever young, remaining active and acquisitive into their golden years. The fragmentation of America divided the mass market into seemingly infinite segments, while blue-collar and black tastes (considered more edgy) began to dominate the mainstream. Only one thing remained constant: the consumer values of comfort, easy care, and individualism shaped people's choices about what to wear, what to drive, and what to buy.

CHAPTER NINE

Electronics "R" Us

Information Snacking

The rising tide of individualism that reshaped housing and fashion in Boomer America played out most noticeably in consumer electronics. In this arena, "cultural hardware"—the things themselves—came to matter far less than "cultural software"—the entertainment experience.

In April 2008, Jeffrey P. Bezos, the founder and chief executive at Amazon.com, Inc., issued a letter to shareholders that rattled some of the fundamental assumptions of the digital age. Bezos compared Johannes Gutenberg's fifteenth-century invention of the printing press, which led to significant cost reductions in book prices, to twentieth-century innovations such as personal computers, laptops, cell phones, and personal digital assistants (PDAs), which have shaped how consumers learn, communicate, have fun, and shop. To Bezos, these new technologies were both assets and liabilities. While networking devices permitted instantaneous communication, they shortened people's attention spans and caused a shift from "long-form reading" into a new mode: *information snacking*." Amazon designed the Kindle, a "purpose-built reading device with wireless access to more than 110,000 books, blogs, magazines and newspapers," as a counterpoint to "info-snacking tools" like the BlackBerry. The Kindle is meant to encourage consumers to enjoy a good long read, much as the Victorians had curled up in the parlor by the gaslight with *Godey's Lady's Book*. The Kindle is thus both backward-looking and forward-looking; its creators hope to re-invigorate the consumer habits of Victorian and Modern times and adapt them to the digitized post-Boomer era.

Whether or not Bezos achieves his missionary goal—reintroducing contemplative reading into the fast-paced digital world—his observations about information snacking are on target. Over the course of the twentieth century, a succession of new communications technologies—beginning with mass-circulation magazines, records, and radio in Modern times—have made it easier, faster, and more convenient for consumers to tailor their recreational time to suit their personal tastes. This trend is epitomized by another device that debuted 2007: the Apple iPhone, a small but powerful multitasker that can perform the duties of record player, telephone, television, personal stereo, computer, radio, two-way radio, and camera. The ultimate tool for "info-snacking," the iPhone gives the consumer the ability to create a portable personal space based on electronic information-entertainment.

As we assess the rise of "info-snacking" and the shift from "cultural hardware" to "cultural software" in this final chapter, it's important to remember that cultural values—the idea of what's important or not—change slowly over time, and that different generations often embrace different values, reflecting their place in the lifecycle. Your grandmother might listen to her favorite music on CDs, enjoy going to the theater to see movies, and browse through flea markets for vintage china, while you prefer to download songs from iTunes, watch videos on YouTube, and buy your shoes online. The fifty-year-old Martha Stewart fan values the things in her home and clothes she wears, while a twenty-year-old college student might define himself by his Facebook profile. By 2005, the endpoint for this book, many of those evanescent experiences were digital.

The Year of Consumer Electronics: 1948

Nineteen-forty-eight was a watershed year in the history of electronics. That year, Bing Crosby, the country's most famous singer and radio host, prerecorded his popular show using a new Ampex Model 200 tape recorder. Not only did this allow Crosby to croon at his convenience, but it also permitted the singer to eliminate less-than-perfect sounds from his performance. After 1948, the sonic quality of the *Bing Crosby Show* was vastly superior to earlier radio programs, and Crosby could play more golf.

The magnetic tape recorder was only one of several major innovations that appeared in 1948, the year of electronic wonders. In New York, Columbia Records released the first vinyl long-playing record, or LP. At Bell Labs, three scientist-inventors—John Bardeen, Walter Brattain, and William Shockley—demonstrated the transistor, a development based on prewar German research. In Cambridge, Massachusetts, Edwin Land introduced the Polaroid camera, which took pictures, developed them before consumers' eyes, and promised instant gratification to amateur photographers. Up and down the East Coast, nearly a million boxing fans watched the fight between Joe Louis and Jersey Joe Walcott on their television sets. Fans learned about where on the dial to find the match by reading *TV Guide*, a new weekly magazine that appeared that year.

Shortly after World War II, tape recorders, electric guitars, vinyl records, transistors, and cable providers made their debut. Despite their critical importance to consumer society, these technical innovations paled before the tidal wave of broadcast television. In the words of Harvard sociologist Robert Putnam, author of *Bowling Alone*, "nothing else in the twentieth century so rapidly and profoundly affected our leisure." In 1947, the NBC network estimated that there were 60,000 television sets in the United States. Three years later, in 1950, nearly 4 million households had television sets, which they watched for more than four hours per day. By 1955, 31 million households, nearly two out of every three, spent five hours a day watching *The Howdy Doody Show*, *The Texaco Star Theatre*, *I Love Lucy*, and weeknight boxing matches.

TV in the Fifties

The television explosion only *seemed* to occur overnight. Television technology had been in place for twenty years, but it took two decades to develop the standards, systems, and infrastructure that resulted in the explosion of 1948–58. With RCA leading the way, manufacturers, wholesalers, and retailers pushed this newest, latest, and greatest technological innovation.

Television followed the path that had been pioneered by radio. The business model was based on corporate sponsorship. Three powerful networks—ABC, CBS, and NBC—controlled the broadcasts, and their programs were based on radio prototypes: variety shows, sports, and soap operas. Radio had also established the idea of gathering people around an electronic device to enjoy entertainment delivered through the air to the home.

Television first appeared in public places in an attempt to attract customers. In 1947–48, neighborhood bars, hotel ballrooms, and appliance retailers introduced consumers in major Northeast cities to the medium. Stereotypical images of men in bars watching boxing and wrestling matches, much like the characters in the 1980s sitcom *Cheers*, were rooted in this first wave of television installations. It wasn't until 1950 that television began to penetrate the household market.

An early television set was a substantial financial and aesthetic investment. On average a set encased in a console retailed for $375 in 1950 ($3,000 in 2005 dollars). Since televisions, like Victrolas and radio consoles in the 1920s and 1930s, were invariably sold as large pieces of furniture, consumers thought carefully about the cost and the style of the console. Catering to diverse tastes, the Chicago-based Motorola Corporation offered the Gainsborough model in blonde or mahogany veneer, the eighteenth-century Raeburn, and the modern-classic Van Dyck.

In these early days, television sets also represented a social investment. The home of the first family in the neighborhood to purchase a television became a magnet for the curious. Friends and neighbors might well "drop in" for a visit when popular shows were on. Magazines and newspapers frequently lampooned this practice, while offering advice to TV-age hostesses who were supposed to prepare and serve snacks. This social phase of collective viewing resembled a similar phase during radio's early days, with a crucial difference. When friends and neighbors gathered around the radio, they interacted, talking, laughing, or singing as they listened. In 1950, television viewers sat in hushed silence in a room darkened to reduce the glare on the screen. The effect was not unlike a miniature movie theater brought into the living room, with snack service complete with popcorn and soft drinks provided by mom or the "lady of the house."

During television's infancy, facing some of the same challenges as the first radio stations of the 1920s, networks had little material to broadcast. Before the take-off period of 1948–50, broadcasters concentrated on sports and news. This choice stemmed from the low cost of broadcasting live unrehearsed events, but it was also driven by the marketers' perception that men made the decisions for big-ticket home purchases. If the networks were to offer programming likely to appeal to men, they reasoned, husbands would invest in televisions. As sales increased, however, the emphasis on sports declined, and children's and variety programming became more prominent.

The Howdy Doody Show, which starred a wooden puppet with 48 freckles, one for each state, and his human co-star, Buffalo Bob Smith, demonstrated the profitability of children's programming. In the spring of the 1948 presidential election year, the program ran a promotion offering a free "Howdy Doody for President" button to any child who wrote to one of the stations carrying the show. Over 60,000 buttons were distributed, one for every three television sets. Originally aired on Saturday night before moving to a five-evening-per-week schedule, *Howdy Doody* was a major reason many parents were among the first consumers to buy television sets.

The first human television star was Milton Berle, whose variety show, *The Texaco Star Theatre*, highlighted NBC's Tuesday evening programming. Berle was a successful New York nightclub comedian, with a history in vaudeville and on Broadway. His hour-long program was copied directly from radio's adaptation of vaudeville. "Uncle Miltie" would tell a few jokes, sing a song, and then introduce different performers: singers, trained animals, jugglers, and other comedians. In between acts, Berle would tell more jokes. His comedy was based on wisecracks, insults, practical jokes, slapstick, physical mugging, and wild costumes, including drag.

Uncle Miltie's antics were perfect for television's early days. By fall 1948, *The Texaco Star Theatre* was so popular that NBC delayed starting election night coverage until 9 PM, so as to not pre-empt Uncle Miltie. Berle's achievement, though, was also an indication of television's immaturity. His jokes focused on life in the big city, which worked as long as most television viewers were located in the Northeast. His popularity and the spread of television in the late 1950s were inversely related. His *shtick* appealed to New Yorkers but didn't resonate with folks in Georgia, California, and points in between.

Berle's appeal, or lack thereof, also highlights the ongoing discussion over television's cultural position. In TV, as with print advertising, records, and radio, debates ensued as to whether the new media should serve "the classes" or kowtow to "the masses." When broadcasting options consisted of the occasional boxing match, the networks didn't give much thought to television's taste level. When the medium started attracting broader attention, tastemakers argued that television was a vehicle for bringing opera, good music, and fine drama to middle America. Highbrows argued that unrefined shows like Uncle Miltie's proved that television could weaken the American character. From the beginning, there were efforts, particularly at NBC, to bring uplifting programs to "the masses."

Televisions themselves also changed during the 1950s. As long as TV prices remained high, manufacturers like the General Electric Company marketed television sets as attractive pieces of furniture, engineering marvels, and sources of entertainment for both men and women. In the push-now age, they worked hard to press Mr. and Mrs. Consumer's hot buttons. The rapid growth of the television business, and the sheer unfamiliarity of consumers with the new technology, forced the entire industry to make things up as it went along.

With more sets in America's living rooms, the networks had to provide new content. When there were only a few thousand sets being watched, a limited number of programs sufficed: sporting and news events, *Howdy Doody,* and *Texaco Star Theatre.* With millions of sets in homes across the country, new types of programs were needed. Soap operas, variety shows, news, and sporting events could move from radio studios to television, but the relationship with the audience changed in the process. A housewife could do her chores while her radio was tuned to *A Guiding Light,* but since her console TV was in the living room, she had to sit down and watch a television broadcast of the same soap opera. TV soap operas thus led to an occasional delay in preparing dinner or doing the ironing. Late afternoon children's programming brought kids, who would normally play outdoors, into the home to watch television. TV became a solitary activity for children; a substitute babysitter.

The older familiar formats were supplemented with newer ones, including talk shows, dramas, and blockbuster spectacles like *Peter Pan* in the evenings. As the program schedule began to expand around the clock, television began segmenting its audience: homemakers during the day, children after school, men on the weekends, and couples in the evening.

This new method of programming inevitably stirred familial conflict over who should decide what to watch, and marketers responded by suggesting people buy more than one TV set per household. In 1955, 2 percent of the 31 million households with a television owned more than one set, a figure that grew to 10 percent by 1958. The introduction of small sets allowed families to buy more than one TV, so that mom, dad, and the kids could watch their favorite programs at the same time. Consumers put televisions in the kitchen so that housewives could follow the soap operas as they prepared meals and in the rec room to contain the mess men made while snacking, drinking, and celebrating during boxing matches.

Curiously, television didn't put other entertainment media out of business. Consumers stayed home more often, partly because it was convenient and partly because—like radio—once the television set was purchased, the programs were free. This resulted in a temporary decline of movie revenues, which rebounded by the late 1950s. Spectator sports and theater didn't show declines in revenue, remaining steady throughout the decade. Instead, the rise in television viewing suggests an increase in available leisure time and a higher demand for entertainment content.

Radio, Records, and High-Fidelity

Television's popularity paralleled major changes in the radio and record industries. The "golden age of radio" ended as TV captured Americans' attention during prime time, and stars like Bing Crosby, Jack Benny, and the husband-and-wife comedy team, George Burns and Gracie Allen, migrated to the new medium. But radio thrived, as formats and listening habits evolved, station revenues expanded, and sales of sets grew. Radio, however, was not the only audio-based growth industry in Boomer America. In the recording industry, improved technologies replaced the brittle shellac disks, which had been the standard since the 1910s. In tandem, the emerging "high-fidelity" business altered the methods by which music was recorded and the way in which consumers listened to it.

Before the rise of television, the networks dominated radio programming. Stations had a format that included a mix of quiz shows, news, variety hours, and drama, filling the gaps with a sprinkling of live music. With the advent of television, the networks channeled their energies into the new medium and national advertisers followed. In turn, radio station owners turned to *local* advertisers, rendering obsolete the old network model of radio programming heavily based on the interweaving of content and commercials as *The King Biscuit Flour Hour* and Maxwell House Coffee's *Showboat*. Radio stations now focused on specific niche audiences that attracted strong local advertising.

New listening habits reinforced this trend toward the standardization of television and the diversification of radio programming. As Americans turned to television in the evening, radio stations began rethinking daytime and late-night broadcasting. By 1953, 60 percent of cars had dashboard radios, and drive time became an important part of the day for commuters, broadcasters, and advertisers. Radio advertisers discovered teenagers in the 1950s, making the after-school and evening hours lucrative for marketers targeting those customers.

Advertisers also found radio a cost-effective way of reaching rural, African Americans, Latino, and other minority listeners. Audience fragmentation continued, as radio stations stopped being identified by their network affiliation and started being associated with the listening preferences of their audiences: rock and roll, rhythm and blues, news and information, classical music, country and western, or religious. Radio's gross advertising revenues increased even as television's income from commercials skyrocketed.

Two major innovations—the invention of the transistor in 1948 and the introduction of the transistor radio in 1955—changed listeners' behavior dramatically. Transistor radios were small, hand-held, and mobile. When Eveready introduced the alkaline battery in the late

1950s, the power problem was solved. Now a listener could have his or her favorite audio entertainment anywhere, on the street, the beach, or lying in bed after lights out. With earphones, nobody else would be bothered by the noise, or hear the magic emanating from the radio.

Transistor radios appealed particularly to teenagers who wanted to take their favorite rock-and-roll music everywhere. As radio programming zoomed in on various market niches, formats fragmented, and pop music became the teen favorite. Music stations played best-selling records that appealed to young listeners who collected 45s, and many of these broadcasters became identified with teenage audiences. During the rock-and-roll explosion, the outrageous antics of radio disc jockeys like Alan Freed and Dick Clark were often as important as the music of singers like Bill Haley, Chuck Berry, and Elvis Presley.

The music and radio businesses became entwined in new ways, largely because of "format wars." To create a 78 rpm (revolutions per minute) record for a Victrola phonograph player in 1947, studio staff used a single microphone to capture live performances. In 1948, New York–based Columbia Records introduced the $33^1/_3$ rpm long-playing album (LP), whose "microgroove" technology could hold twenty minutes of music on a side, as opposed to three minutes on a 78-speed disc. Created by using a multitrack technology, the LP offered improved sound—a better format for the extended works of symphonic music, opera, and jazz. In 1949, archrival RCA used multitrack technology to create an alternative standard: the 45 rpm record. Like the 78, a 45 contained only one song on each side. But the 45 was much cheaper than an LP, and its improved sound and durability set it apart from the old-fashioned 78. In the early 1950s, sophisticated consumers who liked classical music, opera, and jazz embraced the longer playing times of the LP, but pop music fans continued to buy the hit songs one 45 at a time. Initially, the new formats would require new phonographs to play them, but by 1953 inexpensive multispeed portable phonographs were available, and record sales surpassed their previous 1947 peak. Both LPs and 45s were cheaper to manufacture and distribute than were the old 78s.

The proliferation of radio stations specializing in a variety of music formats helped to promote and popularize different musical styles, much more so than the generic network broadcasts of the Great Depression and World War II. By the mid-1950s, when record companies and radio stations were primed to recognize the power of the youth market, Elvis Presley, Pat Boone, and Chuck Berry climbed to the top of the charts. Songs like "Hound Dog," "Tutti Frutti," and "Roll Over Beethoven" poured out of transistor radios, car dashboards, and portable phonographs in basement rec rooms all over America.

The music of the rock-and-roll era jolted the comfortable cardigan-pop of Perry Como and other crooners of the early 1950s. Rock-and-roll musicians freely adapted hillbilly and African American styles in new ways. Elvis Presley synthesized it all, mixing the vibrant realism of country and western, the sexual fire of rhythm and blues, and the sheer vocal quality of all but the best operatic singers.

The sudden changes in the record business and radio were echoed in the movies. Marlon Brando's *The Wild One* and James Dean's best-known film, *Rebel Without a Cause,* focused on the spirit of teenage angst and rebellion, while *Rock Around the Clock, Rock Rock Rock,* and *Don't Knock the Rock* were mostly vehicles to showcase the popular new rock-and-roll genre. Elvis's films, such as *Jailhouse Rock, Love Me Tender*, and *King Creole,* brought the musical and cultural strands together, in a manner not unlike his music.

Dashboard and transistor radios enabled a teenager to create a personalized audio space wherever he or she happened to be. At a drive-in hamburger joint, new shopping mall, soda fountain, or neighbor's rec room, consumers heard the sounds of rock and roll blasting out of the new music boxes. Public space could now be defined by music selections available through multiple technologies.

At the same time that teenage radio, 45 rpm records, and cheap phonographs midwived the rock-and-roll era, high-fidelity fanatics transformed how Americans heard music and purchased audio equipment. Phonographs and radios in the early 1950s were decidedly low-fidelity instruments, equipped with monophonic speakers that had a limited frequency range. However, several technological vectors had started to converge.

One was the development of tape recording, a communications technology created by wartime industrial research. Recording music on tape was significantly superior to the technologies that had preceded it. Reel-to-reel tapes and tape players entered the commercial marketplace in the late 1940s.

Concurrently, Do-It-Yourself audiophiles, akin to the radio hams of the 1920s, decided to reshape their sound environments. Ex-GIs, who had developed expertise in communications technology during World War II, joined thousands of other consumers undertaking Do-It-Yourself projects in their garages, dens, and basements. As a hobby, electronics forged masculine bonds among fathers and sons. The new generation of tinkerers haunted electronic supply houses, like RadioShack, and browsed through mail-order catalogs by Heathkit. Their goal was to find the newest components that would tease louder and more faithful sounds from their equipment. Magazines like *High Fidelity* created a community for these new audiophiles, who labored long into the night with soldering irons, oscilloscopes, and isolation transformers.

The experiments by audio hobbyists developed a market for high-fidelity hardware, and created a new type of consumer: the music aficionado with an appetite for perfect fidelity. The old console phonograph was deemed inadequate for the faithful reproduction of dramatic arias or symphonic crescendos. Technological sophistication or snobbery demanded users purchase a separate turntable equipped with both a specialized tone-arm and a phonograph cartridge housing the needle; a preamplifier; an amplifier; and gargantuan custom-built speakers. As highbrow, high-end consumers developed a taste for high-fidelity sound, engineering entrepreneurs turned their own audio obsessions into state-of-the-art sonic technology companies that produced components to supply the audiophiles' desires. One of these was Henry Kloss, an MIT physics major who never obtained his degree. He turned his fanaticism with speaker design into a series of companies—Acoustic Research, KLH, Advent Corporation, and Cambridge Soundworks—dedicated to improving sound reproduction.

Initially, the high-fidelity market was geared to fanatics, but improvements in sound reproduction soon appeared in mainstream equipment. Console sets sold in furniture stores may have met the mass-market demand for phonographs, but a growing number of sophisticated consumers lusted after concert-hall realism. By the mid-1950s, an ordinary Do-It-Yourself enthusiast could assemble a high-quality component system himself. Even the venerable retailer to middle America, Sears, Roebuck and Company sold separate turntables, amplifiers, and speakers in its stores and mail-order catalogs.

The introduction of stereophonic records in 1958 provided more momentum to the high-fidelity movement. For consumers with the right equipment, stereo provided a more realistic sound experience than mono. Casual consumers simply didn't think the difference between mono and stereo justified an upgrade of their equipment, but some listeners decided that the promise of stereophonic sound definitely warranted replacing their old cabinet phonographs. This gave the man of the house a chance to demonstrate his technical prowess, to assemble a new system from components acquired from multiple manufacturers.

The cover of a 1962 RadioShack catalog illustrates the shift from heavy cabinet phonographs to the new component stereo systems. It shows a young couple lounging in their living room as they listen to a brand-name record player equipped with a brand-name stereo cartridge. Their amplifier is identified by its wattage, and makes no concessions to aesthetics. Two large speakers serve as end tables for lamps. The price of the entire setup — $260 — was far more reasonable than a phonograph-cabinet would have been ten years earlier in 1952. With their stereo system, modern furniture, wall-to-wall carpeting, and form-fitting clothes, the youthful couple invokes the hip urban consumerism of the Kennedy era. Their stripped-down stereo matches their no-nonsense apparel, their overall effect a statement about their stylish and technologically savvy lifestyle.

By 1962, most electronic entertainment was very different than it had been fifteen years earlier. The revolutionary technologies of the late 1940s had taken hold, and many had entered the Average American's life as common household appliances. More than 90 percent of the nation's households had televisions, and many families owned multiple sets. Americans attended fewer movies, plays, and sporting events, staying home to watch TV or listen to the stereo. The proliferation of multiple televisions, radios, and phonographs also enabled consumers to customize domestic entertainment. The home could have one entertainment environment or several. Dad, Mom, and the kids could watch or listen as a family, or as individual consumers. Large, cumbersome pieces of furniture that contained televisions, phonographs, and radios in 1948 had yielded to smaller, more powerful, and high-quality devices that could be easily moved around the house. Most important, lower prices and smaller sizes enabled Americans to take their favorite entertainment along. Dashboard radios in cars and transistor radios in shirt pockets had Americans listening to their favorite songs—whenever and wherever they wanted.

Tape It!

In the 1970s and 1980s, the most important development for the relationship between consumers and sound occurred at the intersection of recording technology and musical genre. Notably, cassette tapes gained popularity among consumers, who appreciated having the freedom to copy material as they saw fit. At the same time, new musical genres—disco, punk, and rap—challenged the dominance of rock and roll and the emphasis on albums. These new genres not only focused on the *song* rather than the LP but also encouraged consumers to bypass the establishment by copying music from any available source—their own collections, their friends' collections, the radio, television, and live concerts—in a way that foreshadowed the internet file sharing of the late 1990s.

Personal tape recorders entered the consumer market in several stages: reel-to-reel, eight-track, and cassette. In the 1950s, companies advertised reel-to-reel tape machines as gadgets for musicians and audiophiles, mostly men. Eight-track tape cartridges appeared in 1965 and, two years later, the Ford Motor Company installed combination radio-tape players as standard equipment in all new cars. The automotive eight-track tape player was a symbol of youthful liberation, a fitting fashion accessory for a car like the Ford Mustang. Now, drivers could purchase eight-tracks of their favorite albums and turn their cars into private sound booths. For the first time, they could listen to talk shows on AM radio, alternative music programs on FM radio, or their favorite rock-and-rollers as they drove along.

Introduced around the same time, cassette players lagged in popularity, but by the mid-1970s, cassettes were the preferred format for home and car stereo systems. Cassettes added a new dimension to electronic entertainment. A consumer could purchase LP albums by his favorite classical, pop, jazz, and rock artists on tape, or could buy blank tapes and use his own equipment to copy records from his personal collection. Reel-to-reel and eight-track technologies had permitted some level of personal recording, but the process was expensive and awkward. With cassettes, a consumer could record anything, and the taped sound would be almost as good as the original LP or 45.

Preoccupied with selling records, the music business missed the long-range cultural significance of the cassette boom. Record companies anguished over the ability of consumers to copy — and share — LPs and 45s on cassette. The British Phonographic Industry, a trade association, campaigned under the slogan, "Home Taping Is Killing Music," a motto eagerly embraced by American companies. Record sales peaked in 1977, as LPs from rock artists like Peter Frampton and pop singers like The Bee Gees set new levels as chart-toppers. At the same time, consumers' insistence on creating their own tapes, combined with budding musical styles based on the individual song, fractured the LP's stronghold on popular music.

Disco, as mentioned, was born in the alternative gay and black cultures of lower Manhattan, but would not have been possible without the high-fidelity fanaticism of the 1950s. Advances in speaker and amplifier design were just as important to nightclub dancers as the music itself. Disco also marked a return to the song as a basic unit of consumption, as opposed to the LP album. Disco songs were produced by hundreds of different artists and record companies. Homemade cassettes, with songs copied from records or the radio, provided consumers with a portable format. In a moment of self-empowerment, consumers could pretend they were producers by creating their own taped albums of songs. Nightclub DJs built their reputations by putting together a distinctive mix of songs.

The bricolage effect again took hold in the punk scene of the late 1970s. Unlike disco, punk didn't make any concessions to sonic fidelity. The music was often harsh, poorly recorded, and played by unskilled musicians. In England, bands like The Sex Pistols, The Clash, The Slits, and The Jam threw up an unmoderated mixture of politics, antifashion, nihilistic philosophy, and loud primitive music.

In America, The Ramones, Dead Kennedys, Blondie, and The Dead Boys skipped the philosophy and offered short, fast, and loud songs. In both countries, antifashion accessories like dog collars, safety pins, and torn T-shirts offered a sharp visual contrast to the glamourous, self-indulgent clothing of the stereotypical rock star. Primitive, self-produced songs on badly pressed 45s became the stock in trade of punk musicians. These, too, were easy to reassemble on homemade cassette collections.

By the late 1970s, consumers could play their cassettes on two new pieces of equipment: the "boom box" and the Walkman. These personal entertainment devices reshaped how people used sound in public spaces just as the transistor radio had fifteen years earlier.

For several years, some models of portable radios featured cassette players, but these tabletop devices were low-fidelity. In the late 1970s, Sony Corporation, Philips [Koninklijke Philips Electronics N.V.], and other high-fidelity manufacturers began making larger, better battery-powered cassette radio players with loud bass woofers, nicknamed "boom boxes." These devices, often the size of a suitcase and ornamented with chrome, delivered sound quality that approached high-fidelity home systems. A boom-box owner proudly carried his music around. The loud, rib-rattling beat of his favorite song was heard by everyone within earshot. Consumers armed with a boom box claimed public space as their own in an act of assertion, if not aggression. Boom boxes became symbols of empowerment for black inner-city youth, who expropriated the new technology and made it a symbol of rap music and a hip-hop style accessory.

Spike Lee's 1989 movie, *Do the Right Thing*, hinges on that boom-box aggression and the subsequent and inevitable reaction to it. The film captures a horrific moment in an African American neighborhood in Brooklyn on the hottest day of the year. It is a classic "slice-of-life" movie with multiple storylines intersecting at various points, all occurring on the block that contains Sal's Famous, a pizzeria operated by an Italian American father and his two sons. One of the key characters is Radio Raheem, a hulking African American who totes his suitcase-sized boom box blasting Public Enemy's "Fight the Power" wherever he goes. Throughout the movie, other African American males celebrate Raheem's bringing Public Enemy's political message to the streets, while the Korean grocery-store owners have trouble coping with his need to immediately replace the twenty D batteries it takes to power this behemoth. A group of Hispanics engage in a "my box is bigger" contest and lose.

The climax in *Do the Right Thing* begins when Raheem brings his boom box, still blasting "Fight the Power," into the pizzeria and Sal yells out "No music, no music, no music!" Radio Raheem's insistence on his right to play his boom box comes into direct conflict with Sal's control over his restaurant. In the end, the disagreement incites a full-scale riot, resulting in the torching of the pizza parlor and Radio Raheem's death at the hands of the police.

The Walkman went in the opposite direction and had a similar, although longer-lasting, effect on how consumers used electronic devices and music to personalize public space. In 1980, Sony introduced the Walkman, a personal cassette player which was no larger than the old-fashioned transistor radio. Its small size marked the Walkman as innovative, as did the earphones that delivered powerful, high-fidelity sound directly to the consumer's ears. Unlike the boom box that blasted sound throughout the neighborhood, the Walkman provided a private listening experience. Subway commuters, joggers, dog-walkers, and teenagers at home could listen to their favorite music without disturbing anyone. Boom-box aficionados redefined public zones as their personal space—Walkman owners carried their private space wherever they went.

Nothing about the shift from records to cassette tapes represented a dramatically new technology. Audio tapes had existed during World War II, but they were not commercialized until consumer demand mobilized the industry. Consumers wanted improved sound, greater convenience, and the ability to customize their choices, which stimulated innovators and manufacturers to make products that were better, smaller, and cheaper. Still, none of this was really revolutionary. The customization of a personal soundscape reflected the "do-your-own-thing" attitude that sparked the individualization of houses and fashion. For breakaway electronic technologies, consumers had to look elsewhere in the home entertainment sector.

Video Games: New Devices and Desires

In 1972, consumers were hooking up *Pong*, the first commercially available video game, to home television sets. This marked the domestic appearance of the personal computer, a truly revolutionary machine. Computers, like many of the other devices of the electronic age, first appeared in the mid-to-late-1940s but for decades lay solely in the domain of universities and the military. Following in the footsteps of radio hams in the 1910s and high-fidelity fanatics of the 1950s, programmers who earned their livelihoods writing codes for the big IBM machines started tinkering with computers as a hobby.

Some of these "geeks" created computer-based games for their own amusement, and the first designed for home use was *Odyssey*, introduced in 1972. It consisted of a basic computer hooked up to a television screen. Others soon followed, including *Pong*, an electronic ping-pong game. Within four years, more than seventy different game manufacturers had entered the U.S. market. *Pong* creators formed Atari, Inc., to market electronic games, selling 100,000 units in 1974 alone. By 1982, 7 million video games were sold to 16 percent of U.S. households.

In the late 1970s and early 1980s, the remarkable thing about video games wasn't their entry into the home but their popularity in public spaces. Atari and other companies sold basic units that worked on home televisions, but they also made sophisticated coin-operated games, complete with glitzy special effects and sounds, for bars, pizza parlors, and arcades. In 1979, Midway Games's *Pac Man* introduced a cute alternative to space conquest games. *Pac Man*'s cuteness broke the gender divide in video games, appealing to women and girls as well as men and boys. By 1982, Americans spent $8 billion dollars annually in video arcades. In a curious recreation of the nickelodeon craze of the early 1900s, young consumers were the primary purchasers of these cheap entertainments outside the home.

The video game industry went through some boom-and-bust cycles, but by the late 1990s, Nintendo Company, Sony, and Microsoft dominated the market. These manufacturers designed games for a range of customers, from very young children to sophisticated fantasy adventurers. They focused on high-quality graphics and sound that provided gaming enthusiasts with constantly challenging excitement. In 2000, video games outsold televisions. Today, video games are a favorite amusement for children and an intellectual challenge for youthful gaming fanatics, two important niche markets in the global electronics business.

The success of video games illustrates the continuing trend of customization. Ever since the 1940s, electronic devices became popular because they allowed users to individualize their own experiences. Whether in arcades in 1982 or at home in 2002, gamers could submerge themselves in a reality of their choosing. Virtual reality became a space for the negotiation of consumer power and the creation of personal identity. Manufacturers tried to offer virtual realities that were more exciting and adventurous than those of their competitors. Gamers defined themselves by virtual wins and losses, and by a new set of imaginary figures that replaced the heroes in dime-store novels and the genies in television sitcoms.

Multinationals like Nintendo, Sony, and Microsoft have created a new, multibillion dollar industry built on gaming. In 1972, *Odyssey* and *Pong* were harbingers of things to come. These early game systems were the first computers used in the home for entertainment, the first application of televisions for something other than broadcasting, and the first example of interactive consumer electronics. They also turned Generation X into a group of consumers for whom interacting with a video screen became second nature.

Personal Computers before the Internet

In the years since the introduction of *Pong,* computers have changed how American consumers listen to music, watch videos, talk to each other, read and write, stay in touch with old friends and make new ones, and find information — from scholarly research to local telephone numbers. Not even television has affected the experience of American consumers as much as have personal computers.

One small device, the transistor, which lay behind the portable radio explosion of the 1950s, also generated the "smaller is better" trend in computers. Starting with the 27-ton ENIAC, computers became increasingly smaller and more powerful. By the late 1960s, mini-computers, which were "mini" only in relation to enormous mainframes that took up an entire office, were becoming prevalent in corporate, military, and university settings.

In 1971, Intel, a Silicon Valley startup co-founded by William Shockley and Gordon Moore, introduced the microprocessor, a tiny chip powerful enough to drive a desktop computer. Four years later, the January 1975 issue of *Popular Electronics* announced the first personal computer, the Altair 8800. Created by Micro Instrumentation and Telemetry Systems (MITS) in a garage in Albuquerque, New Mexico, this new electronic device was available as a $400 Do-It-Yourself kit or as a $498 pre-assembled, pre-tested item. It was devilishly difficult to program, had no display or keyboard, nearly no memory, and no interfaces with other devices. It could run a program, but its only output was a series of flashing lights that an experienced computer programmer had to decipher. In other words, Altair 8800 didn't do very much, but it *was* a small, table-top size, personal computer.

To those in the know, the Altair 8800 was an inspiration sent down to Earth by the electronic gods. Hobbyists and professional programmers, including Bill Gates and Paul Allen, who founded Microsoft in 1975, immediately began playing with the Altair 8800. Over the next two years, different geeks developed storage solutions, interfaces with keyboards and displays, and operating systems that improved its performance. By 1977, RadioShack introduced a commercial variation of the machine, the TRS-80, Commodore launched the PET, and Apple trotted out the Apple II. These three companies targeted slightly different groups of users in the small but growing home-computer market.

This new computer hardware demanded applications, but the only readily apparent uses were games and programs that imitated typewriters, now called word processors. Meanwhile, the influx of minicomputers, mainframes, and memory typewriters into the workplace familiarized Boomers with digital devices, creating the first group of nontechnical consumers who were comfortable with them. In 1979, Visi-Calc changed the landscape, when thousands of people who ran businesses at home purchased computers to run Visi-Calc's new spreadsheet program. A year later, programmers developed standards for word-processers to make them more user-friendly. With spreadsheets and word processing, consumers began using small computers for something other than games.

The next paradigm shift was the introduction of a graphical user interface, or GUI. Before Apple introduced the Macintosh in 1984, a computer user had to know how to execute arcane commands and navigate through complex menus. For the 1984 Super Bowl, Apple's advertising agency, Chiat-Day, and director-producer Ridley Scott, known for the films *Alien* and *Blade Runner*, created a now-iconic television commercial that imprinted the Macintosh's futuristic capabilities in viewers' minds. Echoing themes in George Orwell's dystopian novel, *1984*, a muscular female athlete, dressed in full-blown runner's gear, throws a sledgehammer into a giant screen picturing Big Brother. The commercial's storyline implies that Apple had fractured the mysteries of personal computing and had opened a brave new world of user-friendly personal computers. The Macintosh, with its user-friendly GUI technology, took the desktop computer away from geeks, hobbyists, and tinkerers and put it at the fingertips of ordinary consumers.

After Apple's Macintosh secured a major share of the popular market, personal computer manufacturers woke up to Baby Boomers' desires to domesticate these digital devices and make them part of the yuppie identity kit. Whereas early personal computers had emphasized the power and speed of hardware, the next generation focused on software. Apple's MacPaint software allowed consumers to manipulate graphic images on their computers, while the MacWrite word processor competed with WordPerfect, WordStar, and Microsoft Word. As computers entered the home, gaming attracted new computer users, which further pushed hardware manufacturers to improve their products.

Until the early 1990s, most computers were isolated machines, über-typewriters that could permanently store information (mostly text and spreadsheets) or run simple games. Admittedly, storage and gamesmanship were significant advances, but consumers still preferred to watch television, listen to the radio, and play compact discs (CDs), which had replaced cassettes as the music medium of choice, rather than fiddle around with the home computer. Sometimes people played computer games on digital equipment connected to the television, but for the most part, the personal computer remained an appliance rather than a source of entertainment.

Connecting to the Internet

Then "Tennessee Senator Al Gore invented the internet," or so the mythology goes. Historians know that such claims are simplistic, reducing a complex evolutionary process to the lowest common denominator.

For sure, Gore's 1991 bill to create the "information superhighway"—the High-Performance Computing Act of 1991—laid the foundation for the internet's expansion from a government utility into a commercial entity. Congress initiated a process that not only helped millions of Americans get "online," but also transformed the web into a major commercial tool and communications medium. Nonetheless, by 1991, the internet was already more than thirty years old.

In the 1960s, academic researchers and government agencies had recognized the value of having computers communicate with each other, and for several years, military and university researchers worked on developing networks that would connect distant devices to one another. By 1969, Arpanet, the first electronic network, was linking computers at four west-coast universities. Although Arpanet was created to provide researchers and administrators with remote access and file transfers, programmers soon added three powerful new functions: the capacities to locate electronic mail or email, to locate specific files, and to search their content.

In the military and civilian workplace, potential customers for the personal computer became familiar with email and electronic networks, long before the internet even had a name. To serve these new users, a collection of bulletin board services and then companies like America On-Line, Prodigy, and CompuServe offered a way for users to send emails and search databases for information. This ignited a demand for networked computers outside of the workplace. Developers produced hypertext language, Java programming language, and the graphic integration of it all. New computer operating systems supported the development of web browsers, which gave users the ability to "surf" the brand-new World Wide Web, which is nothing more than all the world's computers linked on a giant network. The web provided a gateway for people to find information on all these computers.

In *The History of Computing*, historian Paul Ceruzzi explains that Alexander Graham Bell never expected his telephone to be used for idle chitchat, and that Thomas A. Edison envisioned the phonograph as a business tool for dictation rather than as an entertainment medium. Similarly, the folks who developed the internet believed that their network could facilitate basic research, not billions of email messages, Christmas shopping, social network sites, easy access to pornography, and endless spam. That, of course, is exactly what happened, as consumers and corporations expropriated digital technology and created new applications for it.

By the early 1990s, many of the technological issues about personal computers, networks, and the web had been addressed, if primitively, but matters of capacity and access hadn't been resolved. When in 1991, Senator Gore, himself a Baby Boomer, secured passage of a bill to create the "information superhighway," the legislation encouraged the development of faster performance and better bandwidth for scientists and other researchers, while removing the government from oversight of the internet. As Gore's bill worked its way through Congress, the chatter it aroused focused attention on the internet as an instrument of commerce.

Opening the information superhighway to commercial entrepreneurs proved to be an important moment in the history of consumer society. The new legislation applied the principles of the American Way to the hottest, newest technology. Advocates like Gore believed that democratizing the internet's use and allowing "free enterprise" to shape cyberspace would best serve researchers, educators, commerce, and consumers. By the mid-1990s, ambitious young entrepreneurs, many from Generation X, were exploring ways to use the information highway as a platform for a new type of business: ecommerce. During the mid-1990s, Boomer Jeffrey P. Bezos and Gen Xer Pierre Omidyar joined hundreds of other entrepreneurs braving these untested waters. In 1995, Bezos opened the internet retailer Amazon.com, while Omidyar unveiled AuctionWeb, the forerunner to eBay, the online auction house. Both ventures were new and risky, but they transformed the face of retailing and the ways in which consumers obtained information.

Initially established as a bookseller, Amazon offered consumers a larger inventory than any "brick-and-mortar" store could imagine. The online store allowed a consumer to search the entire world of books in and out of print, purchase selections at a discount, and have them delivered to her front door. Amazon marketed each book with reviews, customer comments, and links to similar offerings. The online format eliminated the difficulty of going to local bookstores, where consumers couldn't always find what they wanted, assuming they could find a place to park their cars. With Amazon, the contemporary armchair traveler, whose 1940s predecessors eagerly awaited the postal delivery of the *Saturday Evening Post*, *Life*, and *National Geographic*, could turn on the home computer, go online, and order any travelogue, journal, magazine, or novel he wished to own. The package would arrive a few days later, generating almost instant gratification. Building on the popularity of electronic bookselling, Bezos extended his business model to other areas of retailing, including music, clothing, toys, garden furniture, and computers. In 2002, Amazon joined the 1,000 top companies listed by *Fortune*; three years later its rank was 303, as it took in nearly $7 billion in revenues.

Omidyar's model for eBay was different. Ultimately, he created a virtual marketplace that captured the excitement of the ancient bazaars of the Middle East. Anybody with items to sell, new or used, could list them on AuctionWeb; in turn, any consumer with a bank account or credit card was free to bid. Renamed eBay in 1997, the virtual auction format proved to be successful and created a truly global marketplace, unmediated by tariffs, regulations, and layers of middlemen. Hobbyists and collectors shopped at eBay for vintage Oldsmobile convertibles, Chanel jackets, and tapes of old television shows. This eroded sales at conventional antique stores, but it expanded consumers' options. Superstar CEO Margaret C. Whitman joined eBay in the spring of 1998, the year that the company went public. In 2005, eBay was number 529 on the *Fortune* 1000, with revenues topping $3 billion.

Amazon, eBay, and thousands of smaller internet retailers changed the way Americans shopped. By 2000, hundreds of businesses saw ecommerce as the wave of the future. Behind the scenes, internet transactions facilitated global manufacturing, putting materials suppliers, factories, shippers, and retailers within a click of each other. Companies making ingredients for paints, for example, could better manage their supply and distribution chains. Managers could more easily track costs, prices, and the movement of goods and services. Although ecommerce didn't replace shopping malls or big-box retailers, consumers shifted millions of retail transactions from stores to computer screens. With the web, consumers had greater choice and more competitive prices. A shopper who didn't find the right patio furniture at a nearby Target could order the model she liked from Target.com—and get it delivered, all for less than what she would have paid at the store. Or, if she didn't find what she wanted at Target. com, she could search for "patio furniture" with her browser and find other vendors. Web retailing moved shopping from the realm of public social experience and made it more of a solitary entertainment event. Web browsing had become the new window shopping.

Cable Television

In 1995, Cable News Network (CNN), a subscription cable channel and the brainchild of maverick media mogul Ted Turner, introduced CNN.com. Initially, CNN.com provided instantaneous news updates; eventually, it incorporated a novel form of consumer feedback, the web log, or "blog," an opinion forum that welcomed just about anyone. Since its establishment in 1980, CNN had become the country's leading cable news station, and it offered a major challenge to broadcast news networks. Turner's innovations changed the business and distribution models of American television.

Subscription television is another innovation that by serendipity dates to 1948, the year of consumer electronics. That year, Robert J. Tarlton, a Lansford, Pennsylvania, appliance-store owner, hooked up a private antenna-and-wire network so that his television customers in the Pocono Mountains could watch Channel 3 broadcasts from Philadelphia. Tarlton was ahead of the curve because nearly all early television owners lived close to urban areas and relied on rooftop aerial antennas to capture the broadcasts. Nonetheless, the concept of cable subscription persisted. During the 1950s and 1960s, pioneer cable TV operators and government regulators tried to find the proper role for this type of program dissemination. Little content, however, was developed. In 1966 the FCC imposed a freeze on new cable licenses, responding to nervous broadcasters who viewed cable operators as potential competitors.

When the freeze was lifted in 1972, new technologies allowed the operators of subscription television systems to offer something other than better reception. Viewers willing to pay for television could now watch sports, movies, special events, pornography, and local government programs unavailable to consumers who relied solely on antennas. In 1976, Turner Broadcasting System's WTCG in Atlanta became cable television's first super station, serving subscribers across the entire country via satellite. By 1980, 18 million U.S. households had cable access. By 1991, the number had grown to 60 million, and some of the new cable networks provided up to 75 channels.

As subscription television caught on, new channels proliferated, targeting niche markets. Not everyone, however, felt that greater choice led to improved programming. In 1992, New Jersey's homegrown singer Bruce Springsteen put in his 2¢, writing and performing "57 Channels." He satirized the experience of a newly minted millionaire who "bought a bourgeois house in the Hollywood hills." But when he and his wife tucked themselves in and turned on their cable television, they were sorely disappointed. "We switched 'round and 'round 'til half-past dawn," only to find "fifty-seven channels and nothin' on."

Springsteen's observations notwithstanding, consumers flocked to subscription television because these service providers offered more programs than conventional broadcast TV. Consumers could even buy things on cable television; channels like the Home Shopping Network and QVC attracted loyal viewers, prefiguring the internet experiences of eBay and Amazon. Established in 1981 and 1985, respectively, the cable channels MTV and VH1 pioneered the music video format, which featured stars like Prince and Michael Jackson singing and dancing. Imitators followed suit and a proliferation of new cable stations popped up, each focusing on a single format: sports, public affairs, movies, cartoons, Hispanic programs, religion, vintage movies, and reruns of classic comedies or sitcoms from the 1960s, 1970s, and 1980s.

Cable's watershed moment came during the 1991 Gulf War. By investing in news and forging partnerships with local reporters across the world, CNN was able to break stories faster and provide deeper coverage than could traditional networks. When the Gulf War erupted, CNN was uniquely positioned. With staff in Iraq and Kuwait and strong local contacts, CNN reported live from the battlefields days before ABC, CBS, or NBC. The most powerful, and enduring, media images of this conflict showed CNN correspondents Peter Arnett and Christiane Amanpour reporting from Baghdad as shells exploded in the darkness behind them. These images eerily echoed Morley Safer's and Mike Wallace's televised accounts on Vietnam and Edward R. Murrow's voice coming via radio from London during the Blitzkrieg in World War II. But unlike the prerecorded accounts from television and radio, CNN's coverage was live, 24-hours-per-day.

Despite the live-action coverage, it was no longer possible for a single show, or even a war, to capture the attention of an entire country. CNN was competing with the Home Shopping Network, professional wrestling, gardening and cooking shows, and reruns of *M*A*S*H*, a 1970s sitcom about the Korean War, all of which were available for the millions of viewers intent on isolating themselves from the onslaught of the Gulf War coverage. This plethora of choices helped consumers move away from the network programs that had dominated television from its earliest days through the 1980s. As a consequence, viewers' relationships to their televisions changed. The sheer number of choices fragmented the audience into ever smaller niches.

As cable entered more homes, another new technology—videotaping—provided consumers with the ability to customize what they watched and when. Several manufacturers had experimented with methods for making copies of TV programs, but Sony's Beta system, which debuted in 1975, introduced a format that resonated with consumers. The next year, the Japanese firm JVC, which had been established in 1927 as a subsidiary of the Victor Talking Machine Company, countered with the Video Home System, or VHS. During the record industry's format wars of the postwar period, LPs and 45s had vied for consumers' dollars but coexisted by serving different constituencies, until the compact disk (CD) replaced vinyl in the 1990s. In the video-cassette market, consumers chose the VHS, which could record more hours of programming, over the Betamax, which provided a better-quality copy. Introduced in the United States in 1977, the VHS format wiped out the competition within a few short years, suggesting to some observers that consumers preferred convenience over technical virtuosity. The VHS format with its companion hardware, the video cassette recorder or VCR, emerged as the industry standard in the early 1980s. In 1984, nearly 8 million VCRs were purchased in the United States; and by 1990, 75 percent of American households had a VCR connected to their television.

VCRs changed the way consumers used their televisions, obliterating the rigid viewing schedules set by prime-time programs in the 1950s. These devices allowed people to record their favorite television program while they were watching it, viewing another show, or while the TV set was off and they were doing something else. Consumers assembled collections of their favorite shows, movies or sporting events, which could be played back at any time. For those with the right equipment and the ability to understand programming instructions, viewing choices were no longer limited by time.

Recording programs only accounted for a portion of a consumer's leisure time spent with a VCR. Prerecorded tapes gave viewers the opportunity to watch any movie at home anytime. As VCRs became increasingly popular, a new retail format, the video rental store, matched its growth. Many video stores were local or regional operations, but one national chain, the Dallas-based Blockbuster Entertainment Corporation founded in 1982, has dominated the movie rental business since 1985. Video stores stocked popular, classic, and foreign movies; music videos; old television shows; adult movies; and children's programs. Consumers could build a personal video library by purchasing tapes, but most people preferred to rent them for a few days. In 1988, 80 million VHS tapes were sold, and 2.5 billion rented.

During television's early days, viewers' choices were restricted to programs being broadcast by a few stations: the three major networks, a local educational station, and possibly one or two UHF broadcasters. In 1991, as Christiane Amanpour reported live from Iraq, consumers could choose from network and cable channels, the inventory at the neighborhood video stores, and their personal collection of VHS tapes. They could also record Amanpour (or that day's episode of *One Life to Live*) while at work and watch the tape that evening. Television was becoming a highly personalized, highly individual pastime with increasingly diminishing social context.

Everything Is Digital

By 2005, the electronics entertainment business was changing with blinding rapidity, leaving observers aghast with the speed of the digital age. During the early 1980s, a joint venture between the Dutch and Japanese multinationals, Philips and Sony, developed and commercialized the compact disc. The CD debuted in the United States in 1984, eventually becoming the preferred recording format. After the CD forced the LP and the cassette out of the marketplace, it was challenged by digital files, which consumers could find on the internet and move from computer to computer.

By 2005, subscription TV included hundreds of digital channels, some of which were on-demand services for consumers who wanted to watch their favorite shows at any time. Video rental stores like Blockbuster fought for their lives, battling both the proliferation of choice on cable and satellite television, and the more recent availability of movies and music videos on the internet. The Web not only changed the way consumers bought books and deck chairs, it also transformed how they shopped for all types of entertainment. With a high-speed internet connection, consumers could bypass the shopping mall, the video rental store, and long-distance telephone bills. Recording companies, newspapers, theaters, real-estate agents, broadcast television stations, and telephone companies were either threatened or transformed by the digital revolution.

Yet in 2005, two devices stood poised to change the electronics entertainment industry once again: Apple's iPod, a type of digital audio player, and a new generic product called high-definition television, or HDTV. In many respects, the miniature palm-sized devices and overgrown wall-mounted televisions are polar opposites, representing flip sides of the digital age.

Initially released in fall 2001, Apple's iPod captured more than 80 percent of the personal stereo market within four short years. Between 2001 and 2005, Apple introduced several different variations, or "brand extensions," of the iPod. These included the Shuffle, introduced in 2005 as a $99 no-frills product about the size of a cigarette lighter, and the Nano, a 2005 version of the successful "mini," with a color screen and capable of playing four hours of music. Ultimately, the fifth generation iPod was also released in 2005; it had a color screen, video capability, and storage for more than 10,000 songs, the equivalent of 1,000 LPs. It was about one-third the size of a typical transistor radio of the early 1960s with vastly superior capabilities. By 2005, Apple had expanded from its roots in the brave new world of user-friendly word processors, proudly billing itself an entertainment company rather than a computer manufacturer.

On the other hand, HDTV was unveiled in Japan in 1969, but it took more than thirty years of wrangling over standards and formats before manufacturers could produce sets that consumers could purchase without worry. When HDTVs first appeared in stores like Best Buy, they dwarfed the traditional sets on display. Although only a few inches thick, the first sets had giant screens, six times larger than conventional televisions. The image quality of these devices was vivid, with color more realistic than that found in many movie theaters. When an HDTV was combined with a powerful five-speaker audio system, an upper-middle class household—the primary purchasers of these luxury devices—could reproduce a cinematic experience in the comfort of the living room. Here was a virtual movie theater, without the crowds, parking hassles, $9 tickets, and $5 popcorn.

In 2005, iPods represented the ultimate convergence of the consumer electronics revolution of the past three decades. For one, consumers couldn't use an iPod without computers and the internet. The music on an iPod had to be retrieved from a host computer and, more often than not, downloaded for a fee from a companion Apple web site called iTunes. This Apple internet site also sold music videos, audio books, television shows, and movies. It hosted podcasts, a 2004 web development that enabled consumers to produce their own audio creations for on-demand use by anybody with an internet connection, sort of like a Do-It-Yourself radio program. Almost overnight, the number of choices for audio entertainment increased exponentially. With iTunes, content became available to purchasers at all times, without special expertise or guidance.

The audio quality of iPods, while still evolving in 2005, was superior to anything available fifty years earlier. The iPod's video quality, while limited to two-inch screens, was sharper than the broadcasts received by the first television antennas. In essence, every single type of entertainment device discussed in this chapter could be replaced by a single iPod. The world of entertainment had been miniaturized; it fits on an electronic gizmo the size of a glass vacuum tube and retails for less than a 1948 television set, when adjusted for inflation. Like the ideal service worker in the global digital economy, the iPod was maddeningly efficient at multitasking. It was hard to imagine a palm-sized digital device that could better cater to the consumer's whims. The iPod had replaced records, tapes, and CDs as the medium of choice for music, while also developing a market for digital reruns of television shows, audiobooks, podcasts, and second-run movies.

Like other electronic advances of the previous forty years, the iPod continues to make entertainment a private, personal, and isolated experience. The concept of personal audio space originated with the transistor radio that teenagers carried around after 1955. In contrast to those portable devices, the iPod has no speakers, but directs sounds into the listener's head through ear phones. Without its dock, an iPod cannot be heard by anyone else or claim public space, as did transistor radios and boom boxes. It allows the consumer to experience her private aural space on the subway, at the gym, in the shopping mall, in the car, or at home. The iPod emulates the privacy of the Walkman, without the trouble of having to change the tape or the CD.

The versatile iPod stands in stark contrast to the extravagant HDTV, in aspects other than size. Whereas iPods sold for $399 in 2005, the average HDTV retailed for at least three times more. While an iPod can be plugged into a computer, charged, and then used, a HDTV requires a complicated hookup to a computer, a cable system, or a video signal provider. The miniaturized iPod fits in to a consumer's shirt pocket, but an HDTV has to be bolted to the wall or attached to a special stand. One marks the democratization of consumption; the other, the exclusion that has always characterized luxury goods.

In many ways, HDTV represents not the latest generation of television, but the first generation of private big-screen movie theaters transplanted into the home. Six-speaker, surround-sound audio technology has been commercially available since the mid-1990s, but it took several years to perfect. Improvements to video quality were the last piece of the puzzle. Still other reasons explain the timing of HDTV's commercialization. As the King Kong of home entertainment, an HDTV unit would not comfortably fit in the typical Levittown house, even the remodeled ones that were expanded in the 1960s and 1970s. Consumers needed more space or less clutter before they could appreciate the technology's brilliant video and three-dimensional sound. Suburban Ranch Houses, Cape Cod cottages, urban apartments, row houses, mobile homes, and bungalows were unsuitable in size for this technology. Moreover, few moderate-income consumers could afford these expensive luxuries. When introduced, HTDVs were fitting domestic accessories for consumers living in the upscale developments and gated communities in the Edge Cities. For consumers who owned these personal movie theaters, the HDTV symbolized the

American dream. For others, these oversized televisions, along with SUVs and McMansions, seemed like yet another example of egregious "conspicuous consumption."

Hardware to Software, Hearth to HDTV

Back in 1950, a family might have settled in after the dinner dishes were cleared to watch television. This meant gathering around a large wooden cabinet with a glowing black-and-white picture tube in the center, to view one of the three programs being broadcast by the three national networks. Here was the ideal postwar family, sharing the exciting novelty of watching entertainment at home. They didn't just watch television—they watched the television, which was both a piece of furniture and a link to the outside world.

In 2005, the home entertainment experience was conceptually different. Even if an upper-middle-class family did gather after a meal, they weren't looking at a piece of furniture. Their gaze was fixed on the HDTV: a wall display nearly three feet wide but only a few inches deep, connected by black wires to little boxes with red, green, and blue lights. The 1950s housewife would have been repulsed by the tangled wires, blinking lights, and the disharmony with her home décor. But the 2005 family doesn't even notice the aesthetics of the television or their living room. They're focused on the program, or "cultural software" rather than the "cultural hardware."

Television in 1950 represented a significant new piece of hardware, a device that transformed how people entertained themselves and decorated their homes. Over the next several decades, changes in technology and the business models for radio, the music industry, and television led consumers to expect instant gratification and endless entertainment choices. HDTV epitomizes this trend. A level of technological sophistication that would have been unimaginable to a Levittown family, high-definition cable television is not just a novel piece of hardware but a new way for consumers to entertain themselves. The library of audio-visual programs will soon be virtually limitless. The sound and color are often more powerful than real life. The HDTV, as a collection of metals, chemicals, and wires, is unimportant. As a device that offers better-than-life images and near-infinite choice, the HDTV represents a fundamental change in what is valuable to consumers. It is the latest iteration of the shift from material things themselves to meaningful experiences, from hardware to cultural software.

The Victorians, who loved their parlors, would have been stunned to see their knickknacks melt into thin air.

CONCLUSION

Who We Are

In 2003, national newspaper *USA Today* and Claritas, the San Diego–based firm that dominates geodemographic research, created the interactive web site "Who We Are: Redefining Our Demographics." Based on Claritas's classification system for market segments and clusters, Who We Are provided web surfers with a profile of major consumer groups in Columbus, Ohio, just 2½ hours away from Muncie, Indiana. Unlike Robert and Helen Lynd, who chose 1920s Muncie as Middletown for its homogeneity, *USA Today* and Claritas focused on contemporary Columbus because its "demographic landscape" matched "the spectrum of groups seen across the nation." What constituted an Average American community had changed.

Researchers divided the citizens of Columbus using Claritas's framework of 14 segments and 66 clusters. Forty-seven-year old "Greenbelt Sport" Tim Kauffman referred to his fellow suburban Boomers as successful folks who lived "in a comfortable setting around like people." "Multi-Cultural Mosaic" consumers Daryl Lacy, age 42, and Mary Rose, age 37, described their urban cohort as "colors on a painting," and "a big collage of different colors, different walks of life." Lacy identified his traits as "dependable, hard-working," while Rose called herself "an *individual* that makes up a community."

"Young Digerati" Amber Decker, 27, saw herself as a member of Generation X but thought the label "too overused." When asked to define her cluster, Decker said it was comprised of people with "too many digital devices to the point where the devices are actually ruling our lives. I don't know if we could survive without our TiVo and our PalmPilots anymore." "I wouldn't refer to myself by the things that I buy," Decker firmly stated. "We're nothing but a market segment now."

These interviews illuminate some Americans' perceptions of themselves and the place of artifacts in their lives. Decker's remarks reveal a discomfort with materialism and a perception that market segments are new. For the past 150 years, Americans were proud of their bric-a-brac, tailfins, and hi-fi sets. But now, young urban professionals like Decker dislike being identified by their possessions. Decker's unhappiness signifies, perhaps, a new era.

Seven Big Themes

Theorist Marshall Berman defined human experience since the Enlightenment as a process of discovery and reinvention, as people struggled to put themselves at ease in a constantly changing world. The Victorians, the Moderns, and the Boomers all wrestled with social upheavals that made them feel like their worlds were spiraling out of control. The Victorians steadied their ship in the storm by hoisting up the sail of progress, and using material goods as ballast. They charted a course that guided other travelers for the next century.

As people sought to define what it meant to be American, they grappled with abundance and scarcity, neighborhood and mobility, tradition and novelty, and homogeneity and diversity. Over the past 150 years, American-ness became inexorably entwined with the processes of getting and spending. From the Victorian period through the present, seven major themes have shaped the constant evolution of American consumer society.

First, being American became synonymous with being a middle-class consumer.

When Walt Whitman identified the middle class as the most important segment of American society, he probably had no idea how large the middle class would become, and how much they would shape consumer society. Whitman knew that the middle class set the cultural tone and bridged the gap between shop girls and financiers, millhands and mill owners. For most of the nineteenth and twentieth centuries, the middle class was small, limited to about a third of the population in the 1920s; but it was influential far beyond its numbers.

The middle class was not only a place of belonging, but a place of aspiration. Newly arrived Polish peasants knew they might always work in a factory or coal mine, but they dreamed that their sons and daughters would have a better life, providing *their* families with a front parlor. Not everyone dreamt of being middle class, but this popular metaphor helped much of the highly mobile population get its cultural bearing. The streets of America may not have been paved with gold, but they were cobbled in middle-class dreams.

Not until after World War II did a majority of Americans benefit from prosperity and join the middle class. As Polish, Irish, and Italian peasants looked around, they saw the refined manners and respectable homes of families who had "made it" in America. While the middle class was as much about values and beliefs as material things, those tangible badges of belonging showed what was possible. Working people who wanted to move up in the world created parlors and dressed the part, or "made do" with reasonable facsimiles of middle-class possessions. Today, most Americans identify themselves as middle class, whether they make $150,000 or $25,000 per year, and whether they live in an Edge City or on a Texas cattle ranch.

Second, the home and home ownership became the centerpiece of the American dream.

Over the past 150 years, consumers have updated and redefined the types of spaces they found meaningful. If a time machine transported a middle-class Victorian family to a Boomer suburb, they might be astounded by the automobiles, the refrigerators, and the air conditioning. But they would feel "at home" with the single-family house, its welcoming living room, and an entertainment center functioning as its hearth. Whether in 1890 or 2005, the private suburban home was the focal point for the consumer experience, a showpiece of the American dream.

It has never been easy for Americans to buy homes, but it has become progressively less difficult. Nineteenth-century Americans struggled to acquire property, borrowing money from relatives and local savings and loans. The high price of new houses (due to the lack of standardized materials and high labor costs) and the unrealistic terms of mortgages kept home ownership out of reach for many. Home ownership was extended to a wider population with the creation of federally insured mortgages, the benefits of the GI Bill, and the liberalization of private lending practices. Ownership rates hit a record high of 69 percent before the subprime mortgage crisis of 2007–08.

Whether or not they owned a home, many people saw Home, Sweet Home as a consumer sanctuary, and a retreat from the harsh outside world. The Victorian time travelers who visited a contemporary suburb might have been startled by the "horseless" SUV, Lexus, or Subaru, but they would understand the enthusiasm of the soccer mom for her minivan. It would not be dissimilar from the passion that a Victorian housewife would have had for her imported Chinese vases and Waterford crystal, artfully arranged on the mantel or in the china cabinet. Furthermore, these vehicles always carried their owners back to Home, Sweet Home.

Third, consumers assembled personal identity kits that defined themselves and told others who they were.

American consumers didn't talk about their "identity kits," but this phrase, coined by sociologist Erving Goffman, is helpful for describing the things people assembled to present themselves on the stage of life. The contents of the personal identity kit changed over time. No one in Victorian America had a Nash sedan, Nike sneakers, or Nick at Night. No one in Victorian America used Gillette shaving cream or disposable razors. And no one had a walk-in closet filled with a 400 pairs of shoes, à la Carrie Bradshaw. The Victorians lived in the treasure box era, prizing parlors and porcelain rather than the Philadelphia Phillies or Phat Farm.

But the Victorians did establish consumption patterns that have shaped people's choices until this day. They put the single-family home and certain types of rooms and furnishings at the center of the material world. Twenty-first century Americans don't live in gingerbread cottages, but as Martha Stewart knows, they still use the home as a theater for self-presentation.

The domestic spaces that Victorians cherished were: the hall, the parlor, and the dining room. They used the entryway as a buffer against the weather and the outside world, the parlor and dining room as private refuges and showcases for their belongings. The impulse to accumulate and display, which gave birth to world's fairs, department stores, zoos, and museums of dinosaur bones, led homemakers to take up pastimes such as interior decorating, collecting, and "making do." The memory palaces they created may now seem over the top, but the Victorians gloried in Aunt Regine's china painting, the pictures of St. Theresa, the horsehair sofa, the what-not shelf, and the fringed Turkish pillows. For them, more was best.

Victorian consumers had a passion for fashion as well, and they added stylish clothing to the middle-class identity kit. Gender stereotypes dictated the current mode of female silhouette, but consumers had endless choices in fabrics, color, texture, and trim for their attire. Whether a banker or a teller, men could visit a tailor and decide what cut of suit, what fabric, what color, and even what buttons they preferred! Men looked to London, women to Paris, and bank tellers to their bosses for a lead, but nearly everyone tried to dress for their social role.

In Modern times, the identity kit expanded to include personal technologies that linked consumers to the wider world. Many people still lived in tenements, boardinghouses, workers' cottages, rambling farmsteads, and sod houses, but new housing designs like Mission Bungalow and Colonial Revival signaled an end to clutter and brought about the use of electric lights, indoor plumbing, gas stoves, and central heating. The bungalow's technological amenities and spacious floor plan epitomized Modern notions of comfort and convenience. Its openness seemed to encourage new attitudes and behaviors. Whereas Victorian homemakers had orchestrated all their home decorating, Modern couples consulted each other on paint colors, furniture styles, and appliance purchases.

Moderns let go of the idea of "the machine" as a mark of progress, and began to think about how "technology" might overcome the conventional use of time and space. They were the first consumers to live with cars, electricity, and electronics, which helped to expand their worldviews. Modern men, women, and children were the first consumers to share musical experience that was packaged as a tangible object, the record, and to hear sound piped into their homes from a distant place by the radio. The electronics that dominate our world—BlackBerries, cell phones, computers, iPods, iPhones, GPSs, HDTVs, and Xboxes—are just updated versions of the "high-tech" artifacts of the Modern age.

Fourth, consumers shifted from emulating their "social betters" to expressing themselves. In the process, they began to drive innovation.

The Victorian middle-class aspired to a uniform model of taste, modeled after the English country house, the Parisian lady, and the London gentleman. The cozy parlor, the hourglass shape, and the three-piece suit were universal badges of Victorian respectability. One hundred and fifty years later, the idea of a uniform model of taste is, at best quaint—at worst, it is repugnant.

Victorian taste was based on *emulation,* a practice rooted in European social conventions. In ranked societies of the Old World, the royals had set the fashions, which were copied by the aristocrats, the gentry, and the middling sorts. In nineteenth-century America, there was no monarch, but people still admired the trends set by Britain's Queen Victoria, Parisian haute couture, and New York's Fifth Avenue high society. The tastemakers who published *Harper's Bazar,* wrote advice books, and stocked the stores promoted toned-down versions for middle-class consumers who wanted to "keep up with the Joneses."

This top-down style engine never stopped running, but over the course of the twentieth century, it lost some horsepower. Immigration, rural migration, two world wars, prosperity, and the technology explosion all contributed to the change. Modern mass culture—dance halls, movies, the radio, and records—exposed a broad swath of Americans to black music, ethnic tastes, cosmetics, and freewheeling fashions. Rebellious college students shocked their middle- and upper-class parents with their jazz, lipstick, and raccoon coats, borrowed from New Orleans brothels, vaudeville theaters, and frontiersman Davy Crockett. These guttersnipe styles challenged the top-down model and rattled middle-class conventions.

The real watershed in American taste came after World War II, when substantial numbers of blue-collar consumers joined the middle class. Whether they stayed in Brooklyn or moved to New Jersey, newly affluent blue-collar consumers refused to give up their ethnic working-class roots. Accustomed to eating in the kitchen and sitting on the stoop, they remodeled their cookie-cutter Cape Cod cottages, Ranch Houses, and aging rowhomes to suit blue-collar customs, introducing working-class innovations like the rec room and the basement cocktail bar. They also shocked marketers by saying, "I want that!" "That" often was a two-toned Chevrolet, a set of overstuffed Early American chairs, and a big white refrigerator with prominent metal trim. Blue-collar individualism did much to shape the populuxe look.

Vanguard Boomers took consumer-driven innovation to new heights. Beatniks, rock and roll, the Civil Rights movement, the Vietnam War, hippie antimaterialism, and Women's Liberation struck deep at the populuxe moment. These cultural changes produced a climate that rendered populuxe extravagance anachronistic. Market fragmentation found suburban kids listening to The Beach Boys, while blue-collar rock-and-rollers played Led Zeppelin and vice versa. Arty intellectuals might develop affinities for John Coltrane's avant garde jazz, Bob Dylan's beatnik folk-rock, or Emerson Lake and Palmer's electronic version of Modest Mussorgsky's *Pictures at an Exhibition.*

In the late-twentieth century, multicultural influences bubbled up from ethnic enclaves around the world to shape the look of fashion and home décor. Emulation hasn't entirely evaporated, but personal choice determines what many consumers will buy. There were so many possibilities that marketers threw up their hands and declared that the age of the individualist had arrived.

Fifth, producers developed techniques for imagining Mrs. Consumer, and over time evolved a more inclusive model.

One of the most important dynamics in consumer society is the relationship between producers and consumers. Producers learned to harness the persuasive powers of the media to push new goods, brands, and lifestyles on the public, while consumers learned how to decode the advertisements and determined what products to buy. Does capitalism limit consumer choice, or does it create more and better choices? The answer to this question may fall into the realm of philosophy rather than history.

Producers certainly tried to manipulate consumers' insecurities, desires, and aspirations with store displays, advertising, and branding. Victorian trade cards told people how parlors should look, while Modern magazines encouraged consumers to buy national brands. Global brands mastered the art of total immersion, using cable advertising, theme parks, and showcase stores to equate the Disney fantasy world or the Starbucks experience with what it means to have arrived. But these strategies for shaping desire co-existed with techniques for determining what customers wanted.

To figure out what to sell, producers evolved sophisticated methods for deciphering consumers' tastes. Victorian department stores used hit-or-miss techniques, watching people as they browsed and making educated guesses on what to stock. This depended on the observational powers of seasoned tailors, designers, and retailers, who knew how to size up the customers. In 1900, it was possible to look at a man to know something about his occupation, income, and tastes. But as more people stepped through the portal of consumer society, it became more difficult to discern someone's wealth or occupation from what he wore, what she bought, or where they lived.

Businesses inched toward more scientific methods of investigating the market. Dime-store managers, buried under mountains of paper in the Woolworth Building in lower Manhattan, analyzed regional and local sales reports. Modern advertising agencies pioneered the market-research survey, learning to sample representative Mrs. Consumers in whatever Average American communities they could find around Chicago, New York, Philadelphia, or Columbus. Scientists like John B. Watson and Ernest Dichter tried to psychoanalyze them.

By the late-twentieth century, producers looked around and saw the country fragmenting into geographic regions and income groups. Using computers, marketers had the capability of gathering large amounts of data, and they figured out how to crunch the numbers. The new data showed that targets like Mrs. Consumer, the boy hobbyist, the Average American, and the teen market still had some relevance but needed to be updated. The multiethnic consumer, which had been in the peripheral vision of Modern marketers, was deemed the new mainstream.

Sixth, the government played a role as a mediator between producers and consumers.

Another important actor in consumer society was the government, whose role has evolved from the protector of industry to the guardian of the middle class. The contemporary political scene testifies to just how important consumer issues have become. In the 2008 presidential debates, Democratic candidates discussed topics like health care, tax reform, the flight of jobs from Iowa to Asia, and the erosion of middle-class spending power. These concerns about the status of the American dream are a far cry from Gilded Age congressional hearings over whether a tariff on imports of New Zealand wool would hurt Pennsylvania carpet mills.

As the United States industrialized, federal official watched over the economy, tinkering with protectionist tariffs in ways that encouraged domestic production. Victorian muckrakers and Modern progressive reformers pressed lawmakers to deal with consumer issues, beginning with the eight-hour day, lower electric rates, and pure food and drug laws. The New Deal model, from the Franklin Delano Roosevelt to the Lyndon Baines Johnson eras, solidified and refined the government's role. When FDR eloquently spoke of "freedom from want," the New Deal had already created a slate of programs to benefit the people as consumers, including the minimum wage, banking regulations, rural electrification, and mortgage reform. During World War II, rationing, recycling, and price controls taught people to think about the federal government as a conduit that channeled raw materials, goods, and services through the economy. This contributed to the idea that Washington could be a mediator between producers and consumers.

Postwar government initiatives also benefited consumer society. The federal investment in military research had important consequences, generating countless consumer spin-offs like the transistor, the tape recorder, and the microwave oven. Federal subsidies for highway construction and home mortgages provided businesses and white consumers with the means to leave troubled cities. Tax policies encouraged businesses to invest in new plants, office parks, and shopping malls in the Sunbelt and suburbs. Deregulation fostered competition in the telecommunications industry, breaking up the AT&T monopoly and paving the way for new technologies like the cell phone and broadband internet access. Deregulation of the airline industry resulted in lower airfares, making ordinary Americans into jet setters who fly to Europe, Las Vegas, ski resorts, and Caribbean beaches as a matter of course. Victorian consumers, who took the train to seaside resorts like Atlantic City, or Modern Americans, who vacationed in Catskill mountain retreats, would have marveled at these options.

Collectively, these changes fostered the idea that the American standard of living is the birthright of every citizen, and that it's the responsibility of every citizen to be a consumer.

Seventh, the most significant change was the consumer's shift from "hardware" to "software" or from valuing "things" to valuing "content." This paralleled the shift from material goods being regarded first as "treasures" and later as "throwaways."

As the great technological innovations of Victorian and Modern America were commoditized, Americans themselves became more affluent. At the same time, the definition of the Average American became more inclusive, and the meaning of middle-class possessions changed. When a Modern American housewife delighted in her brand-new refrigerator, it was partly because it made her kitchen look up-to-date and partly because it promised to free up her time for other things. In 2007, when a state of the art Sub-zero refrigerator is installed in a remodeled kitchen, it has almost nothing to do with how the kitchen looks or how efficiently the family runs. The new appliance is there to maintain the vintage bottle of wine at the perfect temperature, keep a $50-per pound Prosciutto ham fresh, and feed the fantasy that if the owner had just a little more time, he could prepare gourmet meals every bit as wonderful as Emeril's, Bobby Flay's, and all the other chefs on the Food Channel!

For some people, the purchase of "things" often no longer carries the near-universal significance it did 100 years ago. When a Generation X consumer buys a home entertainment center, the collection of boxes and wires and flashing lights is of little value. The fact that little boxes give nearly unlimited access to music, movies, television programs, news, sporting events, and interactive games is what's important. The potential quality of the entertainment is what motivates someone to buy one set of boxes instead of another.

The devices of the Victorian, Modern, and Boomer eras have matured and converged in ways that makes the experiences they deliver more important than the devices themselves. Post-Boomer consumers crave instantaneous experiences and immediate gratification. Cell phones have replaced telephones, iTunes has replaced record stores, Amazon has replaced bookstores, and L.L. Bean has replaced Sears, all because people want what they want, when they want it, with as little interference as possible.

The joy of a dinner party with the right china and table settings has yielded to ephemeral sensuous delights: a meal prepared at home from gourmet ingredients accompanied by the perfect wine served in the right glass. For some consumers, acquiring beautiful china has been supplanted by the experience of cooking evanescent gourmet cuisine. In this post-Boomer world, "things" merely facilitate the creation of "experiences."

While Martha Stewart caters to Boomers who like to collect and make things, other reality shows, from *Project Runway* to *Millionaire Matchmaker,* target different market segments by focusing on the process of self-transformation through experience. Falling prices for consumer goods, the dominance of the retail scene by big-box retailers like IKEA, Crate and Barrel, Macy's, and Wal★Mart, and the flow of cheap Chinese imports have taught post-Boomer consumers to think less about things as keepsakes and to look elsewhere for satisfaction. The stores are always full of affordable new fashions in clothing, housewares, and toys — so why not replace the dishes every few years? Why not repeatedly transform yourself by eating the right gourmet food, and buy this week's newest outfit, to be replaced next month (or next year) with trends set by Paris Hilton or streetwise hipsters? Just as Martha Stewart has found a niche among wannabe Victorian homemakers, other programs on E! Entertainment Television, Bravo, and ESPN foster and respond to the public's hunger for information snacking and getting it now.

Victorians, Moderns, and Boomers would all be uncomfortable, if not repulsed, at the idea that things merely facilitated experience, or that "hardware" enabled "cultural software." Victorians and Moderns wouldn't have even recognized the words, and Boomers may have felt a bit squeamish about them. Yet all of the previous six themes—with the emphasis on consumer choice, inclusiveness, producers innovating to meet demand, and the importance of consumption to the economy—have fused in a new marketplace where consumers want to create their own experiences and producers strive to meet that demand.

•••

When Young Digerati Amber Decker expresses discomfort with the distribution of wealth and power that seems to rise from consumer culture, she is not alone. Muckrakers like Ida Tarbell and Sinclair Lewis railed against the corporate culture of Victorian and Modern America, and with good reason. Yet for every Tarbell, there were 100 Sister Carries and for every Decker, there are 100,000 Carrie Bradshaws. Although if Carrie Bradshaw were invented today instead of 1996, she'd be spending a lot more time on the internet!

But even when Decker resents being identified by what she buys, she acknowledges that to an extent, she *is* identified by the things and experiences she buys. And in that acknowledgement, she echoes the theme of this book: there is no better lens to examine what it means to be an American than the lens of American consumer culture.

During World War II, the federal government circulated large colorful posters, urging consumers to save, recycle, conserve—and help defeat the enemy. *Courtesy of Hagley Museum and Library.*

Top: The wartime construction industry equated the return of peace and prosperity with wholesome family life and suburban home ownership. *Small Homes Guide* (Washington, DC: National Homebuilders Bureau, 1944), cover. *Author's collection.*

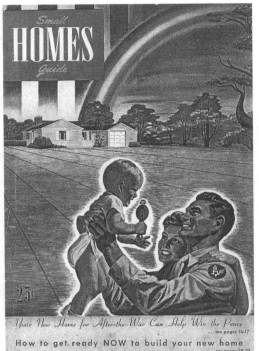

Small
HOMES
Guide

25¢

Your New Home for After-the-War Can Help Win the Peace
...see pages 16-17

How to get ready NOW to build your new home
...see pages 18-19

Bottom: Cape Cod cottages were designed with expansion in mind. *Your New Home* (NY: Archway Press, 1952). Author's collection. *Courtesy, Archway Press, Inc.*

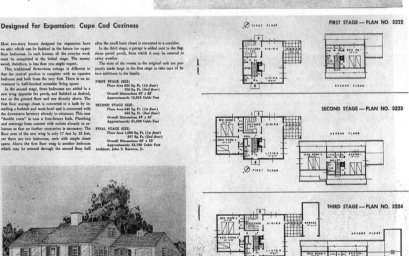

Designed for Expansion: Cape Cod Coziness

Most two-story homes designed for expansion have an attic which can be finished in the future for upper floor bedrooms. In such houses, all the exterior work must be completed at the initial stage. The money saved, therefore, is less than you might expect.

This traditional three-room cottage is different in that the central portion is complete with an upstairs bedroom and bath from the very first. There is no investment in half-finished unusable living space.

In the second stage, three bedrooms are added in a new wing opposite the porch, and finished as desired, two on the ground floor and one directly above. The first floor storage closet is converted to a bath by installing a bathtub and wash bowl and is connected with the downstairs lavatory already in existence. This new "double room" is now a four-fixture bath. Plumbing and sewerage lines connect with outlets already in existence so that no further excavation is necessary. The floor area of the new wing is only 17 feet by 22 feet, yet there are two bedrooms, each with ample closet space. Above the first floor wing is another bedroom which may be entered through the second floor hall

after the small linen closet is converted to a corridor.

In the third stage, a garage is added next to the flagstone paved porch, from which it may be entered in rainy weather.

The sizes of the rooms in the original unit are purposely made large in the first stage to take care of future additions to the family.

FIRST STAGE SIZE:
Floor Area 665 Sq. Ft. (1st floor)
350 Sq. Ft. (2nd floor)
Overall Dimensions 25' x 25'
Approximately 13,315 Cubic Feet

SECOND STAGE SIZE:
Floor Area 645 Sq. Ft. (1st floor)
455 Sq. Ft. (2nd floor)
Overall Dimensions 33' x 25'
Approximately 21,500 Cubic Feet

FINAL STAGE SIZE:
Floor Area 1,000 Sq. Ft. (1st floor)
537 Sq. Ft. (2nd floor)
Overall Dimensions 66' x 25'
Approximately 23,750 Cubic Feet
Architect, John S. Burrows, Jr.

FIRST FLOOR   FIRST STAGE — PLAN NO. 5222

SECOND STAGE — PLAN NO. 5223

THIRD STAGE — PLAN NO. 5224

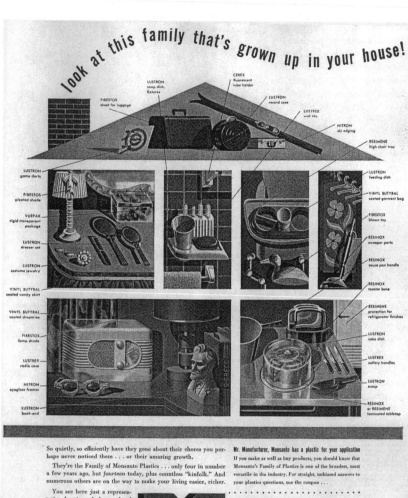

Miracle materials. New types of plastics promised to improve domestic life. Monsanto Chemical Company, advertisement in *Fortune* (April 1948). *Author's collection; courtesy, Monsanto Company.*

Top: Industrial designers like Raymond Loewy used steel, plastic, and vinyl to create colorful dining-room furniture in the Modern mode. Arvin Industries, advertisement in *Better Homes and Gardens* (Oct. 1952). *Author's collection; courtesy, Arvin Industries*

Bottom: Early American furniture in solid maple suggested sturdy comfort to blue-collar consumers. *Hallmark Quality Furniture* (Chicago: Montgomery Ward & Company, 1941), 48. *Author's collection.*

Top: Roadside restaurants like HoJo's taught motorists to "eat on the go" and paved the way for fast-food chains like McDonald's. Howard D. Johnson Co., magazine advertisement, 1950s. Author's collection. *Courtesy, Howard Johnson International.*

Bottom: Early discount stores offered low prices, large inventories, and convenient parking. Cussins & Fearn Co., *Catalog No. 171* (Columbus, OH, 1956), cover. *Author's collection.*

op: Suburban malls, built on
*i*rmlands adjacent to highways,
*i*elped to define the postwar land-
*c*ape. In the heart of Pennsyl-
*i*ania Dutch Country, developers
*i*urchased Amish farms to create
*i*e Park City mall. Park City, ad-
*i*ertisement, Aug. 1972. *Author's*
*c*ollection. *General Growth
Properties.*

They grow 'em big in the land of the Amish . . .

Park City

one of the largest enclosed shopping malls in the nation.

It's a shopping experience you'll long remember. This great canopied city with miles of carpeted streets is one of the biggest attractions in the heart of the popular Pennsylvania Dutch country. And it's a spectacularly beautiful scene. The decorating motif of the four major malls, which run like spokes of a wheel from a towering central mall fountain, depicts the four seasons. "Snow-laden" evergreens, blossoming dogwoods, summery birches and oaks with changing leaves charm the shoppers at every turn. Come anytime—rain, snow or shine—every square foot of Park City is climate-controlled for year 'round comfort.

- Over 160 stores, including 4 major department stores—Gimbels, Penneys, Sears, Watt & Shand.
- Indoor ice skating, miniature golf and health spa.
- 9 restaurants, plus cocktail lounges and many specialty food services.
- Two full-size theaters.
- Parking for over 9,000 cars. Bus depot for charter buses.
- World's largest indoor amusement park.

10:00 A. M. to 9:30 P. M. Monday thru Saturday.
Food services & recreation open Sunday afternoon & evening.
U. S. 30 West Lancaster, Pa.

Park City welcomes group tours all seasons of the year. For help in planning your group's visit, contact any of the below or other tour and charter bus companies serving your area.

Continental Trailways
Washington, D. C.

Monumental Motor Tours, Inc.
Baltimore, Md.

H. E. Cook Bus Lines
Scotland, Pa.

Luther J. Yodel Thornways
Mohnsville, Pa.

Wolf's Bus Lines, Inc.
York Springs, Pa.

Happy's Bus Service
Franconia, Pa.

Triangle Tours, Inc.
Washington, D. C.

Bollman Charter Service
Everett, Pa.

The Baltimore &
Annapolis Rd Co.
Glen Burnie, Md.

Fullington Auto Bus Co., Inc.
Clearfield, Pa.

Penn State Travel
State College, Pa.

Conoll Travel Service
Williamsport, Pa.

Tyrone Y.M.C.A.
Tyrone, Pa.

Blue & White Bus Lines, Inc.
Altoona, Pa.

The Baltimore Motor Coach Co.
Baltimore, Md.

McBeth Bus Company
Walnut Bottom, Pa.

American Sightseeing and
Charter Service
Washington, D. C.

Merris Hill Travel, Inc.
Easton, Pa.

Frisa Bus Company, Inc.
Scranton, Pa.

Carl R. Bieber, Inc.
Kutztown, Pa.

Trans-Bridge Lines, Inc.
Phillipsburg, N. J.

Frank Martz Coach Company
Wilkes-Barre, Pa.

Keystone Tours, Inc.
Bath, Pa.

Conestoga Coach Lines.
Catasauqua, Pa.

Thompson Tours
Scranton, Pa.

Easton Bus Terminal
Easton, Pa.

Wilkes-Barre Transit Corp.
Kingston, Pa.

Capitol Trailways of Penna.
Harrisburg, Pa.

✴ **PARK CITY**
LANCASTER, PENNSYLVANIA

*B*ottom: Malls provided a predict-
ble, climate-controlled environ-
*m*ent all year round. Edgewater
*P*laza Mall, Biloxi, MS, opened
*1*963; postcard by Deep South
*S*pecialties. *Author's collection.*

HOBI

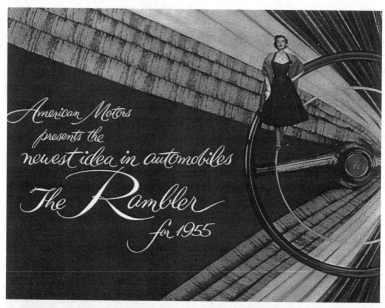

The New Look in clothes and cars. American Motors, formed by the 1954 merger of Nash and Hudson, introduced the Rambler, a small, affordable car with fashion smarts. *American Motors Presents the Newest Idea in Automobiles: The Rambler for 1955,* cover, 6. Author's collection. *Courtesy of Chrysler LLC.*

Top: Pointed bras gave shape to the New Look. Maidenform Inc., "I Dreamed" advertisement, 1960. *Author's collection; courtesy, Maidenform Brands Inc.*

Bottom: In 1955, Air Force sergeant Bill Walls, self-described as oblivious to James Dean, sported the actor's rebel style when he took a date to Pike's Peak in his 1941 Buick. *Courtesy, William W. Walls, Jr.*

Top: Celebrity crooner Frank Sinatra endorsed GE's new portable radio. General Electric, advertisement in the *Saturday Evening Post,* 1946. *Author's collection.*

Bottom: Cartoons, cooking, or sports? Multiple TVs would eliminate squabbles over what to watch. General Electric, advertisement in *Better Homes and Gardens* (Oct. 1955). *Author's collection.*

Top: Reel-to-reel tape recorders were high-tech gadgets for men who loved music. Revere Camera Company, advertisement in *Esquire* (Nov. 1957). *Author's collection. Courtesy: 3M.*

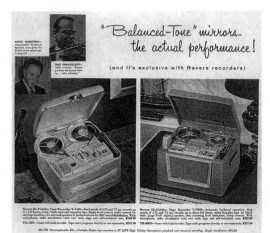

Bottom: Young couples shared a passion for hi-fis. RadioShack Corporation, *Mail Order Catalog No. 111* (Boston: 1962). *Author's collection; courtesy, RadioShack Corporation.*

Top: Ebony targeted the African-American market. Levi's, advertisement in *Ebony* (Sept. 1969). *Author's collection.*

Bottom: The fitness craze gave birth to sexy gym fashions made with Lycra spandex. Puma, advertisement in *Cosmopolitan* (March 1988). *Author's collection. Courtesy, Puma AG.*

In 1984, Apple Computer shocked Americans with a dystopic
Super Bowl commercial and followed up with print advertisements
that touted the user-friendly Macintosh.

Big-box stores became the dominant retailing format by the 1990s.
Top: Target Great Land store, Redondo Beach, CA, 2005; *Image courtesy of Target Stores.*

Bottom: Target offered one-stop shopping for clothing, electronics, toothpaste, and toys.
Interior of Target store, Greeley, CO, 2005; *Image courtesy of Target Stores, photograph by RMA Photography.*

BIBLIOGRAPHICAL ESSAY

The history of American consumer society is a thriving academic discipline dealing with many important topics, from national politics to cultural meaning. This book homes in on important themes that aren't often discussed in U.S. history courses, introducing students to a new way of thinking about the world around them. It also covers historical material that should be helpful to business professionals in management, advertising, design, marketing, retailing, and branding.

Standard Works

American consumer society first captured historians' attention in the postwar era. Two important books laid the foundations for nearly a half century of scholarship. David M. Potter's *People of Plenty: Economic Abundance and the American Character* (Chicago, 1954) introduces the concept of "abundance" and discusses advertising's role in promoting it. Daniel J. Boorstin's *The Americans: The Democratic Experience* (New York, 1973) is a cultural history of the United States from the late 1800s through the post–World War II era. Boorstin writes about "consumption communities," and posits that twentieth-century Americans identified themselves more by the things and experiences they purchased than by their customs, neighborhood, politics, or religion. Although these two books belong to the "consensus" school of American history—an older style of interpretation that didn't consider ethnic groups or subcultures—they offer valuable insights on consumer society. *The Americans: The Democratic Experience* is especially helpful for students interested in the producer-consumer relationship. However, these works should be considered alongside newer, more inclusive interpretations.

The field of consumer history originated in the 1980s and blossomed in the 1990s and 2000s. One strand comes from British economic and social history, where scholars sought to understand the demand side of the English industrial revolution of the 1700s. Some of this work focused on producers and their interface with consumers. Seminal works include Neil McKendrick et al., eds., *The Birth of a Consumer Society: The Commercialization of Eighteenth-Century England* (Bloomington, IN, 1982), which includes essays on manufacturing, retailing, and leisure. Maxine Berg's *The Age of Manufactures,* (New York, 1985), which looks at the Birmingham toy industry, explains the important role of novelty in product design. Peter N. Stearns's *Consumerism in World History: The Global Transformation of Desire* (London, 2001), and Maxine Berg and Helen Clifford, eds., *Consumers and Luxury: Consumer Culture in Europe, 1650–1850* (New York, 1999), situate the rise of European consumer society within the context of the wider world. For developments in British America, a good introduction is Cary Carson et al., eds., *Of Consuming Interests: The Style of Life in the Eighteenth Century* (Charlottesville, VA, 1994), which focuses on material culture. Timothy H. Breen, *The Marketplace of Revolution: How Consumer Politics Shaped Independence* (New York, 2004), argues that anticonsumerist concerns lay at the heart of the American Revolution.

More recently, prominent historians have focused on the unique characteristics of nineteenth- and twentieth-century American consumer society, with reference to politics and the public interest. For the nineteenth century, Lawrence B. Glickman's *A Living Wage: American Workers and the Making of Consumer Society* (Ithaca, NY, 1997) shows how unionized workers fought to be paid wages that were commensurate with their needs as consumers. Dana Frank's *Buy American: The Untold Story of Economic Nationalism* (Boston, 1999), opens the doors onto the world of tariffs versus free trade. Kathleen G. Donohue's intellectual history, *Freedom from Want: American Liberalism and the Idea of the Consumer* (Baltimore, 2003), looks at the concepts of the "producer" and the "consumer" and their roles in transforming free-market liberalism into its more activist form.

For the twentieth century, one important vein of research focuses on the scenery of public affairs, union and grassroots activism, and interest groups on Capitol Hill. Lizabeth Cohen's two books, *Making a New Deal: Industrial Workers in Chicago, 1919–1939,* 2nd ed. (New York, 2008) and *A Consumers' Republic: The Politics of Mass Consumption in Postwar America* (New York, 2003); and Meg Jacobs's *Pocketbook Politics: Eco-*

nomic Citizenship in Twentieth-Century America (Princeton, NJ, 2005), explain how ordinary people's desires for a share in the good life became a central theme for labor leaders and lawmakers, who put consumption atop the national economic policy.

Others have considered the effects of exporting the American Way of Life across the globe. In *Irresistible Empire: America's Advance through Twentieth-Century Europe* (Cambridge, MA, 2005), Victoria de Grazia examines how the ethos of abundance combined with the ideas of free-market economics led to the "Americanization" of Europe. *New York Times* journalist Thomas Friedman, author of *The Lexus and the Olive Tree: Understanding Globalization* (New York, 2000), explores the diffusion of American business practices across the world and the conflicts between modern consumer societies and traditional societies. Some of these themes are also traced in Benjamin R. Barber's best seller, *Jihad vs. McWorld: How Globalism and Tribalism Are Reshaping the World* (New York, 1995).

Critiques of Affluence

Americans have long debated the pros and cons of affluence. While many products have made life warmer, cleaner, and generally easier, widespread consumption has also stirred public anxiety. Historians, economists, political scientists, and social workers have raised concerns about wealth distribution, moral implications, and environmental responsibility. These heated subjects have attracted recent media attention, particularly as Western societies wrestle with the social and environmental costs of globalization.

These concerns, while justifiable, are not new. They stem from a long-standing suspicion of centralized power, embodied for revolutionary-era patriots in the monarchy of King George III and for early U.S. citizens in the economic institutions behind the market revolution. Victorian critics focused their concerns on industrialization, urbanization, and inequitable wealth distribution. The most famous of the progressive critiques is Thorstein Veblen's *The Theory of the Leisure Class: An Economic Study in the Evolution of Institutions* (New York, 1899), which examined "conspicuous consumption" among newly wealthy Americans.

Influential midcentury critics included the journalist Vance Packard, who published three popular works on the business system. *The Hidden Persuaders* (New York, 1957) critiqued the manipulative world of motivational research, public relations, and advertising, while *The Status Seekers* (New York, 1959) described American social stratification and consumer behavior. Most famously, *The Waste Makers* (New York, 1960) focused on Detroit's investment in cosmetic design and introduced the term "planned obsolescence" into popular culture. Packard's contemporary, John Kenneth Galbraith, a Harvard economist, examining the widening gap between rich and poor, and pointed to environmental blight in *The Affluent Society* (Boston, 1958).

Beginning in the 1970s, new generations of sociologists, media scholars, and historians built on these critiques. Classic works include Stuart Ewen's *Captains of Consciousness: Advertising and the Social Roots of the Consumer Culture* (New York, 1976), which describes turn-of-the-century manufacturers, retailers, public-relations men, and advertising agencies as deliberate manipulators of desire. Richard Wightman Fox and T. J. Jackson Lears, eds., *The Culture of Consumption: Critical Essays in American History, 1880–1980* (New York, 1983), offers a series of essays by intellectual historians. William Leach's *Land of Desire: Merchants, Power, and the Rise of a New American Culture* (New York, 1993), explains how strategists of desire like window dresser L. Frank Baum (later author of the *Oz* books) and adman Bruce Barton taught a nation reared on sobriety and asceticism to be consumers.

More recent critics have wondered about the sustainability of mass consumption in the context of global warming, and worry about pollution, toxic waste, and the depletion of natural resources. Juliet B. Schor, *The Overspent American: Why We Want What We Don't Need* (New York, 1998) and Gary S. Cross, *An All-Consuming Century: Why Commercialism Won in Modern America* (New York, 2000), raise important issues along these lines.

Other social questions surface in debates about Wal★Mart, which has consolidated power in big-box retailing, reaping criticism for its environmental indifference and underpaid workers. The essays in Nelson Lichtenstein's edited book, *Wal-Mart: The Face of Twenty-First Century Capitalism* (New York, 2006), are a good introduction to these concerns. News reports about shoddy merchandise from China, sweatshops and illegal immigrants, and the outsourcing of brain work to India raise further questions about the future of the American consumer society. These debates can be traced in the *Atlantic, New York Times,* the *Economist, Fortune,* and *Business Week.*

Intellectual historian Daniel Horowitz has put 100 years of cultural criticism in historical perspective. His book, *The Morality of Spending: Attitudes Toward the Consumer Society in America, 1875–1940* (Baltimore, 1985), highlights the ideas of early social workers who compiled the first standard-of-living surveys. In *The Anxieties of Affluence*, 2d ed. (Amherst, MA, 2004), Horowitz extends his analysis to postwar America, examining how writers like Potter, Packard, Galbraith, and Martin Luther King, Jr., framed popular discussions about the excesses and inequities of consumer culture and their threats to democratic values. Finally, Horowitz's *Vance Packard and American*

Social Criticism (Chapel Hill, NC, 1994), provides a close-up look at this highly influential critic.

Consumer Taste and Middle-Class Culture

The exemplary research on domestic politics, international affairs, and the critique of consumer culture sets the stage for this book, which pursues a complementary set of questions.

Any discussion of consumer taste must consider the idea of what it means to be "middle class," a thorny question that has vexed generations of scholars. Insightful recent interpretations include Catherine E. Kelly, *In the New England Fashion: Reshaping Women's Lives in the Nineteenth Century* (Ithaca, NY, 1999); Burton J. Bledstein and Robert D. Johnston, eds., *The Middling Sorts: Explorations in the History of the American Middle Class* (New York, 2001); Jocelyn Wills, "Respectable Mediocrity: The Everyday Life of an Ordinary American Striver, 1876–1890," in *Journal of Social History* 37 (2003); and id., *Boosters, Hustlers, and Speculators: Entrepreneurial Culture and the Rise of Minneapolis and St. Paul, 1849–1883* (St. Paul, 2005). Marina Moskowitz's insightful book, *Standard of Living: The Measure of the Middle Class in Modern America* (Baltimore, 2004), explains how zoning laws, white bathroom fixtures, bungalows, and silverware sets helped to establish middle-class consumption standards during the early-twentieth century.

These new studies owe much to the first wave of historians to wrestle with the slippery idea of middle-class culture. Classic studies include Karen Halttunen, *Confidence Men and Painted Women: A Study of Middle-class Culture in America, 1830–1870* (New Haven, 1982); Cindy Sondik Aron, *Ladies and Gentlemen of the Civil Service: Middle-class Workers in Victorian America* (New York, 1987); id., *Working at Play: A History of Vacations in the United States* (New York, 1999); Stuart M. Blumin, *The Emergence of the Middle Class: Social Experience in the American City, 1760–1900* (New York, 1989); John F. Kasson, *Rudeness and Civility: Manners in Nineteenth-Century Urban America* (New York, 1990); and Thomas J. Schlereth, *Victorian America: Transformations in Everyday Life, 1876–1915* (New York, 1991). Richard L. Bushman's perceptive book, *The Refinement of America: Persons, Houses, Cities* (New York, 1993), explains how consumers in the early republic built on customs borrowed from the English gentry to define themselves as Americans. This volume has relied heavily on Bushman's many insights.

Some historians have explored the relationship between artifacts and consumer identity. On the importance of things to cultural identity, see Leora Auslander, "Beyond Words," in the *American Historical Review* 110 (October 2005). Simon J. Bronner's edited book, *Consuming Visions: Accumulation and Display of Goods in America, 1880–1920* (New York, 1989), includes introductory essays on world's fairs, mail-order catalogs, and advertising. Victoria de Grazia and Ellen Furlough's edited volume, *The Sex of Things: Gender and Consumption in Historical Perspective* (Berkeley, 1996), puts consumption in a transnational perspective. Michael G. Kammen, *American Culture, American Tastes: Social Change and the 20th Century* (New York, 1999), explores the concepts of highbrow, lowbrow, and middlebrow culture. Jennifer Scanlon's edited volume, *The Gender and Consumer Culture Reader* (New York, 2000), has useful essays on Jewish women in the home, and the postwar Do-It-Yourself fad.

A good deal of useful research on consumer taste, meaning, and identity has come from disciplines outside of American history. Scholars in anthropology, architectural history, business history, cultural studies, fashion history, journalism, sociology, and vernacular architecture studies offer insights, and much of their work is discussed in the topical sections that follow. An excellent introduction to the anthropological scholarship is Daniel Miller, ed., *Material Culture: Why Some Things Matter* (Chicago, 1998). For cultural studies, see Lawrence Grossberg et al., eds., *Cultural Studies* (London, 1992), and Stevi Jackson and Shaun Moores, eds., *The Politics of Domestic Consumption: Critical Readings* (London, 1995). Several works in historical sociology provide accessible introductions to sophisticated theoretical concepts, notably Diana Crane, *The Sociology of Culture: Emerging Theoretical Perspectives* (Cambridge, MA, 1994); Sharon Zukin, *Point of Purchase: How Shopping Changed American Culture* (New York, 2004); and Mark D. Jacobs et al., eds., *The Blackwell Companion to the Sociology of Culture* (Malden, MA, 2005).

Among writers focusing on popular culture, several books offer provocative suggestions on how to think creatively about consumer society and taste: James B. Twitchell, *Carnival Culture: The Trashing of Taste in America* (New York, 1992); id., *Lead Us into Temptation: The Triumph of American Materialism* (New York, 1993); id., *Living It Up: Our Love Affair with Luxury* (New York, 2002); David Brooks, *Bobos in Paradise: The New Upper Class and How They Got There* (New York, 2000); Thomas Hine, *I Want That! How We All Became Shoppers* (New York, 2002); Virginia Postrel, *The Substance of Style: How the Rise of Aesthetic Value is Remaking Commerce, Culture, and Consciousness* (New York, 2003); and Gregg Easterbrook, *The Progress Paradox* (New York, 2003).

Housing, Homes, and Home Furnishings

On the home as consumer dominion, architectural historian Witold Rybczynski's *Home: A Short History of an Idea* (New York, 1986), is a good introduction. The work of cultural historian Clifford Edward Clark, Jr., also provides comprehensive coverage. A fine starting point is his synthesis, *The American Family Home, 1800–1960* (Chapel Hill, NC, 1986). Two of Clark's essays complement his book: "Domestic Architecture as an Index to Social History: The Romantic Revival and the Cult of Domesticity in America, 1840–1870," in *Journal of Interdisciplinary History* 7 (Summer 1976); and "The Vision of the Dining Room: Plan Book Dreams and Middle-class Realities," in Kathryn Grover, ed., *Dining in America, 1850–1900* (Amherst, MA, 1987). Other useful syntheses include David P. Handlin, *The American Home: Architecture and Society, 1815–1915* (Boston, 1979), and Wendell D. Garrett, et al., *American Home: From Colonial Simplicity to the Modern Adventure* (New York, 2001).

Recent work by historians of vernacular architecture focuses on ordinary buildings that aren't designed by famous architects or considered to be masterpieces. Scholars in vernacular architecture studies often examine the houses' layouts and study the social history of the occupants. New research appears in *Perspectives in Vernacular Architecture*, an edited volume published occasionally by the Vernacular Architecture Forum. One recent volume, Alison K. Hoagland and Kenneth A. Breisch, eds., *Constructing Image, Identity, and Place* (Knoxville, TN, 2003), includes essays on drive-in theaters and Mississippi juke joints, topics that convey the flavor of the field.

Exemplary work in vernacular architecture studies has focused on blue-collar and rural homes. Outstanding examples include Margaret M. Mulrooney's *Black Powder, White Lace: The du Pont Irish and Cultural Identity in Nineteenth-Century America* (Hanover, NH, 2002), and Joseph C. Bigott's *From Cottage to Bungalow: Houses and the Working Class in Metropolitan Chicago, 1869–1929* (Chicago, 2001), which considers how Polish Americans adapted traditional housing forms to suit themselves. Other helpful studies of the blue-collar home include Richard M. Candee, *Atlantic Heights: A World War I Shipbuilders' Community* (Portsmouth, NH, 1985); Margaret Crawford, *Building the Workingman's Paradise: The Design of American Company Towns* (New York, 1995), and Margaret Garb, *City of American Dreams: A History of Home Ownership and Housing Reform in Chicago, 1871–1919* (Chicago, 2005). On rural homes, see Sally Ann McMurry, *Families and Farmhouses in Nineteenth-Century America: Vernacular Design and Social Change* (New York, 1988); Ted Ownby, *American Dreams in Mississippi: Consumers, Poverty, & Culture, 1830–1998* (Chapel Hill, NC, 1999); and Susan J. Matt, *Keeping Up with the Joneses: Envy in American Consumer Society, 1890–1930* (Philadelphia, 2003).

For the bungalow as the first national housing style, see Clay Lancaster, *The American Bungalow, 1880–1930* (New York, 1995); and Janet Ore, *The*

Seattle Bungalow: People and Houses, 1900–1940 (Seattle, 2007). Not everyone lived in a rowhouse, cottage, farmhouse, or bungalow. On alternative living spaces, see Paul Erling Groth, *Living Downtown: The History of Residential Hotels in the United States* (Berkeley, CA, 1994), and Wendy Gamber, *The Boardinghouse in Nineteenth-Century America* (Baltimore, 2007).

On twentieth-century housing, see Donald Albrecht, ed., *World War II and the American Dream: How Wartime Building Changed a Nation* (Cambridge, MA: 1995); Barbara M. Kelly, *Expanding the American Dream: Building and Rebuilding Levittown* (Albany, NY, 1993); Regina Lee Blaszczyk, "No Place Like Home: Herbert Hoover and the American Standard of Living," in Timothy Walch, ed., *Uncommon Americans: The Lives and Legacies of Herbert and Lou Henry Hoover* (Westport, CT, 2003); and Andrew Hurley, *Diners, Bowling Alleys, and Trailer Parks: Chasing the American Dream in the Postwar Consumer Culture* (New York, 2001). Scholars in the "new urban history" sometimes discuss the meaning of the home, although it's not their major focus. Kenneth D. Durr's *Behind the Backlash: White Working-Class Politics in Baltimore, 1940–1980* (Chapel Hill, NC, 2003), is most insightful on people who decided to stay in the city. Thomas J. Sugrue's highly acclaimed *Origins of the Urban Crisis: Race and Inequality in Postwar Detroit* (Princeton, 1996) focuses on the unfortunate story of racism and urban decline.

Among the many useful primary sources on the home and its contents, accessible material is found in the dozens of community studies published by twentieth-century social workers and social scientists. For the Progressive era, see, for example, Paul Underwood Kellogg, ed., *The Pittsburgh Survey Findings in Six Volumes* (New York, 1909–1914); and Louise C. Odencrantz, *Italian Women in Industry: A Study of Conditions in New York City* (New York, 1919). Maurine Weiner Greenwald and Margo J. Anderson's wonderful edited volume, *Pittsburgh Surveyed: Social Science and Social Reform in the Early Twentieth Century* (Pittsburgh, 1996), offers essays that can guide scholars through this reform project. Memoirs, such as Mary Antin's *The Promised Land* (Boston, 1912), also vividly describe immigrant and blue-collar positions. Finally, Susan Porter Benson's *Household Accounts: Working-Class Family Economies in the Interwar United States* (Ithaca, NY, 2007) uses raw data collected by U.S. government social workers, primarily in the 1920s and 1930s, to portray the harsh reality of how many working families lived. Benson reminds us that, in the Roaring Twenties, many Americans were still unable to enjoy the fruits of abundance.

On the mid-to-late-twentieth century, see Robert S. Lynd and Helen Merrell Lynd, *Middletown: A Study in Contemporary American Culture* (New York, 1929); id., *Middletown in Transition: A Study in Cultural Conflicts* (New York, 1937); Theodore Caplow and Howard M.

Bahr, *Middletown Families: Fifty Years of Change and Continuity* (Minneapolis, MN, 1982); Lee Rainwater, et al., *Workingman's Wife: Her Personality, World and Life Style* (New York, 1958); Herbert J. Gans, *The Urban Villagers: Group and Class in the Life of Italian-Americans* (New York, 1962); and id.; *The Levittowners: Ways of Life and Politics in a New Suburban Community* (New York, 1967). Historian Sarah Igo contextualizes this material in *The Averaged American: Surveys, Citizens, and the Making of a Mass Public* (Cambridge, MA, 2007).

On the cult of domesticity in its many forms, see Kathryn Kish Sklar, *Catherine Beecher: A Study in American Domesticity* (New Haven, 1973); Glenna Matthews, *"Just a Housewife": The Rise and Fall of Domesticity in America* (New York, 1987); Linda K. Kerber, "Separate Spheres, Female Worlds, Woman's Place: The Rhetoric of Women's History," in *Journal of American History* 75 (June 1988); Elizabeth Clark-Lewis, *Living In, Living Out: African American Domestics in Washington, DC, 1910–1940* (Washington, DC, 1994); Angel Kwolek-Folland, *Engendering Business: Men and Woman in the Corporate Office, 1870–1930* (Baltimore, 1994); id., *Incorporating Women: A History of Women and Business in the United States* (Baltimore, 1998); Sarah Abigail Leavitt, *From Catherine Beecher to Martha Stewart: A Cultural History of Domestic Advice* (Chapel Hill, NC, 2002); Christopher Byron, *Martha Inc.: The Incredible Story of Martha Stewart Living Omnimedia* (New York, 2002); Janice Williams Rutherford, *Selling Mrs. Consumer: Christine Frederick and the Rise of Household Efficiency* (Athens, GA, 2003); and Vicki Howard, *Brides, Inc.: American Weddings and the Business of Tradition* (Philadelphia, 2006).

For Victorian artifacts, several books offer a good starting point. Kenneth L. Ames's *Death in the Dining Room and Other Tales of Victorian Culture* (Philadelphia, 1992), includes essays on the sideboard, the piano, and other household goods. Scholars working in the Ames tradition include Katherine C. Grier, *Culture and Comfort: People, Parlors, and Upholstery, 1850–1930* (Rochester, NY, 1988), revised as *Culture and Comfort: Parlor Making and Middle-class Identity, 1850–1930* (Washington, DC, 1996); Jessica H. Foy and Thomas J. Schlereth, eds., *American Home Life, 1880–1930: A Social History of Spaces and Services* (Knoxville, 1992); and Jessica H. Foy and Karal Ann Marling, eds., *Arts and the American Home, 1890–1930* (Knoxville, TN, 1994), and Shirley Teresa Wajda, "The Commercial Photographic Parlor, 1839–1889," in Carter L. Hudgins and Elizabeth Collins Cromley, eds., *Shaping Communities: Perspectives in Vernacular Architecture* 6 (Knoxville, TN, 1997). Cynthia A. Brandimarte, *Inside Texas: Culture, Identity, and Houses, 1878–1920* (Fort Worth, TX, 1991), walks readers through the Victorian home, using dozens of period photographs. Colleen McDannell has fused cultural and religious history in several enlightening monographs, such as *The Christian Home in Victorian America, 1840–1900* (Bloomington, 1986) and *Material Christianity: Religion and Popular Culture in America* (New Haven, 1995); the latter is especially useful for readers interested in the Catholic home. Craig H. Roell's *The Piano in America, 1890–1940* (Chapel Hill, NC, 1989), is a classic account of music in the home.

On Victorian dining, see Susan Williams, *Savory Suppers and Fashionable Feasts: Dining in Victorian America*, 2d ed. (Knoxville, 1996); Harvey A. Levenstein, *Revolution at the Table: The Transformation of the American Diet* (New York, 1988); id., *Paradox of Plenty: A Social History of Eating in Modern America* (New York, 1993); and Laura Shapiro, *Perfection Salad: Women and Cooking at the Turn of the Century* (New York, 1987).

On women, men, and taste, two of Lizabeth Cohen's early essays offer marvelous insights: "Embellishing a Life of Labor: An Interpretation of the Material Culture of American Working-Class Homes, 1885–1915," *Journal of American Culture* 3 (1980); id., "Respectability at $50.00 Down, 25 Months to Pay! Furnishing a Working-Class Victorian Home," in *Victorian Furniture*, edited by Kenneth L. Ames (Philadelphia, 1983). Chapter One of this book relied heavily on Joan M. Seidl, "Consumers' Choices: A Study of Household Furnishing, 1880–1920," *Minnesota History* (1983), which explains the consumption habits and "make do" strategies of several Minneapolis–St. Paul families. Angel Kwolek-Folland's "The Useful What-not and the Ideal of 'Domestic Decoration,'" *Helicon Nine* 8 (1983), and "The Elegant Dugout: Domesticity and Moveable Culture in the United States, 1870–1900," *American Studies* 25 (1984), thoughtfully blend material culture and social history. Helen Sheumaker, *Love Entwined: The Curious History of Hairwork in America* (Philadelphia, 2007), looks at the history of a forgotten domestic craft that was popular in Victorian times.

The effects of transnational trade on the Victorian home can be traced in several excellent cultural histories. Mary Warner Blanchard's *Oscar Wilde's America: Counterculture in the Gilded Age* (New Haven, 1998) considers the impact of the British Aesthetic Movement on American taste. Mari Yoshihara, *Embracing the East: White Women and American Orientalism* (New York, 2003), explores white Western women's fascination with the East. Kristin L. Hoganson, *Consumers' Imperium: The Global Production of American Domesticity, 1865–1920* (Chapel Hill, NC, 2007), focuses on how that fascination changed interior decoration.

The tastes of nineteenth-century working-class people are described in many excellent community studies by social historians, including Elizabeth Ewen, *Immigrant Women in the Land of Dollars: Life and Culture on the Lower East Side, 1890–1925* (New York, 1985); Kathy Lee Peiss, *Cheap*

Amusements: Working Women and Leisure in Turn-of-the-Century New York (Philadelphia, 1986); and Andrew R. Heinze, *Adapting to Abundance: Jewish Immigrants, Mass Consumption, and the Search for American Identity* (New York, 1990).

The male consumer is an understudied creature. A good place to start is Harvey Green, *Fit for America: Health, Fitness, Sport, and American Society* (New York, 1986), which in part tells the story of men and muscular Christianity at the turn of the century. Mark A. Swiencicki, "Consuming Brotherhood: Men's Culture, Style, and Recreation as Consumer Culture, 1880–1930," *Journal of Social History* 31 (1998), takes a close look at what men bought. Howard P. Chudacoff, *The Age of the Bachelor* (Princeton, NJ, 1999) focuses on single men, their boardinghouses, and their hangouts in the Victorian era. Most recently, John Pettegrew's *Brutes in Suits: Male Sensibility in America, 1890–1920* (Baltimore, 2007), reexamines the evolution of masculinity with reference to men's literature, football, military culture, and sexuality.

On Modern household technologies, see David E. Nye, *Electrifying America: Social Meanings of a New Technology* (Cambridge, MA, 1990); id., *Consuming Power: A Social History of American Energies* (Cambridge, MA, 1998); Ruth Schwartz Cowan, *More Work for Mother: The Ironies of Household Technology from the Open Hearth to the Microwave* (New York, 1983); Susan Strasser, *Never Done: A History of American Housework* (New York, 2000); Carolyn Manning Goldstein, "Mediating Consumption: Home Economics and American Consumers, 1900–1940" (Ph.D. diss., University of Delaware, 1994); id., "From Service to Sales: Home Economics in Light and Power, 1920–1940," *Technology and Culture* 38 (1997); Mark H. Rose, *Cities of Light and Heat: Domesticating Gas and Electricity in Urban America* (State College, PA, 1995); Ronald C. Tobey, *Technology as Freedom: The New Deal and the Electrical Modernization of the American Home* (Berkeley, 1996); Sarah Stage and Virginia B. Vincenti, eds., *Rethinking Home Economics: Women and the History of a Profession* (Ithaca, NY, 1997); Ronald R. Kline, *Consumers in the Country: Technology and Social Change in Rural America* (Baltimore, 2000); Shelley Kaplan Nickles, "'Preserving Women': Refrigerator Design as Social Process in the 1930s," *Technology and Culture* 43 (2002); Thomas P. Hughes, *Networks of Power: Electrification in Western Society, 1880–1930* (Baltimore, 1993); id., *The Human-Built World: How to Think about Technology and Culture* (Chicago, 2004).

For the cultural context of the Modern era, see Larry May, *Screening Out the Past: The Birth of Mass Culture and the Motion Picture Industry* (Chicago, 1983); Harvey Green, *The Uncertainty of Everyday Life, 1914–1945* (Fayetteville, AR, 2000); William L. O'Neill, *A Democracy at War: America's*

Fight at Home and Abroad in World War II (New York, 1993); Lynn Dumenil, *The Modern Temper: American Culture and Society in the 1920s* (New York, 1995), and Steven J. Diner, *A Very Different Age: Americans of the Progressive Era* (New York, 1998).

On Boomer artifacts, see Thomas Hine, *Populuxe* (New York, 1986); id., *The Great Funk: Falling Apart and Coming Together (on a Shag Rug) in the Seventies* (New York, 2007); Karal Ann Marling, *As Seen on TV: The Visual Culture of Everyday Life in the 1950s* (Cambridge, MA, 1994); Carolyn M. Goldstein, *Do It Yourself: Home Improvement in 20th-Century America* (Washington, DC, 1998); Shelley Kaplan Nickles, "Object Lessons: Household Appliance Design and the American Middle Class, 1920–1960" (Ph.D. diss., University of Virginia, 1999); id., "More Is Better: Mass Consumption, Gender, and Class Identity in Postwar America," *American Quarterly* 54 (2002); Glenn Porter, *Raymond Loewy: Designs for a Consumer Culture* (Wilmington, DE, 2002); Per H. Hansen, "Networks, Narratives, and New Markets: The Rise and Decline of Danish Modern Furniture Design, 1930–1970," *Business History Review* 80 (Autumn 2006): 449–83.

The history of plastics is a fascinating area of research. A good introduction by an industry insider is J. Harry DuBois, *Plastics History U.S.A.* (Boston, 1972). Robert D. Friedel's *Pioneer Plastic: The Making and Selling of Celluloid* (Madison, WI, 1983) describes John Wesley Hyatt's quest for an ivory substitute and examines the strategies of early-twentieth-century celluloid manufacturers. Two books provide excellent overviews of plastics in the twentieth century: Jeffrey L. Meikle, *American Plastic: A Cultural History* (New Brunswick, NJ, 1995), and Stephen Fenichell, *Plastic: The Making of a Synthetic Century* (New York, 1996). Alison J. Clarke's *Tupperware: The Promise of Plastic in 1950s America* (Washington, DC, 1999) goes behind the scenes at the Tupperware company to explore how it marketed kitchenware through home shopping parties. Laurie Kahn-Leavitt's award-winning PBS documentary, *Tupperware!*, created for *The American Experience* in 2004, uses interviews and period film clippings to connect plastics, home parties, and 1950s culture. Finally, Robert Kanigel's *Faux Real: Genuine Leather and 200 Years of Inspired Fakes* (Washington, DC, 2007), focuses on the commercial failure of one leather substitute, raising an interesting set of questions about authenticity in materials.

For the cultural context of Boomer America, the work of several historians provide a useful framework. William H. Chafe's *The Unfinished Journey: America Since World War II*, 6th ed. (New York, 2007), and Bruce J. Schulman's *The Seventies: The Great Shift in American Culture, Society, and Politics* (New York, 2001) are good places to start. For the fifties, see

Christina Klein, *Cold War Orientalism: Asia in the Middlebrow Imagination, 1945–1961* (Berkeley, CA, 2003) James Gilbert, *Men in the Middle: Searching for Masculinity in the 1950s* (Chicago, 2005); and Elaine Tyler May's classic study of private life, *Homeward Bound: American Families in the Cold War Era,* rev. ed. (New York, 2008). Sociologist Sam Binkley examines how print culture disseminated countercultural ideals to the middle class in *Getting Loose: Lifestyle Consumption in the 1970s* (Durham, NC, 2007). Susan Smulyan's *Popular Ideologies* (Philadelphia, 2007) tracks the relationship between producers and consumers in mass culture.

Many journalists have published books that focus on the experiences of the middle and working class in the Boomer era. Barbara Ehrenrich is a leading author in this genre. *The Hearts of Men: American Dreams and the Flight from Commitment* (New York, 1983) describes the birth of *Playboy* and new male attitudes in the 1950s. *Fear of Falling: The Inner Life of the Middle Class* (New York, 1990) focuses on the middle class during the Reagan years. Her more recent study, *Nickle and Dimed: On (Not) Getting By in America* (New York, 2001), offers a poignant look at the everyday lives of the working poor.

Consumer Spending and Credit

Several books can steer researchers through the complex history of consumer spending and personal credit. Students should begin with Lendol Calder's immensely readable *Financing the American Dream: A Cultural History of Consumer Credit* (Princeton, 1999). Martha L. Olney's *Buy Now, Pay Later: Advertising, Credit, and Consumer Durables in the 1920s* (Chapel Hill, NC, 1991) offers the in-depth analysis of the Jazz Age durables revolution. For more recent developments, see Lewis Mandell, *The Credit Card Industry: A History* (New York, 1990). Rohit Daniel Wadwhani's "Citizen Savers: The Family Economy, Financial Institutions, and Social Policy in the Northeastern U.S. from the Market Revolution to the Great Depression" (Ph.D. diss., University of Pennsylvania, 2002) focuses on the Victorian and Modern mortgage markets. David P. Handlin's classic, *The American Home: Architecture and Society, 1815–1915* (Boston, 1979), presents useful anecdotal evidence on Victorian consumers and home ownership. For a provocative study that puts the recent credit-card boom in historical perspective, see Robert D. Manning, *Credit Card Nation: The Consequences of America's Addiction to Credit* (New York, 2001).

Additional information on consumers' attitudes toward credit, spending, and home ownership is found in many community studies by social historians. A good starting point is Olivier Zunz, *The Changing Face of Inequality: Ur-*

banization, Industrial Development, and Immigrants in Detroit, 1880–1920 (Chicago, 1982), along with Ronald Edsforth, *Class Conflict and Cultural Consensus: The Making of a Mass Consumer Society in Flint, Michigan* (New Brunswick, NJ, 1987).

For quantitative data, there are several good surveys. An excellent overview of international trade is Ronald Findlay and Kevin O'Rourke, *Power and Plenty: Trade, War, and the World Economy in the Second Millennium* (Princeton, NJ, 2007). For the United States, the place to start is Stanley L. Engerman and Robert E. Gallman, eds., *The Cambridge Economic History of the United States, Vol. II: The Long Nineteenth Century* and *Vol. III: The Twentieth Century* (New York, 2000). Daniel Horowitz's *The Morality of Spending,* mentioned earlier, explains the budget studies done by Progressive-era social workers. Stanley Lebergott's *Pursuing Happiness: American Consumers in the Twentieth Century* (Princeton, 1993) gathers data from diverse sources into useful charts tracing consumption patterns; also see his *Consumer Expenditures: New Measures and Old Motives* (Princeton, 1996). For the late-twentieth century, see Avner Offer, *The Challenge of Affluence: Self-Control and Well-Being in the United States and Britain since 1950* (New York, 2006).

Data sets related to consumption habits are now readily available electronically. Researchers should consult Susan B. Carter et al., eds., *Historical Statistics of the United States: Earliest Times to the Present,* Millennial Edition (New York, 2006), an electronic resource available at most research libraries. Earlier data sets are found in the Bicentennial Edition, U.S. Bureau of the Census, *Historical Statistics of the United States: Colonial Times to 1970,* 2 vols. (Washington, DC, 1976).

Those who want to track consumers' spending habits should also visit the web site of the U.S. Census Bureau, which has posted government reports dating back several decades. This book drew on many such reports, including *Statistical Brief: Who Uses a Computer?* (March 1988); *Statistical Brief: The Growing Use of Computers* (April 1991); Eric C. Newburger, *Computer Use in the United States* (October 1997); Barbara T. Williams, *These Old Houses, 2001* (Feb. 2004); *Electronic Shopping and Mail-order Houses, 2002* (Nov. 2004); and Jennifer Cheeseman Day, et al., *Computer and Internet Use in the United States, 2003* (October 2005).

Urbanization and Suburbanization

A useful one-volume introduction to the history of suburbanization is Delores Hayden's *Building Suburbia: Green Fields and Urban Growth, 1920–2000* (New York, 2003). The classic texts on suburban development include Sam

Bass Warner, Jr., *Streetcar Suburbs: The Process of Growth in Boston, 1870–1900* (Cambridge, MA, 1962); Kenneth T. Jackson, *Crabgrass Frontier: The Suburbanization of the United States* (New York, 1985); and Robert Fishman, *Bourgeois Utopias: The Rise and Fall of Suburbia* (New York, 1987).

In the past few decades, scholars have revised the classic interpretations in dramatic ways. For example, Margaret S. Marsh's *Suburban Lives* (New Brunswick, NJ, 1990), proposed that the retreat to suburbia reflected the triumph of masculine domesticity, with its reverence for agrarian life, rather than a feminization of the home. Robert Bruegmann's *Sprawl: A Compact History* (Chicago, 2005), looks at suburban development in Europe and the United States with fresh eyes. For other new approaches, see Kevin Michael Kruse and Thomas J. Segrue, eds., *The New Suburban History* (Chicago, 2006); Robert A. Beauregard, *When America Became Suburban* (Minneapolis, 2006); and Becky M. Nicolaides and Andrew Wiese, eds., *The Suburb Reader* (New York, 2006). Lizabeth Cohen's masterwork, *A Consumers' Republic*, discussed in an earlier section on Major Works, also offers a detailed case study of one northern New Jersey suburb. Rosalyn Baxandall's and Elizabeth Ewen's *Picture Windows: How the Suburbs Happened* (New York, 2000), focuses on Long Island, with wider implications.

On the changing face of cities, see Joel Garreau's *Edge City: Life on the New Frontier* (New York, 1991); Robert M. Fogelson, *Downtown: Its Rise and Fall, 1880–1950* (New Haven, 2001); and Alison Isenberg, *Downtown America: A History of the Place and the People Who Made It* (Chicago, 2004).

Fashion and Clothing

Scholarship on fashion and clothing has exploded in the New Millennium, with historians, curators, anthropologists, sociologists, and journalists making vital contributions. Useful overviews include Lois W. Banner, *American Beauty* (Los Angeles, 2006); Valerie Steele, *Fashion and Eroticism: Ideals of Feminine Beauty from the Victorian Era to the Jazz Age* (New York, 1985); id., *Paris Fashion: A Cultural History*, rev. ed. (New York, 1998); Elizabeth Ann Coleman, *The Opulent Era: Fashions of Worth, Doucet, and Pingat* (Brooklyn, NY, 1989); Christopher Breward, *The Culture of Fashion: A New History of Fashionable Dress* (New York, 1995); Kathy Lee Peiss, *Hope in a Jar: The Making of America's Beauty Culture* (New York, 1998); Valerie Steele, *Fifty Years of Fashion: New Look to Now* (New Haven, 1997); id., *The Corset: A Cultural History* (New Haven, 2001); Philip B. Scranton, ed., *Beauty and Business: Commerce, Gender, and Culture in Modern America* (New York, 2001), which includes Carole Turbin's essay on the Arrow man; Linda Welters and Patricia A. Cunningham, eds., *Twentieth-Century American Fashion* (New York, 2005); and Christopher Breward et al., eds., *Swinging Sixties: Fashion in London and Beyond, 1955–1970* (New York, 2006). On the importance of casting a broad net when defining fashion, see Regina Lee Blaszczyk, ed., *Producing Fashion: Commerce, Culture, and Consumers* (Philadelphia, 2008), which discusses a range of style goods from haute couture to houses.

On professional dressmakers versus home sewing, see Wendy Gamber, *The Female Economy: The Millinery and Dressmaking Trades, 1860–1930* (Urbana, IL, 1997); Barbara Burman, ed., *The Culture of Sewing: Gender, Consumption and Home Dressmaking* (New York, 1999); Susan Hay, ed., *From Paris to Providence: Fashion, Art, and the Tirocchi Dressmakers' Shop, 1915–1947* (Providence, RI, 2000); and Cynthia Amnéus, *A Separate Sphere: Dressmakers in Cincinnati's Golden Age, 1877–1922* (Cincinnati, 2003). On the industrialization of the garment industry, see Claudia Brush Kidwell and Margaret C. S. Christman, *Suiting Everyone: The Democratization of Clothing in America* (Washington, DC, 1974); Nancy L. Green, *Ready-to-Wear and Ready-to-Work: A Century of Industry and Immigrants in Paris and New York* (Durham, NC, 1997); Andrew Godley, *Jewish Immigrant Entrepreneurship in New York and London, 1880–1914: Enterprise and Culture* (New York, 2001); and Rob Schorman, *Selling Style: Clothing and Social Change at the Turn of the Century* (Philadelphia, 2003).

Men's clothing is discussed in many general works on fashion, including the books by Christopher Breward and Rob Schorman. British historians and literary scholars examine the intriguing history of the dark suit, mostly in the English context: John Harvey, *Men in Black* (Chicago, 1995); David Kuchta, *The Three-Piece Suit and Modern Masculinity: England, 1550–1850* (Berkeley, CA, 2002); and Brent Shannon, *The Cut of His Coat* (Athens, OH, 2006). Michael Zakim's *Ready-Made Democracy: A History of Men's Dress in the American Republic, 1760–1860* (Chicago, 2003) addresses questions about men's tailoring, masculine attire, and national identity in the decades leading up to the Civil War.

For readers interested in New York's role as a fashion center, a good place to start is Caroline Rennolds Milbank's *New York Fashion: The Evolution of American Style* (New York: Abrams, 1996), a *tour de force* of high-end styles over a broad time period. For mass-market designs, the best treatment is Gabriel M. Goldstein and Phyllis Dillon, et al., *A Perfect Fit: The Garment Industry and American Jewry* (New York, 2005). On synthetic fabrics, see Susannah Handley, *Nylon: The Story of a Fashion Revolution* (Baltimore, 2000), and Regina Lee Blaszczyk, "Styling Synthetics: DuPont's Marketing of Fabrics and Fashions in Postwar America," *Business History Review* 80

(Autumn 2006: 485–582). On recent designers and brands, see Teri Agins, *The End of Fashion: The Mass Marketing of the Clothing Business* (New York, 1999), which in part compares Ralph Lauren and Tommy Hilfiger; and Veronica Manlow, *Designing Clothes: Culture and Organization of the Fashion Industry* (New Brunswick, NJ, 2007).

For the meaning of clothing and fashion, it is helpful to bring in the work of scholars in other social sciences. Sociologists doing important work on the fashion and cultural values include Diana Crane, *Fashion and Its Social Agendas: Class, Gender, and Identity in Clothing* (Chicago, 2000); id., "Globalization, Organizational Size, and Innovation in the French Fashion Industry: Production of Culture Theory Revisited," *Poetics* 24 (1997: 393–414); and Yuniya Kawamura, *Fashion-ology: An Introduction to Fashion Studies* (New York, 2005). Geographer Norma Rantisi is insightful on contemporary innovation networks in "The Local Innovation System as a Source of 'Variety': Openness and Adaptability in New York City's Garment District," *Regional Studies* 36 (2002: 587–600), and "The Ascendance of New York Fashion," *International Journal of Urban and Regional Research* 28 (March 2004): 86–106.

On the role of retailers and magazines in the fashion-industrial complex, there are several good places to start: Leigh Eric Schmidt, *Consumer Rites: The Buying and Selling of American Holidays* (Princeton, 1995); Thomas Frank, *The Conquest of Cool: Business Culture, Counter-Culture, and the Rise of Hip Consumerism* (Chicago, 1997); Bill Osgerby, *Playboys in Paradise: Masculinity, Youth and Leisure-style in Modern America* (New York, 2001); and Daniel Delis Hill, *As Seen in Vogue: A Century of American Fashion in Advertising* (Lubbock, TX, 2004).

On fashion icons, see Debora Silverman, *Selling Culture: Bloomingdale's, Diana Vreeland, and the New Aristocracy of Taste in Reagan's America* (New York, 1986); Marling, *As Seen on TV*, for Mamie Eisenhower; Hamish Bowles, ed., *Jacqueline Kennedy: The White House Years* (Boston, 2001); and Rosalind Coward, *Diana: The Portrait* (Kansas City, MO, 2007).

This study drew on several types of resources to fill in the gaps in the business history of fashion: the Nike Collection and the Estelle Ellis Papers at the Smithsonian National Museum of American History, Washington, DC, the Ernest Dichter Papers at the Hagley Museum and Library, Wilmington, DE, and original mail-order catalogs from Sears, Roebuck and Company, Montgomery Ward, and other firms, and oral history interviews.

Retailing

For the history of mass merchandising, Boorstin's *The Americans* offers an insightful analysis of department stores as "palaces" and five-and-tens as "bazaars." Alfred D. Chandler, Jr.'s *The Visible Hand: The Managerial Revolution in American Business* (Cambridge, MA, 1977) discusses the shift from wholesalers to mass retailers. On traditional distribution channels, see Bill Reid Moeckel, *The Development of the Wholesaler in the United States, 1860–1900* (New York, 1986); Glenn Porter and Harold C. Livesay, *Merchants and Manufacturers: Studies in the Changing Structure of Nineteenth-Century Marketing* (Chicago, 1989); Timothy B. Spears, *100 Years on the Road: The Traveling Salesmen in American Culture* (New Haven, 1995); and Walter A. Friedman, *Birth of a Salesman: The Transformation of Selling in America* (Cambridge, MA, 2004).

Students interested in the department store should begin with Jan Whitaker's *Service and Style: How the American Department Store Fashioned the Middle Class* (New York, 2006), a national survey of this important retailing institution from the mid-1800s to the present. A fine case study of locally operated department stores in Buffalo, NY, is Sarah Elvins, *Sales and Celebrations: Retailing and Regional Identity in Western New York State, 1920–1940* (Athens, OH, 2004). Early scholarship often focused on the biographies of entrepreneurs and their firms: Ralph M. Hower, *History of Macy's of New York, 1858–1919: Chapters in the Evolution of the Department Store* (Cambridge, MA, 1943); Harry E. Resseguie, "Alexander Turney Stewart and the Development of the Department Store," *Business History Review* 39 (1965: 301–22); Robert W. Twyman, *History of Marshall Field & Co., 1852–1906* (New York, 1976); and Robert Hendrickson, *The Grand Emporiums: The Illustrated History of America's Great Department Stores* (New York, 1979). The best study of store displays is William L. Bird, Jr., *Holidays on Display* (Princeton, NJ, 2007), a whirlwind tour of urban centers from the 1920s to the 1960s. Combining the study of business archives, trade journals, and images of displays, Bird's lavishly illustrated book is a model study of retailing and consumer culture.

Historians of labor, women, and consumer culture have produced several important books on department stores: Susan Porter Benson, *Counter Cultures: Saleswomen, Managers, and Customers in American Department Stores, 1890–1940* (Urbana, IL, 1986); Elaine S. Abelson, *When Ladies Go A-Thieving: Middle-class Shoplifters in the Victorian Department Store* (New York, 1989), and William Leach, *Land of Desire*. Although the title suggests that it's about shoplifting, Abelson's book contains a good deal of business and consumer history that isn't found in other places. For example, her careful reading of consumers' diaries makes the Victorian shopping experience come alive. Herbert Ershkowitz's *John Wanamaker: Philadelphia Merchant* (Conshohocken, PA, 1999) effectively blends business biography with cultural history.

For mail-order houses, the place to begin is with an encyclopedic business history: Boris Emmet and John E. Jeuck, *Catalogues and Counters: A History of Sears, Roebuck and Company* (Chicago, 1950). Using interviews with employees, popular writer Gordon L. Weil picked up where they left off in *Sears, Roebuck USA: The Great American Catalog Store and How It Grew* (New York, 1977). Tom Mahoney and Leonard Sloane's *The Great Merchants: America's Foremost Retail Institutions and the People Who Made Them Great* (New York, 1974) contains succinct accounts of Sears, Wards, and other mail-order houses. For the social history, see Thomas J. Schlereth's "Country Stores, County Fairs and Mail-order Catalogs: Consumption in Rural America," in Bronner, *Consuming Visions*. Curator JoAnne Olian has published several Dover picture books that open the doors onto the world of mass-produced fashion sold by mail-order retailers. Volumes such as *Everyday Fashions, 1909–1920, as Pictured in Sears Catalogs* (New York, 1995), and *Children's Fashions, 1900–1950, as Pictured in Sears Catalogs* (New York, 2003), contain introductory essays followed by period illustrations.

The literature on chain stores falls into several categories. The first group of books focuses on the business history of early chains. On the seminal role of tea stores in creating the chain store, see the account of one former executive, William I. Walsh, *The Rise and Decline of the Great Atlantic and Pacific Tea Company* (Secaucus, NJ, 1986). The literature on dime stores includes classic works such as John K. Winkler, *Five and Ten: The Fabulous Life of F. W. Woolworth* (New York, 1970); William Thomas Grant, *The Story of W. T. Grant and the Early Days of the Business He Founded* (New York, 1962); and F. W. Woolworth Company, *Woolworth's First 75 Years: The Story of Everybody's Store* (New York, 1954). Bernice L. Thomas, *America's 5 & 10 Cent Stores: The Kress Legacy* (New York, 1997), is an architectural history of one southern store, making good use of visual materials at the National Building Museum in Washington, DC. Karen Plunkett-Powell's *Remembering Woolworth's: A Nostalgic History of the World's Most Famous Five-and-Dime* (New York, 1999) offers a fun-filled trip down memory lane, suggesting wonderful ideas for further research.

Another body of literature focuses on the public critique of these first chain stores. Godfrey M. Lebhar, publisher of the trade journal *Chain Store Age*, responded to this criticism with a book, *Chain Stores in America, 1859–1959* (New York, 1963), while Jonathan J. Bean supplies historical perspective in *Beyond the Broker State: Federal Policies toward Small Business, 1936–1961* (Chapel Hill, NC, 1996). The rise of big-box retailers has yet to be studied by business historians, but a flurry of books followed the recent controversy over Wal★Mart's labor practices; see, for example, John Dicker, *The United States of Wal-Mart* (New York, 2005); Nelson Lichtenstein, ed.,

Wal-Mart: The Face of Twenty-First-Century Capitalism (New York, 2006); and Charles Fishman, *The Wal-Mart Effect* (New York, 2006). For the management perspective on early big-box stores, see Stuart U. Rich and Bernard Portis, "Clues for Action from Shopper Preferences," *Harvard Business Review* 41 (March–April 1963: 147–53); and for a journalist's account of one store, Laura Rowley, *On Target: How the World's Hottest Retailer Hit a Bull's Eye* (New York, 2003). On fair trade laws, see L. Louise Luchsinger and Patrick M. Dunne, "Fair Trade Laws—How Fair?" *Journal of Marketing* 42 (January 1978: 50–53); and David W. Boyd, "From 'Mom and Pop' to Wal-Mart: The Impact of the Consumer Goods Pricing Act of 1975 on the Retail Sector in the United States," *Journal of Economic Issues* 31 (March 1997: 223–32).

Several recent Ph.D. dissertations promise to fill some of the holes in the historical literature on retailing, once they appear as books: Paul Schmitz, "D'Agostino Supermarkets, From Pushcart to Product: Family and Ethnicity as Cultural Currency" (Ph.D. diss., Boston University, 2006); Tracey Ann Deutsch, "Making Change at the Grocery Store: Government, Grocers, and the Problem of Women's Autonomy in the Creation of Chicago's Supermarkets, 1920–1950" (Ph.D. diss., University of Wisconsin, 2001); Stephanie Dyer, "Markets in the Meadows: Department Stores and Shopping Centers in the Decentralization of Philadelphia, 1920–1980" (Ph.D. diss., University of Pennsylvania, 2000); Thomas David Beal, "Selling Gotham: The Retail Trade in New York City from the Public Market to Alexander T. Stewart's Marble Palace, 1625–1860" (Ph.D. diss., State University of New York at Stony Brook, 1998); Bethany Moreton, "The Soul of the Service Economy: Wal-Mart and the Making of Christian Free Enterprise" (Ph.D. diss., Yale University, 2006).

Insightful work on retail buildings and the commercial landscape comes from urban planning, geography, architectural history, and business history. Planner Ann Satterthwaite's *Going Shopping: Consumer Choices and Community Consequences* (New Haven, 2001) is a whirlwind tour of shopping spaces through the ages, with special attention to the late-twentieth century. For the Victorian era, see Mona Domosh, "Shaping the Commercial City: Retail Districts in Nineteenth-Century New York and Boston," *Annals of the Association of American Geographers* 80 (1990). Architectural historian Richard Longstreth has produced an admirable *oeuvre* on commercial space that is an asset to students of consumer society: see *City Center to Regional Mall: Architecture, the Automobile, and Retailing in Los Angeles, 1920–1950* (Cambridge, MA, 1997); *The Drive-in, the Supermarket, and the Transformation of Commercial Space in Los Angeles, 1914–1941* (Cambridge, MA, 1999); "The Mixed Blessings of Success: The Hecht Company and the Department Store Branch Development after World War II," in Hudgins and

Cromley, eds., *Shaping Communities*; and "Sears, Roebuck and the Remaking of the Department Store, 1924–42," in *Journal of the Society of Architectural Historians* 65 (2006: 238–79). M. Jeffrey Hardwick's *Mall Maker: Victor Gruen, Architect of an American Dream* (Philadelphia, 2004) is a biography that also documents the evolution of mall architecture. Thomas S. Dicke's *Franchising in America: The Development of a Business Method, 1840–1980* (Durham, NC, 1992) is a readable account of the franchise, including car dealers and gas stations.

On the impact of globalization on retailing and clothing, readers should begin with Pietra Rivoli's *The Travels of a T–Shirt in the Global Economy: An Economist Examines the Markets, Power and Politics of World Trade* (Hoboken, NJ, 2006); James Sullivan, *Jeans: A Cultural History of an American Icon* (New York, 2006); and Rachel Louise Snyder, *Fugitive Denim: A Moving Story of People and Pants in the Borderless World of Global Trade* (New York, 2007). Two marvelous studies on the transformation of shipping are also helpful to understanding the integration of the global economy: Marc Levinson, *The Box: How the Shipping Container Made the World Smaller and the World Economy Bigger* (Princeton, 2006), and Brian J. Cudahy, *Box Boats: How Container Ships Changed the World* (New York, 2006).

Readers interested in retailing during World War II should begin with Jan Whitaker's study of the department store, *Service and Style*. Rationing is dealt with in Barbara McLean Ward's edited volume, *Produce and Conserve, Share and Play Square: The Grocer and the Consumer on the Home-Front Battlefield during World War II* (Portsmouth, NH, 1994). This exhibition catalog, published in conjunction with the Strawbery Banke Museum's restoration of a corner grocery store, contains illustrated essays on the home front, rationing, chains versus mom-and-pop stores, and national advertising. Amy Bentley's *Eating for Victory: Food Rationing and the Politics of Domesticity* (Urbana, IL, 1998) explores the role of government propaganda in creating the wartime homemaker.

Good primary sources on retailing include Malcolm P. McNair and Eleanor G. May, *The American Department Store, 1920–1960: A Performance Analysis Based on the Harvard Reports* (Boston, 1963), and the websites of The National Retail Federation and the International Council of Shopping Centers (ICSC). With a staff of professional librarians and researchers, the ICSC has used the web to make public a wealth of late-twentieth-century data, much of which was invaluable for this book. (See http://www.icsc. org/rsch/research.php?page=e-data, accessed March 8, 2008). I supplemented these sources with research in major archival collections: the John Wanamaker Papers at the Historical Society of Pennsylvania, Philadelphia, the Strawbridge and Clothier Archives at the Hagley Museum and Library in Wilmington, Delaware, and other retail collections.

Advertising and Marketing

Since the 1970s, the history of advertising has attracted a good deal of attention from media scholars, cultural historians, and practitioners. The most comprehensive historical overview is Stephen R. Fox's *The Mirror Makers: A History of American Advertising and Its Creators* (Urbana, IL, 1997), which covers a broad time span. An underappreciated classic is Michael Schudson's *Advertising, the Uneasy Persuasion: Its Dubious Impact on American Society* (New York, 1984). Advertising professor Juliann Sivulka's *Soap, Sex, and Cigarettes: A Cultural History of American Advertising* (Belmont, CA, 1998) highlights memorable slogans, brand names, and favorite jingles.

Two outstanding works on the Victorian era are T. J. Jackson Lears, *Fables of Abundance: A Cultural History of American Advertising* (New York, 1994), which offers provocative insights on cultural hegemony, and Pamela Walker Laird's *Advertising Progress: American Business and the Rise of Consumer Marketing* (Baltimore, 1998). Laird expands and deepens earlier works by Daniel Pope, *The Making of Modern Advertising* (New York, 1983), and James D. Norris, *Advertising and the Transformation of American Society, 1865–1920* (New York, 1990), which has useful case studies of the bicycle and the Kodak camera. Her work is distinctive for the scope and the use of original sources, including trade journals such as *Advertiser's Gazette, Judicious Advertising, Inland Printer, Printers' Ink,* and *Profitable Advertising.*

For more on Victorian trade cards, good places to begin are Peter C. Marzio, *The Democratic Art: Pictures for a 19th-Century America, Chromolithography, 1840–1900* (Boston, 1979); Robert Jay, *The Trade Card in Nineteenth-Century America* (Columbia, MO, 1987); and Jay T. Last, *The Color Explosion: Nineteenth-Century American Lithography* (Santa Ana, CA, 2005). Literary scholar Ellen Gruber Garvey examines how trade cards and scrap booking trained people to be consumers in *The Adman in the Parlor: Magazines and the Gendering of Consumer Culture, 1880s to 1910s* (New York, 1996).

On mass-circulation magazines and national advertising, Richard M. Ohmann's *Selling Culture: Magazines, Markets, and Class at the Turn of the Century* (New York, 1996) surveys the golden age of national magazines like *Saturday Evening Post, Collier's,* and *Ladies' Home Journal.* The best overview of women's magazines is Mary Ellen Zuckerman's *A History of Popular Women's Magazines in the United States, 1792–1995* (Westport, CT,

1998). Literary scholar Jennifer Scanlon offers a close-up look at the J. Walter Thompson agency's relationship to one magazine in *Inarticulate Longings: The Ladies' Home Journal, Gender, and the Promises of Consumer Culture* (New York, 1995). For the business history of Modern advertising, the classic work is Roland Marchand's *Advertising the American Dream: Making Way for Modernity, 1920–1940* (Berkeley, 1985). Jonathan Augustus Silva, "The Development of American Marketing Thought and Practice, 1902–1940" (Ph. D. diss., Ohio State University, 1998), goes behind the scenes at J. Walter Thompson.

Historians have started to analyze niche markets that emerged in this period; see, for example, Gary Cross, *Kids' Stuff: Toys and the Changing World of American Childhood* (Cambridge, MA, 1997); id., *Cute and Cool: Wondrous Innocence and Modern American Children's Culture* (New York, 2004); id., *Men to Boys: The Making of Modern Immaturity* (New York, 2008); Steven M. Gelber, *Hobbies: Leisure and the Culture of Work in America* (New York, 1999); Daniel Thomas Cook, *The Commodification of Childhood: The Children's Clothing Industry and the Rise of the Child Consumer* (Durham, NC, 2004); and Lisa Jacobson, *Raising Consumers: Children and the Mass Market in Early Twentieth Century America* (New York, 2005), which is terrific on the boy consumer. Jacobson's edited volume, *Children and Consumer Culture in American Society: A Historical Handbook and Guide* (Westport, CT, 2008), contains essays and primary sources that illuminate the formation of children's consumerism. Also informative on the youth market is Paula S. Fass, *The Damned and the Beautiful: American Youth in the 1920's* (New York, 1979), and Jon Savage, *Teenage: The Creation of Youth Culture* (New York, 2007).

Two historians have focused on advertising practice and the business ethos known as the American Way of Life. Charles F. McGovern's *Sold American: Consumption and Citizenship, 1890–1945* (Chapel Hill, NC, 2006) examines the tensions between producers and consumers, with reference to early consumer advocacy groups and the American Way as a backlash against organized labor, the consumers' movement, and the New Deal. Cynthia Lee Henthorn's book, *From Submarines to Suburbs: Selling a Better America, 1939–1959* (Athens, OH, 2006), traces the evolution of the American Way through World War II and the early Cold War in a detailed analysis of advertising imagery and the papers of the National Association of Manufacturers. A complement to McGovern's discussion of the consumers' movement is Inger L. Stole's *Advertising on Trial: Consumer Activism and Corporate Public Relations in the 1930s* (Urbana, IL, 2006).

On world's fairs as commercial extravaganzas, see Robert C. Post, ed., *1876: A Centennial Exhibition* (Washington, DC, 1976); Robert W. Rydell, *All the World's a Fair: Visions of Empire at American International Expositions, 1876–1916* (Chicago, 1984); id., *World's Fairs: The Century-of-Progress Expositions* (Chicago, 1993); Joseph J. Corn, *Imagining Tomorrow: History, Technology, and the American Future* (Cambridge, MA, 1986); Robert W. Rydell, et al., eds., *Fair America: World's Fairs in the United States* (Washington, DC, 2000); and Bruno Giberti, *Designing the Centennial: A History of the 1876 Centennial Exhibition in Philadelphia* (Lexington, KY, 2002). Researchers seeking primary sources on local and world's fairs will find no better source than *The Books of the Fairs*, a multireel microfilm set published for the Smithsonian Institution Libraries, Washington, DC (Chicago, 1992).

The history of marketing and market research has several excellent surveys. Susan Strasser's *Satisfaction Guaranteed: The Making of the American Mass Market* (Washington, DC, 1995) explores marketing, branding, and advertising in the 1880–1920 period. Richard S. Tedlow's *New and Improved: The Story of Mass Marketing in America*, rev. ed. (Boston, 1996) is built around case studies of A&P, Ford and GM, Sears, and Pepsi and Coca-Cola. Richard S. Tedlow and Geoffrey Jones, eds., *The Rise and Fall of Mass Marketing* (New York, 1993), offers new insights into the evolution of marketing practice in the twentieth century. Nancy F. Koehn's *Brand New: How Entrepreneurs Earned Consumers' Trust from Wedgwood to Dell* (Boston, 2001) is a series of case studies on Wedgwood, H. J. Heinz, Marshall Field, Estée Lauder, Starbucks, and Dell. For the history of demographic surveys by an insider, see Jean M. Converse, *Survey Research: Roots and Emergence, 1890–1960* (Berkeley, CA, 1987).

Several cultural historians have put the history of marketing practice within the context of business developments and consumer history. For an introduction to this approach, see Regina Lee Blaszczyk, *Imagining Consumers: Design and Innovation from Wedgwood to Corning* (Baltimore, 2000), and id., "Rethinking Fashion," in Regina Lee Blaszczyk, ed., *Producing Fashion*. Kathy Lee Peiss's *Hope in a Jar* explains how women drove changes in the cosmetics and beauty products industries. Roger Horowitz and Arwen P. Mohun, eds., *His and Hers: Gender, Consumption, and Technology* (Charlottesville, VA, 1998), includes essays on hotels, chocolate, and glassware. Coleman Harwell Wells examines the lives of forgotten marketing pioneers in "Remapping America: Market Research and American Society, 1900–1940" (Ph.D. diss., University of Virginia, 1999).

Advertising geared to black consumers has attracted its share of historians. Robert E. Weems, Jr., set the stage with his important work: "The Revolution Will Be Marketed: American Corporations and Black Consumers during the 1960s," *Radical History Review* 59 (1994: 94–107); id., *Desegregating the Dollar: African-American Consumerism in the Twentieth Century* (New York, 1998). M. M. Manring's *Slave in a Box: The Strange Career of Aunt Jemima* (Charlottesville, VA, 1998) examines how one early twentieth century advertising icon mirrored and created white fantasies about race relations. Journalist Stephanie Capparell explores early target marketing in *The Real Pepsi Challenge: The Inspirational Story of Breaking the Color Barrier in American Business* (New York, 2007). Jason Chambers explores how black professionals positioned themselves within the advertising industry as experts on African American taste, and then used their status to alter racial stereotypes; see *Madison Avenue and the Color Line* (Philadelphia, 2008).

Those interested in the recent history of marketing should turn to the work of journalists and industry practitioners. A professor of marketing and international business, Robert Bartels surveyed American developments in advertising, credit, retailing, and management in *The History of Marketing Thought*, 3d ed. (Columbus, OH, 1988). Although a textbook, Bartels's volume is an invaluable survey for business and cultural historians. On brands, the best overview is Naomi Klein, *No Logo: Taking Aim at the Brand Bullies* (New York, 2000). On market segments, see Madhav N. Segal and Lionel Sosa, "Marketing to the Hispanic Community," *California Management Review* 26 (Fall 1983: 120–34); Michael J. Weiss, *The Clustering of America* (New York, 1988); Regis McKenna, "Marketing in an Age of Diversity," *Harvard Business Review* (1988: 88–95); John H. Johnson with Lerone Bennett, Jr., *Succeeding Against the Odds* (New York, 1992); Faith Popcorn and Lys Marigold, *EVEolution: The Eight Truths of Marketing to Women* (New York, 2000); and Guy Garcia, *The New Mainstream: How the Multicultural Consumer Is Transforming American Business* (New York, 2004). Marketing gurus like Regis McKenna and Ronald D. Michman have published numerous books that advance their approaches to the contemporary consumer. Books like Michman's *Lifestyle Marketing* (Westport, CT, 2003) and McKenna's *Total Access* (Boston, 2002) are useful as primary sources.

Luxury brands have attracted a good deal of attention from marketers. Recent books include Ronald D. Michman and Edward M. Mazze, *The Affluent Consumer: Marketing and Selling the Luxury Lifestyle* (Westport, CT, 2006). Journalist Dana Thomas offers an incisive critique of the dark side of the luxury industry in *Deluxe: How Luxury Lost Its Luster* (New York, 2007).

To supplement these secondary sources, additional research for this book's discussion of marketing and advertising was conducted in major trade journals (e.g., *Printers' Ink, Printers' Ink Monthly, Magazine of Wall Street*), the Goya Foods Collection and the Campbell Soup Collection at the Smithsonian National Museum of American History, and the J. Walter Thompson Archives at Duke University's John W. Hartman Center for Sales, Advertising, and Marketing History.

Automobiles

Comprehensive coverage of Detroit's business history is found in Sally H. Clarke, *Trust and Power: Consumers, the Modern Corporation, and the Making of the United States Automobile Market* (New York, 2007); Thomas K. McCraw, *American Business, 1920–2000: How It Worked,* 2d ed. (Wheeling, IL, 2008); Richard S. Tedlow, Chap. 3 in *New and Improved*; David A. Hounshell, *From the American System to Mass Production, 1800–1932* (Baltimore, 1984); and Allan Nevins and Frank Ernest Hill, *Ford,* 3 vols. (New York, 1954–63).

On automotive styling, the best treatment is David Gartman, *Auto Opium: A Social History of American Automobile Design* (New York, 1994), which draws on corporate archives, national magazines, and trade journals. For Ford, see Henry L. Dominguez, *Edsel Ford and E. T. Gregorie: The Remarkable Design Team and Their Classic Fords of the 1930s and 1940s* (Warrendale, PA, 1999). On GM's 1920s color efforts, see Regina Lee Blaszczyk, "The Importance of Being True Blue: DuPont and the Color Revolution," in Elspeth H. Brown, et al., eds. *Cultures of Commerce: Representation and American Business Culture, 1877–1860* (New York, 2006), and "True Blue: DuPont and the Color Revolution," *Chemical Heritage Magazine* 25 (Fall 2007: 20–25). For streamlining, see Jeffrey L. Meikle, *Twentieth Century Limited: Industrial Design in America, 1925–1939,* 2d ed. (Philadelphia, 2001), and Christina Cogdell, *Eugenic Design: Streamlining in America in the 1930s* (Philadelphia, 2004).

The social history of the automobile is addressed by several recent books: Rudi Volti, *Cars and Culture: The Life Story of a Technology* (Baltimore, 2004); Kevin L. Borg, *Auto Mechanics: Technology and Expertise in Twentieth-Century America* (Baltimore, 2007); Kathleen Franz, *Tinkering: Consumers Reinvent the Early Automobile* (Philadelphia, 2005); Roger B. White, *Home on the Road: The Motor Home in America* (Washington, DC, 2000); Clay McShane, *Down the Asphalt Path: The Automobile and the American City* (New York, 1994); Virginia Scharff, *Taking the Wheel: Women and the Coming of the Motor Age* (Albuquerque, NM, 1992); and David A. Kirsch, *The Electric Vehicle and the Burden of History* (New Brunswick, NJ, 2000). Classic texts include John B. Rae, *The American Automobile Industry* (Boston, 1984), and James J. Flink, *The Automobile Age* (Cambridge, MA, 1988).

These secondary sources were supplemented by research in the automotive trade journals, the Ford Motor Company Archives at The Henry Ford, Dearborn, Michigan, and the General Motors Collection at the Kettering/GMI Alumni Foundation of Industrial History, in Flint, Michigan.

Consumer Electronics

For an excellent analysis of American audiences, see Richard Butsch, *The Making of American Audiences: From Stage to Television, 1750–1990* (New York, 2000); *The Audience: Crowds, Publics, and Individuals* (New York, 2008); and his edited volume, *For Fun and Profit: The Transformation of Leisure into Consumption* (Philadelphia, 1990). Another good source for how mass and personal entertainment affects social interactions is Robert D. Putnam, *Bowling Alone: The Collapse and Revival of American Community* (New York, 2000). For an overview of many different devices and media, see Steven D. Lubar, *Info Culture: The Smithsonian Book of Information Age Inventions* (Boston, 1993).

On television, James L. Baughman's *Same Time, Same Station: Creating American Television 1948–1961* (Baltimore, 2007) is a good resource on early programming, business development, and viewer experience. The medium's cultural impact is explored in Lynn Spigel, *Make Room for TV: Television and the Family Ideal in Postwar America* (Chicago, 1992). Extending through later years is Richard E. Caves, *Switching Channels: Organization and Change in TV Broadcasting* (Cambridge, MA, 2005). Sarah Banet-Weiser analyzes how the Nickelodeon cable channel addresses young viewers in *Kids Rule! Nickelodeon and Consumer Citizenship* (Durham, NC, 2007).

For radio, the best historical analysis of consumers' experience and the construction of meaning is Susan J. Douglas, *Listening In: Radio and the American Imagination* (New York, 1999). Lizabeth Cohen's *Making a New Deal* discusses radio use among Chicago's blue-collar workers. Susan Smulyan's *Selling Radio: The Commercialization of American Broadcasting, 1920–1934* (Washington, D.C, 1994), explains the rise of the networks. In Michele Hilmes and Jason Loviglio, eds., *Radio Reader: Essays in the Cultural History of Radio* (New York, 2002), two essays consider how radio reacted to the rise of television: Eric W. Rothenbuhler and Tom McCourt, "Radio Redefines Itself, 1947–1962," and Jennifer Hyland Wang, "'The Case of the Radio-Active Housewife': Relocating Radio in the Age of Television." In the same book, Michael C. Keith's chapter, "Turn On . . . Tune In: The Rise and Demise of Commercial Underground Radio," discusses FM radio in the 1960s. Kathy M. Newman documents the popular response to commercial radio in

Radio Active: Advertising and Consumer Activism, 1935–1947 (Berkeley, CA, 2004). Anthropologist Michael Brian Schiffer's *The Portable Radio in American Life* (Tucson, 1991) analyzes consumers' response to these devices and is a good source of illustrations.

A. J. Millard, *America on Record: A History of Recorded Sound,* 2d ed. (New York, 2005); David Morton, *Off the Record: The Technology and Culture of Sound Recording in America* (New Brunswick, NJ, 2000); Hans-Joachim Braun, ed., *Music and Technology in the Twentieth Century* (Baltimore, 2002); and Mark Coleman, *Playback: From the Victrola to MP3, 100 Years of Music, Machines, and Money* (Cambridge, MA, 2005) all discuss the changing formats, patterns, use, and culture of music. Russell Sanjek and David Sanjek, *American Popular Music Business in the 20th Century* (New York, 1991), delves into the business aspects of the music industry, as do other books by the late Russell Sanjek.

Most studies of the computer focus on innovators and manufacturers. Good overviews include Martin Campbell-Kelly and William Aspray, *Computer: A History of the Information Machine,* 2d ed. (Boulder, CO, 2004), and Paul E. Ceruzzi, *A History of Modern Computing,* 2d ed. (Cambridge, MA, 2003). Also useful are several books written, edited, or co-edited by the late Alfred D. Chandler, Jr., best known for a Pulitzer Prize–winning survey of big business: *The Visible Hand: The Managerial Revolution in American Business* (Cambridge, MA, 1977). Also important are his *Inventing the Electronic Century: The Epic Story of the Consumer Electronics and Computer Industries* (Cambridge, MA, 2005); and with James W. Cortada, *A Nation Transformed by Information* (New York, 2000). Although not focused on consumers, some of Cortada's other books outline the basics and point to areas ripe for research. See *Making the Information Society: Experiences, Consequences, and Possibilities* (Upper Saddle River, NJ, 2002); *The Digital Hand: How Computers Changed the Work of American Manufacturing, Transportation, and Retail Industries* (New York: 2004); *The Digital Hand, Volume II: How Computers Changed the Work of American Financial, Telecommunications, Media, and Entertainment Industries* (New York, 2006); and *The Digital Hand, Volume III: How Computers Changed the Work of American Public Sector Industries* (New York, 2008).

The birth of the high-fidelity hobby and industry is the subject of Jeffrey Tang's "Sound Decisions: Systems, Standards, and Consumers in American Audio Technology, 1945–1975" (Ph.D. diss., University of Pennsylvania, 2004). James Paul Gee, *What Video Games Have to Teach Us about Learning and Literacy* (New York, 2003), offers a semiotic perspective on video games. *In Doing Cultural Studies: The Story of the Sony*

Walkman (Thousand Oaks, CA, 1997), Paul du Gay and his co-authors use the portable stereo as a case study for demonstrating the evanescence of the postmodern experience.

Scholarship on the internet is just beginning to emerge, and much of the literature is written by journalists and entrepreneurs. Journalist John Cassidy relates the stories of Netscape, Yahoo, Amazon, and other internet firms in *Dot.con: The Greatest Story Ever Told* (New York, 2002). Another journalist, Karen Angel, focuses on one important company in *Inside Yahoo! Reinvention and the Road Ahead* (New York, 2002). Journalist-turned-entrepreneur Tom Ashbrook, founder of HomePortfolio.com, recounts his personal experiences in *The Leap: A Memoir of Love and Madness in the Internet Goldrush* (Boston, 2000). William Aspray and Paul E. Ceruzzi offer an historical perspective in *The Internet and American Business* (Cambridge, MA, 2008). Tom Standage suggests that, as with communications technologies, history does indeed repeat itself in *The Victorian Internet: The Remarkable Story of the Telegraph and the Nineteenth Century's On-Line Pioneers* (New York, 1998).

Finally, a good source for historical data on consumers and electronics is the website of the U.S. Census Bureau, which has posted countless government reports on this subject. Some of these reports have been described in the section of this essay subtitled "Consumer Spending and Credit."

ACKNOWLEDGMENTS

When the late Abraham S. Eisenstadt invited me to contribute a volume to the American History Series, he envisioned a short book on advertising, but I convinced him that consumer society was a better fit for the liberal-arts curriculum. Following my initial discussions with Abe, the historical literature on consumer society exploded and some scholars shifted their focus from cultural history to the political economy. This book looks at American consumer society by synthesizing the work of countless scholars pursuing very different lines of inquiry. Like other recent books in the American History Series, it draws on secondary sources and the author's own original research to offer a new synthesis.

Early in this project, many colleagues shared with me their syllabi for courses on consumer society, which helped me sketch the outlines of this book. For detailed comments on various drafts and chapters, I am grateful to Catherine E. Hutchins, Jonathan Bean, Joseph C. Bigott, Dilys Blum, Nathan Ensmenger, Ann N. Greene, Roger Horowitz, Pamela Walker Laird, Charles F. McGovern, Susan J. Matt, Margaret M. Mulrooney, William R. Scott, Barbara Clark Smith, Theresa Snyder, R. Daniel Wadhwani, and Steve Zdatny.

Several friends and colleagues contributed extra time and effort. Robert Dallek helped with the book proposal. Steven D. Lubar and Pam Laird read the very first draft and pushed me to deepen my analysis and lengthen the book, while Bruce J. Schulman and Glenn Porter read the penultimate manuscript and offered collegial suggestions for reining it back in. Jon Bean shared his enthusiasm for the business history of consumer society and some wonderful primary sources on market research. Phyllis Dillon, a leading costume historian who, like me, has a passion for everyday fashion, went beyond the call of duty and contributed her knowledge of the clothing industry, while Nina de Angeli Walls, William W. Walls, and Robert D. Hicks described their personal clothing choices. An accomplished music journalist, Lee O'Neill steered me through the history of popular sound and recent developments from the digital age.

Special kudos go to Mark Rose and his students at Florida Atlantic University, who read the book's introduction as an assignment in their course on American consumer culture. I am grateful to Shannon Burton, Rachel Christie, Jennifer Goosen, David Hollingsworth, and Matthew Uttal for their excellent suggestions. Professor Rose deserves extra credit for his comments on earlier versions of the introduction and the conclusion and his reminders to keep it simple.

Written from an interdisciplinary vantage point, this book has benefited from students' ongoing enthusiasm for the study of consumer society, advertising, business culture, and material life. At Boston University and Rutgers University-Camden, dozens of imaginative seniors and graduate students in history and American studies completed first-rate theses, term papers, and class presentations that advanced my thinking on the central themes. While a BU professor, I accumulated debts to Fred Spears, Jennifer Vilaga, Prairie Rose Clayton, Elysa Engelman, Ruth Murray, Aysha Ghadiali, Devon Hansen, Paul Schmitz, Brendan F. Sheehan, and Elif Sinanoglu, whose ideas steered me in new directions. More recently at Rutgers-Camden, I have learned much from the dozens of bright students in my graduate seminars on American advertising and consumer culture. As a teacher, I have encouraged these students to think for themselves and carefully evaluate the scholarship on consumer culture. In turn, these students have passed on their gusto for popular culture and the "stuff" of history, pushing me to think farther outside the box. Often, we agreed that some of the most provocative and insightful interpretations of consumer society and the meaning of artifacts come from fields like anthropology, business history, design history, journalism, and sociology, and this book reflects that perspective. I am especially indebted to Ruth Murray, Claire Schmieder and Walter J. Hajduk III for sharing their research materials on patent medicines, trade cards, and Vance Packard.

As a visiting professor at the École des Hautes Etudes en Sciences Sociales, I had the chance to discuss this project with French professors and graduate students in business history and American studies. I thank my dear colleague Patrick Fridenson for inviting me to Paris, the beautiful city of light; Pap Ndiaye and François Weil for hosting my lectures in American studies; and Diana Crane, Nancy L. Green, Michele Ruffat, Paul Schor, Julie Thomas, Dominique Veillon, and Jean-Christian Vinel for making me feel welcome. The French comments on several chapters led me to deepen the discussion of themes that many Americans take for granted. As a result, I hope this book will be useful to American history and culture programs outside of the United States.

Similarly, this book owes much to resources at several first-rate research universities and libraries in the United States. At the University of Pennsylvania, Ruth Schwartz Cowan has welcomed me to the Department of the History and Sociology of Science, where as a Visiting Scholar I've had the opportunity to interact with professors and graduate students who share my enthusiasm for the history of technology, capitalism, and culture. At the Hagley Center for Business, Technology and Society, Roger Horowitz, Philip B. Scranton, Theresa Snyder, and Susan Strasser have been stalwart colleagues who have provided me with access to their institution's wonderful resources. As always, the Smithsonian National Museum of American History has offered outstanding primary sources that supplemented the scholarly literature, thanks to John Fleckner, Fath Ruffins, and other staff in the archives and collections. At Duke University, I visited the John W. Hartman Center for Sales, Advertising, and Marketing History, courtesy of the J. Walter Thompson Fellowship, and studied business records relating to several important ad campaigns. Elsewhere, several professional librarians, archivists, and corporate publicists have been especially helpful with illustrations and permissions: Tony Jahn at

Target, Lisa Backman at The Cable Center, Jon Williams at the Hagley Museum and Library, and Charles Hodges at RadioShack Corporation, who graciously granted Harlan Davidson, Inc., permission to use the 1962 hi-fi image on the cover.

On the publishing front, Andrew Davidson, Abe Eisenstadt, John Hope Franklin, and Glenn Porter have been supportive of this project from the outset, and I am grateful for their faith in me. Andrew Davidson is a model editor and publisher, gifted with enduring patience. Lucy Herz is a wonderful production editor blessed with good sense. Others at Harlan Davidson who made this book a reality include Claudia Siler and Linda Gaio. Closer to home, Nina and Bill Walls have served as this project's devoted grandparents, watching lovingly from a distance. This book is dedicated to Lee O'Neill, my muse and manager, who makes it possible for me to pursue my own ideas, set my own research agenda, and write consumer history with a different twist.

Regina Lee Blaszczyk
Philadelphia

INDEX

American Consumer Society, 1865–2005: From Hearth to HDTV
Developmental Editor: Andrew J. Davidson
Production Editors: Lucy Herz and Linda Gaio
Typesetter: Bruce Leckie
Proofreader: Claudia Siler
Indexer: Regina Lee Blaszczyk
Printer: Versa Press